Microsoft®

Word 97

Illustrated PLUS Edition

Microsoft®

Word 97

Illustrated PLUS Edition

Marie L. Swanson

COURSE
TECHNOLOGY

ONE MAIN STREET, CAMBRIDGE, MA 02142

an International Thomson Publishing company I(T)P®

Cambridge • Albany • Bonn • Boston • Cincinnati • London • Madrid • Melbourne • Mexico City
New York • Paris • San Francisco • Singapore • Tokyo • Toronto • Washington

Microsoft Word 97—Illustrated PLUS Edition
is published by Course Technology

Managing Editor:	Nicole Jones Pinard
Product Manager:	Jeanne Herring
Production Editor:	Nancy Shea
Developmental Editor:	Meta Chaya Hirschl
Composition House:	GEX, Inc.
QA Manuscript Reviewers:	John McCarthy, Gail Massey, Brian McCooey
Text Designer:	Joseph Lee
Cover Designer:	Joseph Lee

© 1997 by Course Technology — I(T)P®

For more information contact:

Course Technology
One Main Street
Cambridge, MA 02142

International Thomson Publishing Europe
Berkshire House 168-173
High Holborn
London WC1V 7AA
England

Thomas Nelson Australia
102 Dodds Street
South Melbourne, 3205
Victoria, Australia

Nelson Canada
1120 Birchmount Road
Scarborough, Ontario
Canada M1K 5G4

International Thomson Editores
Campos Eliseos 385, Piso 7
Col. Polanco
11560 Mexico D.F. Mexico

International Thomson Publishing GmbH
Königswinterer Strasse 418
53277 Bonn
Germany

International Thomson Publishing Asia
211 Henderson Road
#05-10 Henderson Building
Singapore 0315

International Thomson Publishing Japan
Hirakawacho Kyowa Building, 3F
2-2-1 Hirakawacho
Chiyoda-ku, Tokyo 102
Japan

ISBN 0-7600-4698-0

Printed in the United States of America

10 9 8 7 6 5

From the
Illustrated Series™ Team

At Course Technology we believe that technology will transform the way that people teach and learn. We are very excited about bringing you, instructors and students, the most practical and affordable technology-related products available.

▶ The Development Process

Our development process is unparalleled in the educational publishing industry. Every product we create goes through an exacting process of design, development, review, and testing.

Reviewers give us direction and insight that shape our manuscripts and bring them up to the latest standards. Every manuscript is quality tested. Students whose backgrounds match the intended audience work through every keystroke, carefully checking for clarity and pointing out errors in logic and sequence. Together with our own technical reviewers, these testers help us ensure that everything that carries our name is as error-free and easy to use as possible.

▶ The Products

We show both how and why technology is critical to solving problems in the classroom and in whatever field you choose to teach or pursue. Our time-tested, step-by-step instructions provide unparalleled clarity. Examples and applications are chosen and crafted to motivate students.

▶ The Illustrated Series™ Team

The Illustrated Series™ Team is committed to providing you with the most visual introduction to microcomputer applications. No other series of books will get you up to speed faster in today's changing software environment. This book will suit your needs because it was delivered quickly, efficiently, and affordably. In every aspect of business, we rely on a commitment to quality and the use of technology. Each member of the Illustrated Series™ Team contributes to this process. The names of all our team members are listed below.

The Team

Cynthia Anderson	Mary-Terese Cozzola	Jeanne Herring	Elizabeth Eisner Reding
Chia-Ling Barker	Carol Cram	Meta Chaya Hirschl	Art Rotberg
Donald Barker	Kim T. M. Crowley	Jane Hosie-Bounar	Neil Salkind
Ann Barron	Catherine DiMassa	Steven Johnson	Gregory Schultz
David Beskeen	Stan Dobrawa	Bill Lisowski	Ann Shaffer
Ann Marie Buconjic	Shelley Dyer	Chet Lyskawa	Dan Swanson
Rachel Bunin	Linda Eriksen	Kristine O'Brien	Marie Swanson
Joan Carey	Jessica Evans	Tara O'Keefe	Jennifer Thompson
Patrick Carey	Lisa Friedrichsen	Harry Phillips	Sasha Vodnik
Sheralyn Carroll	Jeff Goding	Nicole Jones Pinard	Jan Weingarten
Brad Conlin	Michael Halvorson	Katherine T. Pinard	Christie Williams
Pam Conrad	Jamie Harper	Kevin Proot	Janet Wilson

Preface

Welcome to *Microsoft Word 97— Illustrated PLUS Edition*! This book in our highly visual new design offers new users a comprehensive hands-on introduction to Microsoft Word 97 and is appropriate for a full semester course. It also includes a brief introduction to Windows 95 in order to get students quickly up and running in the Windows 95 environment.

▶ Organization and Coverage

This book is divided into two sections that are made up of two units on Microsoft Windows 95 and sixteen units on Microsoft Word 97. The Windows section provides a brief introduction to the Windows 95 environment and helps students learn basic Windows skills. The next section concentrates on Word 97 and moves from beginning coverage to the most advanced topics. In the Word 97 units students learn how to design, create, edit, and enhance Word documents. They learn how to work with tables, charts, graphs, and forms, as well as how to create macros and templates. In addition, they learn how to create a Web page and how to integrate documents created in other Microsoft programs into Word 97.

This book has been approved by Microsoft as courseware for the Certified Microsoft Office User (CMOU) program. After completing the tutorials and exercises in this book, you will be prepared to take the Proficient level CMOU Exam for Microsoft Word 97. By passing the certification exam for a Microsoft software program, you demonstrate your proficiency in that program to employers. CMOU exams are offered at participating test centers, participating corporations, and participating employment agencies. For more information about certification, please visit the CMOU program World Wide Web site at http://www.microsoft.com/office/train_cert/

▶ About this Approach

What makes the Illustrated approach so effective at teaching software skills? It's quite simple. Each skill is presented on two facing pages, with the step-by-step instructions on the left page, and large screen illustrations on the right. Students can focus on a single skill without having to turn the page. This unique design makes information extremely accessible and easy to absorb, and provides a great reference for students after the course is over. This hands-on approach also makes it ideal for both self-paced or instructor-led classes. The modular structure of the book also allows for great flexibility; you can cover the units in any order you choose.

Each lesson, or "information display," contains the following elements:

This icon indicates a CourseHelp 97 slide show is available for this lesson. See the Instructor's Resource Kit page for more information.

Each 2-page spread focuses on a single skill.

Concise text that introduces the basic principles in the lesson and integrates the brief case study.

Excel 97

Changing Attributes and Alignment of Labels

Attributes are font styling features such as bold, italics, and underlining. You can apply bold, italics, and underlining from the Formatting toolbar or from the Font tab in the Format Cells dialog box. You can also change the alignment of text in cells. Left, right, or center alignment can be applied from the Formatting toolbar, or from the Alignment tab in the Format Cells dialog box. See Table C-2 for a description of the available attribute and alignment buttons on the Formatting toolbar. Excel also has predefined worksheet formats to make formatting easier. ◀━━━ Now that he has applied the appropriate fonts and font sizes to his worksheet labels, Evan wants to further enhance his worksheet's appearance by adding bold and underline formatting and centering some of the labels.

Steps

CourseHelp

The camera icon indicates there is a CourseHelp available with this lesson. Click the Start button, point to programs, point to CourseHelp, then click Word 97 Illustrated. Choose the CourseHelp that corresponds to this lesson.

QuickTip

Highlighting information on a worksheet can be useful, but overuse of any attribute can be distracting and make a document less readable. Be consistent by adding emphasis the same way throughout a workbook.

Time To

➤ Save

1. Press [Ctrl][Home] to select cell A1, then click the Bold button **B** on the Formatting toolbar
   The title "Advertising Expenses" appears in bold.

2. Select the range A3:J3, then click the Underline button **U** on the Formatting toolbar
   Excel underlines the column headings in the selected range.

3. Click cell A3, click the Italics button **I** on the Formatting toolbar, then click **B**
   The word "Type" appears in boldface, italic type. Notice that the Bold, Italics, and Underline buttons on the Formatting toolbar are indented. You decide you don't like the italic formatting. You remove it by clicking **I** again.

4. Click **I**
   Excel removes italics from cell A3.

5. Add bold formatting to the rest of the labels in the range B3:J3
   You want to center the title over the data.

6. Select the range A1:F1, then click the Merge and Center button **▦** on the Formatting toolbar
   The title Advertising Expenses is centered across six columns. Now you center the column headings in their cells.

7. Select the range A3:J3 then click the Center button **▤** on the Formatting toolbar
   You are satisfied with the formatting in the worksheet. Compare your screen to Figure C-8.

TABLE C-2: Attribute and Alignment buttons on the Formatting toolbar

icon	description	icon	description
B	Adds boldface	**▤**	Aligns left
I	Italicizes	**▥**	Aligns center
U	Underlines	**▦**	Aligns right
	Adds lines or borders	**▦**	Centers across columns, and combines two or more selected adjacent cells into one cell.

▶ EX C-6 **FORMATTING A WORKSHEET**

Quickly accessible summaries of key terms, toolbar buttons, or keyboard alternatives connected with the lesson material. Students can refer easily to this information when working on their own projects at a later time.

Hints as well as trouble-shooting advice right where you need it – next to the step itself.

Clear step-by-step directions, with what students are to type in red, explain how to complete the specific task.

Every lesson features large, full-color representations of what the screen should look like as students complete the numbered steps.

The innovative design draws the students' eyes to important areas of the screens.

Brightly colored tabs above the program name indicate which section of the book you are in. Useful for finding your place within the book and for referencing information from the index.

Other Features

The two-page lesson format featured in this book provides the new user with a powerful learning experience. Additionally, this book contains the following features:

▶ **Real-World Case**
The case study used throughout the textbook, a fictitious company called Nomad Ltd, is designed to be "real-world" in nature and introduces the kinds of activities that students will encounter when working with Microsoft Word 97. With a real-world case, the process of solving problems will be more meaningful to students.

▶ **End of Unit Material**
Each unit concludes with a Concepts Review that tests students' understanding of what they learned in the unit. A Skills Review follows the Concepts Review and provides students with additional hands-on practice of the skills they learned in the unit. The Skills Review is followed by Independent Challenges, which pose case problems for students to solve. At least one Independent Challenge in each unit asks students to use the World Wide Web to solve the problem as indicated by a Web Work icon. The Visual Workshops that follow the Independent Challenges help students to develop critical thinking skills. Students are shown completed documents and are asked to recreate them from scratch.

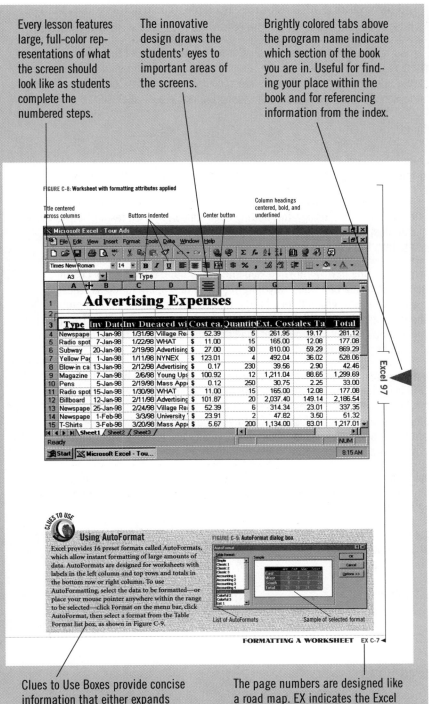

FIGURE C-8: Worksheet with formatting attributes applied

Title centered across columns

Buttons indented

Center button

Column headings centered, bold, and underlined

Excel 97

Using AutoFormat

Excel provides 16 preset formats called AutoFormats, which allow instant formatting of large amounts of data. AutoFormats are designed for worksheets with labels in the left column and top rows and totals in the bottom row or right column. To use AutoFormatting, select the data to be formatted—or place your mouse pointer anywhere within the range to be selected—click Format on the menu bar, click AutoFormat, then select a format from the Table Format list box, as shown in Figure C-9.

FIGURE C-9: AutoFormat dialog box

List of AutoFormats

Sample of selected format

FORMATTING A WORKSHEET EX C-7

Clues to Use Boxes provide concise information that either expands on the major lesson skill or describes an independent task that in some way relates to the major lesson skill.

The page numbers are designed like a road map. EX indicates the Excel section, C indicates Excel Unit C, and 7 indicates the page within the unit. This map allows for the greatest flexibility in content — each unit stands completely on its own.

Instructor's Resource Kit

The Instructor's Resource Kit is Course Technology's way of putting the resources and information needed to teach and learn effectively into your hands. With an integrated array of teaching and learning tools that offer you and your students a broad range of instructional options, we believe this kit represents the highest quality and most cutting edge resources available to instructors today. Many of these resources are available online at www.course.com. The resources available with this book are:

CourseHelp 97 CourseHelp 97 is a student reinforcement tool offering online annotated tutorials that are accessible directly from the Start menu in Windows 95. These on-screen "slide shows" help students understand the most difficult concepts in a specific program. Students are encouraged to view a CourseHelp 97 slide show before completing that lesson. This text includes the following CourseHelp 97 slide shows:
- Moving and Copying Data
- Creating and Formatting Sections
- Understanding Mail Merge
- Displaying Data as a Chart

Adopters of this text are granted the right to post the CourseHelp 97 files on any standalone computer or network.

Course Test Manager Designed by Course Technology, this cutting edge Windows-based testing software helps instructors design and administer tests and pre-tests. This full-featured program also has an online testing component that allows students to take tests at the computer and have their exams automatically graded.

Course Faculty Online Companion This new World Wide Web site offers Course Technology customers a password-protected Faculty Lounge where you can find everything you need to prepare for class. These periodically updated items include lesson plans, graphic files for the figures in the text, additional problems, updates and revisions to the text, links to other Web sites, and access to Student Disk files. This new site is an ongoing project and will continue to evolve throughout the semester. Contact your Customer Service Representative for the site address and password.

Course Student Online Companion This book features its own Online Companion where students can go to access Web sites that will help them complete the WebWork Independent Challenges. This page also contains links to other Course Technology student pages where students can find task references for each of the Microsoft Office 97 programs, a graphical glossary of terms found in the text, an archive of meaningful templates, software, hot tips, and Web links to other sites that contain pertinent information. These new sites are also ongoing projects and will continue to evolve throughout the semester.

Student Files To use this book students must have the Student Files. See the inside front or inside back cover for more information on the Student Files. Adopters of this text are granted the right to post the Student Files on any stand-alone computer or network.

Instructor's Manual This is quality assurance tested and includes:
- Solutions to all lessons and end-of-unit material
- Unit notes with teaching tips from the author
- Extra Independent Challenges
- Transparency Masters of key concepts
- Student Files
- CourseHelp 97

CLUES TO USE

The Illustrated Family of Products

This book that you are holding fits in the Illustrated Series – one series of three in the Illustrated family of products. The other two series are the Illustrated Projects Series and the Illustrated Interactive Series. The Illustrated Projects Series is a supplemental series designed to reinforce the sills learned in any skills-based book through the creation of meaningful and engaging projects. The Illustrated Interactive Series is a line of computer-based training multimedia products that offer the novice user a quick and interactive learning experience. All three series are committed to providing you with the most visual and enriching instructional materials.

Contents

 ▶ Windows 95

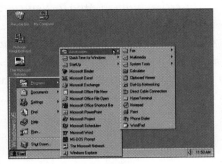

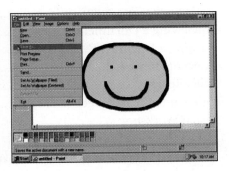

Contents

Word 97

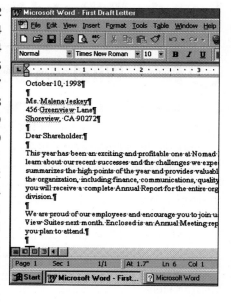

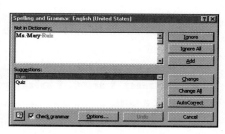

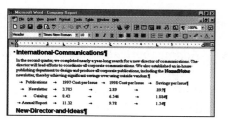

Working with Tables

Formatting Pages

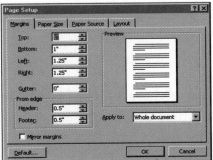

Contents

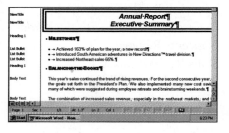

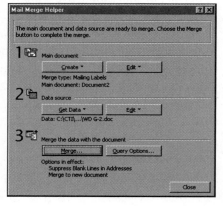

Sharing Information with Other Programs

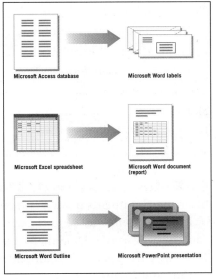

Creating a Web Site with Word

Contents

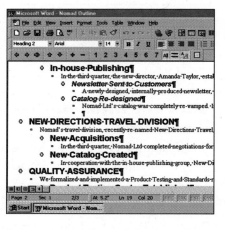

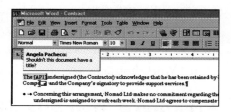

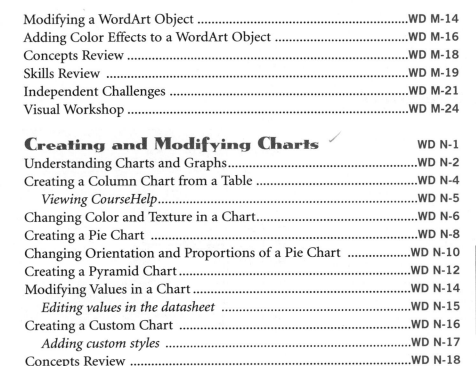

Contents

✓ Customizing Word with AutoText and Macros

Getting
Started with Microsoft Windows 95

Objectives

- ► **Start Windows and view the desktop**
- ► **Use the mouse**
- ► **Start a program**
- ► **Resize a window**
- ► **Use menus and toolbars**
- ► **Use dialog boxes**
- ► **Use scroll bars**
- ► **Get Help**
- ► **Close a program and shut down Windows**

Microsoft Windows 95 is an operating system that controls the basic operation of your computer and the programs you run on it. Windows has a graphical user interface (GUI) which means you can use pictures (called icons) in addition to words to carry out tasks and operations. Windows 95 also helps you organize the results of your work (saved as files) and coordinates the flow of information among the programs, files, printers, storage devices, and other components of your computer system. ◆ This unit introduces you to basic skills that you can use in all Windows programs.

Starting Windows and Viewing the Desktop

Microsoft Windows 95 is an operating system designed to help you get the most out of your computer. You can use Windows 95 to run **programs**, also known as **applications**, which are software tools you use to accomplish tasks. When you first start Windows, you see the **desktop**, which is the area on your screen where you organize your computer work. See Figure A-1. The small pictures you see on the desktop are called icons. Icons represent a program you use to carry out a task, or a document, or a set of files or documents. The **My Computer** icon represents a program you use to organize the files on your computer. The **Recycle Bin** icon represents a storage area for deleted files. Below the desktop is the taskbar, which shows you the programs that are running (at the moment, none are running). At the left end of the taskbar is the **Start button**, which you use to start programs, find files, access Windows Help and more. Use Table A-1 to identify the icons and other key elements you see on your desktop. ✒️ If Windows 95 is not currently running, follow the steps below to start it now.

Steps 123 4

1. **Turn on your computer and monitor**
   Windows automatically starts, and the desktop appears as shown in Figure A-1. If you are working on a network at school or at an office, you might see a password dialog box. If so, continue to step 2.

2. **Type your password, then press [Enter]**
   If you don't know your password, see your instructor. Once the password is accepted, the Windows desktop appears on your screen, as shown in Figure A-1.

FIGURE A-1: Windows desktop

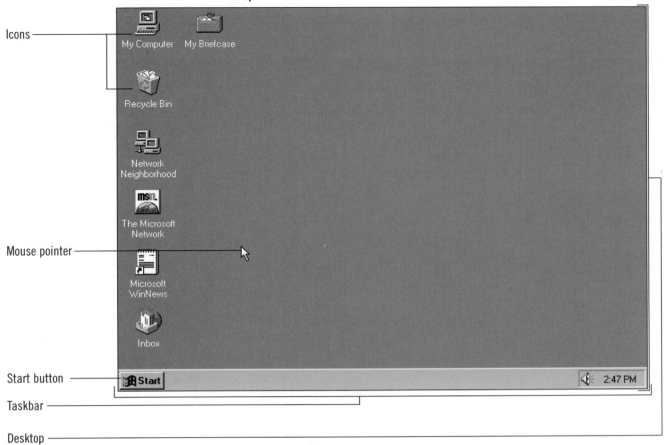

Icons

Mouse pointer

Start button

Taskbar

Desktop

More about operating systems

Windows95 is one of several operating systems. The operating system you use depends to some degree on the kind of computer you are using. For example, the Apple Macintosh computer uses an operating system that only runs on Macintosh computers. Other computers might run other operating systems such as UNIX and OS/2. Each operating system has its own unique features and benefits, causing different user communites to prefer one over the other based on their computing needs. Before Windows, many personal computers ran an operating system called MS-DOS. This character-based operating system required that you enter commands very carefully when you used the computer. With the development of Windows (and more powerful computers), personal computers can now run programs that take advantage of a graphical user interface. As a result computers have become easier to use.

TABLE A-1: Elements of the Windows desktop

desktop element	description
Icon	Picture representing a task you can carry out, a program you can run, or a document
Mouse pointer	Arrow indicating the current location of the mouse on the desktop
Taskbar	Area that identifies any programs currently open (that is, running); by default, the taskbar is always visible
Start button	Provides main access to all Windows operations and programs available on the computer

Windows 95

Using the Mouse

The mouse is a handheld input device that you roll on a smooth surface (such as your desk or a mousepad) to position the mouse pointer on the Windows desktop. When you move the mouse, the mouse pointer on the screen moves in the same direction. The buttons on the mouse, shown in Figure A-2, are used to select icons and commands. You also use the mouse to select options and identify the work to be done in programs. Table A-2 shows some common mouse pointer shapes. Table A-3 lists the five basic mouse actions. ✎ Begin by experimenting with the mouse now.

Steps

1. **Locate the mouse pointer ▷ on the Windows desktop and then move the mouse across your desk**
   Watch how the mouse pointer moves on the desktop in response to your movements. Practice moving the mouse pointer in circles, and then back and forth in straight lines.

2. **Position the mouse pointer over the My Computer icon**
   Positioning the mouse pointer over an icon is called pointing.

3. **With the pointer over the My Computer icon, press and release the left mouse button**
   Unless otherwise indicated, you will use the left mouse button to perform all mouse operations. Pressing and releasing the mouse button is called clicking. When you position the mouse pointer over an icon and then click, you select the icon. When an icon is selected, both it and its title are highlighted. Practice moving an icon by dragging it with the mouse.

4. **With the icon selected, press and hold down the left mouse button, then move the mouse down and to the right and release the mouse button**
   The icon becomes dimmed and moves with the mouse pointer. When you release the mouse button, the icon relocates on the desktop. Next, you will use the mouse to display a pop-up menu.

5. **Position the mouse pointer over the My Computer icon, then press and release the right mouse button**
   Clicking the right mouse button is known as right-clicking. Right-clicking an item on the desktop displays a pop-up menu, as shown in Figure A-3. This menu displays the commands most commonly used for the item you have clicked.

6. **Click anywhere outside the menu to close the pop-up menu**
   Now use the mouse to open a window.

7. **Position the mouse pointer over the My Computer icon, then press and release the left mouse button twice quickly**
   Clicking the mouse button twice quickly is known as double-clicking. Double-clicking this icon opens a window. The My Computer window displays additional icons that represent the drives and system components that are installed on your computer.

8. **Click the Close button ☒ in the upper-right corner of the My Computer window**

FIGURE A-2: The mouse

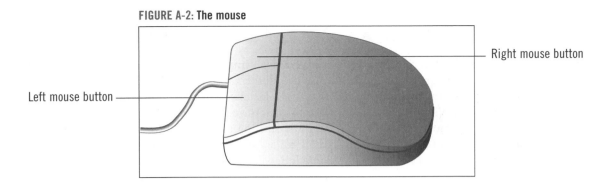

Left mouse button

Right mouse button

FIGURE A-3: Displaying a pop-up menu

Selected icon

Pop-up menu

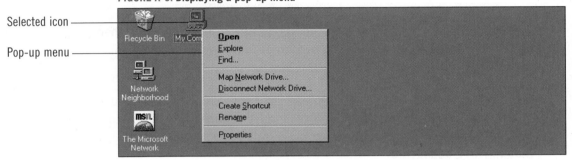

TABLE A-2: **Common mouse pointer shapes**

shape	used to
⬉	Select items, choose commands, start programs, and work in programs
I	Position mouse pointer for editing or inserting text; called the insertion point or cursor
⧗	Indicate Windows is busy processing a command
↔	Change the size of a window; appears when mouse pointer is on the border of a window

TABLE A-3: **Basic mouse techniques**

technique	what to do
Pointing	Move the mouse to position the mouse pointer over an item on the desktop
Clicking	Press and release the left mouse button
Double-clicking	Press and release the left mouse button twice quickly
Dragging	Point to an item, press and hold the left mouse button, move the mouse to a new location, then release the mouse button
Right-clicking	Point to an item, then press the right mouse button

Windows 95

Starting a Program

Clicking the Start button on the taskbar displays the all-important Start menu. You use the Start menu to start a program, find a file, or display help information. Table A-4 describes the **default** categories of items available on this menu that are installed with Windows 95. As you become more familiar with Windows you might want to customize the Start menu to include additional items that you use most often. ◀ Begin by starting the **WordPad** program, an Accessory that comes with Windows 95. You can use WordPad to create and edit simple documents. See Table A-5 for a description of other popular Windows Accessories.

Steps 1 2 3 4

1. Position the mouse pointer over the **Start button** on the taskbar, then click
The Start menu appears. Next, you need to open the Programs submenu.

2. Point to **Programs**
An arrow next to a menu item indicates a **cascading menu**. Pointing at the arrow displays a submenu from which you can choose additional commands, as shown in Figure A-4.

3. Point to **Accessories**
This is the Accessories menu, containing several programs to help you complete day-to-day tasks. You want to Start WordPad, which should be at the bottom of the list.

4. Click **WordPad**
The WordPad program opens and a blank document window appears, as shown in Figure A-5. WordPad is a simple word processor provided with Windows 95 that you can use to write and edit documents. Note that when a program is open, a program button appears on the taskbar indicating that it is open. An indented button indicates the program that is currently active. Leave the WordPad window open for now, and continue to the next lesson.

TABLE A-4: Start menu categories

category	description
Programs	Opens programs included on the Start menu
Documents	Opens documents most recently opened and saved
Settings	Allows user preferences for system settings, including control panels, printers, Start menu, and taskbar
Find	Locates programs, files, and folders not included on the Start menu
Help	Displays Windows Help information by topic, alphabetical index, or search criteria
Run	Opens a program or file based on a location and filename that you type or select
Shut Down	Provides options to shut down the computer, restart the computer in Windows mode, restart the computer in MS-DOS mode, or log on to the system as a different user

FIGURE A-4: Cascading menus

Arrow indicates cascading menu will open

WordPad program

Cascading menus

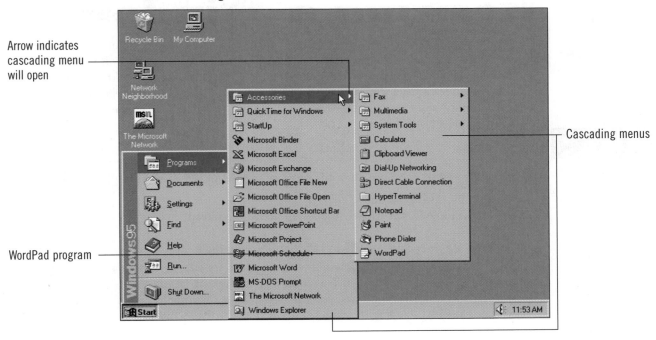

FIGURE A-5: WordPad document window

Indented program button indicates active program

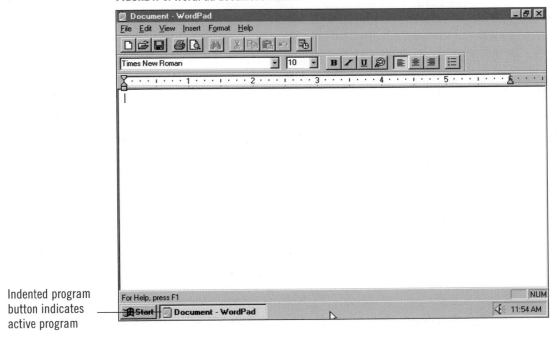

TABLE A-5: Common Windows Accessories

accessory	description
Calculator	Use to add, subtract, divide, and multiply numbers
Paint	Use to draw and edit graphic images
WordPad	Use to create and edit documents

Resizing a Window

The Windows desktop can quickly get cluttered with icons and windows. One of the ways to keep your desktop organized is by changing the size of the windows. Each window is surrounded by a standard border and sizing buttons that allow you to change the size of windows by minimizing, maximizing, and restoring windows as needed. You can also drag a window's border to size it. See the related topic "More about sizing windows" for more information. Practice sizing the WordPad window now.

Steps

1. **In the WordPad window, click the Maximize button ▣, if the WordPad window does not already fill the screen**
When a window is maximized, it takes up the whole screen.

2. **Click the Restore button ▣ in the WordPad window**
The Restore button returns a window to its previous size, as shown in Figure A-6. The Restore button only appears when a window is maximized. In addition to minimizing, maximizing, and restoring windows, you can also change the dimensions of any window. Next, experiment with changing the dimensions of the WordPad window.

3. **Position the pointer on the right edge of the WordPad window until the pointer changes to ↔, then drag it to the right**
The width of the window increases. You can size the height and width of a window by dragging any of the four sides individually. You can also size the height and width of the window simultaneously by dragging the corner of the window.

4. **Position the pointer in the lower-right corner of the WordPad window, as indicated in Figure A-6, then drag down and to the right**
The height and width of the window are increased at the same time. You can also position a restored window wherever you wish on the desktop by dragging its title bar.

5. **Click the title bar on the WordPad window and drag up and to the left**
The window is repositioned on the desktop. At times, you might wish to close a program's window, yet keep the program running and easily accessible. You can accomplish this by minimizing a window.

6. **In the WordPad window, click the Minimize button ▬**
When you minimize a window, it shrinks to a program button on the taskbar, as shown in Figure A-7. The WordPad program is still open and running; however, it is not active.

7. **Click the WordPad program button on the taskbar to restore the window to its previous size**
The WordPad program is now active; this means that any actions you perform will take place in this window. Next, return the window to its full size.

8. **Click the Maximize button ▣ in the upper-right corner of the WordPad window**
The window fills the screen. Leave the WordPad window maximized and continue with the next lesson.

FIGURE A-6: **Restored WordPad window**

Title bar

Sizing buttons

Drag here to size
both height and
width

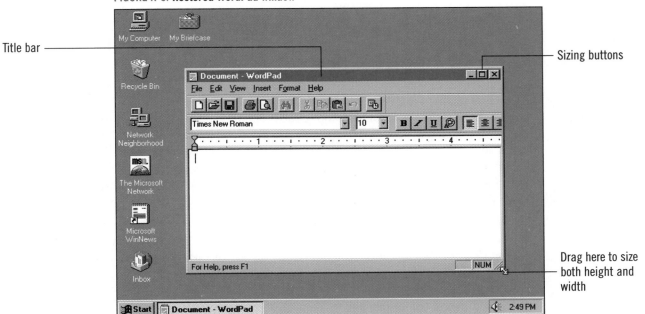

FIGURE A-7: **Minimized WordPad window**

Indicates program
is running but not
active

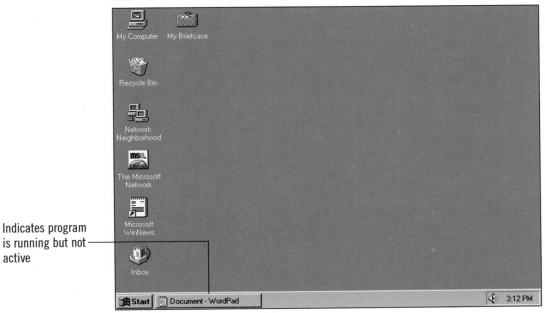

CLUES TO USE

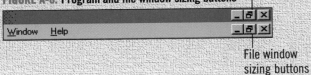

More about sizing windows

More programs contain two sets of sizing buttons: one that controls the file which can be a document, spreadsheet, database, or presentation window within the program. The program sizing buttons are located in the title bar; the file sizing buttons are located below them in the menu bar. See Figure 1-8. When you minmize a file window within a program, the file window is reduced to an icon in the lower-left coner of program window. The size of the program window remains intact.

Program window
sizing buttons

FIGURE A-8: **Program and file window sizing buttons**

File window
sizing buttons

Using Menus and Toolbars

A **menu** is a list of commands that you use to accomplish certain tasks. You've already used the Start menu to start WordPad. Each Windows program also has its own set of menus, which are located on the **menu bar** along the top of the program window. The menus organize commands into groups of related operations. See Table A-6 for examples of what you might see on a typical menu. Some of the commands found on a menu can also be carried out by clicking a button on a **toolbar**. Toolbar buttons provide you with convenient shortcuts for completing tasks. Open the Control Panel program, then use a menu and toolbar button to change how the window's contents are displayed.

Steps 1 2 3 4

1. Click the Start button on the taskbar, point to Settings, then click Control Panel
The Control Panel window contains icons for various programs that allow you to specify your preferences for how your computer environment looks and performs.

2. Click View on the menu bar
The View menu appears, displaying the View commands, as shown in Figure A-9. When you click a menu name, a general description of the commands available on that menu appears in the status bar. On a menu, a check mark identifies a feature that is currently selected (that is, the feature is enabled). To disable the feature, you click the command again to remove the check mark. A bullet mark can also indicate that an option is enabled. To disable this option, however, you must select another option in its place. In the next step, you will select a command.

3. On the View menu, click Small Icons
The icons are now smaller than they were before, taking up less room in the window. You can also use the keyboard to access menu commands. Next, open the View menu by pressing [Alt] on the keyboard and then the underlined letter of the menu on the menu bar.

4. Press and hold [Alt], then press [V] to open the View menu, then release both keys
The View menu appears. Notice that a letter in each command is underlined. You can select these commands by pressing the underlined letter. Now, select a command using the keyboard.

5. Press [T] to select the Toolbar command
The Control Panel toolbar appears below the menu bar. This toolbar includes buttons for the commands that you use most frequently while you are in the Control Panel program. When you position the mouse pointer over a button, the name of the button – called a ToolTip – is displayed. Pressing a button displays a description of the button in the status bar. Use the ToolTip feature to explore a button on the toolbar.

Trouble?

If you cannot see the Details button on the toolbar, you can resize the Control Panel window by dragging the right border to the right until the button is visible.

6. On the Control Panel toolbar, position the pointer over the Details button ▦ as shown in Figure A-10, then click
The Details view includes a description of each Control Panel program. If you were to click the View menu now, you would see that the Details command is now checked.

FIGURE A-9: View menu on Control Panel menu bar

Menu bar ──────

Commands in menu ──────

Description of menu in status bar ──────

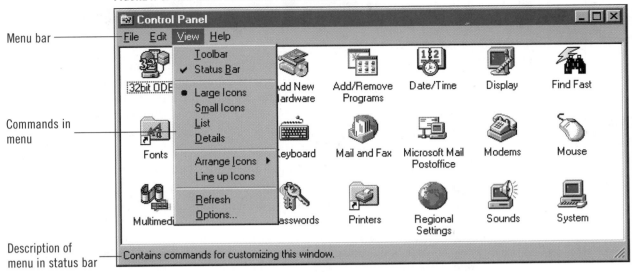

FIGURE A-10: Control Panel toolbar

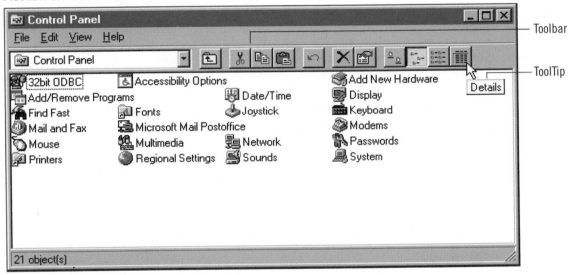

── Toolbar

── ToolTip

TABLE A-6: Typical items on a menu

item	description
Dimmed command	A menu command that is not currently available
Ellipsis	Choosing this menu command opens a dialog box that allows you to select different or additional options
Triangle	Choosing this menu command opens a cascading menu containing an additional list of menu commands
Keyboard shortcut	A keyboard alternative for executing a menu command
Underlined letter	Pressing the underlined letter executes the menu command

Using Dialog Boxes

A command from a menu that is followed by an ellipsis (…) requires more information before it can complete its task. When you select this type of command a **dialog box** opens for you to specify the options you want. See Figure A-11 and Table A-7 for some of the typical elements of a dialog box. Practice using a dialog box to control your mouse settings.

Steps

1. **In the Control Panel window, double-click the Mouse icon** (you might need to resize the Control Panel window to find this icon)
   The Mouse Properties dialog box opens, as shown in Figure A-12. The options in this dialog box allow you to control the way the mouse buttons are configured, select the types of point-ers that are displayed, choose the speed of the mouse movement on the screen, and specify what type of mouse you are using. **Tabs** at the top of the dialog box separate these options into related categories.

2. **Click the Buttons tab if it is not the frontmost tab, then in the Button configuration area, click the Left-handed radio button to select it**
   If the Left-handed radio button is already selected, click the Right-handed radio button. Use this option to specify which button is primary (controls the normal operations) and which is secondary (controls the special functions, such as context-sensitive pop-up menus). Next, select an option which shows pointer trails when you move the mouse.

3. **Click the Motion tab, then in the Pointer trail area click the Show pointer trails check box to select it**
   This option makes the mouse pointer easier to see on certain types of computer screens such as laptop computers. The slider feature, located below the check box, lets you specify the degree to which the option is in effect, in this case, the length of the pointer trail.

4. **Drag the slider below the check box all the way to the right**
   As you move the mouse, notice the longer pointer trails.

5. **Click the other tabs in the Mouse Properties dialog box and experiment with the options that are available in each category**
   Finally, you need to select a command button to carry out the options you've selected. The two most common command buttons are OK and Cancel. Clicking OK accepts your changes and closes the dialog box; clicking Cancel leaves the settings intact and closes the dialog box. The third command button in this dialog box is Apply. Clicking the Apply button accepts the changes you've made and keeps the dialog box open so that you can select additional options. Because you might share this computer with others, it's important to return the dia-log box options back to the original settings.

6. **Click Cancel to leave the original settings intact and close the dialog box**

QuickTip

You can also use the key-board to carry out com-mands in a dialog box. Pressing [Enter] is the same as clicking OK; pressing [Esc] is the same as click-ing Cancel.

FIGURE A-11: Dialog box elements

Spin box

Radio button

Check box

List box

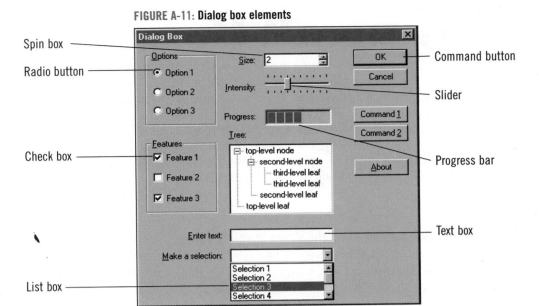

Command button

Slider

Progress bar

Text box

FIGURE A-12: Mouse Properties dialog box

Tabs

Button configuration area

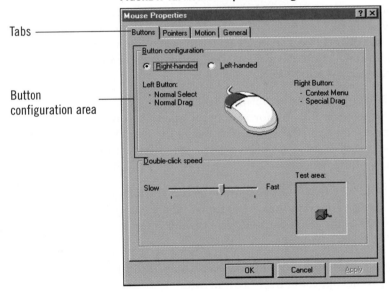

TABLE A-7: Typical items in a dialog box

item	description	item	description
Check box	Clicking this square box turns a dialog box option on or off	**List box**	A box containing a list of items; to choose an item, click the list arrow, then click the desired item
Text box	A box in which you type text	**Spin box**	Allows you to scroll or type numerical increments
Radio button	Clicking this small circle selects a single dialog box option	**Slider**	Allows you to set the degree to which an option is in effect
Command button	Clicking this button carries out a command in a dialog box	**Progress bar**	Indicates how much of a task is completed

Using Scroll Bars

When you cannot see all of the items available in a window, scroll bars will appear on the right and/or bottom edges of the window. Using the scroll bars, you can move around in a window to display the additional contents of the window. There are several ways you can scroll in a window. When you need to scroll only a short distance, you can use the scroll arrows. Clicking in the scroll bar above or below the scroll box scrolls the window in larger increments, while dragging the scroll bar moves you quickly to a new part of the window. See Table A-8 for a summary of the different ways to use scroll bars. ◤ With the Control Panel window in the Details view, you can use the scroll bars to view all of the items in this window.

Steps 1 2 3 4

1. **In the Control Panel window, click the down scroll arrow, as shown in Figure A-13**
   Clicking this arrow moves the view down one line. Clicking the up arrow moves the view up one line at a time. So that you can better explore other scrolling features in this lesson, you will resize the window to show fewer items.

2. **Drag the bottom border of the Control Panel window up so that only 6 or 7 items appear in the window**
   Notice that the scroll box appears smaller than in the previous step. The size of the scroll box changes to reflect the amount of items available, but not displayed in a window. For example, a larger scroll box indicates that a relatively small amount of the window's contents is not currently visible; therefore you need to scroll only a short distance to see the remaining items. A smaller scroll box indicates that a relatively large amount of information is currently not visible. To see the additional contents of the resized window, you can click in the area below the scroll box in the vertical scroll bar.

3. **Click the area below the scroll box in the vertical scroll bar**
   The view moves down one window full of information; for example, you see another 6 or 7 items further down in the window. Similarly, you can click in the scroll bar above the scroll box to move up one window full of information. Next, you will display the information that appears at the very bottom of the window.

4. **Drag the scroll box all the way down to the bottom of the vertical scroll bar**
   The view displays the items that appear at the very bottom of the window. Similarly, you can drag the scroll box to the top of the scroll bar to display the information that appears at the top of the window.

5. **Drag the scroll box all the way up to the top of the vertical scroll bar**
   This view displays the items that appear at the top of the window. Next, you will explore the horizontal scroll bar, so you can see all of the icons near the right edge of the window.

6. **Click the area to the right of the scroll box in the horizontal scroll bar**
   The far right edge of the window comes into view. Next, you will redisplay the left edge of the window.

7. **Click the area to the left of the scroll box in the horizontal scroll bar**

8. **Resize the Control Panel window so that the scroll bars no longer appear**

Trouble?

If you cannot see both the vertical and horizontal scroll bars, make the window smaller (both shorter and narrower) until both scroll bars appear.

FIGURE A-13: Control Panel window in Details view

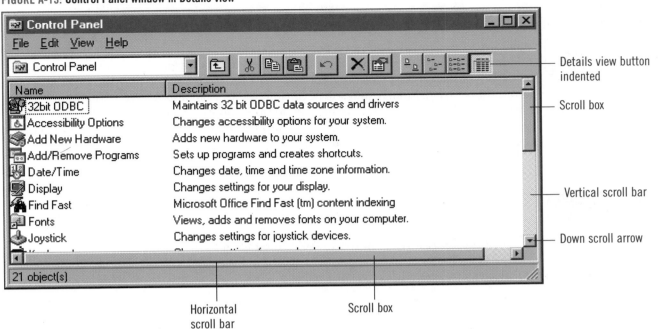

TABLE A-8: Using scroll bars in a window

to	do this
Move down one line	Click the down arrow at the bottom of the vertical scroll bar
Move up one line	Click the up arrow at the top of the vertical scroll bar
Move down one window	Click in the area below the scroll box in the vertical scroll bar
Move up one window	Click in the area above the scroll box in the vertical scroll bar
Move up a greater distance in the window	Drag the scroll box up in the vertical scroll bar
Move down a greater distance in the window	Drag the scroll box down in the vertical scroll bar
Move a short distance side to side in a window	Click the left or right arrows in the horizontal scroll bar
Move to the right one screenful	Click in the area to the right of the scroll box in the horizontal scroll bar
Move to the left one screenful	Click in the area to the left of the scroll box in the horizontal scroll bar
Move left or right a greater distance in the window	Drag the scroll box in the horizontal scroll bar

Windows 95

Getting Help

Windows 95 comes with a powerful online Help system that allows you to obtain help information in several ways, depending on your current needs. The Help system provides guidance on many Windows features, including detailed steps for completing a procedure, definitions of terms, lists of related topics, and search capabilities. You can also receive assistance in a dialog box; see the related topic "More about Help" for more information. In this lesson, you'll get Help on how to start a program. You'll also get information on the taskbar. You start the online Help system from the Start menu.

Steps

1. **Click the Start button on the taskbar, then click Help**
   The Help Topics dialog box opens, as shown in Figure A-14. Verify that the Contents tab is selected.

2. **Click the Contents tab if it isn't the frontmost tab, double-click How To in the list box, then double-click Run Programs**
   The Help window displays a selection of topics related to running programs.

3. **Click Starting a program, then click Display**
   A Windows Help window opens. At the bottom of the window, you can click the Related Topics button to display a list of topics that may also be of interest. Some help topics also allow you to display additional information about important words; these words are identified with a dotted underline.

4. **Click the dotted underlined word taskbar**
   A pop-up window appears with a definition of the underlined word.

5. **Read the definition, then click anywhere outside the pop-up window to close it**

6. **Click the Help Topics button to return to the Help Topics window**
   You can use the Find tab to search for a specific word or phrase for which you want to display help topics. As you type the word or phrase in the first list box, any available words that match appear in the second list box. In the next step, search for help topics on the word "taskbar."

7. **Click the Find tab, then in the first list box, type taskbar**
   Two word matches are displayed in the second list box, as shown in Figure A-15. The third list box displays help topics related to the selected word.

8. **In the third list box, click Customizing the taskbar or Start menu, then click Display**
   The Help window that appears lists the steps for completing this task. Close the Windows Help window for now.

9. **In the Windows Help window, click the Close button ☒ in the upper-right corner of the window**
   Clicking the Close button closes the active window.

FIGURE A-14: Help Topics dialog box

Click this tab to display an alpha- betical index of Help topics

Click this tab to search for words and phrases in the Help topics

Prints contents of help topic on a printer connected to your computer

FIGURE A-15: Find tab in Help Topics dialog box

Type the word you are searching for here

List word matches

Lists the help topics for word matches

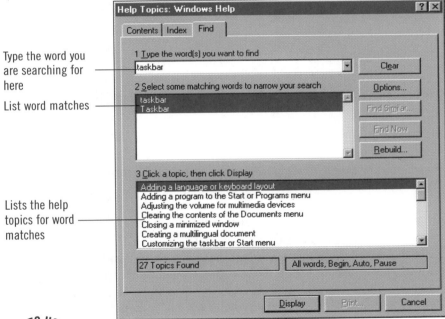

More about Help

To receive online help in a dialog box, click the Help button ☒ in the upper-right corner of the dialog box. The mouse pointer changes to ☒? . Click the Help pointer on the item for which you need addi- tional information. A pop-up window provides a brief explanation of the selected feature. You can also click the right -mouse button on an item in a dialog box. Then click the What's This? button to display the help explanation. In addition, when you click the right mouse button in a help topic window, you can choose commands to annotate, copy, and print the contents of the topic window. From the Help pop-up menu, you can also choose to have topic windows always appear on top of the currently active window, so you can see help topics while you work.

Closing a Program and Shutting Down Windows

When you are finished working with Windows, close all the open programs and windows, and then exit Windows using the Shut Down command on the Start menu. Do not turn off the computer while Windows is running; you could lose important data if you turn off your computer too soon. ▄▄▄▄▄ Close all your active programs and exit Windows.

1. Click the WordPad program button on the taskbar to make the WordPad program active

To close a program and any of its currently open files, you select the Exit command on the File menu. You can also click the Close button in the program window. See the related topic "Closing programs and files with the Close button" for more information. If you have made any changes to the open files, you will be prompted to save your changes before the program quits. Some programs also give you the option of choosing the Close command on the File menu. This command closes the active file but leaves the program open, so you can continue to work in it. In the next step, you will quit the WordPad program and return to the Windows desktop.

2. Click File on the menu bar, then click Exit

3. If you see a message asking you to save changes to the document, click No

4. In the Control Panel window, click the Close button ☒ in the upper-right corner of the window

The Control Panel window closes. *Complete the remaining steps to shut down Windows and your computer only if you have been told to do so by your instructor.*

5. Click the Start button on the taskbar, then click Shut Down

The Shut Down Windows dialog box opens, as shown in Figure A-16. In this dialog box, you have the option to shut down the computer, restart the computer in Windows mode, restart the computer in MS-DOS mode, or log on to the computer as another user.

6. Verify that the first option, "Shut down the computer?," is selected

7. If you are working in a lab click No; if you are working on your own machine or if your instructor told you to shut down Windows, click Yes to exit Windows and shut down the computer

QuickTip

Some programs allow you to close multiple files simultaneously by pressing [Shift], then clicking File on the menu bar. Click Close All to close all open files at once.

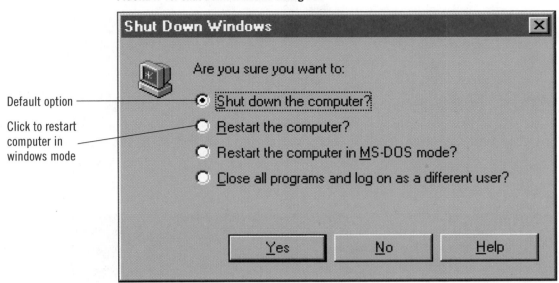

Default option ——————

Click to restart
computer in
windows mode

Closing programs and files with the Close button

You can also close a program and its open files by clicking the Close button ⊠ on the title bar in the upper-right corner of the program window. If there is a second set of sizing buttons in the window, the Close button that is located on the menu bar will close the active file only, leaving the program open for continued use.

Practice

► Concepts Review

Without referring to the unit material, identify each of the items in Figure A-17.

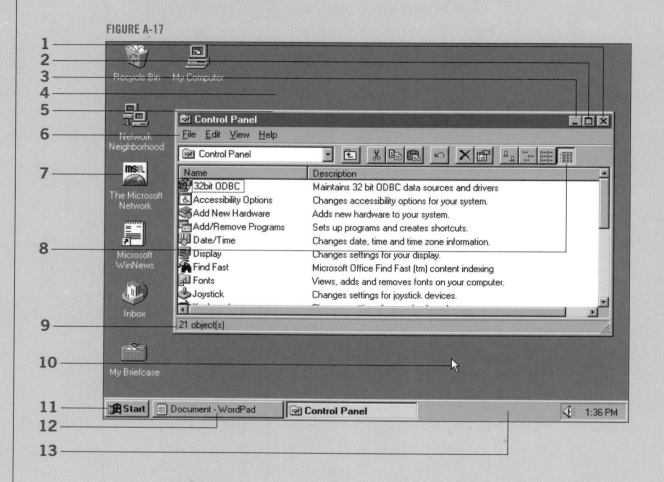

FIGURE A-17

Match each of the statements with the term it describes.

C 14. **Start button**
D 15. **Dialog box**
E 16. **Taskbar**
F 17. **Mouse**
B 18. **Title bar**
A 19. **Minimize button**
G 20. **Icon**

a. Shrinks a window to a button on the taskbar
b. Displays the name of the window or program
c. Displays list of programs you can run
d. Requests more information that you supply before carrying out command
e. Displays Start button and currently open programs
f. Lets you point to and make selections
g. Graphic representation of program you can run

▶ Skills Review

1. **Start Windows and identify items on the screen.**
   a. Turn on the computer, if necessary.
   b. After Windows loads, try to identify as many items on the desktop as you can, without referring to the lesson material. Then compare your results with Figure A-1.
2. **Practice dragging, maximizing, restoring, sizing, and minimizing windows.**
   a. Drag the Recycle Bin icon to the bottom of the desktop.
   b. Double-click the My Computer icon to open the My Computer window.
   c. Maximize the window, if it is not already maximized.
   d. Restore the window to its previous size.
   e. Size the window by dragging the window borders until you see both horizontal and vertical scroll bars.
   f. Size the window until the horizontal scroll bar no longer appears.
   g. Click the Minimize button. Now try restoring the window.
3. **Run a program.**
   a. Click the Start button on the taskbar, then point to Programs.
   b. Point to Accessories, then click Calculator.
   c. Minimize the Calculator program.
4. **Practice working with menus and dialog boxes.**
   a. Click the Start button on the taskbar, then point to Settings, then click Control Panel.
   b. Click View on the menu bar, then click Toolbar twice to practice hiding and displaying the toolbar.
   c. Double-click the Display icon.
   d. Click the Appearance tab.
   e. Write down the current settings you see in this dialog box.
   f. Try out different selections in this dialog box to change the colors on your desktop and click the Apply button.
   g. Return the options to their original settings and click OK to close the dialog box.
5. **Use online Help to learn more about Windows.**
   a. Click the Start button on the taskbar, then click Help.
   b. Click the Contents tab.
   c. Double-click Introducing Windows.
   d. Double-click each of the following topics (click Help Topics to return to the Contents window after reading each topic):
   Welcome, then A List of What's New, then A new look and feel
   Getting Your Work Done, then The basics
   Keyboard Shortcuts, then General Windows keys
   Using Windows Accessories, then For General Use
   Using Windows Accessories, then For Writing and Drawing
6. **Close all open windows.**
   a. Click the Close button to close the Help topic window.
   b. Click File on the menu bar, then click Exit to close the Control Panel window.
   c. Click Calculator in the taskbar to restore the window.
   d. Click the Close button in the Calculator window to close the Calculator program.
   e. Click the Close button in the My Computer window to close the window.
   f. If you are instructed to do so by your instructor, use the Shut Down command on the Start menu to exit Windows. Otherwise, be sure all windows and programs are closed and you have returned the desktop to its original appearance as it appeared before you began this unit.

▶ Independent Challenges

1. Microsoft Windows 95 provides an extensive help system designed to help you learn how to use Windows effectively. In addition to step-by-step instructions, there are also tips that you can try to gain even greater confidence as you become acquainted with Windows features. In this challenge, you start Help, double-click Tips and Tricks, then double-click Tips of the Day. Read each of the following topics (click Help Topics to return to the Contents window after reading each topic):

Getting your work done
Personalizing Windows
Becoming an expert
Optional: If you have a printer connected to your computer, click the Print button to print the tips described in each Help topic window.
Close all the Help topic windows and return to the desktop.

2. Use the skills you have learned in this unit to create a desktop that looks like the desktop in Figure A-18. It's OK if your desktop contains more items than in this figure.

FIGURE A-18: Shut Down Windows dialog box

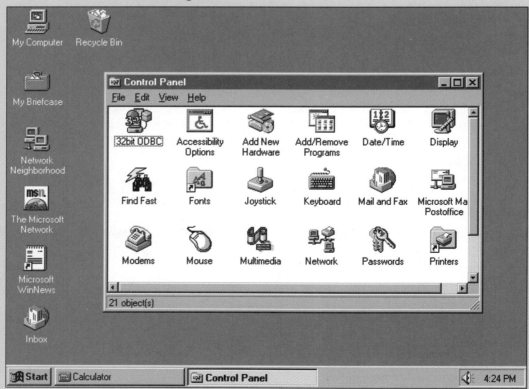

Be sure to return your settings and desktop back to their original arrangement when you complete this challenge.

Managing
Files, Folders, and Shortcuts

Objectives

► **Format a disk**
► **Create a Paint file**
► **Save a Paint file**
► **Work with multiple programs**
► **Understand file management**
► **View files and create folders with My Computer**
► **Move and copy files using My Computer**
► **View files and rename folders with Windows Explorer**
► **Delete and restore files**
► **Manage files on the desktop**

In this unit, you will explore the file management features of Windows 95. In this unit you will learn how to format a floppy disk, so that you can permanently store your work. You will then create and save files using a drawing program called Paint. Next, you will learn how to use the Clipboard to copy and paste your work from one program to another. Then, you will learn two methods for managing the files you create: using My Computer and Windows Explorer. Finally, you will learn how to work more efficiently by managing files directly on your desktop.

Windows 95

Formatting a Disk

When you use a program, your work is temporarily stored in your computer's random access memory (RAM). When you turn off your computer, the contents of RAM are erased. To store your work permanently, you must save your work as a file on a disk. You can save files either on an internal **hard disk** (which is built into your computer, usually drive C) or on a removable 3.5 or 5.25 inch **floppy disk** (which you insert into a drive on your computer, usually drive A or B). Before you can save a file on a floppy disk, you must prepare the disk to receive your file by first **formatting** the disk. To complete the steps below, you need a blank disk or a disk containing data you no longer need. Formatting erases all data on a disk, so be careful which disk you use.

Steps

1. **Place a blank, unformatted disk in drive A:**
   If your disk does not fit in the drive A, try drive B and substitute drive B wherever you see drive A.

2. **Double-click the My Computer icon on the desktop**
   The My Computer window appears, as shown in Figure B-1. This window displays all the drives and printers that you can use on your computer; depending on your computer system, your window might look different. You can use My Computer for managing your files as well as for formatting your disk. You will learn more about My Computer later in this unit. For now, locate the drive that contains the disk you want to format in the My Computer window.

3. **Right-click the 3½ Floppy (A:) icon**
   This icon is usually the first icon in the upper-left corner of the window. Clicking with the right mouse button displays a pop-up menu of commands that apply to using drive A, including the Format command.

4. **Click Format on the pop-up menu**
   The Format dialog box opens, as shown in Figure B-2. In this dialog box, you specify the capacity of the disk you are formatting and the kind of formatting you want to do. See Table B-1 for a description of formatting options.

5. **Click the Full radio button, then click Start**
   Windows is now formatting your disk. By selecting the Full option, you ensure that the disk can be read by your computer. Once a disk is formatted you will not need to format it again. After the formatting is complete, you see a summary about the size of the disk. Now that the disk is formatted, you are ready to save files on it. From now on, we will refer to this disk as your **Work Disk**. Before you continue with this unit, close each of the open dialog boxes.

6. **Click Close in the Format Results dialog box, then click Close in the Format dialog box**
   You can keep the My Computer window open for now; you will return to it later in this unit.

Trouble?

Windows cannot format a disk if it is write-protected, therefore, you need to remove (on a 5.25 disk) or move (on a 3.5 disk) the write-protect tab to continue. See Figure B-3 to locate the write-protect tab on your disk.

FIGURE B-1: **My Computer window**

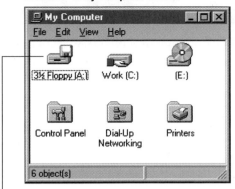

Drive containing
disk

FIGURE B-2: **Format dialog box**

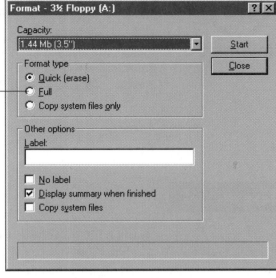

Click to format a
new, blank disk

FIGURE B-3: **Write-protect tabs**

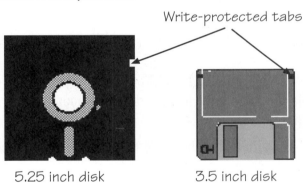

Write-protected tabs

5.25 inch disk   3.5 inch disk

TABLE B-1: **Formatting options**

Option	Description
Capacity	Click the Capacity list arrow to specify the amount of information your disk is made to hold; for a high-density disk, choose 1.44 Mb, for double-density disks, choose 720Kb
Quick (erase)	Choose this option if your disk contains files that you want to erase; it takes less time than the Full option
Full	Choose this option if you are using a new, blank disk; this option initializes, as well as formats, the disk, requiring more time to complete than the Quick option
Copy System	Use this option when you want to make the disk you are formatting bootable; this means you will be able to start Files Only
Label	Choose this option to give your disk a name; this will help you keep track of the files you save on a disk

Creating a Paint File

Most of your work on a computer involves creating files in programs. When you use a program, you can use many of the Windows skills you have already learned. In this lesson, you'll work with **Paint**, a drawing program located on the Accessories submenu that you use to create simple graphics. ▬▬▬ Launch Paint and create the drawing shown in Figure B-4.

Steps ¹²³⁴

1. **Click the Start button on the taskbar, point to Programs, point to Accessories, then click Paint**
   The Paint program window opens. Notice the title and menu bars across the top of the screen. Along the left side of the window is the Toolbox. The white rectangular area, called the **drawing area**, is where you draw. The **color palette**, which contains the colors you use to paint with, is at the bottom of the window.

2. **Click the maximize button, if necessary, to maximize the window, then click the Brush tool** 🖌
   A Linesize box appears under the Toolbox where you choose the line size of the brush stroke you want. The Brush tool is a freehand drawing tool that you will control with your mouse. See Table B-2 for description of each of the Paint tools.

3. **In the Linesize box, click the thickest line width, then move the mouse pointer on the drawing area of the Paint window**
   Your pointer changes to ▪ and you are now ready to create a simple picture.

4. **Press and hold the left mouse button, drag the mouse in a large circle, then release the mouse button**

5. **Add eyes and a mouth inside the circle to create a smiling face**
   Next, you will add color to the image.

Trouble?
If you make a mistake while painting, choose Undo from the Edit menu.

6. **Click the Fill With Color tool** 🪣**, click the bright yellow color in the bottom row of the color palette as shown in Figure B-4, then click on your smiling face with the Fill With Color pointer** 🪣
   The Fill With Color tool fills the area with the currently selected color and your drawing is complete; compare it to Figure B-4. Don't worry if your file looks slightly different. In the next lesson, you will save your work.

FIGURE B-4: Paint window with graphic

Toolbox

Fill with color pointer

Color palette

TABLE B-2: Paint Toolbox tools

tool	description	tool	description
Free-Form Select	Selects a free-form section of the picture to move, copy, or edit	Airbrush	Produces a circular spray of dots
Select	Selects a rectangular section of the picture to move, copy, or edit	Text	Inserts text in to the picture
Eraser/Color Eraser	Erases a portion of the picture using the selected eraser size and foreground color	Line	Draws a straight line with the selected width and foreground color
Fill With Color	Fills closed shape or area with the current drawing color	Curve	Draws a wavy line with the selected width and foreground color
Pick Color	Picks up a color off the picture to use for drawing	Rectangle	Draws a rectangle with the selected fill style; also used to draw squares by holding down [Shift] while drawing
Magnifier	Changes the magnification; displays list of magnifications under the toolbar	Polygon	Draws polygons from connected straight-line segments
Pencil	Draws a free-form line one pixel wide	Ellipse	Draws an ellipse with the selected fill style; also used to draw circles by holding down [Shift] while drawing
Brush	Draws using a brush with the selected shape and size	Rounded Rectangle	Draws rectangles with rounded corners using the selected fill style; also used to draw rounded squares by holding down [Shift] while drawing

Reversing actions

With the Undo feature (available in most Windows applications), you can reverse the result of the last action. For example, if you are creating a drawing in Paint and you draw a rectangle when you intended to draw a straight line, you can click Edit on the menu bar and then click Undo. In this case, this command will remove the rectangle from the graphic, so you can click a new tool and try again.

Saving a Paint File

Much of your work with Windows will involve saving different types of files. The files you create using a computer are stored in the computer's random access memory (RAM). **RAM** is a temporary storage space that is erased when the computer is turned off. To store a file permanently, you need to save it to a disk. You can save your work to a 3.5 inch disk, also know as a **floppy disk**, which you insert into the drive of your computer (i.e., drive A or B), or a hard disk, which is built into your computer (usually drive C). Now, save the Paint file you created in the last lesson in two different forms.

Steps 1 2 3 4

1. Click **File** on the menu bar, then click **Save As**, as shown in Figure B-5

   The Save As dialog box opens, as shown in Figure B-6. In this dialog box, you give your work a file name and specify where you want the file saved. Specify the location first.

2. Click the **Save In list arrow**, click **3½ Floppy (A:)** (or whichever drive contains your Work Disk), then click the **Save as type list arrow** and click **16 color Bitmap**

   The drive containing your Work Disk is now active. This means that the file you save will be saved on the disk in this drive.

3. Double-click the text in the File Name box, type **My first Paint file**, then click **Save**

   Your drawing is now saved as a Paint file with the name "My first Paint file" on your Work Disk in drive A. When you name a file, you can type up to 255 characters (including spaces and punctuation) in the File Name box. You can also use both upper and lowercase. Next, you will modify the Paint file and save the changed file with a new name.

4. Click a **light blue color** on the color palette, then click on the smiling face

   The face is now filled with the light blue color. To save this modified drawing in a new file (so you can keep the original unchanged), you can use the Save As command. If you wanted to save a change in the original file, you could use the Save command.

5. Click **File** on the menu bar, then click **Save As**

   The Save As dialog box opens, as shown in Figure B-7. Because Windows "remembers" where you last saved a file, you do not need to specify a location this time. Enter a new file-name to create a new file.

6. With the text in the File Name box selected, type **My second Paint file**, then click **Save**

   Your revised drawing is now saved as a new Paint file with the name "My second Paint file" on your Work Disk. The original file closes automatically when you use the Save As command. There are now two Paint files on your Work Disk.

FIGURE B-5: The Save As command

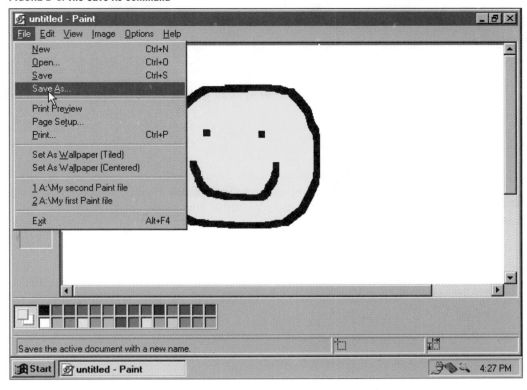

FIGURE B-6: Save As dialog box

Click to select a new location for a file

Existing files (if any) appear in list

Enter filename

FIGURE B-7: Save As dialog box for saving your second Paint file

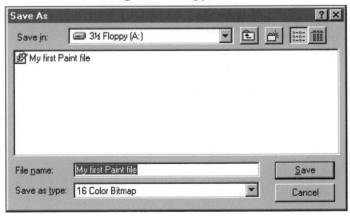

Working with Multiple Programs

Occasionally, you might want to work with more than one program at a time. For example, perhaps you have created a graphic file that you want to include with text in a document file. With Windows 95 you can copy objects onto the Clipboard. The Clipboard is a temporary area in your computer's memory for storing text or graphics. Once you place something on the Clipboard, you can paste it into other locations. Using the taskbar or keyboard, you can switch to another program quickly so that you can paste the contents of the Clipboard into another file without closing the original program. Next, you will copy the logo graphic you created in the previous lesson into a WordPad document.

Steps

1. **Click the Start button on the taskbar, point to Programs, point to Accessories, then click WordPad**
   The WordPad program window opens. If the WordPad program window does not fill your screen, click the Maximize button. The blinking insertion point, also called the cursor, indicates where the text you type will appear.

2. **In the WordPad window, type This is the new logo I created for our company brochure., then press [Enter] twice**
   Pressing [Enter] once places the insertion point at the beginning of the next line. Pressing [Enter] again creates a blank line between the first line of text and the graphic you will copy from the Paint program.

3. **Click the Paint program button on the taskbar**
   The Paint program becomes the active program in the window. Next, you will select the logo graphic in the Paint window.

4. **Click the Select tool ▢, then drag a rectangle around the entire graphic**
   When you release the mouse button, the dotted rectangle indicates the contents of the selection. The next action you take will affect the entire selection.

5. **Click Edit on the menu bar, then click Copy**
   The selected logo graphic is copied to the Clipboard. When you copy an object onto the Clipboard, the object remains in its original location, and is also available to be pasted into another location. Now you will switch to the WordPad window using the keyboard.

6. **Press and hold down [Alt], press [Tab] once, then release [Alt]**
   A box appears, as shown in Figure B-8, indicating which program will become active when you release the Alt key. If you have more than two programs open, you press the Tab key (while holding down [Alt]) until the program you want is selected. The WordPad program becomes the active program in the window.

7. **Click Edit on the menu bar, then click Paste**
   The contents of the Clipboard, in this case the Paint graphic, are pasted into the WordPad window at the location of the insertion point.

8. **Click File on the menu bar, then click Save As, and save the file to your Work Disk with the name My WordPad file**
   Be sure to select the Work Disk in the Save In box before naming the file.

9. **Click the Close buttons in both the WordPad and Paint programs to close the open files and exit the programs**
   You return to the desktop and the My Computer window.

Trouble?

If you make the wrong program active, hold down [Alt] and press [Tab] to redisplay the box. Then (while holding down [Alt]), press [Tab] to move the selection box from program to program. When the program you want to make active is selected, then release both keys.

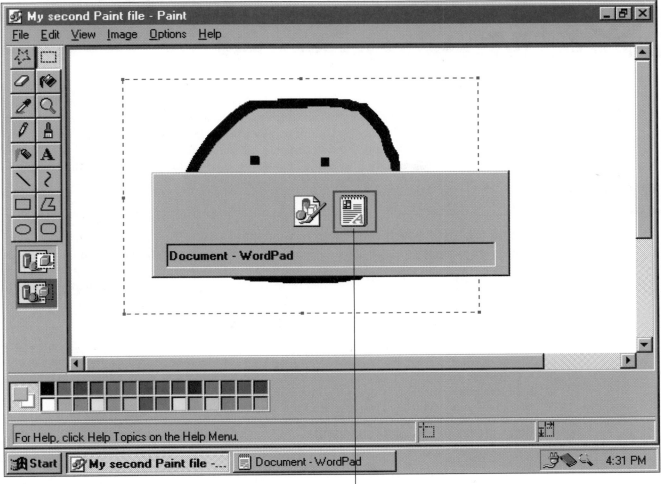

For Help, click Help Topics on the Help Menu.

Start | My second Paint file -... | Document - WordPad | 4:31 PM

Indicates which
program will
become active

Windows 95

Understanding File Management

After you have created and saved numerous files while working in various programs, it can be a challenge to keep track of all of your files. Fortunately, Windows 95 provides the tools you need to keep everything organized so you can quickly locate the files you need. There are two main tools for managing your files: My Computer (which you have already opened when you formatted your Work Disk) and Windows Explorer. You'll learn more about Windows Explorer later in this unit. No matter which tool you use, Windows 95 gives you the ability to:

Details

Create folders in which you can save your files

Folders are areas on your disk (either a floppy disk or a hard disk) in which you can save files. For example, you might create a folder for your documents and another folder for your graphics. Folders can also contain additional folders, so you can create a more complicated structure of folders and files, called a hierarchy. See Figure B-9 for an example of your Work Disk hierarchy.

Examine the hierarchy of files and folders

When you want to see the overall structure of your folders and files, you can use either My Computer or Windows Explorer. By examining your file hierarchy with these tools, you can better organize your files by adding new folders, renaming folders, deleting folders, and adjusting the hierarchy to meet your needs. Figures B-10 and B-11 illustrate sample hierarchies for your Work Disk, one using My Computer and the other using Windows Explorer.

Copy, move, delete, and rename files

For example, if you decide that a file belongs in a different folder, you can move the file to another folder. You can also rename a file if you decide a new name is more descriptive. If you want to keep a copy of a file in more than one folder, you can copy files to new folders. With the same files in two different folders, you can keep track of previous versions of files, so that they are available in the event of data loss. You can also delete files you no longer need, as well as restore files you delete accidentally.

Locate files quickly with the Windows 95 Find feature

With Find you can quickly locate files by providing only partial names or by other factors, such as by file type (for example, a WordPad document, a Paint graphic, or a program) or by the date the file was created or modified.

Preview the contents of a file without opening the file in its program

For example, if after locating a particular file, you want to verify that it is the file you want, you can use the Preview feature to quickly look at the file. The Preview feature saves you time because you do not need to wait for the program to open the file. Other options help you get additional information about your files so you can better organize your work.

FIGURE B-9: Sketch of Work Disk hierarchy

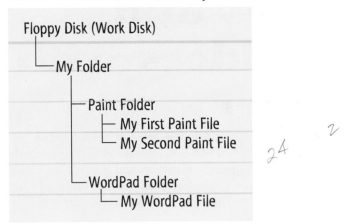

Floppy Disk (Work Disk)
└─ My Folder
   ├─ Paint Folder
   │ ├─ My First Paint File
   │ └─ My Second Paint File
   └─ WordPad Folder
      └─ My WordPad File

24   2

FIGURE B-10: Sample hierarchy in My Computer

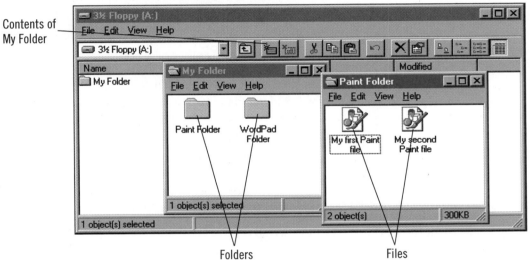

Contents of My Folder

Folders

Files

FIGURE B-11: Sample hierarchy in Windows Explorer

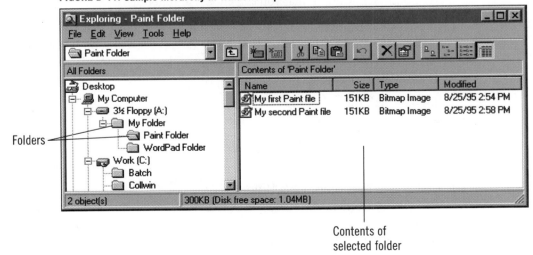

Folders

Contents of selected folder

Viewing Files and Creating Folders with My Computer

The My Computer window displays the contents of the selected drive or folder. When you double-click a drive or folder, its contents appear in a new window. ✒ Begin by using My Computer to move around in the system's file management hierarchy and then create a new folder on your Work Disk that will contain the files you create. First, you need to turn on the My Computer toolbar if it is not currently displayed. See Figure B-12 if you're not sure what the toolbar looks like.

Steps

1. **Click the Maximize button in the My Computer window, if My Computer does not already fill the screen**
   If your toolbar is visible, skip Step 2 and continue with Step 3.

2. **Click View on the menu bar, then click Toolbar**

3. **Click the drive list arrow, then click the drive icon for your hard disk**
   Now you are ready to view the hierarchy of your hard drive. You can do this using any one of the four view buttons on the My Computer toolbar.

4. **Click the Details button ▦ on the My Computer toolbar**
   In addition to the drive and folder icons, Details view also displays the type of drive or folder, the amount of total available space on the hard disk, and the remaining free space, as shown in Figure B-12. The List button provides a slightly smaller amount of information, but still mostly text-based. Let's try viewing the files and folders using a more graphical view.

5. **Click the Large Icons button ▫ on the My Computer toolbar**
   This view offers less information but provides a large, clear view of the contents of the disk.

6. **Click the Small Icons button ▫ on the My Computer toolbar**
   This view provides the same amount of information as the large icons except that the icons are smaller and take up less space in the window. Next, you want to display the contents of My Computer again, so that you can choose another drive.

7. **Click the Up One Level button ▣ on the My Computer toolbar**
   Clicking the Up One Level button displays the next level up the file hierarchy, in this case My Computer. Now, you are ready to create a folder on your Work Disk so you need to select the drive that contains your Work Disk.

8. **Double-click the 3½ Floppy (A:) icon (or B if that drive contains your Work Disk)**
   You can now create a folder that will contain the files you create in this unit.

9. **Click File on the menu bar, point to New, then click Folder**
   A new folder is created on your Work Disk. Finally, give the folder a unique name.

10. **Type My Folder, then press [Enter]**
    Verify that the contents contained in the window are the same as those shown in Figure B-13. Depending on the selections used by the previous user, your window might not match the one in the illustration. If you wish, you can match the illustration by resizing the window, displaying the toolbar, and clicking the Details button.

FIGURE B-12: Using Details view to examine the hard disk

Toolbar

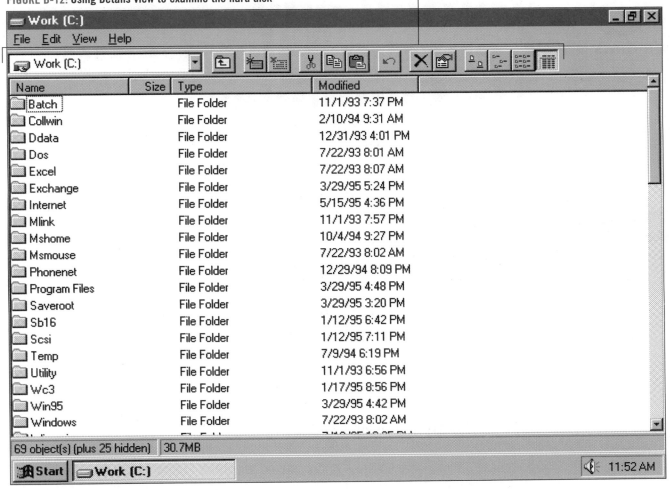

69 object(s) (plus 25 hidden)   30.7MB

FIGURE B-13: New folder in A: window

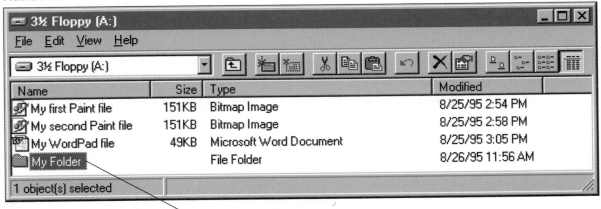

New folder

Moving and Copying Files Using My Computer

At times you might want to change the hierarchy of your files within a particular drive. For example, to better organize your files, you might decide to place files in a folder whose name reflects the name of a project or the program in which the file was created. My Computer allows you to quickly move or copy files and folders to another location. In this lesson you will create two folders within the folder you created in the previous lesson. Then you will move the appropriate files into these new folders.

Steps

1. **Double-click the My Folder to open it**
   The My Folder window opens. Before you can create a folder, you have to make sure you are creating it in the right place—in this case within the My Folder. Now you will create two folders, one named Paint Folder and the other named WordPad Folder.

2. **Right-click in an empty area of the My Folder window (away from files, folder, and buttons)**

3. **Point to New in the pop-up menu, then click Folder**
   A new folder appears in the My Folder window. Next, you'll name it.

4. **Type Paint Folder, then press [Enter]**
   Now you need to repeat these steps to create another folder.

5. **Repeat Steps 2-4 to create a folder named WordPad Folder**
   Compare your My Folder window to Figure B-14. Next, you will move the Paint files to the Paint Folder, removing them from the original location at the root of drive A:.

6. **In the 3½ Floppy (A:) window, click My first Paint file, then press [Shift] and click My second Paint file, then drag both files on top of the Paint Folder icon in the My Folder window**
   Windows displays the Moving window which shows the names of the files being moved and how much of the move operation is complete. See Table B-3 for a description of the different file selection techniques. Instead of dragging files or folders to a new location, you can use the cut, copy, and paste commands on the Edit menu or the Cut, Copy, and Paste toolbar buttons. Next, you will move the WordPad file to the WordPad folder.

7. **Click My WordPad file to select it, then drag the file over the WordPad Folder icon and release the mouse button**
   The My WordPad file is moved to the WordPad Folder. Next, you will close all of the open windows including the 3½ Floppy (A:) window.

8. **Click the Close buttons in all open windows**
   All open windows are closed and you return to the Windows desktop.

QuickTip

To cut a selected file, you can press [Ctrl] [X]. To copy a selected file, you can press [Ctrl] [C]. To paste a selected file, you can press [Ctrl] [V].

FIGURE B-14: **Contents of My Folder**

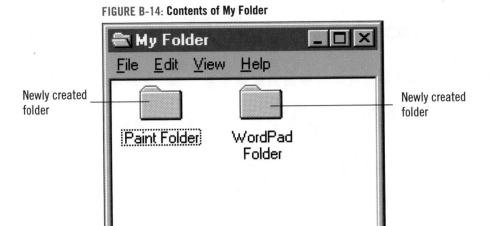

Newly created folder

Newly created folder

TABLE B-3: **File/folder selection techniques**

To Select This	Use This Technique
Individual objects not grouped together	Click the first object you want to select, then press [Ctrl] as you click each additional object you want to add to the selection
Objects grouped together	Click the first object you want to select, then press [Shift] as you click the last object in the list of objects you want to select; all the objects listed between the first and last objects are selected

CLUES TO USE

Using Edit commands to copy and move files

An alternative to dragging files is to use the Cut, Copy, or Paste commands on the Edit menu or the Cut, Copy and Paste buttons on the toolbar. The Cut and Copy commands or Cut and Copy buttons 🔪 📋 place the selected files on the Clipboard.

Once on the Clipboard, the files can be pasted into the destination folder with the Paste command or Paste button 📋. Be sure to select the destination folder before you paste your files. You can also use keyboard shortcuts to cut, copy, and paste files.

Viewing Files and Renaming Folders with Windows Explorer

You've seen how to view, copy, and move files and create folders with My Computer. Windows 95 also provides another tool, Windows Explorer, that is particularly useful when you need to establish a hierarchy or move and copy files between multiple drives. You can also use Windows Explorer to view files without opening them. In this lesson, you will copy a folder from your Work Disk onto the hard drive, and then rename it.

Steps 1 2 3 4

1. **Click the Start button, point to Programs, click Windows Explorer, then click the Maximize button in the Windows Explorer window**
   The Windows Explorer window appears, as shown in Figure B-15. You can see right away that unlike My Computer, the window is divided into two sides called panes. The left pane displays the drives and folders on your computer. The right pane displays the contents of the drive or folder selected in the left pane. A plus sign next to a folder in the left pane indicates there are additional files or folders located within a drive or folder. A minus sign indicates that all folders of the next level of hierarchy are displayed.

2. **In the left pane, right-click the hard drive icon, then click Properties on the pop-up menu**
   The Properties dialog box opens with the General tab the frontmost tab. Here, you see the capacity of your hard drive and how much free space you have available. After you've examined the properties of your hard drive you can close this window.

3. **Click the Close button in the Properties dialog box**
   Next, you will use Windows Explorer to examine your Work Disk.

4. **In the left pane double-click the 3½ Floppy (A:) icon**
   The contents of your Work Disk are displayed in the right pane as shown in Figure B-16. The plus sign next to My Folder indicates that it contains additional folders. Try expanding My Folder in the next step.

5. **In the left pane, click the plus sign next to My Folder**
   The folders contained within the My Folder now appear in the left pane.

6. **In the left pane, click the WordPad folder**
   The contents of the WordPad folder appear in the right pane of Windows Explorer. In the next step, you'll copy the WordPad folder to the hard drive in order to have a backup copy for safe keeping.

7. **In the left pane, drag the WordPad folder on top of the icon for the hard drive, then release the mouse button**
   The WordPad folder and the file in it are copied to the hard disk. Check to see if the copy of this folder is on the hard drive.

8. **In the left pane, click the icon representing your hard drive**
   The WordPad Folder should now appear in the list of folders in the right pane. You might have to scroll to find it. Now let's rename the folder so you can tell the original folder from the backup.

9. **Right-click the WordPad folder in the right pane, click Rename in the pop-up menu, then type Backup WordPad Folder and press [Enter]**
   Leave the Windows Explorer window open and continue with the next lesson.

FIGURE B-15: Windows Explorer window

Menu bar

Sizing buttons

Toolbar

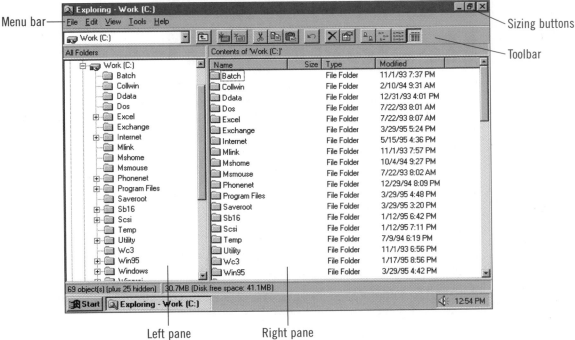

Left pane

Right pane

FIGURE B-16: Contents of your Work Disk

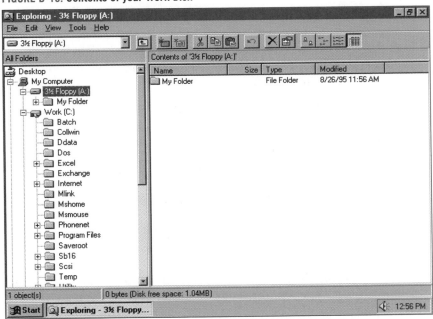

Quick View

At times you might want to preview a document to get an idea of what is in the file before opening it. It is much faster to preview the document using either My Computer or Windows Explorer than opening the program in which the file was created, then opening the file. To preview the file, simply right-click the selected file, then click Quick View on the pop-up menu. A preview of the file appears in the Quick View box. If the Quick View command does not appear on the pop-up menu, it means that this feature was not installed on your computer; see your instructor or technical support person for additional information.

Windows 95

Deleting and Restoring Files

To save disk space and to manage your files more effectively, you should delete files you no longer need. Because all files deleted from your hard drive are stored in the Recycle Bin (until you remove them permanently), you can restore files you might have deleted accidentally. There are many ways to delete files in Windows 95. In this lesson, you'll use two different methods for removing files you no longer need. Then you will learn how to restore a deleted file.

1. Click the **Restore button** on the Windows Explorer title bar
Now you should be able to see the Recycle Bin icon on your desktop. If you can't see it, resize or move the Windows Explorer window until it is visible.

2. Drag the folder called **Backup WordPad Folder** from the right pane to the **Recycle Bin** on the desktop
The folder no longer appears in the Windows Explorer window because you have moved it to the Recycle Bin. The Recycle Bin looks as if it contains paper. If you see an "Are you sure you want to delete" confirmation box, click No and see the Trouble? on the next page. Next, you will examine the contents of the Recycle Bin.

3. Double-click the **Recycle Bin** icon on the desktop
The Recycle Bin window appears, as shown in Figure B-17. Depending upon the number of files already deleted on your computer, your window might look different. The folder doesn't appear in the Recycle Bin window but the file does. Use the scroll bar if you can't see it. Next, you'll try restoring a deleted folder.

4. Click **Edit** on the Recycle Bin menu bar, then click **Undo Delete**
The Backup WordPad folder is restored and should now appear in the Windows Explorer window. You might need to move or resize your Recycle Bin window if it blocks your view of the Windows Explorer window. Next, you can delete the Backup WordPad folder for good using a Windows Explorer toolbar button.

5. Click the **Backup WordPad Folder** in the left pane, then click the **Delete button** ❎ on the Windows Explorer toolbar
The Confirm Folder Delete dialog box opens as shown in Figure B-18.

6. Click **Yes**
When you are sure you will no longer need files you've moved into the Recycle Bin, you can empty the Recycle Bin. You won't do this now, in case you are working on a computer that you share with other people. But, when you're working on your own machine, simply right-click the Recycle Bin icon, then click Empty Recycle Bin in the pop-up menu.
Leave both the Recycle Bin and the Windows Explorer windows open and continue to the next lesson.

Trouble?

If you are unable to recycle a file, it might be because your Recycle Bin is full, or too small, or the properties have been changed so that files are not stored in the Recycle Bin, they are deleted right away. Right-click the Recycle Bin icon, then click Properties on the pop-up menu to change the settings for storage and capacity.

FIGURE B-17: Contents of Recycle Bin

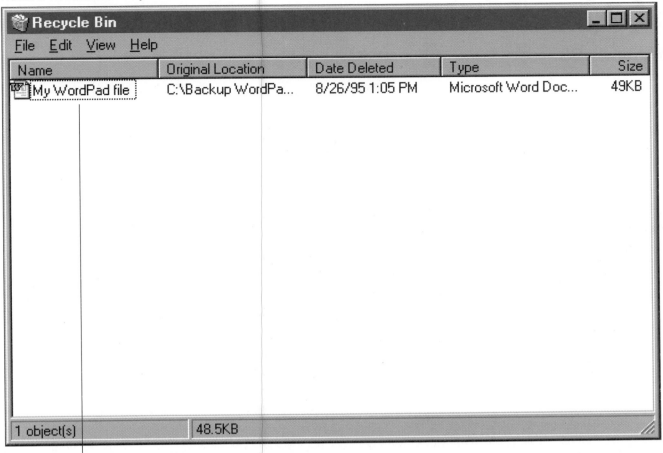

File you just
deleted

FIGURE B-18: Confirm Folder Delete dialog box

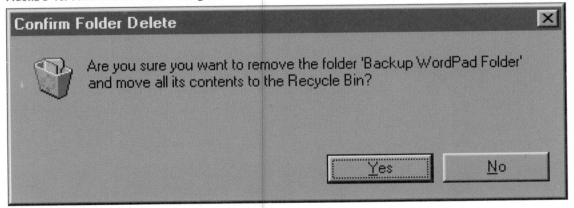

CLUES TO USE

Important note about deleting files on a floppy disk

You cannot restore files deleted from a floppy disk. Once a file on a floppy disk is sent to the Recycle Bin, it is permanently removed from the floppy disk and cannot be retrieved.

Managing Files on the Desktop

You've now learned two different tools for managing files in Windows 95: My Computer and Windows Explorer. There is yet another Windows 95 feature you can use to make it easier to access files, folders, or programs you frequently use. A pop-up menu on the Windows desktop allows you to create folders and shortcuts on the desktop itself. **Shortcuts** are icons that point to an object that is actually stored elsewhere in a drive or folder. When you double-click a shortcut, you open the object without having to find its actual location. In this lesson, you will create a shortcut to the My WordPad file. Creating shortcuts to files you use frequently and placing them on the desktop allows you to work more efficiently.

QuickTip

Windows 95 enables you to customize your desktop to suit your work habits. For example, you can create a folder on the desktop that you can use to store all of your shortcuts. You can even create a shortcut folder on the desktop.

1. **In the left pane of the Windows Explorer window, click the WordPad folder**
   You need to select the file you want to create a shortcut to, first.

2. **In the right pane, right-click the My WordPad file**
   A pop-up menu appears as shown in Figure B-19.

3. **Click Create Shortcut in the pop-up menu**
   The file named Shortcut to My WordPad file appears in the right pane. Now you need to move it to the desktop so it will be at your fingertips whenever you need it. If you drag it using the left mouse button you will copy it to the desktop. If you drag it using the right mouse button you will have the option to copy or move it. Let's try dragging it using the right mouse button.

4. **Right-drag the Shortcut to My WordPad file to an empty area of the desktop**
   When you release the mouse button a pop-up menu appears.

5. **Click Move Here in the pop-up menu**
   A shortcut to the My WordPad file now appears on the desktop as shown in Figure B-20. When you double-click this shortcut icon, you will open both WordPad and the My WordPad file document. Now let's delete the shortcut icon in case you are working in a lab and share the computer with others. Deleting a shortcut does not delete the original file or folder to which it points.

6. **On the desktop, click the Shortcut to My WordPad file, then press [Delete]; click Yes to confirm the deletion**
   The shortcut is removed from the desktop and now appears in the Recycle Bin; however, the file itself remains intact in the WordPad folder. (See the Windows Explorer window to make sure it's still there.)

7. **Close all open windows**

FIGURE B-19: Pop-up menu

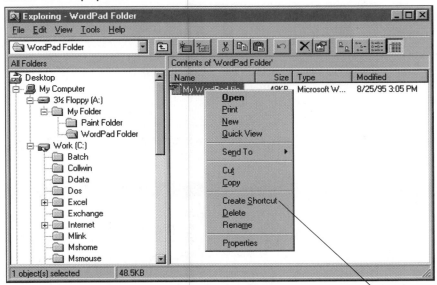

Click to create a
shortcut to the file

FIGURE B-20: Shortcut on desktop

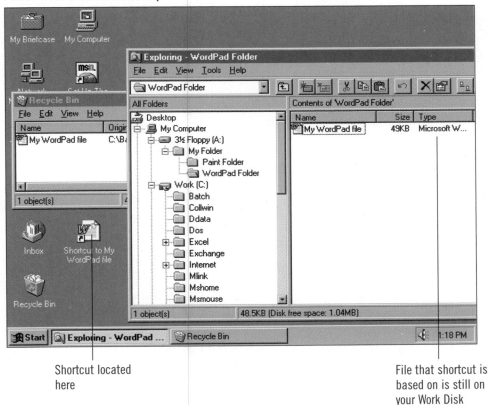

Shortcut located
here

File that shortcut is
based on is still on
your Work Disk

Adding shortcuts to the Start menu

If you do not want your desktop to get cluttered with icons, but you would still like easy access to certain files, programs, and folders, you can create a shortcut on the Start menu or any of its cascading menus.

Drag the file, program, or folder that you want to add to the Start menu from the Windows Explorer window to the Start button. The file, program, or folder will appear on the first level of the Start menu.

Practice

► Concepts Review

Label each of the elements of the Windows Explorer window shown in Figure B-21.

FIGURE B-21

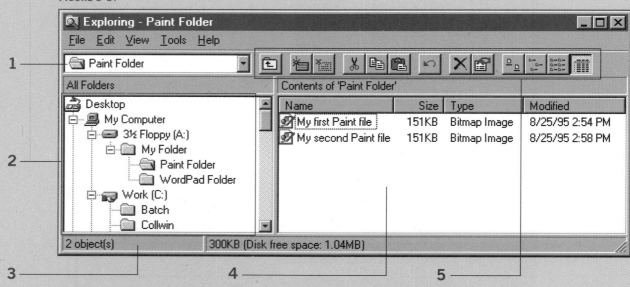

Match each of the descriptions with the correct term.

6. **RAM**
7. **Folders**
8. **Files**
9. **Hierarchy**
10. **Clipboard**

a. Permanent storage of your work in programs
b. Temporary location of your work as you use a program
c. Temporary location of information you wish to paste into another program
d. Storage area for organizing files or folders by type, project, or whatever you wish
e. Structure of files and folders revealing organization of a disk

Select the best answer from the list of choices.

11. **To prepare a floppy disk to receive your files, you must first do which of the following?**
    a. Copy work files to the disk
    b. Format the disk
    c. Erase all the files that might be on the disk
    d. Place the files on the Clipboard

12. **To view the contents of a folder, you can use which of the following tools?**
    a. The desktop   **b.** Windows Explorer   **c.** My Computer   **d.** Either b or c

13. **You can use the My Computer program to:**
    a. Create a drawing of your computer.
    b. View the contents of a folder.
    c. Customize the Start menu.
    d. Determine what programs begin automatically when you start Windows.

14. **While you are working in a program, where is your work stored?**
    a. On a hard drive   **b.** In RAM   **c.** In the monitor   **d.** On the Clipboard

15. **What is the correct sequence for starting the Paint program?**
    a. Double-click the Paint shortcut on the desktop
    b. Click Start, Programs, Accessories, Paint
    c. Click Start, Programs, Paint
    d. Click Start, Accessories, Paint

16. **Which of the following best describes the WordPad program?**
    a. A program for pasting in graphics
    b. A program for performing complex financial analysis
    c. A program that is a simple text editor for creating basic documents
    d. A program for creating graphics

17. **For most Windows programs, the Save As command is located on which menu?**
    a. File
    b. Edit
    c. Help
    d. Save

18. **Which of the following is NOT a way to move files from one folder to another?**
    a. Opening the file and using the Save As command to save the file in a new location.
    b. In My Computer or the Windows Explorer, drag the selected to the new folder.
    c. Use the Cut and Paste commands on the Edit menu while in the My Computer or the Windows Explorer windows.
    d. Use the [Ctrl] [X] and [Ctrl] [V] keyboard shortcuts while in the My Computer or the Windows Explorer windows.

19. **Which of the following is a way to rename the selected file in either the My Computer window or the Windows Explorer window?**
    a. Click Edit on the menu bar, then click Rename.
    b. Click File on the menu bar, then click Rename.
    c. Click the Rename button on the toolbar.
    d. You can only rename files in the program in which the file was created.

20. **In which of the following can you view the hierarchy of drives, folder, and files in a split pane window?**
    a. The Windows Explorer window
    b. The Programs window
    c. The My Computer window
    d. The WordPad window

▶ Skills Review

1. **Format a disk.**
   a. Insert a new blank disk in a drive.
   b. Open My Computer and use the right mouse button to click on the drive.
   c. Format the disk using the Format command on the pop-up menu. Check that the capacity and format type are correct.

2. **Create a WordPad file.**
   a. Launch WordPad.
   b. Type a short description of your artistic abilities and press [Enter] several times to create extra space between the text and the graphic you are about to create.
   c. Insert your Work Disk in the appropriate disk drive, then save the document as My New Document to the My Folder on your Work Disk.
   d. Minimize the WordPad program.

3. **Create and save a Paint file.**
   a. Launch Paint.
   b. Create your own unique, colorful design using several colors. Use a variety of tools. For example, create a filled circle and then place a filled square inside the circle. Use the Text button to create a text box in which you type your name.
   c. Save the picture as My Art to the My Folder on your Work Disk.
   d. Select the entire graphic and copy it onto the Clipboard.

    e. Switch to the WordPad program.

    f. Place the insertion point below the text and paste the graphic into your document.

    g. Save the changes to your WordPad document.

    h. Switch to the Paint program.

    i. Using the Fill With Color button, change the color of a filled area of your graphic.

    j. Save the revised graphic with a new name, My Art2 to the My Folder on your Work Disk.

    k. Select the entire graphic and copy it to the Clipboard.

    l. Switch to the WordPad program and above the picture type "This is an improved graphic."

    m. Select the old graphic by clicking the picture, then paste the new contents of the Clipboard. The new graphic replaces the old graphic that was selected.

    n. Save the changed WordPad document with a new name, My Second Document to the My Folder on your Work Disk.

    o. Exit the Paint and WordPad programs.

4. Manage files and folders with My Computer.

    a. Open My Computer.

    b. Be sure your Work Disk is in either drive A or drive B.

    c. Double-click the drive icon that contains your Work Disk to prepare for the next step.

5. Create new folders on the Work Disk and on the hard drive.

    a. Create a folder called My Review Folder on your Work Disk by clicking File, New, then clicking Folder.

    b. Open the folder to display its contents in a separate window.

    c. Create another folder (at the root of C on the hard drive) called My Temporary Folder.

    d. In the My Review Folder window, click File, New, then click Folder. Create two new subfolders (under My Review Folder), one called Documents and the other called ArtWork.

    e. In the My Computer window, double-click the drive C icon to display the contents of your hard drive in a new window.

6. Move files to the new folders in the My Review Folder.

    a. Open the ArtWork folder on your Work Disk.

    b. From the root of the Work Disk, drag the two Paint files into the ArtWork folder window on your Work Disk. Close the ArtWork folder window.

    c. Open the Documents folder on your Work Disk.

    d. From the root of the Work Disk, drag the two WordPad files into the Documents folder window on your Work Disk. Close the Documents folder window.

    e. Close all of the open windows in My Computer.

7. Copy files to the My Temporary Folder on the hard drive.

    a. Open the Windows Explorer.

    b. Copy the four WordPad and Paint files from the folders on the Work Disk to the My Temporary Folder.

8. Delete files and folders.

    a. Drag the My Temporary Folder to the Recycle Bin icon.

    b. Click the My Review Folder and press [Del]. Then confirm that you want to delete the file.

    c. Double-click the Recycle Bin icon and restore the My Temporary Folder and its files. Delete the folder again.

9. Create a shortcut that opens Windows Explorer.

    a. Use Windows Explorer to locate the Windows folder on your hard drive. In the right side of the window, scroll through the list of objects until you see a file called Explorer.

    b. Drag the Explorer file to the desktop.

    c. Close the Windows Explorer.

    d. Double-click the new shortcut to test the shortcut for starting Windows Explorer. Then close the Explorer again.

    e. Delete the shortcut for Windows Explorer. Then use the Start button to verify that the Windows Explorer program is still available on the Programs menu.

Independent Challenges

1. It is important to develop a sound, organized plan when you manage files and folders. Practice your skills by organizing the following list of names into a coherent and logical hierarchy. Begin by identifying folders. In each folder, identify the files you could expect to find in them. Sketch a hierarchical structure like the one you would see in the right side of a Windows Explorer window.

- Projects
- My Resume
- Recommendation letter
- First Qtr Bulletin
- Marketing
- Finance
- Sales 95
- Sales 96
- Personal
- Employee Profile article
- Sales 94
- Project Plan Second Qtr
- Project Plan First Qtr
- Sales Summary
- Performance Review 1996

2. It is important to develop a sound, organized plan when you manage files and folders. Practice your skills by organizing the following list of names into a coherent and logical hierarchy. Begin by identifying folders. Then in each folder, identify the files you could expect to find in them. Sketch the series of windows containing the folders and files you would display using My Computer. For example, one of the windows might represent the contents of a folder designated for non-work related files.

- Projects
- My Resume
- Recommendation letter
- First Qtr Bulletin
- Marketing
- Finance
- Sales 95
- Sales 96
- Personal
- Employee Profile article
- Sales 94
- Project Plan Second Qtr
- Project Plan First Qtr
- Sales Summary
- Performance Review 1996

3. On your computer's hard drive (at the root of C:), create a folder called My Review Folder. Then using the files on your Work Disk, create the file hierarchy indicated below. Follow these guidelines to create the files you need to place in the correct folders.

1. Create a new file using WordPad that contains a simple list of things to do. Save the file as To Do List.
2. Create two copies of any WordPad files and rename them New WordPad Article and Copy of Article.
3. Copy any Paint file and rename the copy Sample Logo.
4. Copy the To Do List, and rename the copy Important.

After you have placed the files in their correct folders, copy the My Review Folder (and its contents) to your Work Disk. Then on your hard drive, delete the My Review Folder. Using the Recycle Bin icon, restore the file called Important. To remove all your work on the hard drive, delete this file again.

4. To make working with files on a floppy disk easier, create a shortcut to a Windows Explorer window that displays the contents of a disk in the drive that currently contains your Work Disk. (*Hint*: Open Windows Explorer as shown in Figure B-23 and drag the icon representing your floppy drive to the desktop). Next, capture a picture of your desktop (with the new shortcut) onto the Clipboard by pressing the [Prnt Scrn] key (located on the upper-right side of your keyboard). With the picture on the Clipboard, open the Paint program and paste the contents of the Clipboard into the drawing window as shown in Figure B-24. Save the Paint file as My Desktop Picture on your Work Disk. Finally, delete the shortcut.

FIGURE B-22

My Review Folder
    ➥Projects
        ➥To Do List
        ➥Communications (folder)
            ➥New WordPad Article
            ➥Copy of Article
        ➥Graphics (folder)
            ➥Sample Logo
            ➥CTI Important

Getting
Started with Word 97

Objectives

► **Define word processing software**
► **Launch Word 97**
► **View the Word program window**
► **Enter and save text in a document**
► **Insert and delete text**
► **Select and replace text**
► **Get Help and with the Office Assistant**
► **Preview, print, close a document, and exit Word**

Welcome to Microsoft Word 97. Microsoft Word is a powerful computer program that helps you create documents that communicate your ideas clearly and effectively. More than an automated typewriter, it provides graphics, sophisticated formatting, proofing tools, and charts, to name just a few of its features. The lessons in this unit introduce you to the basic features of Word and familiarize you with the Word environment as you create a new document. ◢▬ Angela Pacheco is the marketing manager at Nomad Ltd, an outdoor sporting gear and adventure travel company. Angela's responsibilities include communicating with new and current customers about the company. To make her job easier, she'll be using Word to create attractive and professional-looking documents. She'll begin by exploring the Word environment while creating a letter to her shareholders.

Defining Word Processing Software

Microsoft Word is a full-featured **word processing** program that allows you to create attractive and professional-looking documents quickly and easily. You'll find that word processing offers many advantages over typing. Because the information you enter in a word processing document is stored electronically by your computer, it is easy to revise and reuse text in documents that you (or others) have already created. In addition, you can enhance your documents by giving text a special appearance, adding lines, shading, and creating tables. Figure A-1 illustrates the kinds of features you can use in your documents. ▰ Angela is eager to learn about some of the benefits she can expect by using Word. Table A-1 describes additional features she will use as she learns about working in Word.

Details

Locate and correct spelling mistakes and grammatical errors
As you use Word to create documents use Word's proofreading tools to identify errors and correct them. The AutoCorrect feature even corrects many typing mistakes as you make them.

Copy and move text without retyping
You can save time by copying text from other documents and using it again in the current document. Within the same document, you can easily reorganize and edit text.

Enhance the appearance of documents by adding formatting
By applying different types of formatting (including shading and borders) to important parts of documents, you can create documents that convey your message effectively to your readers. Word features, such as the Formatting toolbar, styles, and AutoFormat, help you do this quickly.

Align text in rows and columns using tables
Although you can use another program such as Microsoft Excel, for complex financial analysis, you can also use tables in Word to present small amounts of financial information in an easy-to-read format. You can also format the tables to emphasize important points.

FIGURE A-1: Features in a Word document

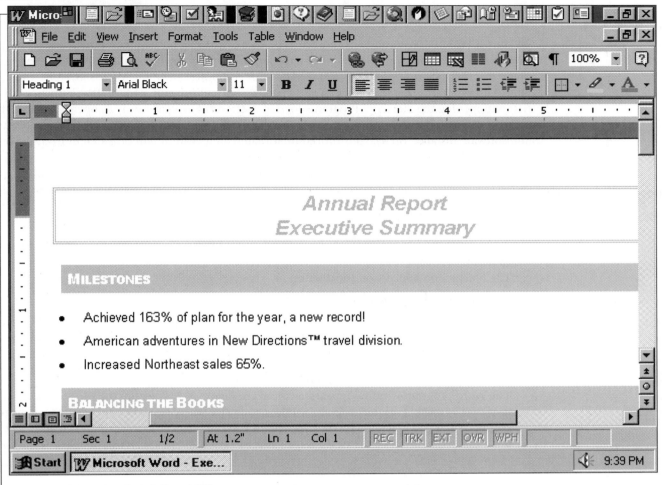

If you had a previous installation of Office on your computer, your screen may contain the Office 97 shortcut bar. Click the Close button on the shortcut bar.

TABLE A-1: Additional Word Features

feature	description	example
AutoSummarize	Allows you to see important ideas in a document	When you use the AutoSummarize command, Word highlights important words, phrases, sentences in the document. This feature helps you learn about the main ideas without requiring you to read the entire document.
Templates and Wizards	Provides the ability to create standard business documents using professionally designed formats	Word provides a number of preformatted business documents that help you quickly create the documents you need, including memos, letters, and faxes. You can even create your own templates for customized company documents.
AutoComplete	After you type a few characters of a word you use often, Word suggests the word it expects you to insert	This feature can save you a lot of time. As you work in Word, it keeps track of words and phrases you use often. Then when you type just a few characters, Word displays a word it expects you to type. When you press [Enter] Word inserts the remaining text.
AutoText	Allows you to store and insert frequently used words and phrases for fast document creation	By storing frequently used words and phrases as AutoText entries, such as a standard closing to letters, you can work faster and with fewer errors.
Document Map	Combines Outline view with Normal view	In a large document, use the Document Map to view the overall structure of the document and quickly locate headings and text you want to edit.

Word 97

Launching Word 97

To launch Word 97, you must first launch Windows by turning on your computer. You get to the Word program by clicking Start and then choosing Word from the Programs menu. The Programs menu displays the list of programs installed on your computer, including Microsoft Word. You can launch all programs this way. You can also create a shortcut on your desktop that launches Word without opening the Start and Programs menus. A **shortcut** is a faster way to open a program or a document. Because each computer system can have a different setup (depending on the hardware and software installed on it), your procedure for launching Word might be different from the one described below, especially if your computer is part of a network. See your instructor or technical support person for additional instructions. The marketing department at Nomad has installed Word 97 on all their computers, including Angela's. Angela's first step in learning to use Word 97 is to launch the program.

1. **Make sure the Windows desktop is open, then click the Start button**  **on the taskbar**
   The Start menu appears on the desktop.

2. **On the Start menu, point to Programs**
   Each menu remains open as you point, as shown in Figure A-2. Depending on the programs installed on your computer, the programs you see on the Programs menu might be different from the ones shown in the figure.

3. **On the Programs menu, click Microsoft Word**
   The Word program window appears, as shown in Figure A-3. The blinking vertical line, called the **insertion point,** | in the program window, indicates where text will appear when you begin typing. When you first launch Word, by default you can begin entering text and creating a new document right away. In the next lessons, you will continue to explore basic Word features.

Trouble?

If you have installed Microsoft Office on your computer, you might need to click Microsoft Office on the Programs menu, before you click Microsoft Word.

Creating Shortcuts

You can create a shortcut on the desktop to launch Word without going through all the menus. You just double-click a shortcut, and the program starts. To create a shortcut on the desktop, use either My Computer or Windows Explorer to locate the Program Files folder. In this folder, open the Winword folder, and locate the application file called Winword. Drag this file out of the window and onto the desktop. To eliminate the shortcut, just drag the shortcut to the Recycle Bin and confirm that you want to remove the shortcut from the desktop. Note: If you are working on a network or you share your computer with others, get permission from your instructor or technical support person before creating shortcuts on the desktop.

FIGURE A-2: Menus on the Windows desktop

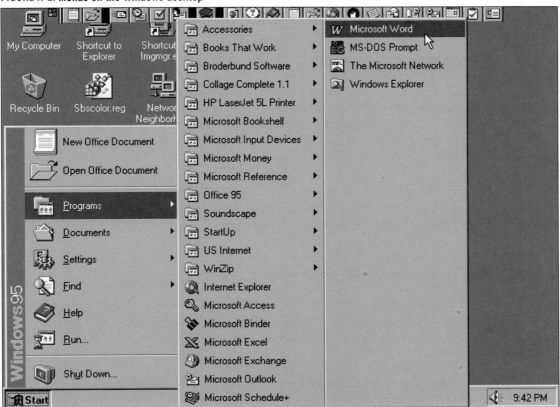

FIGURE A-3: Word program window

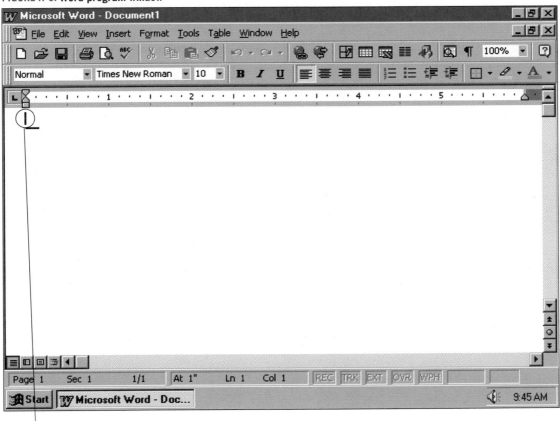

Insertion point

Viewing the Word Program Window

Now that you are in the Word **program window**, you can see some of the key features of Word. Word provides different views that allow you to see your document in different ways. In default view (called normal view), you see the features described below. On your computer, locate each of the elements described below using Figure A-4 for reference.

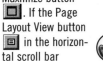

Details

 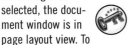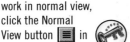
 The **title bar** displays the name of the program and the document. Until you save the document and give it a name, the temporary name is Document1.

The **menu bar** lists the names of the menus that contain Word commands. Clicking a menu name on the menu bar displays a list of commands from which you can choose.

The **Standard toolbar** contains buttons for the most frequently used commands, such as the commands for opening, saving, and printing documents. This toolbar is one of the two default toolbars. Clicking buttons on a toolbar is often faster than using the menu bar.

The **Formatting toolbar** contains buttons for the most frequently used formatting commands, such as applying bold to text or aligning text. This toolbar is the other default toolbar. Other toolbars related to other features are also available.

The **horizontal ruler** displays tab settings, left and right paragraph margins, and document margins.

 The **document window** displays the work area for typing text and working with your document. The blinking insertion point is the location where your text appears when you type. When the mouse pointer is in the text area of the document window, the pointer changes to an **I-beam**, I . You can have as many document windows open as your computer's memory will hold. You can minimize, maximize, and resize each window. When only one document is open, maximize the document window so that you see more of the document.

 The **vertical and horizontal scroll bars** display the relative position of the currently displayed text in the document. You use the scroll bars and **scroll boxes** to view different parts of your document.

 The **view buttons**, which appear in the horizontal scroll bar, allow you to display the document in one of four views: normal, online layout, page layout, and outline. Each view offers features that are useful in the different phases of working with a document.

 The **status bar** displays the current page and section numbers, the total number of pages, and the position of the insertion point (in inches and in lines from the upper-left corner of the document).

When you position the pointer over a button, a **ScreenTip** appears showing the name of the button. You can customize the ScreenTips to display keyboard shortcuts. You also have the option to hide the ScreenTips.

FIGURE A-4: Elements of the Word program window

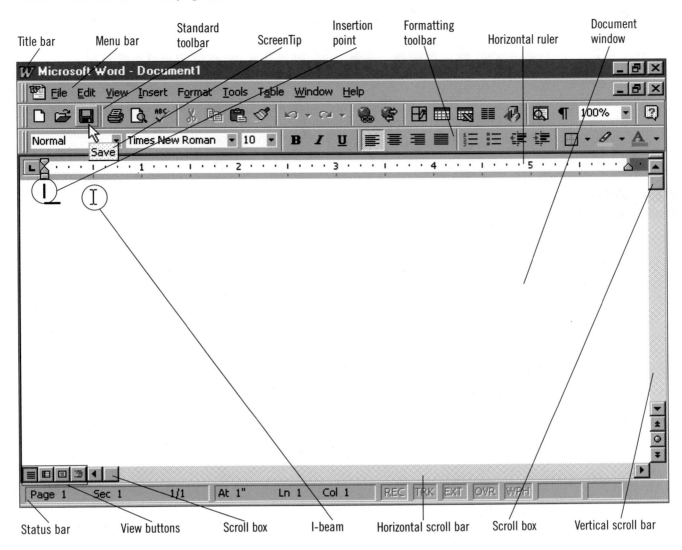

Title bar   Menu bar   Standard toolbar   ScreenTip   Insertion point   Formatting toolbar   Horizontal ruler   Document window

Status bar   View buttons   Scroll box   I-beam   Horizontal scroll bar   Scroll box   Vertical scroll bar

Customizing ScreenTips

To display or hide ScreenTips, click Toolbars on the View menu, click Customize, click the Options tab, then select or clear the Show ScreenTips on toolbars check box. You can also hide or display keyboard shortcuts as part of the ScreenTip by deselecting the Show shortcut keys in ScreenTips check box.

Word 97

Entering and Saving Text in a Document

When you launch Word, the program opens a document window in which you can create a new document. You can begin by simply typing text at the insertion point. When you reach the end of a line as you type, Word automatically moves the insertion point to the next line. This feature is called **word-wrap**. To insert a new line or start a new paragraph simply press [Enter]. It is also a good idea to save your work shortly after writing your first paragraph and every 10 or 15 minutes and before printing. You can save a document using the Save button on the Standard toolbar, or the Save or Save As commands on the File menu.   Angela begins by typing the first two paragraphs in the body of her letter to Nomad Ltd's shareholders.

Steps 1 2 3 4

1. At the insertion point, type the following paragraph:

   The year has been an exciting and profitable year, at Nomad Ltd. As a shareholder, you will be interested to learn about our recent successes and the challenges we expect in the coming year and beyond. This letter includes the high points of the year and provides valuable details about our work in individual areas of the organization, including finance, communications, quality assurance, and travel. In the next few days you will receive a complete Annual Report for the entire organization and detailed profiles for each division.

   Do not press [Enter] when you reach the end of a line. Just keep typing.

2. Insert your Student Disk in drive A, then click the **Save button** 🖫 on the Standard toolbar

   The Save As dialog box opens, as shown in Figure A-5. In this dialog box, you need to assign a name to the document you are creating, replacing the default filename supplied by Word.

3. In the File name text box, type **First Draft Letter**

   Next, you need to instruct Word to save the file to your Student Disk. The name of the currently active drive or folder appears in the Save in list box.

4. Click the **Save in list arrow**, then click $3\frac{1}{2}$**Floppy (A:)**, and then click **Save.**

   These lessons assume your Student Disk is in drive A. If you are using a different drive or storing your practice files on a network, click the appropriate drive.

5. Press **[Enter]** twice

   The first time you press [Enter], the insertion point moves to the start of the next line. The next time you press [Enter], you create a blank line before the text you type next.

6. Type the following paragraph:

   We are proud of our employees and encourage you to join us at the Annual Meeting to be held at the Ocean View Suites next month. Enclosed please find an Annual Meeting reply card, which you can return to let us know if you plan to attend.

7. At the end of the second paragraph, press **[Enter]** once

   Don't be concerned about making typing mistakes. Also, don't be concerned if your text wraps differently from the text shown in the figure. How text wraps depends on your monitor or printer. Next display the number of spaces between words and paragraphs, by displaying non-printing characters.

8. Click the Show/Hide button ¶ on the Standard toolbar

   The spaces between words appear as dots. New lines are represented by ¶ at the end of a paragraph. Compare your screen to Figure A-6 then click Save.

9. Click 🖫

   The document is saved with the name First Draft Letter on your Student Disk.

FIGURE A-5: **Save As dialog box**

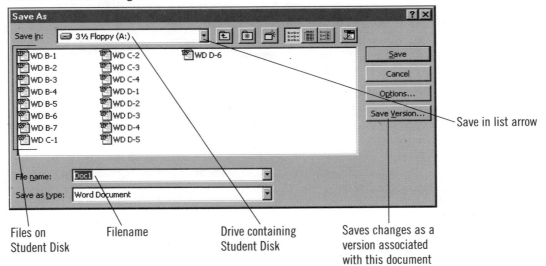

Files on
Student Disk

Filename

Drive containing
Student Disk

Saves changes as a
version associated
with this document

Save in list arrow

FIGURE A-6: **Text in a Word document**

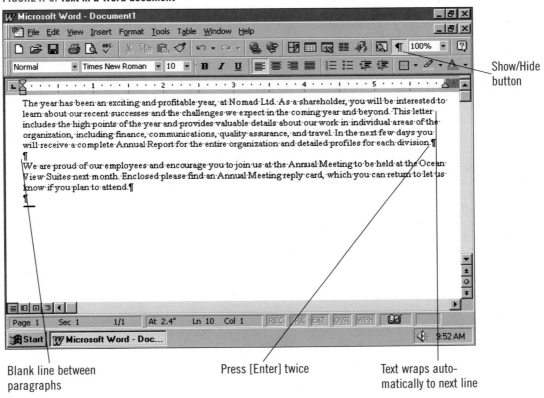

Show/Hide
button

Blank line between
paragraphs

Press [Enter] twice

Text wraps auto-
matically to next line

Working with Automatic Corrections

If you make certain kinds of spelling or typographical errors, you might notice that Word automatically makes the necessary corrections as you type. This feature is called AutoCorrect. For example, some common spelling mistakes (such as typing 'adn' instead of 'and') are corrected as soon as you type the first space after the word. Similarly, if you type two capitalized letters in a row, Word automatically changes the sec-ond character to lower case as you continue typing (except in a state's abbreviation, such as 'WA'). If you misspell a word that is not corrected right away, Word underlines the word with a red, wavy underline. If you make a potential grammatical error, Word underlines the error with a green, wavy underline. After you finish typing, click the right mouse button on the word to display a pop-up menu of correction options.

Inserting and Deleting Text

After typing text, you often need to edit it by inserting new text or deleting text you want to remove. To insert text, place the insertion point where you want the new text to appear, then start typing. You can delete text to the left or the right of the insertion point. Word also offers commonly used AutoText entries that can be inserted in your documents for more information. Whenever you insert or delete text, Word adjusts the spacing of the existing text. First, Angela adds the inside address to her letter, then she'll make a few corrections by removing individual characters.

Trouble?

If your typing overwrites existing text, check to see if the indicator "OVR" appears in black in the status bar. Press [Insert] or double-click OVR in the status bar to switch back to Insert mode, so that text you type does not overwrite existing text.

QuickTip

The Letter Wizard is a fast and easy way to create letters. Just click the Letter Wizard option in the Office Assistant balloon-shaped dialog box and complete the dialog boxes according to your preferences.

1. Press [Ctrl][Home] to place the insertion point at the beginning of the document and type the following address, pressing [Enter] after each line:
   Ms. Malena Jeskey [Enter]
   456 Greenview Lane [Enter]
   Shoreview, CA 90272 [Enter]
   Notice that a wavy, red underline appears under the word "Malena" and other proper names. This means that these words are not in Word's dictionary.

2. Press [Enter] again to insert a blank line and type **Dear Shareholder:** and press [Enter] twice

3. If the Office Assistant appears asking if you want to create a letter using a wizard, click **Cancel** in the Office Assistant balloon-shaped dialog box
   If you create a letter using the Letter Wizard, you simply respond to a series of dialog boxes. So that you can learn a lot more about using Word, for now type this letter without the aid of the wizard. Next, you want to change the word "The" in the first sentence to "This."

4. Place the insertion point after the word **The** (but before the space) in the first sentence, press [Backspace], then type **is**
   This removes the "e" and inserts "i" and "s." Next, you will delete an unnecessary comma.

5. Place the insertion point after the second occurrence of the word **year** (but before the comma) in the first sentence, then press [Delete]
   This removes the comma. Next, you will add today's date to the beginning of the letter. First, move to the beginning of the document.

6. Press [Ctrl][Home]
   With the insertion point at the beginning of the document, you can insert the date.

7. Click **Insert** on the menu bar, then click **Date and Time**
   The Date and Time dialog box opens. Word displays the date based on your computer's system clock. Before you proceed, verify that the Update Automatically check box is cleared, so that the date is not updated each time you save or print the document. For formatting dates in letters and other business correspondence, choose the third option in the list.

8. In the dialog box, click the third option in the list, then click **OK**
   Today's date automatically appears in the document.

9. Press [Enter] twice
   Compare your document to Figure A-7. The date you see might be different.

FIGURE A-7: Letter after inserting and deleting text

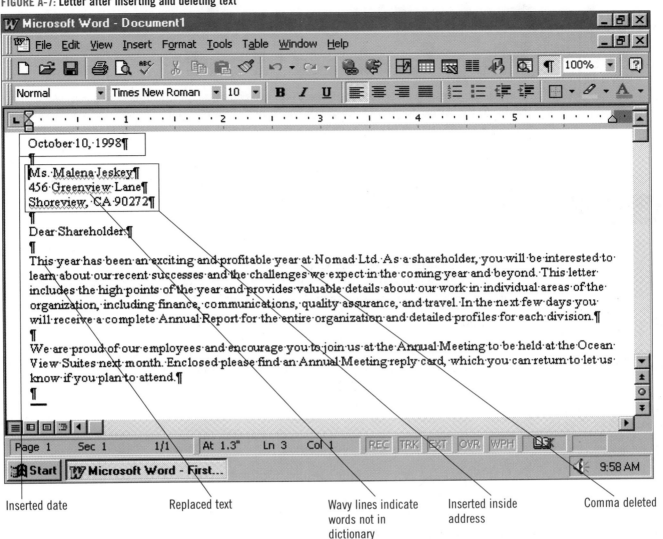

Inserted date   Replaced text   Wavy lines indicate words not in dictionary   Inserted inside address   Comma deleted

Inserting built-in AutoText entries

AutoText entries are words or phrases that are frequently used, such as company names or greetings and closings in letters. Word includes various built-in AutoText entries which are arranged by subject, such as closings and salutations. To insert a built-in AutoText entry, point to AutoText on the Insert menu, click the desired subject, then click the desired AutoText entry as shown in Figure A-8. The AutoText entry is inserted at the place of the insertion point.

FIGURE A-8: Built-in AutoText entries on the Insert menu

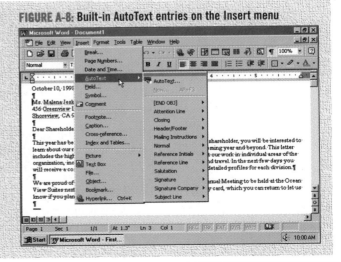

Word 97

Selecting and Replacing Text

In addition to editing characters one at a time, you can also edit multiple characters, words, paragraphs, or the entire document. Most Word editing techniques require that you first select the text you want to edit. For example, to delete existing text and replace it with new text, you first select the text you want to remove, then type the new text. This feature is called **Typing Replaces Selection.** Table A-2 describes the different ways to select text with a mouse. You can also change your mind about the revisions you make with the Undo and Redo features. Next, Angela uses various techniques to select and replace text.

Trouble?
If text you type does not replace selected text, click Tools, click Options, click the Edit tab, then click to select the Typing Replaces Selection check box. Click OK to return to the document.

1. **Place the insertion point in front of the second occurrence of the word year in the first sentence and drag across the word**
The highlighting indicates that the word is selected. You want to replace the selection so that the word "year" is not used twice in the same sentence.

2. **Type one**
The word "one" replaces the selected word. Now you will replace several words with one word.

3. **Place the insertion point in front of the word please in the last sentence and drag across it and the next word, find, then release the mouse button and type is**
Both words and the spaces that follow the words are selected. If you drag across too many words, drag back over the text to deselect it. The word "is" replaces the selected text. Word inserts the correct spacing and reformats the text after the insertion point. You will replace the word "includes" in the third sentence.

4. **Double-click the word includes in the third sentence, then type summarizes**
The word "summarizes" replaces the selected text, along with the correct spacing. If you change your mind about a change, you can reverse it. You will reinsert the word "includes."

5. **Click the Undo Typing button on the Standard toolbar**
The word "includes" replaces the word "summarizes." Clicking the Undo Typing button reverses the most recent action. The arrow next to the Undo Typing button displays a list of all the changes you've made since opening the document, so you can undo one or more changes. You can also reverse a change you have undone.

6. **Click the Redo Typing button on the Standard toolbar**
The word "summarizes" reappears. As with the Undo Typing feature, the arrow next to the Redo Typing button displays a list of changes you can redo.

7. **Position the pointer to the far left of the first line of the body of the letter until the pointer changes to , then click the mouse button**
Clicking next to the line in the selection bar selects the text. The **selection bar** is the area to the left of the text in your document, as shown in Figure A-9.

8. **Click anywhere in the document to deselect the text**
The first line is no longer selected. Whenever you want to deselect text, simply click in the document window. Compare your screen to Figure A-10.

9. **Click the Save button on the Standard toolbar.**
Your document is now saved.

FIGURE A-9: Selected text and selection bar

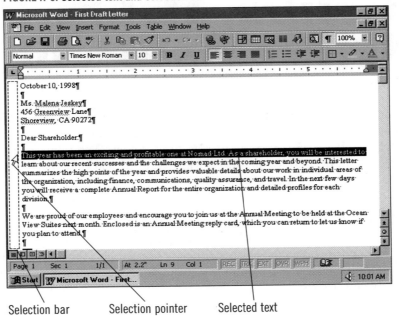

Selection bar   Selection pointer   Selected text

FIGURE A-10: Completed document

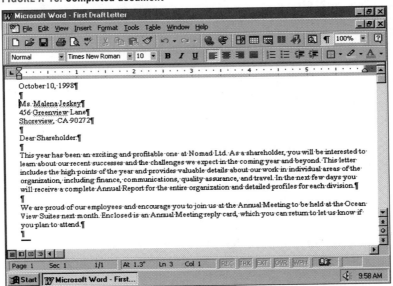

TABLE A-2: Mouse selection techniques

to select text with the mouse	do this
A word	Double-click the word
A sentence	Press and hold [Ctrl] and click in the sentence
A paragraph	Triple-click in the paragraph, or double-click in the selection bar next to the paragraph
A line of text	Click in the selection bar next to the line
An entire document	Press and hold [Ctrl] and click anywhere in the selection bar, or triple-click in the selection bar
A vertical block of text	Press and hold [Alt] and drag through the text
A large amount of text	Place the insertion point at the beginning of the text, move to the end of the desired selection, then press and hold [Shift] and click

Getting Help with the Office Assistant

The Word program includes an online Help system that provides information and instructions on Word features and commands while you are using Word. You can get as little or as much information as you want, from quick definitions to detailed procedures. The **Office Assistant** is just one way to find help while working in Word. Using this animated assistant is an easy way to display Help windows and discover new features. Other Help commands are on the Help menu. In the next lesson, Angela will save, print, and close the document. Before she does this, she will use the Office Assistant to learn more about saving a document.

Steps 1 2 3 4

1. **Click the Office Assistant button ❓ on the Standard toolbar**
   The Office Assistant appears, as shown in Figure A-11. Your animated assistant may look different depending on which assistant is selected on your computer. If this is the first time the Office Assistant has been used on your computer, you will see the message "preparing Help file for first use."

2. **Type saving documents under Type your question here, and then click Search**
   In this area you can type key words or whole questions for which you would like more information.

3. **Click Search**
   The Office Assistant offers various topics related to saving documents from which you can choose.

4. **Click the Save a document option button**
   A Help window opens detailing various save features.

5. **Scroll through the Help window and read about saving documents**
   At the bottom of the Help window you will find a list of related topics from which you can choose. These topics will give detailed instructions on performing certain operations.

6. **Position the pointer over the topic Save a new, unnamed document, until the pointer changes to 👆 and click**
   A new Help window opens displaying the steps necessary for saving a document. When the pointer changes to 👆 once you've placed the pointer over a word or button, you can click to display more information.

7. **Click the Save button 💾 in the Help window**
   A message appears describing the function of this button.

8. **Click outside of the Help window in the letter document**
   The Save button message is hidden, but the Help window is still visible. The letter document is active again. A window is active when the title bar is highlighted. An inactive window will have a dimmed title bar. Compare your screen to Figure A-12.

9. **Click the Close button ❎ in the Help window, and then click the Close button in the Office Assistant window**

FIGURE A-11: Office Assistant in Word document

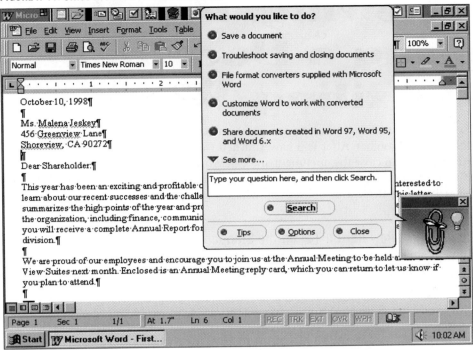

FIGURE A-12: Visible Help window

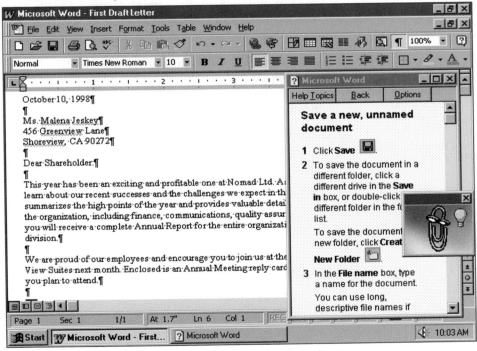

More about using Help

You can also use commands on the Help menu when searching for Help information. Click Help on the menu bar, then click Contents and Index. The Help Topics dialog box will open. You can use the Contents tab to choose from various Help topics or you can use the Find and Index tabs to search for key words that you provide. You can also use the What's This pointer ▶? to find information. Click What's This on the Help menu, then click the What's This pointer over buttons, formatting, and features. To turn off the pointer, click What's This on the Help menu again.

Previewing, Printing, Closing a Document, and Exiting Word

Once you have saved your document, you can print one copy of the document using the Print button on the Standard toolbar. After you have finished working in a document and it has been saved and printed, you can close the document and exit Word. Angela has finished working with her letter for now. She would like to save, print, and close the document before exiting Word. Angela will use the directions in the Help window to save her document.

1. **Click the Print Preview button 🔍 on the Standard toolbar**
   The document appears in the Preview window, as shown in Figure A-13. The size of the page you see depends on the number and size of pages displayed the last time the Print Preview command was issued.

2. **Click the Close button on the Print Preview toolbar to return to your document**

3. **Click the Save button 💾 on the Standard toolbar to save your document**

4. **Click the Print button 🖨 on the Standard toolbar**
   The Print button prints the current document to the default printer connected to your computer. If you are not connected to a printer, ask your technical support person or instructor for assistance. You are now ready to close your document.

QuickTip

Clicking the Close button on the right end of the menu bar closes the document. Clicking the Close button on the right end of the title bar exits the program.

5. **Click File on the menu bar, then click Close**
   When you close a document that has changes you have not saved, Word asks if you want to save your changes. If you get a message asking if you want to save changes, click Yes. The documents closes.

6. **Click File on the menu bar, then click Exit**
   The Exit command closes the Word program and returns you to the Windows desktop.

FIGURE A-13: Document in Print Preview

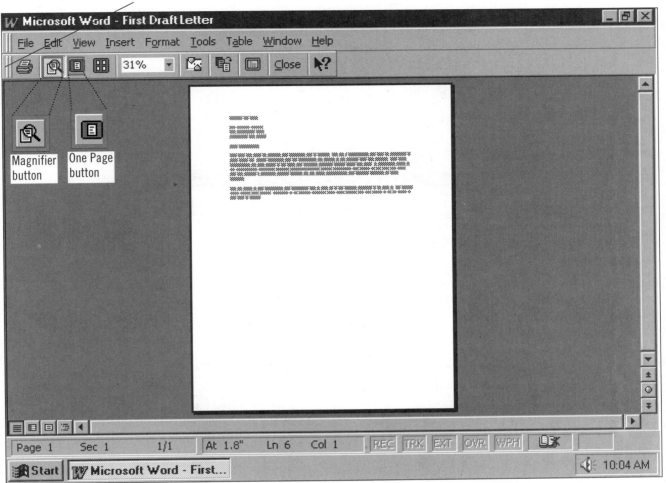

Practice

► Concepts Review

Label each option in the Save As dialog box shown in Figure A-14.

FIGURE A-14

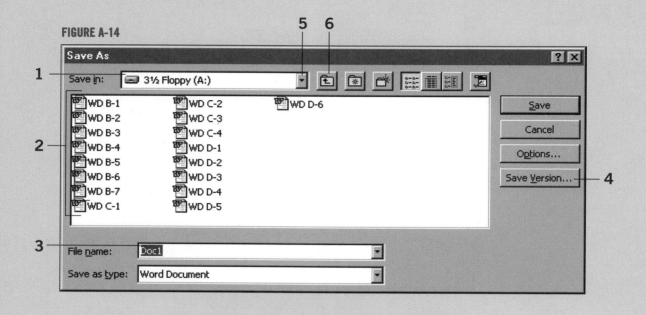

Match each of the following terms with the statement that best describes its function.

7. Standard toolbar
8. Formatting toolbar
9. Document window
10. Ruler
11. Status bar
12. Deleting
13. Inserting
14. AutoText

a. Displays area in which you enter text
b. Identifies location of insertion point and command status
c. Contains buttons for easy access to general commands such as Open and Print
d. Removing the text to the right or left of the insertion point
e. Displays tab settings, paragraph and document margins
f. Typing text between existing text
g. Contains buttons for easy access to commands that affect the appearance of text in a document
h. Standard text and expressions you can insert instead of typing

Select the best answer from the list of choices.

15. **Word processing is most similar to:**
    a. Performing financial analysis
    b. Filling in forms
    c. Typing
    d. Forecasting mortgage payments

16. **To display another part of a document, you:**
    a. Click in the Moving toolbar
    b. Scroll with a scroll bar
    c. Drag the ruler
    d. Select the Close box

17. **You can get Help in any of the following ways, except:**
    a. Clicking the Help box in a dialog box
    b. Double-clicking anywhere in the document window
    c. Clicking the Help button on the Standard toolbar
    d. Clicking Help on the menu bar

18. **What keys do you press to move the insertion point to the first character in a document?**
    a. [Ctrl][Home]
    b. [Home]
    c. [Alt][PgUp]
    d. [Shift][Tab]

19. **The Close command on the File menu:**
    a. Closes Word without saving any changes
    b. Closes the current document and, if you have made any changes, asks if you want to save them
    c. Closes all currently open Word documents
    d. Closes the current document without saving changes

20. **To leave the Word program window, you must:**
    a. Close all open documents or lose your work when you close Word
    b. Click the Exit button on the Standard toolbar
    c. Click the Close command on the File menu, which closes documents and closes Word
    d. Click the Exit command on the File menu, which closes documents and closes Word

21. **Which of the following methods is not a way to select text?**
    a. Clicking in the selection bar
    b. Dragging across the text
    c. Double-clicking a word with the left mouse button
    d. Dragging text to the selection bar

22. **Which key do you press to remove text to the left of the insertion point?**
    a. [Backspace]
    b. [Delete]
    c. [Cut]
    d. [Overtype]

▶ Skills Review

1. **Launch Word, then identify the parts of the window.**
    a. Click the Start button on the Windows desktop taskbar.
    b. Point to Programs.
    c. Click Microsoft Word.
    d. Identify as many elements of the Word window as you can without referring to the unit material.

2. Explore the Word program window.

    a. Click each of the menus and drag the mouse button through all the commands on each menu. To close a menu without making a selection, drag the mouse away from the menu, then release the mouse button.

    b. Point to each of the buttons on the toolbars, and read the ScreenTips and descriptions.

    c. Click Tools, then click Options. In the Options dialog box, click the Edit tab and make sure that the first three options are selected. Click any of these three check boxes that are not selected.

    d. Click OK to close the dialog box.

3. Enter and save text in a new document.

    a. At the insertion point, type a short letter to a local business describing your interest in learning more about the company.

    b. Don't type the inside address or a closing yet. For a greeting, type "To Whom It May Concern:". (If the Office Assistant appears offering Help in writing your letter, click Cancel.)

    c. Be sure to state that you are looking for a position in the company.

    d. Mention that you have been encouraged to investigate opportunities at the company by counselors, instructors, and alumni.

    e. Request a copy of the company's annual report to understand the scope of the company's business. For a closing, type "Sincerly," then press [Enter] twice. Notice that Word corrects your typing for you.

    f. Save the document on your Student Disk as Information Letter.

4. Insert and delete text.

    a. Place the insertion point at the beginning of the document.

    b. Insert today's date and press [Enter] twice.

    c. Type the name of the company contact and press [Enter]. Use whatever contact name you want.

    d. Type the company name and press [Enter]. Use whatever company name you want.

    e. Type the company address and press [Enter].

    f. Type the city, state, and postal code, then press [Enter].

    g. Press [Enter] twice, then type your name and press [Enter].

    h. Type your street address and press [Enter].

    i. Type your city, state, and postal code and press [Enter] again.

    j. Type your phone number.

    k. Use [Backspace] to delete your phone number. Press [Enter] once more.

5. Select and replace text.

    a. Select the text "To Whom It May Concern:", then type "Dear" followed by the name of the recipient of the letter; for example, Mr. Martin.

    b. Select the last word of the document, then press [Delete] to delete the entire word.

    c. Click the Undo button to restore the original text.

    d. Use selecting and replacing techniques to correct any mistakes in your letter.

6. Explore Word Help.
   a. Click the Office Assistant button on the Standard toolbar.
   b. Type "Print" under What would you like to do?.
   c. Click Search.
   d. Click the option button next to Print a document.
   e. Click Print a range of pages.
   f. Click Options, Print Topic.
   g. Click the What's This? button, then click Properties.
   h. Click Cancel.
   i. Click the Close button in the Help window.
   j. Click the Close button in the Office Assistant window to close this Help option.

7. Print and close the document and exit Word.
   a. Save the document, and then click the Print button on the Standard toolbar.
   b. Click File on the menu bar, then click Close.
   c. Click No if you see a message asking if you want to save your changes.
   d. Click File on the menu bar, then click Exit.

► Independent Challenges

1. Using the Contents and Index command on the Help menu, learn more about Keyboard shortcuts. Use the Show Me button in the Help windows to see an animated demonstration of the features. Print the Help windows as you go using the Print Topic command on the Options menu. Figure A-15 displays an example of one of the windows that you can print.

FIGURE A-15

Keys for working with documents	
To	**Press**
Create a new document	CTRL+N
Open a document	CTRL+O
Close a document	CTRL+W
Split a document	ALT+CTRL+S
Save a document	CTRL+S
Quit Word	ALT+F4
To	**Press**
Find text, formatting, and special items	CTRL+F
Repeat find	ALT+CTRL+Y
Replace text, specific formatting, and special items	CTRL+H
Go to a page, bookmark, footnote, table, comment, graphic, or other location	CTRL+G
Go back to a page, bookmark, footnote, table, comment, graphic, or other location	ALT+CTRL+Z
Browse a document	ALT+CTRL+HOME
To	**Press**
Cancel an action	ESC
Undo an action	CTRL+Z
Redo or repeat an action	CTRL+Y
To	**Press**
Switch to page layout view	ALT+CTRL+P
Switch to outline view	ALT+CTRL+O
Switch to normal view	ALT+CTRL+N
Move between a master document and its subdocuments	CTRL+\

2. As a co-chair for the Lake City High School 1993 class reunion planning committee, you are responsible for recruiting classmates to help with reunion activities. Using Figure A-16 as a guide, draft a letter to the 1993 graduates asking for volunteers to aid the four reunion committees: entertainment, hospitality, meals, and transportation. For the inside address, use any name and address you wish. Save this document as "1993 Letter". Be sure to insert today's date and salutation. (If the Office Assistant appears offering Help in writing your letter, click Cancel.)

FIGURE A-16

June 25, 1998

Ms. Sandy Carter
8899 Lakeshore Boulevard
Minneapolis, MN 56789

Dear Sandy:

As a member of the Lake City High School class of 1993, I often think of the people who made our school such a rewarding experience for me. Of course, there are the close friends I made and kept throughout the years, but also I think about the people I somehow lost track of since graduation. The instructors, students, and administrative staff all contribute to the richness of the memories.

Now is your opportunity to play an important role in helping bring Lake City High School memories alive not only for yourself, but for your fellow classmates as well. As the co-chair of the 1998 Reunion planning committee, I am looking for ambitious, organized alumni who are interested in working on various reunion activities.

We need people for the following areas: meeting coordination for all committees, computer consulting to help us use technology to work efficiently, meals and entertainment planning for the three-day event, and logistics coordination for getting everyone to Lake City and lodging them once they return to campus. All committees need as many volunteers as possible, so you are sure to be able to work in any area you choose.

If you are interested and available to work five hours a month for the next 10 months, please let me know. You can leave me a message at (555)555-4321. I look forward to hearing from you soon.

[your name]
Lake City High School Reunion 1993
Co-Chair

3. As a recent graduate, you are scouring the planet for job opportunities. Log on to the Internet and use your browser to go to http://www.course.com. From there, click Student On Line Companions, and then click the Microsoft Office 97 Professional Edition—Illustrated: A First Course page, then click on the Word link for Unit A. Click on the link that takes you to a list of employment opportunities. After downloading a file of interesting positions, create a cover letter that describes your qualifications or the qualifications such a position would require. Use Figure A-17 as a guide for the content of this letter. Save the document as "Job Letter". Be sure to insert today's date and an inside address and salutation. (If the Office Assistant appears offering Help in writing your letter, click Cancel.)

FIGURE A-17

June 7, 1998

Ms. Kelly Grand
Hewlett Packard
HP Circle W406
Cupertino, CA 98007

Dear Ms. Grand:

I am interested in working as a Senior Programmer for your organization. I am an expert programmer with over 10 years of experience to offer you. I enclose my resume as a first step in exploring the poossibilities of employment with Hewlett Packard.

My most recent experience was designing an automated billing system for a trade magazine publisher. I was responsible for the overall product design, including the user interface. In addition, I developed the first draft of the operator's guide.

As a Senior Programmer with your organization, I would bring a focus on quality and ease of use to your system development. Furthermore, I work well with others, and I am experienced in project management.

I would appreciate your keeping this inquiry confidential. I will call you in a few days to arrange an interview at a convenient time for you. Thank you for your consideration.

Sincerely,

[your name]

4. As a co-chair for the Lake City High School class of 1993 planning committee, you have received a telephone message from a classmate volunteering to serve on the entertainment committee. Use the Letter Wizard, which appears after you type a salutation and press [Enter], to create a thank you letter to this volunteer that provides details about the entertainment committee members, meeting place, and schedule. Enter your letter preferences in each of the Letter Wizard dialog boxes. For the inside address, use any name and address you wish. Save the document with the name "Thank You Letter". Be sure to insert today's date and an inside address and salutation. Compare your letter to the one shown in Figure A-18.

FIGURE A-18

September 15, 1996

Mr. Oliver Randall
Vice President/Marketing
InterSysData Corp.
4440 Pacific Boulevard
San Francisco, CA 94104

Dear Mr. Randall:

Thank you for volunteering to participate on the entertainment committee for the Lake City High School 1990 class reunion. We are looking forward to working with you on these events.

So that you can arrange your time accordingly, please block out the first Thursday of each month for the next six months for planning meetings. All meetings will take place at 7:30 p.m. at the Comfort Corner Coffee Shop in Middleburg (on Highway 95, next to the Burger Palace drive-in). Our first meeting will be next month; please come prepared to discuss your ideas for entertainment events at the reunion.

Please let me know by noon on the meeting date if you are unable to attend any of these meetings.

[your name]
Lake City High School Reunion 1990
Co-Chair

Visual Workshop

You are currently planning an International Communications conference and have been contacting independent consultants to deliver short presentations. Type a thank you letter to a consultant who has agreed to demonstrate new online features to conference attendees. Be sure to misspell some words so you can observe the automatic corrections provided by Word. You can view AutoCorrect entries with the AutoCorrect command on the Tools menu. Try to use as many inserting, selecting, and replacing techniques as possible. Save the document as "International Voices". Compare your document to Figure A-19. You can either use the Letter Wizard or create your own letter from scratch.

FIGURE A-19

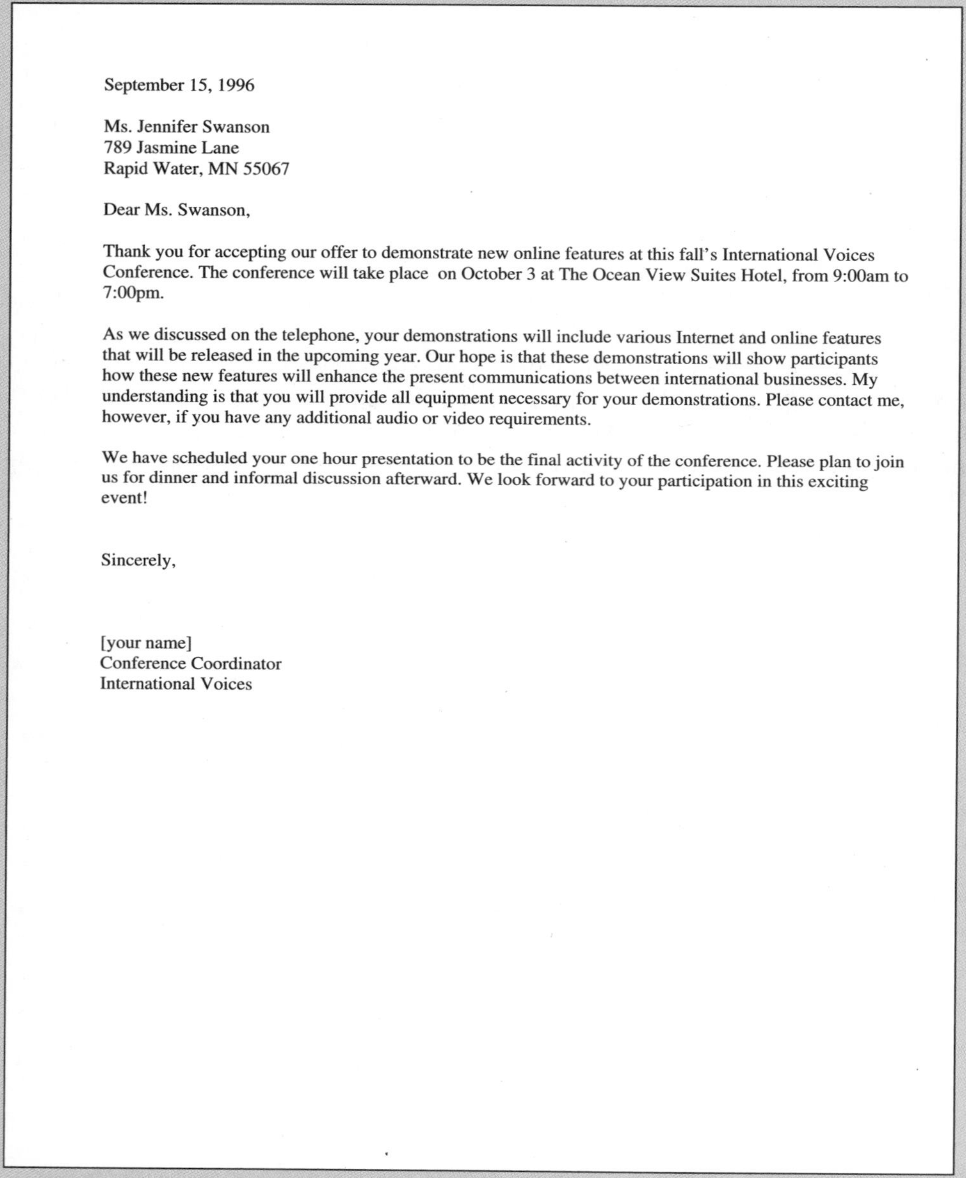

September 15, 1996

Ms. Jennifer Swanson
789 Jasmine Lane
Rapid Water, MN 55067

Dear Ms. Swanson,

Thank you for accepting our offer to demonstrate new online features at this fall's International Voices Conference. The conference will take place on October 3 at The Ocean View Suites Hotel, from 9:00am to 7:00pm.

As we discussed on the telephone, your demonstrations will include various Internet and online features that will be released in the upcoming year. Our hope is that these demonstrations will show participants how these new features will enhance the present communications between international businesses. My understanding is that you will provide all equipment necessary for your demonstrations. Please contact me, however, if you have any additional audio or video requirements.

We have scheduled your one hour presentation to be the final activity of the conference. Please plan to join us for dinner and informal discussion afterward. We look forward to your participation in this exciting event!

Sincerely,

[your name]
Conference Coordinator
International Voices

Editing
and Proofing Documents

► **Plan a document**
► **Open a document and save it with a new name**
► **Copy text**
► **Move text**
► **Correct spelling and grammatical errors**
► **Find and replace text**
► **Preview a document**
► **Print a document**

In this unit, you will save a document with a new name so that the original document is unchanged. Using a variety of copying and moving techniques, you will learn how to make fast work of reusing and rearranging text in a document. You will also use Word's proofing tools to find and correct misspelled words and grammatical errors. In addition, Word's find and replace capabilities enable you to locate specific occurrences of text and replace each instance consistently throughout a document. After proofreading a document, you can preview it, make any necessary adjustments, then print it. ✎ At Nomad Ltd, Angela drafted a letter to Nomad shareholders that will serve as a cover letter to the annual report. Angela would like to copy text from another document to add to the letter and proof this letter before printing it.

Planning a Document

Although Word makes it easy to modify documents after you have created them, it is always a good idea to plan the document. Planning involves identifying the audience and purpose, developing the content and organization, and then matching the tone to all these elements. After identifying the audience and the purpose of the document, which form the foundation of the plan, determine what you want to say. Once you have listed the main ideas of the document, it's important to organize these ideas into a logical sequence. When you begin writing, use a tone that matches the audience, purpose, content and organization. For example, the tone in an announcement to a company picnic will be different from a business letter requesting payment for an overdue invoice. Finally, make the document visually appealing, by using formatting that emphasizes the ideas presented. If you are working on a document for someone else, it is a good idea to verify your plan with your supervisor before you continue. ✒ Angela wants to inform shareholders of an upcoming Annual Meeting and provide an overview of the year's highlights.

Steps 1234

1. Identify the intended audience and purpose of the document
Jot down general ideas for each of these elements, as shown in Figure B-1.

2. Choose the information and important points you want to cover in the document
You write down your ideas for the document.

3. Decide how the information will be organized
Because the information about the meeting is most important, you decide to present it first. The company highlights are included next. Later, if you decide to rearrange the structure of the document, you can use Word's editing features to move, copy, and cut text as needed.

4. Choose the tone of the document
Because the document is being sent to corporate shareholders, you will use a businesslike tone. In addition, it has been a good year at Nomad Ltd, so you will also use a positive, enthusiastic tone intended to encourage shareholders to feel good about their investments in the company. You can edit the document as needed until you achieve exactly the tone you want.

5. Think about how you want the document to look
To best communicate this information to your readers, you plan to use a straightforward business letter format for the document. The letter will include lists, directions, and a signature block. Each part will require special formatting to distinguish it from the rest of the letter. If you change your mind about the format of the document, you can make adjustments later.

6. After you have completed the planning you'll want to verify the document plan with your supervisor.
You can save much time later and avoid confusion about key elements before you begin the document. Be sure to clarify any elements you are unsure about. The planning stage is a good point at which to clarify your plan.

FIGURE B-1: A possible document plan

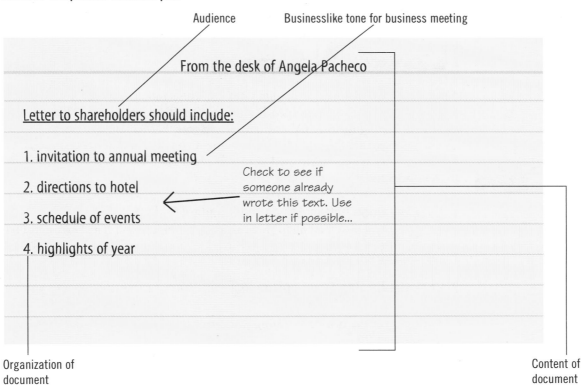

Audience

Businesslike tone for business meeting

From the desk of Angela Pacheco

Letter to shareholders should include:

1. invitation to annual meeting

2. directions to hotel

3. schedule of events

4. highlights of year

Check to see if someone already wrote this text. Use in letter if possible...

Organization of document

Content of document

CLUES TO USE

Creating new documents using wizards and templates

You can use Word's document wizards and templates to create a variety of professionally-designed business documents, including resumes, memos, faxes, and business letters. These wizards and templates take into account the planning techniques described above to create documents that are consistent in tone, purpose, and formatting. All you do is provide the text. To create such a document, click the New command on the File menu, and double-click the icon for the type of document you want to create. You can use either a wizard (which guides you through a series of dialog boxes regarding your preferences for the document) or you can use a template in which you replace placeholder text with your own text. Either method gives you a great head start in developing attractive and effective documents.

Opening a Document and Saving it with a New Name

Using text from existing documents saves you time and energy. To prevent any changes to the original document, you can open it and save it with a new name. This creates a copy of the document, leaving the original unchanged. Earlier Angela reviewed a document created by a colleague at Nomad Ltd. This document contains additional text Angela wants to use in the shareholder letter she created earlier. So that she does not alter the original documents, Angela opens the documents and saves both with new names.

Steps

Time To

✔ Start Word 97

1. **Click the Open button 🖼 on the Standard toolbar**
   Word displays the Open dialog box, as shown in Figure B-2. The Look in list box displays the name of the drive or folder you accessed the last time you saved or opened a file. Table B-1 describes the buttons in this dialog box.

2. **Click the Up One Level button 🖼 until you see the drive where you save your files for this book**
   The name of the drive containing your Student Disk appears in the large box.

3. **Double-click the drive to display its contents**
   The Look in box displays the drive containing your Student Disk and the lesson files appear in the large box.

4. **Click the document named WD B-1 in the file list box, then click Open**
   The document WD B-1 appears in the document window. To keep this original file intact, you will save it with a new name, Shareholder Letter.

5. **Click File on the menu bar, then click Save As**
   The Save As dialog box opens, in which you can enter a new name for the document. Make sure the Save in list box displays the drive where you want to save your files.

6. **In the File name text box, type Shareholder Letter, then click Save**
   The document is saved with the new name, and the original document is closed. You can now safely use Shareholder Letter without changing the original document. You now need to open and save another document before beginning revisions.

7. **Repeat steps 1–6, opening the document WD B-2 and saving the document as Report**
   The document is saved with the new name, as shown in Figure B-3, and the original document is closed. The Shareholder Letter is still open in a document window behind the newly saved Report document.

QuickTip

You can double-click a filename in the Open dialog box to open the document. This is faster than clicking the filename then clicking Open.

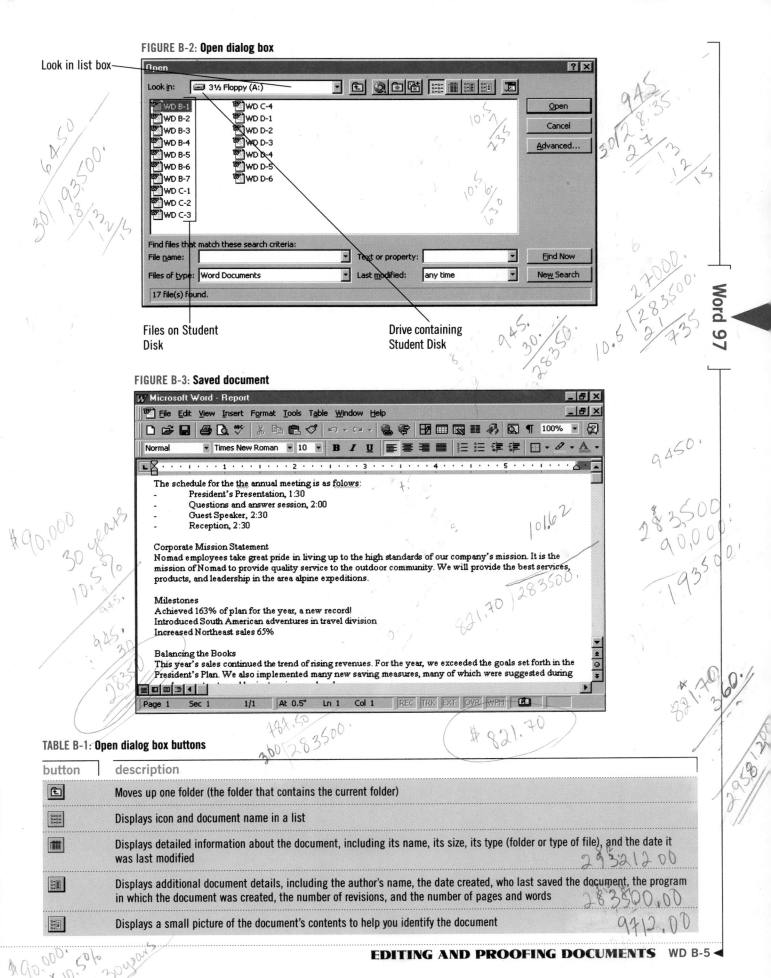

FIGURE B-2: Open dialog box

Look in list box

Open

Look in: 3½ Floppy (A:)

WD B-1
WD B-2
WD B-3
WD B-4
WD B-5
WD B-6
WD B-7
WD C-1
WD C-2
WD C-3

WD C-4
WD D-1
WD D-2
WD D-3
WD D-4
WD D-5
WD D-6

Open
Cancel
Advanced...

Find files that match these search criteria:
File name:
Files of type: Word Documents

Text or property:
Last modified: any time

Find Now
New Search

17 file(s) found.

Files on Student Disk

Drive containing Student Disk

FIGURE B-3: Saved document

Microsoft Word - Report

File Edit View Insert Format Tools Table Window Help

Normal | Times New Roman | 10

The schedule for the the annual meeting is as folows:
- President's Presentation, 1:30
- Questions and answer session, 2:00
- Guest Speaker, 2:30
- Reception, 2:30

Corporate Mission Statement
Nomad employees take great pride in living up to the high standards of our company's mission. It is the mission of Nomad to provide quality service to the outdoor community. We will provide the best services, products, and leadership in the area alpine expeditions.

Milestones
Achieved 163% of plan for the year, a new record!
Introduced South American adventures in travel division
Increased Northeast sales 65%

Balancing the Books
This year's sales continued the trend of rising revenues. For the year, we exceeded the goals set forth in the President's Plan. We also implemented many new saving measures, many of which were suggested during

Page 1 | Sec 1 | 1/1 | At 0.5" | Ln 1 | Col 1 | REC TRK EXT OVR WPH

TABLE B-1: Open dialog box buttons

button	description
	Moves up one folder (the folder that contains the current folder)
	Displays icon and document name in a list
	Displays detailed information about the document, including its name, its size, its type (folder or type of file), and the date it was last modified
	Displays additional document details, including the author's name, the date created, who last saved the document, the program in which the document was created, the number of revisions, and the number of pages and words
	Displays a small picture of the document's contents to help you identify the document

Word 97

Copying Text

You can copy existing text that you want to reuse in a document. You can use the Copy command or Copy button to copy text to the Clipboard so that the text is available to be pasted in other locations in the document. The Clipboard (available in any Windows program) is a temporary storage area in computer memory for text and graphics. You can also drag selected text to a new location using the mouse. Dragging is a great way to copy text when both the text and its new location are visible in the window at the same time. ◀━━ Next Angela will copy text from her colleague's document to her shareholder letter. Angela displays both documents at once, in separate windows, so that she can work in both documents at the same time.

QuickTip

Display paragraph marks by clicking the Show/Hide button ¶ on the Standard toolbar.

CourseHelp

The camera icon indicates there is a CourseHelp available with this lesson. Click the Start button, point to programs, point to CourseHelp, then click Word 97 Illustrated. Choose the CourseHelp that corresponds to this lesson.

Time To

✔ Save

1. **Click Window on the menu bar, then click Arrange All**
   Both documents appear in the program window, as shown in Figure B-4. You want to copy all the text from the Report document to the Shareholder Letter.

2. **With the pointer in the selection bar of the Report document, triple-click the left mouse button**
   Triple-clicking in the selection bar selects the entire document.

3. **Click the Copy button 📋 on the Standard toolbar**
   The selected text is copied to the Clipboard. By placing text on the Clipboard (with either the Cut or Copy command), you can insert the text as many times as you want. You want to place this text before the last sentence in the Shareholder Letter.

4. **Click in the Shareholder Letter document window to make it active, then place the insertion point in front of the first sentence in the paragraph before the signature block**

5. **Click the Paste button 📋 on the Standard toolbar**
   The copied text is inserted. It remains on the Clipboard until you copy or cut new text. To make it easier to work in the document, maximize the Shareholder Letter document window.

6. **In the Shareholder Letter document window, click the Maximize button, 🔲 then scroll to the top of the document**
   You can see more of the document at once with the window maximized. Compare your document to Figure B-5.

FIGURE B-4: Two open documents in the Word program window

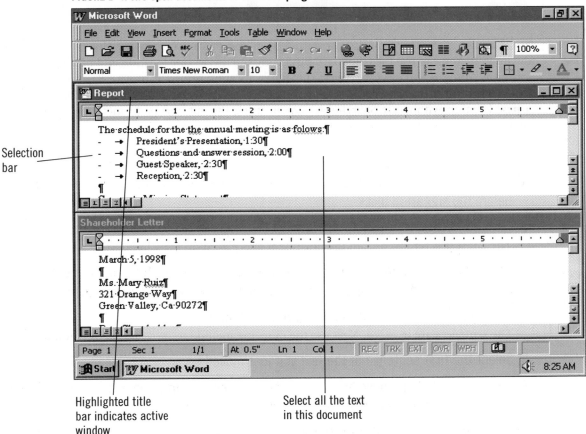

Selection bar

Highlighted title
bar indicates active
window

Select all the text
in this document

FIGURE B-5: Completed document

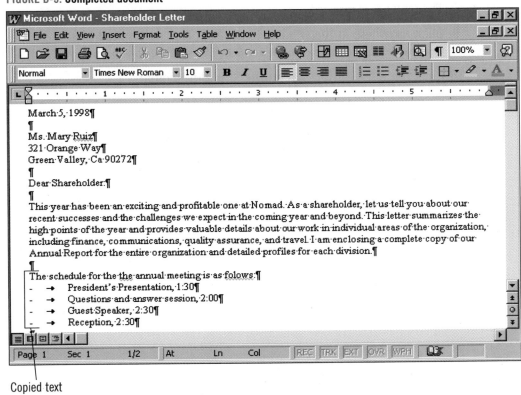

Copied text

Word 97

Moving Text

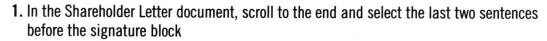

You can also move text from its current location and place it in new locations, even in other documents. You can use the Clipboard by cutting the text in one location and pasting it in new locations. You can also drag selected text to a new location using the mouse. Be sure to view the CourseHelp for this lesson before completing the steps.  Next Angela will move text to a new location within her Shareholder Letter, using the cut and paste method. She will also move text by dragging it to a new location.

CourseHelp

The camera icon indicates there is a CourseHelp available with this lesson. Click the Start button, point to programs, point to CourseHelp, then click Word 97 Illustrated. Choose the CourseHelp that corresponds to this lesson.

QuickTip

If you want to copy selected text rather than move it when you drag, press and hold [Ctrl] first. The pointer changes to the Copy pointer when you copy text by dragging.

1. In the Shareholder Letter document, scroll to the end and select the last two sentences before the signature block

2. Click the Cut button on the Standard toolbar
   The cut text is removed from the document and placed on the Clipboard.

3. Scroll through the document until you see the schedule for the annual meeting, and then place the insertion point in the first line below the last event (Reception, 2:30)

4. Click the Paste button on the Standard toolbar
   The sentences are inserted. Next use the dragging method to move text to the new location.

5. Select the first sentence of the text you just moved

6. Press and hold the mouse button over the selected text until the pointer changes from ↗ to ↖, *do not release the mouse button*

7. Drag the mouse up, placing the vertical bar of the pointer in the first line of text above the schedule

8. Release the mouse button
   The sentence is inserted.

9. Click anywhere in the window to deselect the highlighted text
   Compare your document to Figure B-6. The sentence has been moved.

10. Click the Save button on the Standard toolbar

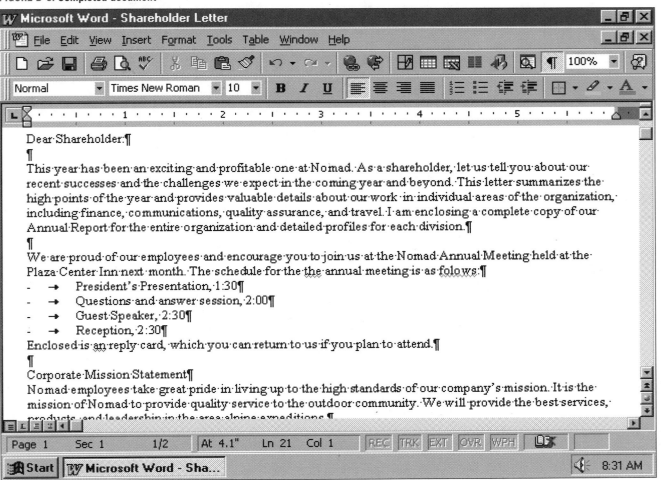

Viewing CourseHelp

The camera icon on the opposite page indicates there is a CourseHelp available for this lesson. CourseHelps are on-screen "movies" that bring difficult concepts to life, to help understand the material in this book. Your instructor received a CourseHelp disk and should have installed it on the machine you are using.

Because CourseHelp runs in a separate window, you can start and view a movie even if you're in the middle of completing a lesson. Once the movie is finished, you can click the Word program button on the taskbar and continue with the lessons, right where you left off.

Word 97

Correcting Spelling and Grammar Errors

Word's Spelling and Grammar command identifies and corrects spelling mistakes and repeated words (such as "the the"). When you use this command, Word highlights any word that is not in its standard dictionary and displays suggested spellings from which you can choose. This command also allows you to review your document for grammatical errors such as mistakes in punctuation, sentence fragments, or agreement errors. ✏️ Angela will proofread her Shareholder Letter using the Spelling and Grammar command to correct any spelling or grammatical errors.

1. Press [Ctrl][Home] to move to the top of the document, then click the Spelling and Grammar button 📝 on the Standard toolbar
Clicking this button is the same as choosing Spelling and Grammar from the Tools menu. The Spelling and Grammar dialog box opens, as shown in Figure B-7. The dialog box identifies the word "Ruiz" as a possible misspelling. The highlighted word is a proper noun, so you can ignore this occurrence.

2. Click Ignore in the Spelling and Grammar dialog box
Next, the dialog box indicates that "the" word the is repeated.

3. Click Delete to delete the second occurrence of the word the
The Spelling command next identifies "folows" as a misspelled word. Suggested spellings appear in the Suggestions list. The spelling that most closely resembles the misspelled word is highlighted in the Suggestions list. You can choose any one of the suggested spellings.

4. Click Change in the Spelling dialog box
The highlighted text in the Suggestions list replaces the misspelled word. Next, the Spelling and Grammar dialog box suggests using the word "a" in place of "an." To learn more about the error, you view an explanation.

5. Click the Office Assistant button ❓ in the Spelling and Grammar dialog box
The Office Assistant displays an explanation of the rule that applies to this error.

6. After reading the explanation, click the Close box ❌ in the right corner of the Office Assistant window
According to the information in the explanation, you decide that a change is necessary.

7. Click Change
The word "a" is substituted for the incorrect word "an." The Spelling and Grammar command finishes searching for errors.

8. Click OK
The message box closes. Compare your corrected document to Figure B-8.

9. Save your work

FIGURE B-7: **Spelling and Grammar dialog box**

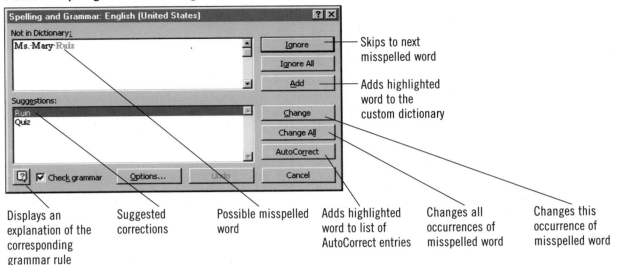

Skips to next misspelled word

Adds highlighted word to the custom dictionary

Displays an explanation of the corresponding grammar rule

Suggested corrections

Possible misspelled word

Adds highlighted word to list of AutoCorrect entries

Changes all occurrences of misspelled word

Changes this occurrence of misspelled word

FIGURE B-8: **Proofed document**

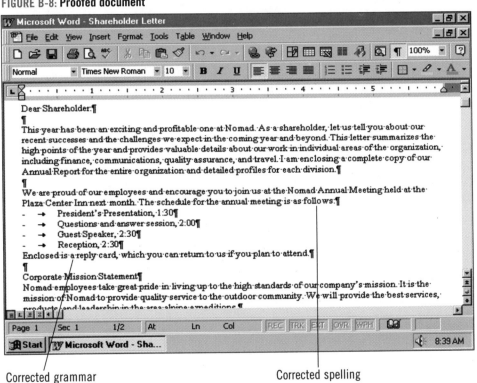

Corrected grammar

Corrected spelling

Using the Thesaurus

You can use the Thesaurus to look up synonyms of overused or awkward words in your document. Select the overused word, click Tools on the menu bar, point to Language, then click Thesaurus. The Thesaurus dialog box opens, listing synonyms of the selected word. This dialog box also displays antonyms for appropriate words. Choose a desired word in the Replace with Synonym list and click Replace to replace the selected word in your document.

FIGURE B-9: **Thesaurus dialog box**

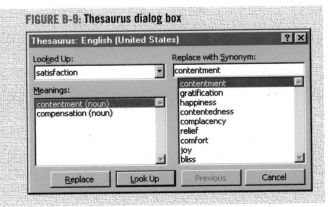

Finding and replacing text

Sometimes you need to find and replace text throughout a document. For example, you might need to make a product name change, company name change, or change an abbreviation to a full name. In a long document, doing this manually would be time-consuming and prone to error. Word's Replace command automates this process, locating each occurrence of the text you want to replace. You can replace all occurrences at once or choose to replace specific occurrences individually. Word's Find command is also a useful searching tool.  Angela's letter refers to the company name as simply Nomad. However, Angela believes the letter will sound more professional if she uses the company's full name, Nomad Limited. She'll use the Replace command to correct all instances of the company name at one time.

Steps

QuickTip

Click the More button in the Find and Replace dialog box to include formatting in your searches.

1. If necessary, press [Ctrl][Home] to move to the top of the document, then click Edit on the menu bar, then click Replace
The Find and Replace dialog box opens with the Replace tab selected, as shown in Figure B-10. There are many ways to specify the text for which you want to search. See Table B-2 for a summary of search and replace options that are available when you click More. Unless you click the More button, you will not see these additional options.

2. In the Find what box, type Nomad
You need to replace all occurrences of "Nomad" with "Nomad Limited" so that the correct company name will appear in the letter.

3. Press [Tab] to move to the Replace with box, then type Nomad Limited

4. Click Replace All
Word changes all occurrences of "Nomad" to "Nomad Limited" in the document. A message appears telling you the number of occurrences (6) of the text in the document that were changed.

5. Click OK
The message box closes and you return to the Find and Replace dialog box.

6. Click Close
The dialog box closes and you return to the document. Compare your document to Figure B-11.

7. Save your work

CLUES TO USE

Using the Find command

The Find command on the Edit menu allows you to locate specified text. If after finding the text, you decide you want to replace this and other occurrences, you can click the Replace tab. If you want to choose the individual occurrences of text to change, click Find Next in the Replace dialog box to locate the next occurrence. Then click Replace to change it or click Find Next again to skip to the next occurrence.

FIGURE B-10: Find and Replace dialog box

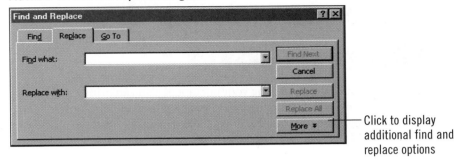

Click to display
additional find and
replace options

FIGURE B-11: Document after changes

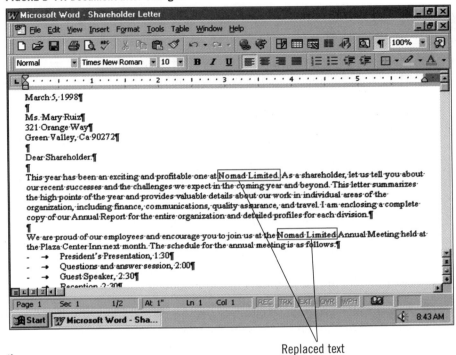

Replaced text

TABLE B-2: Replace options

replace option	description
Find What	Identifies the text to be replaced
Replace With	Identifies the text to use as a replacement
Search	Specifies the direction of the search from the current position of the insertion point: Down, Up, All (default)
Match Case	Locates only text with uppercase and lowercase letters that match exactly the entry in the Find what box
Find Whole Words Only	Locates only words that are complete and are not included as part of a larger word
Use Pattern Matching	Searches for a group of characters located at the beginning of specified text, at the end of specified text, or within specified text
Sounds Like	Locates words that sound like the text in the Find what box, but have different spellings
Find All Word Forms	Replaces all forms of a word. For example, specifying "find" in the Find what box locates "find," "finds," "found," and "finding" and replaces each with the comparable form of the replacement word.
No Formatting	Removes any formatting specifications noted in the Find what or Replace with box
Format	Displays a list of formatting specifications to find and replace
Special	Allows you to search for and replace special characters, such as a tab character or a paragraph mark

Previewing a Document

After proofreading and correcting your document, you can print it. Before you do, it is a good idea to display the document using the Print Preview command. In print preview, you can easily check the overall appearance of your document. You can also get a close-up view of the page and make final changes before printing. Next, Angela previews the document before printing it.

Steps

QuickTip

The keyboard shortcut for the Print Preview command is [Ctrl][F2].

1. Click the **Print Preview button** 🔍 on the Standard toolbar
The document appears in the Preview window. The size of the page you see depends on the number and size of pages displayed the last time the Print Preview command was issued. You want to see both pages of the document.

2. Click the **Multiple Pages button** ▦ on the Print Preview toolbar and drag to show two pages, as shown in Figure B-12
As you view the document, you notice that something is missing in the signature block. Get a close-up view of this part of the letter to examine it more carefully.

3. Move the pointer over the page until it changes to 🔍 , then click near the signature block of the letter
The document is magnified, allowing you to read and edit the text. For example, you can change the abbreviation "VP" to a more official title, "Vice President." You can make this change without first returning to the document window.

4. If necessary, click the **Magnifier button** 🔍 on the Print Preview toolbar
The Magnifier pointer changes to I. Now you can edit the text.

5. Select the text **VP**, then type **Vice President**
While you are near the end of the document, you add some additional text.

6. Place the insertion point in the line just above the text "Sincerely" and press [Enter] to create a new blank line

QuickTip

Although it is convenient to edit in Print Preview, unlike page layout view, print preview does not display non-printing characters. Therefore, do not use print preview when you are doing a lot of editing that requires rearranging text.

7. Type the following sentence, then press [Enter]
We hope to see you at the upcoming Annual Meeting.
You can see that the letter spills only a few lines onto the second page. You would like the letter to fit on one page, which is a change you can make in Print Preview.

8. Click the **Shrink to Fit button** 🔲 on the Print Preview toolbar
The text is adjusted to fit on one page. Next, you display the full page of the document.

9. Click the **One Page button** 🔲 on the Print Preview toolbar to see the full page of the document and compare your document to Figure B-13
With the document complete, you can now save the document and print it without returning to the document window.

10. Save your document.

FIGURE B-12: **Two pages in Print Preview**

Print Preview toolbar

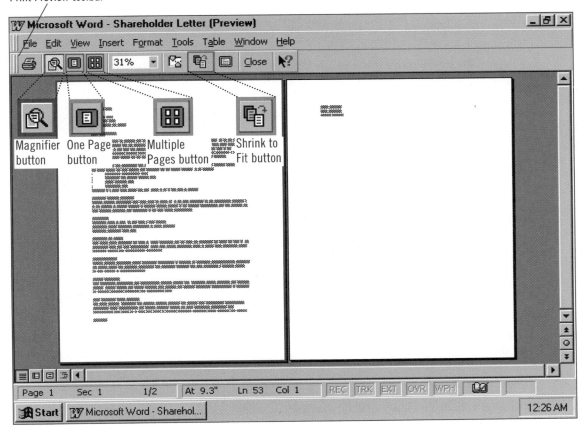

FIGURE B-13: **Document fit to one page**

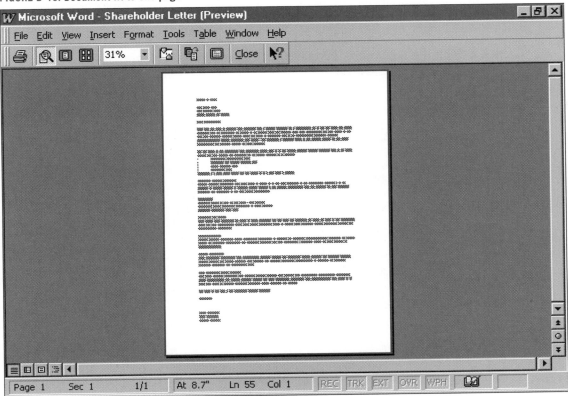

Printing a Document

After proofreading and correcting a document, you're ready to print it. Printing a document is as simple as clicking the Print button on the Print Preview toolbar or the Standard toolbar. However, to take advantage of many printing options, use the Print command on the File menu. See Table B-3 to learn more about printing options. ✐ Angela uses the Print command to print two copies of her letter. In general, it is a good practice to save your document before printing it (to prevent loss of work if there are printer problems, for example). However, Angela saved her work at the end of the previous lesson, so she can continue without saving.

Steps 1234

1. Click **File** on the menu bar, then click **Print**

The Print dialog box opens, as shown in Figure B-14. In this dialog box, you can specify the print options you want to use when you print your document. The name of the printer and the options you have available might be different, depending on the kind of printer you have set up with your computer.

2. In the Number of copies box, type **2**

If applicable, you can submit the second copy of the document to your instructor. In general, avoid using the printer as a copier to produce multiple copies of larger documents.

Trouble?

If you are not connected to a printer, ask your technical support person or instructor for assistance.

3. Click **OK**

The Print dialog box closes and Word prints your document. You may notice a printer icon at the bottom of the screen while the document prints. Compare your document to Figure B-15.

4. Click the **Close button** on the Preview toolbar

You leave Print Preview and return to the document window.

5. Press and hold down **[Shift]**, click **File** on the menu bar, then click **Close All**

Your document no longer appears in your document window and the other document that was open closes as well.

6. If you see a message box asking if you want to save changes, you can click **Yes**

7. Click **File** on the menu bar, then click **Exit** to close the Word

TABLE B-3: Printing options

print options	description
Name	Displays the name of the selected printer
Properties	Displays dialog box which specifies other options that vary based on the features available with your printer, such as the size or type of paper loaded in the printer, and the resolution of the graphics in the document (if any).
Print to File	Prints a document to a new file instead of a printer
Page Range	All: prints the complete document Current page: prints the page with the insertion point or the selected page Selection: prints selected text only Pages: prints user-specified pages (separate single pages with a comma, a range of pages with a hyphen)
Number of Copies	Specifies the number of copies to print
Collate	Prints all pages of the first copy before printing subsequent copies, (not available on all printers)
Print What	Prints the document (default), or only comments, annotations, styles, or other text associated with the document
Print	Specifies the print order for the page range: All Pages in Range, Odd Pages, Even Pages

FIGURE B-14: **Print dialog box**

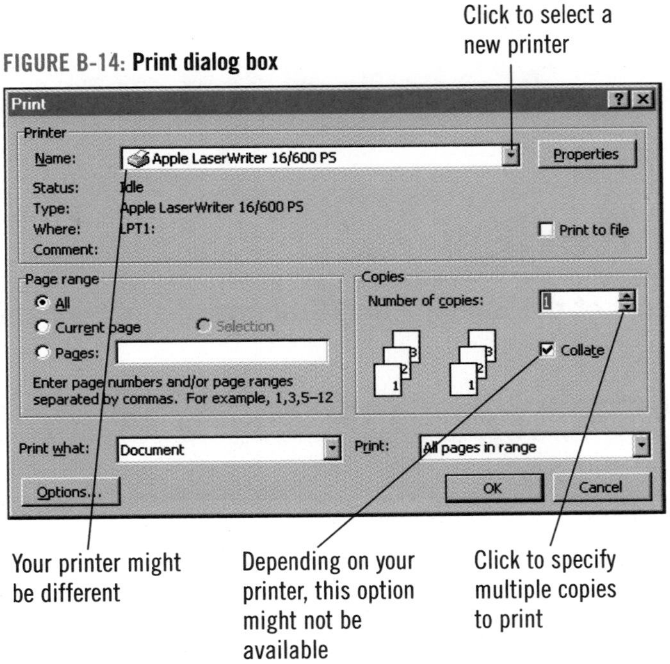

Click to select a
new printer

Print

Printer
Name: Apple LaserWriter 16/600 PS   Properties
Status: Idle
Type: Apple LaserWriter 16/600 PS
Where: LPT1:   ☐ Print to file
Comment:

Page range   Copies
● All   Number of copies: [1]
○ Current page   ○ Selection
○ Pages: [   ]   ☑ Collate
Enter page numbers and/or page ranges
separated by commas. For example, 1,3,5–12

Print what: [Document]   Print: [All pages in range]

[Options...]   [OK]   [Cancel]

Your printer might
be different

Depending on your
printer, this option
might not be
available

Click to specify
multiple copies
to print

FIGURE B-15: **Shareholder Letter**

March 5, 1998

Ms. Mary Ruiz
321 Orange Way
Green Valley, Ca 90272

Dear Shareholder:

This year has been an exciting and profitable one at Nomad Limited. As a shareholder, let us tell you about our recent successes and the challenges we expect in the coming year and beyond. This letter summarizes the high points of the year and provides valuable details about our work in individual areas of the organization, including finance, communications, quality assurance, and travel. I am enclosing a complete copy of our Annual Report for the entire organization and detailed profiles for each division.

We are proud of our employees and encourage you to join us at the Nomad Limited Annual Meeting held at the Plaza Center Inn next month. The schedule for the annual meeting is as follows:
-        Presidentís Presentation, 1:30
-        Questions and answer session, 2:00
-        Guest Speaker, 2:30
-        Reception, 2:30
Enclosed is a reply card, which you can return to us if you plan to attend.

Corporate Mission Statement
Nomad Limited employees take great pride in living up to the high standards of our companyís mission. It is the mission of Nomad Limited to provide quality service to the outdoor community. We will provide the best services, products, and leadership in the area alpine expeditions.

Milestones
Achieved 163% of plan for the year, a new record!
Introduced South American adventures in travel division
Increased Northeast sales 65%

Balancing the Books
This yearís sales continued the trend of rising revenues. For the year, we exceeded the goals set forth in the Presidentís Plan. We also implemented many new saving measures, many of which were suggested during employee retreats and brainstorming weekends.

Communications
Nomad Limited developed office publishing department to produce all corporate communications including the annual report, the corporate newsletter, and corporate catalogs. We also completed a yearlong search for new director of communications.

Quality Assurance
This department normalized and implemented Product Testing and Standards review process. QA installed Product Testing Center. QA started working with guiding and outdoor leadership organizations to field-test all products including outerwear and recreational gear.

New Directions Travel Division
The travel division purchased two national guiding services and another with international connections. Combined, these organizations will deliver services through the New Directions subsidiary. This diversification will allow us to offer new tours in exciting locations, including South America and Africa.

We hope to see you at the upcoming Annual Meeting.

Sincerely,

Chris Peterson
Vice President
Nomad Limited

Practice

► Concepts Review

Label each of the elements of the Spelling and Grammar dialog box in Figure B-16.

FIGURE B-16

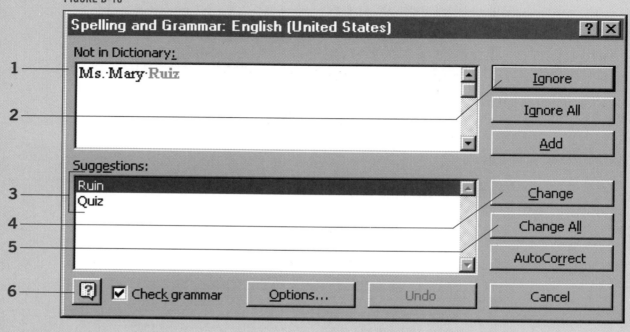

Match each of the following commands or features with the statement that best describes its function.

7. Copy command

8. Paste command

9. Spelling and Grammar command

10. Thesaurus command

11. Cut command

12. Replace command

13. Find command

13 — **a.** Locates each occurrence of specified text

9 — **b.** Reviews a document for correct spelling, punctuation, and usage errors

10 — **c.** Lists synonyms and antonyms

11 — **d.** Removes text from the document and places it on the Clipboard

7 **e.** Copies text to the Clipboard

12 — **f.** Locates each occurrence of specified text and replaces all occurrences or those occurrences you specify

8 — **g.** Copies text from the Clipboard into a document

14. To place text on the Clipboard, you must first
   a. Click the Copy button
   b. Click the Cut button
   c. Click the Paste button
   d. Select the text

15. To display two open documents at once, you use which menu and command?
   a. Click Window on the menu bar, then click Arrange All
   b. Click Window on the menu bar, then click Split
   c. Click Window on the menu bar, then click New Window
   d. Click File on the menu bar, click Print Preview, then click Multiple Pages

16. Which option is NOT available in the Spelling and Grammar dialog box when a spelling error is identified?
   a. Add the word to the dictionary
   b. Add an AutoCorrect entry
   c. Select a synonym for the word
   d. Choose a suggested spelling

17. Which statement does not describe the Spelling and Grammar command?
   a. Provides a way to learn about a grammatical error
   b. Suggests revisions to make a sentence correct
   c. Revises your document based on the style of the document
   d. Checks for spelling errors

18. Which tool will identify as misspelled the word "your" when the word "you're" should be the correct word?
   a. The Spelling and Grammar command
   b. The Preview command
   c. The Thesaurus command
   d. The AutoCorrect command

19. Using the Find and Replace command you can do all of the following EXCEPT:
   a. Check for all usages of the passive voice in your document.
   b. Search the document for specified text in a certain direction only.
   c. Replace all occurrences of a word or words with another word.
   d. Find all of the different forms of a word.

20. In print preview, how do you get a close-up view of a page?
   a. Click the Print Preview button.
   b. Click the Close button.
   c. Click the page with the Magnifier pointer.
   d. Click the One Page button.

21. **Which of the following is NOT true about printing?**

   a. You can choose to print only the current page of a document.

   b. You can print a range of pages in a document.

   c. You can print all the open documents from the Print dialog box.

   d. The Print button automatically prints your document without displaying the Print dialog box.

▶ Skills Review

1. **Open a new document and save it with a new name.**

   a. Open the document named WD B-3, then save it as "Road Map."

   b. Insert today's date at the top of the document.

   c. Add an extra line after the date.

   d. Edit the signature block to contain your name.

2. **Copy and move text.**

   a. Using the mouse, copy the text "Open Roads, Inc." from the first sentence to the last line in the signature block.

   b. Using the Clipboard, move the last two sentences of the first body paragraph to the paragraph mark under the text "How does it work?"

3. **Correct spelling and grammatical errors.**

   a. Click the Spelling and Grammar button on the Standard toolbar.

   b. Correct any spelling and grammatical errors.

   c. Click OK after Word has finished searching for spelling and grammar errors.

   d. Save your changes.

4. **Find and replace text.**

   a. Click Edit, then click Replace.

   b. Type "Inc." in the Find what box.

   c. Type "Intl." in the Replace with box.

   d. Click Replace All to substitute the new company name.

   e. Click OK, then click Close.

   f. Save your changes.

5. **Preview a document.**

   a. Click the Print Preview button on the Standard toolbar.

   b. Click the One Page button.

   c. Click the page near the signature.

   d. Click the Magnifier button on the Print Preview toolbar.

   e. Select Account Representative, then type "Corporate Sales."

   f. Click the One Page button on the Print Preview toolbar.

   g. Click Close to return to normal view.

6. Print a document.

a. Save your document.

b. Click File, then click Print.

c. In the copies box, type "2."

d. Click OK.

e. Click File, then click Close.

f. Click File, then click Exit.

▶ Independent Challenges

1. As the co-chair for the Lake City High School class of 1993 reunion planning committee, you are responsible for recruiting classmates to help with reunion activities. Open the draft letter WD B-4 and save it as "Lake City Reunion Letter". Using Figure B-17 as your guide, use Word's proofing tools to make the following changes to the letter. To complete this independent challenge:

1. Use the Find command to locate the word "ambitious," and then use the Thesaurus to substitute another word of your choice.
2. Preview the document and edit the signature block to display your name.
3. Check the spelling and grammar in the document. Ignore your name if Word identifies it as a possible misspelled word.
4. In Print Preview, modify the title in the signature block.
5. Save your changes and print the document.

FIGURE B-17

September 17, 1998

Mr. Chris Randall
Randall and Associates
4440 Pacific Boulevard
San Francisco, CA 94104

Dear Chris:

As a member of the Lake City High School class of 1993, I often think of the people that made our school such a rewarding experience for me. Of course, there are the close friends I made and kept throughout the years, but also I think about the people that I somehow lost track of since graduation. The instructors, students, and administrative staff all contribute to the richness of the memories.

Now is your opportunity to play a important role in helping bring Lake City High memories alive not only for yourself, but for your fellow classmates as well. As the co-chair of the Lake City High Reunion 1998 planning committee,

I am looking for resourceful, organized alums that are interested in working on various reunion activities. We need people for the following areas: meeting coordination for all committees, computer consulting to help us use technology to work efficiently, meals and entertainment planning for the three-day event, and logistics coordination for handling getting everyone to Lake City and lodging them once they return to campus. All committees need as many volunteers as they can get, so you are sure to get to work in any area you choose.

If you are interested and available to work five hours a month for the next 10 months, please let me know. You can leave me a message at (555) 555-4321. I look forward to hearing from you soon.

Angela Pacheco
Lake City High Reunion 1998
Co-Chair

2. As an account representative for Lease For Less, a company that leases various office equipment such as fax machines and large copiers, you previously drafted a proposal describing the corporate discount program to a current customer. Open the document named WD B-5 and save it as "Discount Proposal." Using Figure B-18 as your guide, use Word's proofing tools to make the following changes to the letter. To complete this independent challenge:

1. Check the spelling and grammar in the document.
2. Use the Find command to locate the word "sequential."
3. Use the Thesaurus to look up an alternative word for "sequential" and replace it with a word of your choice.
4. Add the company before the text "Discount Proposal" at the top of the document.
5. Preview the document and edit the "From" line to display your name, followed by your title "Account Representative".
6. Save your changes and print the document.

3. You are the fund-raising coordinator for a nonprofit organization called Companies for Kids. In response to a potential corporate sponsor, you have previously drafted a short letter describing the benefits of being a sponsor. Open the document named WD B-6 and save it as "Kids Fund Raising." Using Figure B-19 as your guide, use Word's proofing tools to make the following changes to the letter. To complete this independent challenge:

1. Move the last sentence of the first paragraph to the start of the second paragraph.
2. Check the spelling and grammar in the document. Insert spaces between periods and the start of the next sentence as needed.
3. Use the Replace command to locate all occurrences of the word "valuable" and replace it with "important" throughout.
4. Preview the document and edit the signature block to display your name. Also, add the title "Companies for Kids" and your title to the signature block.

FIGURE B-18

LEASE FOR LESS DISCOUNT PROPOSAL

TO: MS. SANDY YOUNGQUIST
FROM: KIM LEE, ACCOUNT REPRESENTATIVE
SUBJECT: DISCOUNT PRICING
DATE: SEPTEMBER 17, 1998
CC: MARION WEST, SALES DIRECTOR

  Thank you for your inquiry about a corporate discount for our temporary office services company. Enclosed is the information you requested. In addition, I have also include the premier issue of *EasyLeasing*, our exclusive newsletter.

  You must use our services for at least 100 days each year, for two consecutive years to be eligible for the corporate discount. As a corporate customer, you will receive a 20% discount on general office temps and a 30% discount for our professional personnel. As your account representative, I would be pleased to discuss your temporary requirements with you. I will call you to arrange a time when we can meet.

FIGURE B-19

Companies for Kids Needs Your Help!

September 17, 1998

Celia Warden
Goff Associates
567 Ash Lane
Spring Lake, MN 55667

Dear Ms. Ward:

To complete our mission of collecting toys, clothing, and various necessary materials for children in local shelters, we would like to request your important assistance.

We depend largely on local businesses to help fund our efforts. Your company's time, services, and donations will benefit children in need. You can choose to donate time and services. Each weekend *Companies for Kids* sends out a number of teams to collect clothing and toys from the community. We desperately need organized teams to help us in this effort. Your company may also choose to make monthly donations, which will be put towards furnishing the shelters and paying various staff members that touch the lives of these children daily.

No matter how your company decides to participate in this program, you will no doubt benefit the lives of all the children who enter these shelters. I hope we can look forward to Goff Associates's participation in this important community program.

Sincerely,

Daniel Montreux
Companies for Kids
Fund Raising Coordinator

5. Save your changes and print the document.
6. Log on to the Internet and use your browser to go to http://www.course.com. From there, click Student On Line Companions, and then click the link to go to the Microsoft Office 97 Professional Edition—Illustrated: A First Course page, then click on the Word link for Unit B and locate the United Way home page. After reviewing the text and tone of a few pages, insert into your letter a few phrases or sentences that you think are especially effective and then paste them into the document. Edit the text as required to reflect the name of the Companies for Kids organization.

4. As a co-chair for the Lake City High School class of 1993 planning committee, you have received a telephone message from a classmate volunteering to serve on the entertainment committee. Open the thank you memo named WD B-7 and save it as "Volunteer Thanks Memo." Using Figure B-20 as your guide, use Word's proofing tools to make the following changes to the letter. To complete this independent challenge:

1. Move the last sentence of the second paragraph to the start of the second paragraph.
2. Check the spelling and grammar in the document.
3. Ignore the classmate's name if Word identifies it as a possible misspelled word.
4. Use the Replace command to replace all occurrences of the year "1980" with "1993."
5. Preview the document and edit the "From:" line to display your name and title.
6. Save your changes and print the document.

FIGURE B-20

Memo

To: Mr. Chris Randal
        Randal Associates
        4440 Pacific Boulevard
        San Francisco, CA 94104
From: Andy Ortega, Lake City High, Class of 1993 Reunion Co-Chair
Date: September 17, 1998
Re: Entertainment Committee

Thank you for volunteering to participate on the entertainment committee for the Lake City 1993-class reunion. We are looking forward to working with you on these events.

Please let me know by noon on the meeting date if you are unable to attend any of these meetings. So that you can arrange your time accordingly, please block out the first Thursday of each months for the next six months for planning meetings. All meetings will take place at 7:30 p.m. at the Corner Coffee Shop in Lake City (on Highway 95, next to the Big Eight drive-in). Our first meeting will be next month; please come prepared to discuss your ideas for entertainment events at the reunion.

▶ Visual Workshop

As the conference coordinator for International Voices' upcoming conference, you are in charge of organizing the details for the informal dinner that will complete the Communications Conference. Use the Letter Wizard to type a letter to the banquet caterer at the conference site. Use Figure B-21 as a guide when selecting options in the wizard dialog boxes to decide how the banquet letter should look. Save the document with the name "Conference Dinner." Use the Spelling and Grammar command to identify any errors you may have made. Experiment with the Thesaurus. Try moving and copying text to arrange the letter more logically. Preview the document and make required edits. Finally, print the document, then close it and exit Word.

FIGURE B-21

October 24, 1998

Ms. Leslie Ryden
Banquet Caterer
Lakeside Center
North Bay, MN 55509

Dear Ms. Ryden:

I would like to take this opportunity to reaffirm how delighted we are to be conducting this fall's Communications Conference at the Lakeside Center on January 4. We at International Voices believe it is the perfect setting for our conference objectives.

As you requested, here are my ideas for the informal dinner that will wrap-up the day's events. I would be interested in having a low-fat, healthful cuisine for this meal. Since we will not be serving any alcoholic beverages, perhaps we could offer an array of fruit juices and sparkling mineral waters. Regarding floral decorations, I particularly liked your idea of international flags drawn by children. I believe this finishing touch will contribute to a wonderful, relaxing environment.

I hope these general guidelines will be helpful to you as you develop your menu and price proposal. I look forward to confirming our plans by late October.

Sincerely,

[your name]
[title]
[company name]

Formatting
a Document

Objectives

- ► Apply font effects using the toolbar
- ► Apply special font effects
- ► Align text with tabs
- ► Change paragraph alignment
- ► Indent paragraphs
- ► Change paragraph spacing
- ► Create bulleted and numbered lists
- ► Apply borders and shading

Using Microsoft Word's formatting capabilities, you can change the appearance of text on the page to emphasize important points and make the text easier to read. You can change the appearance of characters and words by applying **font formatting**, and you can change the appearance of entire paragraphs to improve the appearance of your documents. **Paragraph formatting** refers to the spacing, indentation, and alignment of text in paragraphs. ✐ Angela needs to format a Company Report of accomplishments to Nomad Ltd shareholders. Using a variety of methods, she will change the character and paragraph formatting to emphasize the important topics and ideas.

Applying Font Effects Using the Toolbar

You can emphasize words and ideas in a document by applying special effects to text, such as making text darker (called **bold**), slanted (called *italics*), or underlined. These options are available on the Formatting toolbar. See Figure C-1 for the buttons on the Formatting toolbar that you can use to format text. ◢▬▬ Angela wants to draw attention to the name of a newsletter described in the Company Report and to the headings, so she applies special formatting to these words.

1. Start Word

2. Open the document named WD C-1 and save it as Company Report
   First locate the text you want to emphasize.

3. In the first body paragraph, select the text NomadNotes, then click the Italic button [*I*] on the Formatting toolbar
   Deselect the text to see that it now appears italicized. To give special emphasis to the headings for each topic, apply bold formatting to them.

4. Select the first line in the document, International Communications, click the Bold button [**B**] on the Formatting toolbar, and then deselect the text
   The text now appears in bold. You decide to emphasize this text even more using a sans serif font.

5. Select the text again, click the Font list arrow on the Formatting toolbar, then scroll to and click Arial
   The text appears in the Arial font. The fonts available in the Font list box depend on the fonts installed on your computer. Next, increase the font size of the heading.

6. With the same text still selected, click the Font Size list arrow on the Formatting toolbar, then click 14
   The physical size of the text is measured in points (pts). A point is 1/72". The bigger the number of points, the larger the font size. The selected text appears in 14 point type. Because you want all headings to be formatted this way, copy the formatting to the other occurrences.

7. With the same words still selected, double-click the Format Painter button [🖌] on the Standard toolbar
   Double-clicking this button allows you to copy the same formatting multiple times. You can also click the Format Painter button once to copy formatting only once. Notice that the pointer changes to 🖌I .

8. Drag the 🖌I across each of the remaining five headings in the document: New Director and Ideas, In-House Publishing, Newsletter Update, Catalog Redesigned, Shareholder Meeting
   The font effects of the formatted text are copied to the text you select. Scroll toward the top of the screen and compare your document to Figure C-2.

9. Click 🖌 to deactivate the Format Painter, then save the document
   Notice that the Format Painter button is no longer indented.

Trouble?

If you see red or green wavy lines, it means that Word is identifying possible spelling and grammatical errors. To help you focus on formatting features in this unit, you can hide the wavy lines. Click Tools on the menu bar, and then click Options. On the Spelling & Grammar tab, click the check boxes that hide spelling and grammar errors in this document. Then click OK.

QuickTip

With the Format Painter pointer you can drag across or double-click to copy formatting. If you move the pointer into the selection bar, the pointer changes to a selection pointer. With the Format Painter button still active, you can also click with this pointer in the selection bar to copy formatting.

FIGURE C-1: Text formatting buttons on the Formatting toolbar

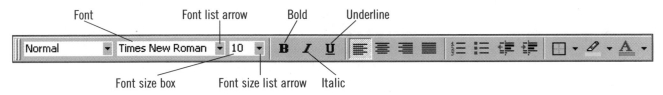

Font   Font list arrow   Bold   Underline

Font size box   Font size list arrow   Italic

FIGURE C-2: Formatted document

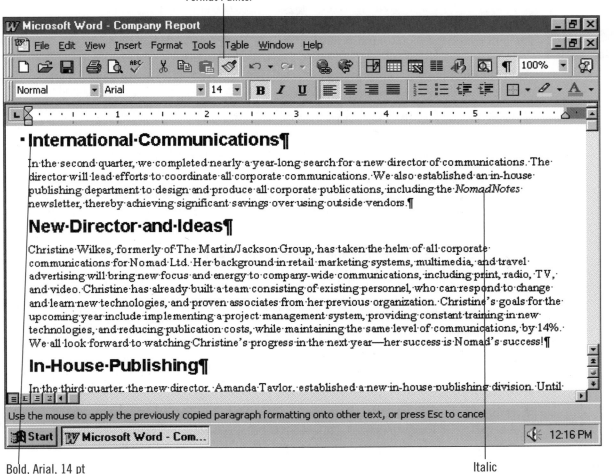

Format Painter

Bold, Arial, 14 pt   Italic

Serif vs. sans serif fonts

Serifs are the small strokes at the ends of a character, as shown in Figure C-3. A **serif font**, such as Times New Roman, has a small stroke at the ends of its characters. Simple fonts without serifs, such as Arial, are known as **sans serif fonts**. Typically, sans serif fonts are used for headings in a document, and serif fonts are used for the body text.

FIGURE C-3: Serif vs. sans serif fonts

Serif

Serif font

Sans serif font

Applying Special Font Effects

Font formatting options are also available with the Font command. For example, you can apply several different kinds of underlining, as well as format text to appear in all capital letters. The Font tab in the Font dialog box also includes special options such as applying shadow, engraved, or outline effects to text. The Animation tab provides additional font effects that can be used to emphasize text when viewed on screen. ✒️ Angela wants to apply formatting to the name of the newsletter to draw even more attention to this new offering. She will use the options with the Font command to accomplish this.

Steps 123 4

1. In the first body paragraph, double-click the text NomadNotes to select it
With the text selected, you can format it.

2. Click Format on the menu bar, then click Font
The Font dialog box opens, as shown in Figure C-4. Distinguish the name of the newsletter from the surrounding text by having it appear in a larger font.

3. In the Size list, select 11
The name of the newsletter appears in 11 point type. In the Preview area of the dialog box, you can see a sample of the font formatting changes. Next, experiment with other font effects.

4. In the Effects section, click the Engrave check box
Notice in the Preview area that this option formats the text so the text has an engraved appearance. However, the text does not show up clearly, so change the color.

5. Click the Color list arrow, then select Black
The text appears in black in the Preview area. Try the Outline effect.

6. In the Effects section, click Outline
The text now appears outlined in the Preview area. With the Outline formatting, your text no longer needs to be italicized.

7. In the Font style list, click Regular
The text is no longer italicized. Now close the dialog box.

Time To

✔ Save

8. Click OK, then deselect the text
View the formatting applied in the document, as shown in Figure C-5.

CLUES TO USE

Applying special effects using the Character Spacing and Animation tabs

To adjust character spacing, click Font on the Format menu and choose the desired option on the Character Spacing tab. You can adjust the spacing between the individual characters. For example, you can create dramatic text effects by expanding the space between characters with the Expanded option. On this same tab, you can adjust the width of individual characters, making the characters themselves narrower or wider as needed to achieve the effect you want. You can also draw attention to text using animated text effects— text that moves or flashes—for documents that will be read online. You can highlight the headline using animated font effects such as a blinking background or red dotted lines moving around the selected text. The animated effects can only be seen online and do not appear in the printed document. Click the Animation tab in the Font dialog box to see the animation effects you can use in an online document.

FIGURE C-4: Font dialog box

Currently selected font | Fonts available on your computer | Font style options | Font Size options

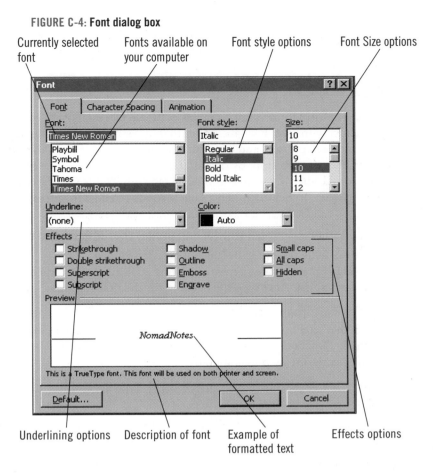

Underlining options | Description of font | Example of formatted text | Effects options

FIGURE C-5: Font formatting

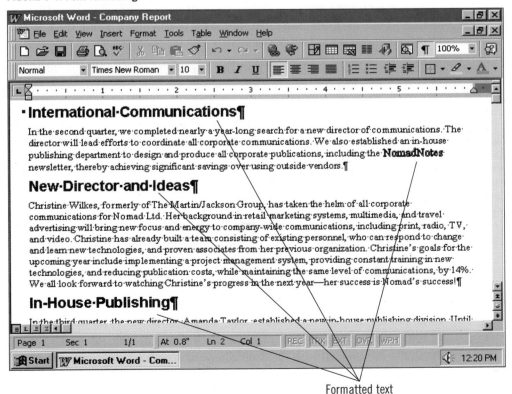

Formatted text

Aligning Text with Tabs

Numerical information (such as tables of financial results) are often easier to read when you align the text with tabs. Use tabs rather than the spacebar to align your text because tab settings are faster, more accurate, and easier to change. When you press the Tab key, the insertion point moves to the next tab stop. By default, tab stops are located at every half inch, but you can use the horizontal ruler to create and modify tab stops. Table C-1 describes the four different types of tabs. In her document, Angela wants to add a list identifying estimated cost savings.

Steps

1. Place the insertion point after the period that follows the word **vendors** at the end of the first body paragraph, then press **[Enter]**
   Pressing [Enter] creates a new blank line. This line will contain the column headings in the cost savings list. Next type the heading for the first column.

2. Press **[Tab]**, then type **Publications**, and press **[Tab]** again
   A tab character appears before and after the word and the insertion point moves to the right to the 1½" mark on the ruler, as shown in Figure C-6. Next type the remaining headings, separating each one by pressing [Tab].

3. Type **1997 Cost per Issue**, press **[Tab]**, type **1998 Cost per Issue**, press **[Tab]**, then type **Savings per Issue**
   Currently, the headings are aligned with the default tab stops located every half inch on the horizontal ruler. To space the headings evenly, create new tab stops on the ruler.

Trouble?

You can remove a tab stop by dragging it off the ruler.

4. With the insertion point in the line of column headings, click the **tab alignment indicator** at the left end of the ruler until you see the **right-aligned tab marker** 🔳, then click the **1" mark** on the ruler
   The right edge of the word "Publications" is now aligned with the new tab stop. Format the remaining columns to be left-aligned.

Trouble?

If you see no change in the alignment of the column headings, it means that the text was already aligned at the default tab stop. Placing a tab stop there anyway ensures the proper alignment, even if the amount of text in the line changes.

5. With the insertion point still in the line of column headings, click the **tab alignment indicator** until you see the **left-aligned tab marker** 🔳, then click the 1½", 3", and 4¼" marks on the ruler
   Left-aligned tab stops appear at the locations you clicked. To adjust a tab stop, just drag it with the mouse. Next add additional lines.

6. Press **[End]** to place the insertion point at the end of the line, then press **[Enter]**
   The tab stops you created for the previous paragraph are still in effect in the new paragraph. Now you can enter additional text for your list.

7. Type the following information in the document, press **[Tab]** as indicated, and remember to press **[Enter]** at the end of each line except after the last line
   [Tab] Newsletter   [Tab] 3.785   [Tab] 2.89   [Tab] .895 [Enter]
   [Tab] Catalog   [Tab] 8.43   [Tab] 6.546   [Tab] 1.884 [Enter]
   [Tab] Annual Report   [Tab] 11.32   [Tab] 9.78   [Tab] 1.54

Time To

✔ Save

8. Select all the text in the columns, drag the last **left tab stop** (currently at 4¼" on the horizontal ruler) to the **4½" mark**, then deselect the text
   All the text aligned with this stop is moved. Compare your screen to Figure C-7.

FIGURE C-6: **Working with tabs**

Tab alignment
indicator

Default tab stops

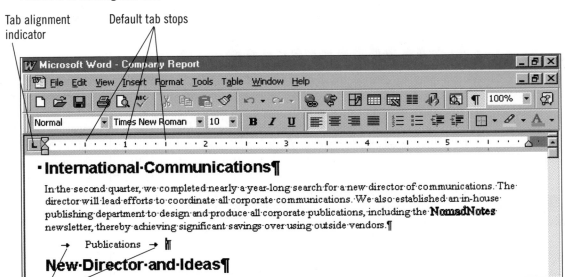

Nonprinting
tab marks

FIGURE C-7: **Using tabs**

Right-aligned
tab stop

Left-aligned
tab stop

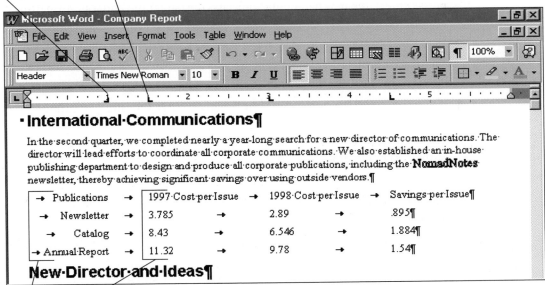

Text aligned with
right-aligned tabs

Text aligned with
left-aligned tabs

TABLE C-1: **Different types of tabs**

alignment	description	Button
Left	Text aligns at the left and extends to the right of the tab stop	⌊
Center	Text aligns at the middle of the tab stop, extending an equal distance to the left and right of the stop	⊥
Right	Text aligns at the right and extends to the left of the tab stop	⌋
Decimal	Text aligns at the decimal point. Text before the decimal extends to the left; the text after the decimal extends to the right	⊥

Changing Paragraph Alignment

Another way to change the appearance of text in a document is to change the alignment of paragraphs. By default your text is left-aligned. However, you can center a paragraph (usually done in a title, or in menus or invitations), or you can right-align a paragraph so that its right edge is even with the right margin (usually seen in dates and signatures of letters). You can also justify a paragraph so that both the left and right edges are even with both margins (as in reports or textbooks). All these alignment options are available on the Formatting toolbar or with the Paragraph command on the Format menu, as shown in Figure C-8. Angela wants the title to stand out, as well as to convey that the document is a first draft. She will use the buttons on the Formatting toolbar to improve the appearance of the document by changing the alignment of specific paragraphs.

1. Place the insertion point in the first line, International Communications, then click the Center button ⊟ on the Formatting toolbar
   The first line is centered evenly between the left and right margins of the page. Note that you do not need to select the text in a paragraph to apply paragraph formatting. Next, add a second line of text to the title.

2. Press [End] to place the insertion point at the end of the current line, then press [Enter]
   This inserts a new blank line that is centered between the left and right margins. When you press [Enter], the new paragraph "inherits" the paragraph and font formatting from the previous paragraph.

3. Type First Draft
   The text is centered automatically as you type. Next, use justified formatting to give the report a more formal appearance.

4. Place the insertion point in the first body paragraph and click the Justify button ⊟ on the Formatting toolbar
   This formatting creates even left and right edges of the paragraph. Continue formatting each of the remaining body paragraphs.

5. Repeat step 4 in each of the remaining five body paragraphs
   Compare your document to Figure C-9. Next align the closing text at the end of the document so that it is aligned at the right margin.

6. Press [Ctrl] [End] to place the insertion point at the end of the document, then click the Align Right button ⊟ on the Formatting toolbar
   This formatting places the right edge of the text "Nomad Ltd" at the right margin. Include the month and year as part of the closing.

7. Press [Enter] and type Sept, press [Enter], press [Spacebar] and then type 1998
   The AutoComplete feature allows you to type the first few characters of a word and a tag above the text displays the word that Word will insert if you press [Enter]. Notice that the text in the new line remains right-aligned. Compare the end of your document to Figure C-10.

8. Save the document

FIGURE C-8: Paragraph dialog box

Click here to
display paragraph
alignment options

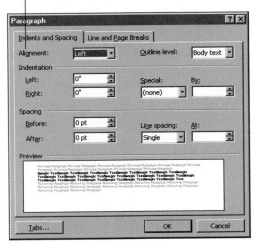

FIGURE C-9: Paragraph formatting changes

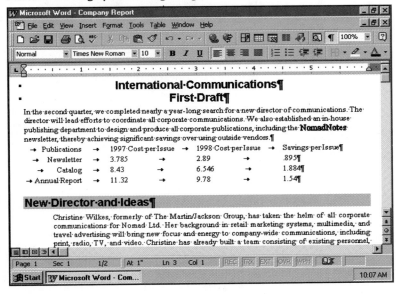

FIGURE C-10: Additional formatting changes

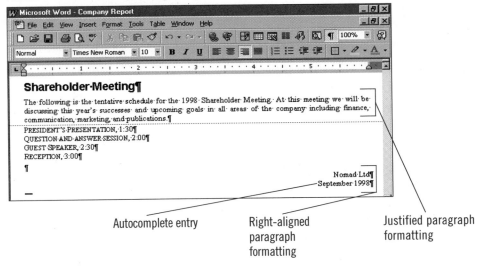

Autocomplete entry   Right-aligned   Justified paragraph
                             paragraph   formatting
                             formatting

Indenting Paragraphs

One way to add structure to the appearance of a document is to increase the white space by changing the indentation of individual paragraphs. When you indent a paragraph you are changing the width of each line in the paragraph. You can modify the indentation from the right or left edge of the document, or both. You can indent paragraphs using three methods: with the buttons on the Formatting toolbar, the Paragraph command on the Format menu, and the horizontal ruler. ▨ Angela would like to indent several paragraphs in her document to reflect the structure of her document. For example, she wants subtopics to be indented under main ideas.

1. Place the insertion point in the paragraph under the heading New Director and Ideas and click the Increase Indent button ▤ on the Formatting toolbar
   Clicking the Increase Indent button indents the left edge of the paragraph to the first tab stop. To give your document structure, make the "In-House Publishing" heading a subtopic under the heading "New Director and Ideas."

2. Place the insertion point in the heading In-House Publishing and click ▤
   Next change the left and right indentation of the next heading and two body paragraphs using the Paragraph command.

3. Select the body paragraph under the heading In-House Publishing through the body paragraph under Newsletter Update, click Format on the menu bar, and then click Paragraph
   The Paragraph dialog box appears. Make sure the Indents and Spacing tab appears foremost in the dialog box.

4. In the Indentation area, click the up arrow in the Left box until you see 1" and in the Right box click the up arrow until you see 0.5"

5. Click OK, then deselect the text
   Word changes the left and right indentation for these paragraphs, as shown in Figure C-11

Trouble?

Word hides settings in a dialog box when you have selected text that includes different format settings for the same feature.

6. Select the heading Catalog Re-designed and the body paragraph that follows, drag the First Line Indent marker ▽ on the ruler to the half-inch mark Dragging the first line indent marker indents only the first line of text in a paragraph. To have all the lines in the paragraph be indented the same amount, adjust the indentation for the remaining lines of the paragraph.

7. Drag the Hanging Indent marker △ to the half-inch mark
   Dragging the hanging indent marker indents the remaining lines of the paragraph (the first line of the paragraph does not move). Although this formatting indents all the lines in these paragraphs in the same way, they are not indented enough to identify the text as a subtopic.

8. Drag the Left Indent marker ▢ to the 1" mark
   Dragging this marker indents all the lines of the paragraph at once. The next heading, body paragraph, and list should also be indented.

9. Select the heading Shareholder Meeting through the end of the list, and then drag the Left Indent marker ▢ to the half-inch mark

Time To

✔ Save

10. Select all the text from Catalog Re-designed through the last body paragraph, and drag the Right Indent marker △ to the 5.5" mark, then deselect the text
    You have completed changing the indentation of the paragraphs in the document. Compare your document to Figure C-12.

FIGURE C-11: **Indented paragraphs**

First Line Indent marker

Hanging Indent marker

Left Indent marker

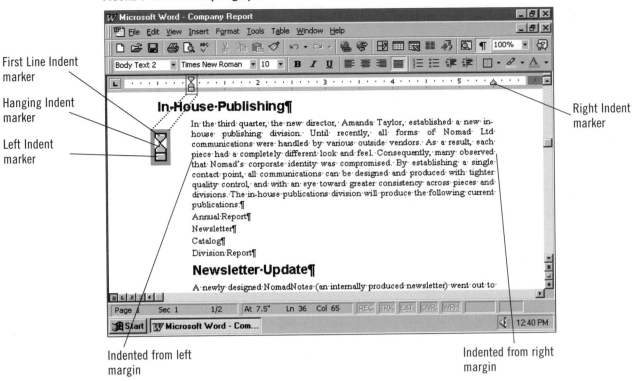

Right Indent marker

Indented from left margin

Indented from right margin

FIGURE C-12: **More indented paragraphs**

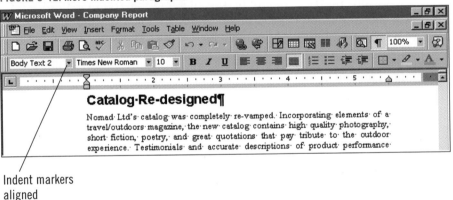

Indent markers aligned

Using Hanging Indent Paragraph Formatting

FIGURE C-13: Hanging indent

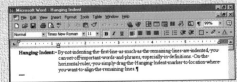

Sometimes you want a paragraph formatted so that the first line of paragraph is not indented as much as the text in the remaining lines. This formatting is known as a **hanging indent**, as shown in Figure C-13. Hanging indent formatting is usually seen in product or features lists or in glossaries. Notice the arrangement of the indent markers on the horizontal ruler and the indentation of the first and remaining lines of the paragraph. You can create a hanging indent by dragging the hanging indent marker on the horizontal ruler.

Changing Paragraph Spacing

Another way to make a document easier to read is to increase the amount of spacing between lines. For example, increase the line spacing in documents where you expect readers to add written comments (as in thesis papers or draft versions of a document). Line spacing options are available with the Paragraph command on the Format menu. You can also increase the amount of space between paragraphs to better separate ideas in paragraphs. Angela would like to provide space in this draft document for comments from her colleagues in the Marketing Department. She'll increase the line spacing and the spacing before and after the list of publications for written feedback.

1. Select the entire document by pressing [Ctrl][A]

2. Click Format on the menu bar, then click Paragraph
   The Paragraph dialog box opens where you can change the line spacing from the default single spacing.

QuickTip

You can also press [Ctrl][5] to format text with 1.5 spacing.

3. Click the Line spacing list arrow, click 1.5 lines, then click OK
   The dialog box closes and the paragraphs appear with 1.5 line spacing between the lines. So that the list below the "In-House Publishing" heading is easier to read, you can increase the space after the list.

4. Place the insertion point in the line Annual Report, right-click the mouse, click Paragraph in the pop-up menu, and then click the Indents and Spacing tab
   Using the right mouse button is a handy way to format paragraphs.

5. Click the up arrow next to the Spacing After box three times until you see 18 pt in the box
   Each time you click the arrow, the value in the box increases by 6 points. As you click, notice that the Preview area of the dialog box displays the effect of your changes.

6. Click OK
   The space between the list and the following body paragraph increases. Next increase the space before the tabbed list.

7. Place the insertion point in the first line of the tabbed list, click Format on the menu bar, then click Paragraph

Time To

✔ Save

8. Click the up arrow next to the Spacing Before box twice until you see 12 pt in the box and click OK
   Compare your screen to Figure C-14. You have finished adjusting paragraph spacing for now.

FIGURE C-14: Increased spacing in a document

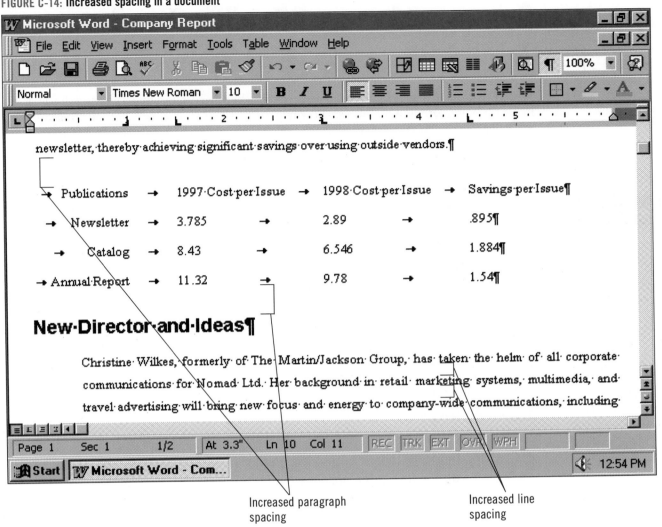

Increased paragraph
spacing

Increased line
spacing

Creating Bulleted and Numbered Lists

When you group paragraphs in a list, you can create a bulleted list. In a bulleted list, each paragraph in the list is preceded by a **bullet**, a small symbol such as a circle or square. With the Bullets button on the Formatting toolbar, you can insert a bullet in front of each item in a list. When you want to show items in a sequence, a numbered list best reflects the order or priority of the items. To create a simple numbered list (starting with the numeral "1"), you can use the Numbering button on the Formatting toolbar. You can also use the Bullets and Numbering command on the Format menu to specify additional bullet and numbering formatting options. ▰▰▰ Angela decides to draw attention to the lists in her document by formatting them with bullets and numbering.

1. Select the list of four publications starting with Annual Report, click the Bullets button ▤ on the Formatting toolbar, and then deselect the text
A bullet character appears in front of each item in the list as shown in Figure C-15. Next change the type of bullet shape.

2. Select the four items in the list, click Format on the menu bar, then click Bullets and Numbering
The Bullets and Numbering dialog box opens, as shown in Figure C-16. In this dialog box, you can choose from seven different bullet styles. You can also change any of the seven styles to use whatever shape you prefer. Change to the arrow style.

3. Click the third box in the second row and click OK
The list appears as a bulleted list with a small arrow in front of each line.

4. Click the Increase Indent button ▤ on the Formatting toolbar until the bullets are aligned with the text in the previous paragraph
Next add numbering to the schedule at the end of the document.

5. Select the four items in the meeting schedule at the end of the document, then click the Numbering button ▤ on the Formatting toolbar
The schedule is now a numbered list. Because you would like to view alternate numbering formats, use the Bullets and Numbering command available on a pop-up menu.

6. If necessary, select the four lines of the schedule, then right-click the selected text
A pop-up menu appears, from which you can select the Bullets and Numbering command.

7. Click Bullets and Numbering on the pop-up menu, then click the Numbered tab, if necessary, in the dialog box
The Numbered tab in the Bullets and Numbering dialog box displays additional numbering options. To impart a more formal tone to the text, choose a Roman numeral format.

8. In the first row, click the Roman numeral (the fourth) option and click OK
The bullets in the list change to Roman numerals.

Time To
✔ Save

9. Click the Increase Indent button ▤ until the numbers are aligned with the text in the previous paragraph, then deselect the text
Compare your document to Figure C-17.

FIGURE C-15: **Bulleted list**

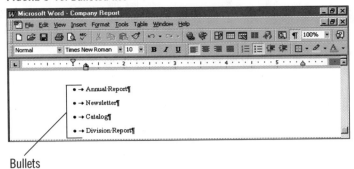

Bullets

FIGURE C-16: **Bulleted tab in Bullets and Numbering dialog box**

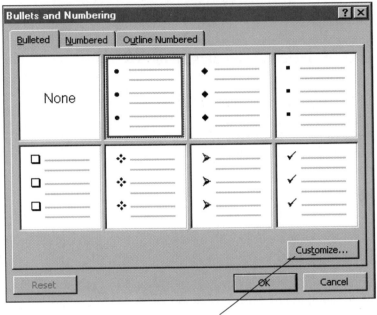

Click to create your
own bullet style

FIGURE C-17: **Numbered list**

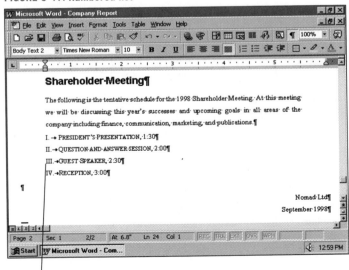

Roman numerals

Applying Borders and Shading

Borders add visual interest to paragraphs of text. **Borders** are lines you can add to the top, bottom, or sides of paragraphs. Preset border settings make it easy to create a box around a paragraph. You can also use shading to offer even more visual interest to paragraphs of text. **Shading** is a background color or pattern you add behind the text of a paragraph. With the Tables and Borders toolbar you can apply borders and shading options you use most often, or you can use the Borders and Shading command to select from additional border and shading options. Angela wants to use borders and shading to emphasize the title and main topics in the document. First, she'll add a double-lined box around the title to give the document a more formal appearance.

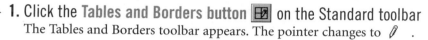

Steps

Trouble?

If you see the Office Assistant, click the Cancel button in the Office Assistant window to work without the Office Assistant.

1. **Click the Tables and Borders button ⊞ on the Standard toolbar**
   The Tables and Borders toolbar appears. The pointer changes to ✐ .

2. **Click the Draw Table button ✐ on the Tables and Borders toolbar to deactivate the Draw Table feature for now**
   You can move the toolbar anywhere you want by dragging it to a new location. The document now appears in Page Layout view, as shown in Figure C-18. Now you can select the text you want to format.

3. **Select the first two lines (the title) of the document**
   Next select the style of border you want to apply.

4. **Click the Line Style list arrow on the Tables and Borders toolbar and scroll to select the double line**

QuickTip

You can quickly remove a border for a selected paragraph by verifying that the line style matches the border you want to remove and then clicking the button that corresponds to the line you want to remove.

5. **Click the Outside Border button ⊞ on the Tables and Borders toolbar**
   A double-line box border surrounds the text, spanning the width of the margins. Next emphasize the main headings in the document by adding shading.

6. **Select the New Director and Ideas heading and the paragraph mark, then click the Shading Color list arrow**
   Change the shaded background to gray.

7. **Click Gray 25% (the third option in the second row)**
   The text appears with a gray background. To apply the same shading to the other main headings in the document, repeat the last command to selected text.

QuickTip

A fast way to repeat the previous command is to press [F4].

8. **For each of the remaining four headings, select the heading and its paragraph mark and click Edit on the menu bar, and then click Repeat Shading Color**
   The other main headings are formatted with shading. You have finished formatting your document for now, so hide the Tables and Borders toolbar.

9. **Click the Close button ☒ on the Tables and Borders toolbar**
   The Tables and Borders toolbar is no longer displayed. Compare your document to Figure C-19.

10. **Save your work, then close and exit Word.**

FIGURE C-18: Tables and Borders toolbar

Tables and Borders toolbar

Line Style list arrow

Shading Color list arrow

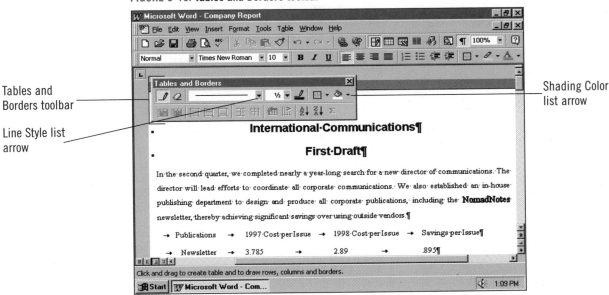

FIGURE C-19: Gray shading in a document

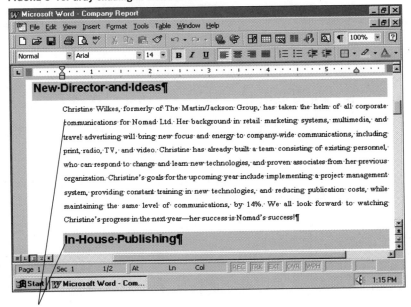

Light gray shading applied

CLUES TO USE

Creating borders with the Borders and Shading command

The Tables and Borders toolbar provides the most frequently used border and shading options. However, even more border and shading options are available with the Borders and Shading command on the Format menu. This command displays the Borders and Shading dialog box. On the Borders tab, you can select box and shadowed box preset borders, as well as specify the color of the border. You can also indicate how far away from the text the border should appear. On the Shading tab, you can specify the color of both the foreground and background of the shaded area. This feature allows you to customize the intensity of the shading you apply to text.

Practice

► Concepts Review

Label each of the formatting elements shown in Figure C-20

FIGURE C-20

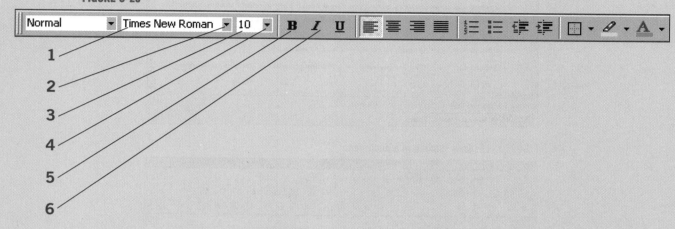

1
2
3
4
5
6

Match each of the following terms with the statement that best describes it or its function.

C 7. Font
C 8. Bold
  9. Font effect
E 10. Bullets
D 11. Numbering
  12. Borders
G 13. Paragraph formatting

a. Character formatting such as hidden text and small caps
b. The design set of characters
c. Text which appears darker
d. Used to reflect a sequence of events or importance in a list
e. Symbols or graphics preceding items in a list
f. Lines added to paragraphs of text
g. Changes the line spacing, alignment, and space between paragraphs

Select the best answer from the list of choices.

14. Which paragraph formatting feature is not available on the Formatting toolbar?
   a. Paragraph alignment
   b. Line spacing
   c. Decrease indentation
   d. Increase indentation

15. To add a specific amount of space between paragraphs, the best solution is to:
   a. Press [Enter] until you get the amount of space you want
   b. Use the Spacing Before and After options in the Paragraph dialog box
   c. Adjust the top margin for each paragraph
   d. Use the Line Spacing options in the Paragraph dialog box

16. Which of the following automatically adds a bullet to selected text?
   a. Right-clicking in a bulleted list
   b. Clicking Format on the menu bar, then clicking Bullets and Numbering
   c. Clicking the Bullets button on the Formatting toolbar
   d. Pressing [Ctrl][B] on the keyboard

17. **A hanging indent refers to formatting in which:**
   a. The text in the first line is not indented as much as the remaining lines of a paragraph
   b. All lines of a paragraph are indented more than the paragraph above it
   c. All lines of a paragraph are aligned under the same tab stop
   d. The text in the first line is indented more than the remaining lines of a paragraph

18. **You can choose alternative bullet graphics from which of the following dialog boxes?**
   a. Bullets and Numbering
   b. Change Bullets
   c. WingDings
   d. Symbol

19. **Which button do you click when you want to apply shading to text?**
   a. Borders
   b. Tables and Borders
   c. Borders and Shading
   d. Shading

20. **You can access the shading feature by**
   a. Clicking Format on the menu bar, then clicking Paragraph
   b. Clicking the Border button on the Formatting toolbar
   c. Clicking the right mouse button in a paragraph
   d. Clicking Format on the menu bar, then clicking Borders and Shading

► Skills Review

1. **Apply font effects using the toolbar.**
   a. Launch Word.
   b. Open the document named WD C-2, then save the document as "Shipping Letter".
   c. Select the text "RoadMap" and click the Italic button on the Formatting toolbar.
   d. With the text still selected, click the Underline button. Then click the Italic button to remove the italic formatting.
   e. With the text still selected, click the Font list arrow and choose Arial.
   f. Click the Font Size box on the Formatting toolbar and type "10.5" and press Enter.
   g. Repeat Steps c-f for the second occurrence of the word RoadMap.

2. **Apply special font effects using the Font command.**
   a. Select the first occurrence of "Open Roads, Inc."
   b. Click Font on the Format menu, choose Arial, then 12 pts, then Bold.
   c. In the Effects area, click the Outline box and All caps box, then click OK.
   d. With the text still selected, double-click the Format Painter button on the Standard toolbar. With the Format Painter pointer, select each occurrence of the company name, "Open Roads, Inc." in the document.
   e. Click the Format Painter button on the Standard toolbar.

3. Align text with tabs

  a. Place the insertion point in the blank line above "Our Promise to You..." and press [Enter].

  b. Press [Tab] then type "Weight"; press [Tab] then type "Cost", then press [Enter] to create a new blank line.

  c. Press [Tab] then type "Under 1 lb"; press [Tab] then type "5.25", then press [Enter] to create a new blank line.

  d. Press [Tab] then type "1 - 10 lbs"; press [Tab] then type "10.75".

  e. Select all three lines of the list and place a left-aligned tab stop at the 2" mark.

  f. With the same three lines selected, click the tab alignment indicator at the left end of the ruler until you see the decimal tab marker.

  g. Place a decimal-aligned tab stop at the 4.5" mark.

  h. Press [End] to place the insertion point at the end of the last item, then press [Enter].

  i. Press [Tab] and type "More than 10 lbs", press [Tab] and type "14.50", save your changes.

4. Apply paragraph formatting

  a. Press [Ctrl][Home] to place the insertion point at the beginning of the document.

  b. Type today's date and press [Enter].

  c. Place the insertion point in the date line, then click the Center button on the Formatting toolbar.

  d. Select the text of the signature block. Click Format on the menu bar, then click Paragraph. In the Indentation area, scroll the Left up arrow until you see 4.5". Click OK to return to your document.

  e. Select all of the body paragraphs (including the list).

  f. Click Format on the menu bar, then click Paragraph.

  g. In the Line Spacing area, choose 1.5 lines, then click OK.

  h. Select the "Generate pre-printed. . . ." line, and then click Paragraph on the Format menu.

  i. In the After box, click the up arrow until you see 12, then click OK.

  j. Select the three body paragraphs, from "Thank you. . ." to ". . . you have."

  k. Click the Justify button on the Formatting toolbar.

  l. Be sure to select the placeholder "[Your Name]" and replace it with your name.

  m. Save your changes.

5. Create bulleted and numbered lists

  a. Select the list of three items starting with "track the location. . ." and ending with "generate pre-printed. . . . "

  b. Click the Numbers button on the Formatting toolbar, then click to deselect the text.

  c. Select the same three lines of text and right-click the selected text.

  d. Click the Bullets and Numbering command on the pop-up menu, then click the Bulleted tab.

  e. Choose a bullet pattern you like, then click OK.

6. Apply borders and shading

  a. Click Toolbars on the View menu, then choose Tables and Borders.

  b. With the insertion point in the line containing the date, choose the 1½ pt line from the Line Style box on the Tables and Borders toolbar.

  c. Click the Bottom Border button on the Tables and Borders toolbar.

  d. Select the list of shipping prices, starting with the line containing "Weight" and "Cost."

  e. Choose the ¾ pt line from the Line Style box on the Borders toolbar.

  f. Click the Outside Border button on the Tables and Borders toolbar.

  g. Select the first line of the list and choose the 1½ pt line from the Line Style box on the Borders toolbar.

h. Click the Bottom Border button on the Tables and Borders toolbar.
i. Select the paragraph under the heading in the middle of the document, and choose 25% shading from the Shading box on the Tables and Borders toolbar.
j. Click Toolbars on the View menu, then choose Tables and Borders to hide the Tables and Borders toolbar.
k. Save your changes to the document, print the document, and exit Word.

Independent Challenges

1. As a committee member assigned to plan the Carson Associates Family Weekend, you have been asked to design the announcement for the Carson Classic golf tournament. Another committee member has begun the document by entering some of the tournament information. Open the document WD C-3 and save it as "Golf Classic". Using Figure C-22 as your guide, enhance the appearance of the document using font and paragraph formatting.

To complete this Independent Challenge:

1. Center the title of the document, and change the font to Arial, Bold, Italics, 18 pt.
2. Add 25% Gray shading to the title.
3. Center the paragraph after the title.
4. Add the information about time and location in a list in the center of the document using tabs. Press [Tab] before and after the word "Where".
5. Place a right tab stop at the 1½" mark and a left tab stop at the 2" mark for the tournament information.
6. Center the heading "Schedule". Format this heading in Bold, Arial.
7. Add numbers to the schedule of events. Left align this list.
8. Place a 1½ pt line above the line "Complete and send the attached..."
9. Preview the document and click the Shrink to Fit button if the document does not appear on one page.
10. Save, and print the memo, then close it.

FIGURE C-21

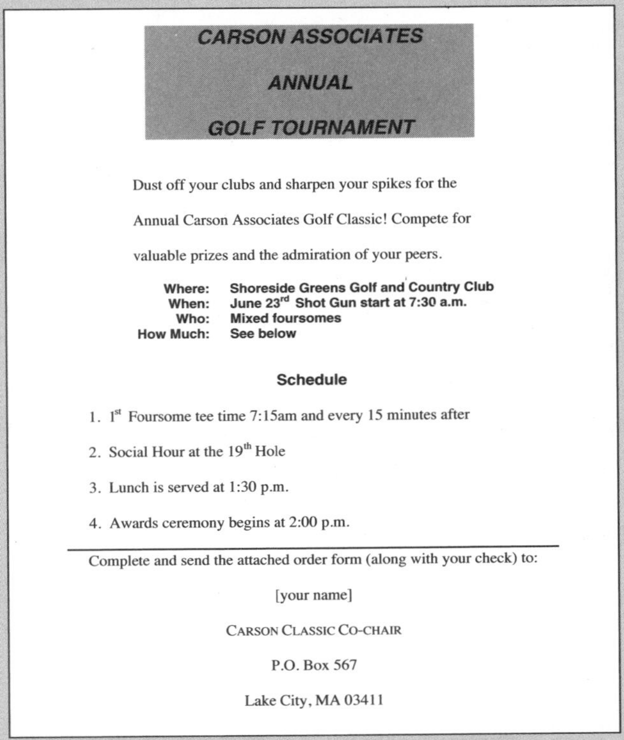
CARSON ASSOCIATES

ANNUAL

GOLF TOURNAMENT

Dust off your clubs and sharpen your spikes for the Annual Carson Associates Golf Classic! Compete for valuable prizes and the admiration of your peers.

Where:	**Shoreside Greens Golf and Country Club**
When:	**June 23rd Shot Gun start at 7:30 a.m.**
Who:	**Mixed foursomes**
How Much:	**See below**

Schedule

1. 1st Foursome tee time 7:15am and every 15 minutes after
2. Social Hour at the 19th Hole
3. Lunch is served at 1:30 p.m.
4. Awards ceremony begins at 2:00 p.m.

Complete and send the attached order form (along with your check) to:

[your name]

CARSON CLASSIC CO-CHAIR

P.O. Box 567

Lake City, MA 03411

2. As coordinator for the Carson Associates Golf Classic, you have been asked to create a certificate to be awarded to the golfer with the longest drive. Open the document WD C-4 and save it as "Golf Certificate". Enhance the appearance of the certificate using font and paragraph formatting. After completing the certificate, access the World Wide Web to plan a golfing vacation in Arizona.

To complete this Independent Challenge:

1. Center all the text.
2. Format the title with 36 pt, bold, italicized, Comic Sans Ms font. In the Font dialog box, apply the shadow effect.
3. Use 1.5 line spacing in all paragraphs.
4. Use 24 pt font on all the text except the title and the text "Longest Drive". Use 36 pt font on this text.
5. Use 12 pt line spacing before and after the date and before the line "for the." Use 12 pt line spacing before and after the line "Presented".
6. Place a 1½ pt line under the line "Recipient" for writing the winner's name.
7. Type your name and title at the bottom of the award. Right align this text and Format it at 24points.
8. Place a ½ pt border above your name for your signature.
9. Drag the Indent marker to the 2" mark.
10. Preview, save, and print the certificate, then close it.
11. Log on to the Internet and use your browser to go to http://course.com. From there, click Student On Line Companions, and then click the link to go to the Microsoft Office 97 Professional Edition-Illustrated: A First Course page, then click on the word link for Unit C.

3. As co-chair for the Lake City High School class of 1993 reunion, you need to draft a memo to the planning committee members informing them of the place and times of committee meetings. Since you are unsure of how to format this memo, you will use the Memo Wizard which will request information about your memo and will format it for you. After the memo is created, you can adjust the formatting to your own preferences. You will save this memo as "Reunion Memo".

To complete this Independent Challenge:

1. Create a new document using the Memo Wizard on the Memo tab in the New dialog box. Choose the Professional memo style.
2. After you answer the questions on each page of the Wizard dialog boxes, then click Next.
3. Enter "Reunion Memo" for the Title.
4. Enter the date, your name, and the topic "Meeting dates". Clear the CC check box.
5. Clear all boxes except Writer's initials and page numbers on the next two pages. Click Finished on the last page.
6. Format the title with Arial, Bold, 14 pt font. Underline the title with a 1½ pt line.
7. Center the title.
8. Create appropriate paragraph text and meeting dates and times.
9. Format the document attractively with borders, shading, bullets, and paragraph formatting a double-line 1½ pt border and 20% gray shading and 6 pt After paragraph formatting.
10. Preview, save, and print the memo, then close it.

4. As an account representative for Lease For Less, a company that rents various office equipment such as fax machines and large copiers, you need to draft a letter explaining the corporate discount program to a current customer. Instead of formatting your letter from scratch, you can use one of Word's letter templates to automatically format parts of the letter for you. You can modify the formatting after the letter is complete. Save this document as "Discount Letter". Use Figure C-22 as a guide to complete the letter.

To complete this Independent Challenge:

1. Use the Professional Letter Template on the Letter tab in the New dialog box.
2. Type the company name and format it with 100% Black shading.
3. Type the return address. Format the Font Size to 9 pt.
4. Type the customer name, address, and body of the letter.
5. Add the bulleted list at the bottom of the letter. Choose any bulleted style you like. Then indent the bulleted list to the 1" mark.
6. Format the Bulleted list to have 6 pt spacing after each line. (Hint: Select all lines at one time.)
7. Add the company name to the signature.
8. Format the letter and company name font in Bold and Shadowed.
9. If you are asked to save changes to the wizard, click No.
10. Preview, save, and print the document, then close it.

FIGURE C-22

Lease for Less

7809 South Washington Drive
Suite 13B
Sandy Hills, MN 56789

September 25, 1998

Ms. Louise Rand
River Industries
1 Main St.
Upton, NY 54005

Dear Ms. Rand:

Thank you for your inquiry about a corporate discount for our copier rentals. Enclosed is the information you requested. In addition, I have also included the premier issue of **WorkADay**, our newsletter.

To be eligible for a corporate discount, you must contact to rent 2 or more of our fax or copier machines for at least six months. Of course all of our machines come with unlimited service by our highly trained technicians. As a corporate customer, you will receive a 10% discount on general office rentals and a 15% discount for our industrial copiers including color copy machines. As your account representative, I would be pleased to discuss your office requirements with you. I will call you to arrange a time when we can meet.

With a corporate discount you can rent any of the following office machines:

- Industrial copy machines with correlating, automatic feed, and stapling features.
- Basic copy machines
- Color copiers
- Fax machines
- Binders
- Laminating machines

Sincerely,

[your name]
Lease for Less
Account Representative

Visual Workshop

As fundraising coordinator for Companies for Kids, you have been asked to create a letter to local company owners asking for donations of money and time. Use the Letter Wizard and choose the Elegant letter style to create your letter. After entering text, modify the formatting to improve the appearance of the letter even further. Save the document as "Elegant Kids Letter". Using Figure C-23 as a guide, complete the formatting for the document. Preview, save, and print your document before closing it.

FIGURE C-23

COMPANIES FOR KIDS

October 24, 1998

Jake Wilson
Wilson Jewelers
1014 Farmington Drive
Hillside, CA 92407

Dear Mr. Wilson:

Thank you for your recent inquiry into the COMPANIES FOR KIDS corporate sponsorship program. We are a non-profit community program that attempts to collect toys clothing, and various necessary materials for children in local shelters. We depend largely on local businesses to help fund our efforts.

Your company's time, services, and donations will benefit children in need. You may choose to donate time and services. Each weekend COMPANIES FOR KIDS sends out a number of teams to collect clothing and toys from the community. We are desperately in need of organized teams to help us in this effort. Your company may also choose to help our children in need in any or all of the following ways:

- Monetary donation.

- Teams of company workers to sort or collect clothing and toys.

- Time spent with children in local shelters

I hope we can look forward to your company's support participation in this valuable community program.

Sincerely,

[your name]
COMPANIES FOR KIDS
Fundraising Coordinator

[STREET ADDRESS] • [CITY/STATE] • [ZIP/POSTAL CODE]
PHONE: [PHONE NUMBER] • FAX: [FAX NUMBER]

Working
with Tables

Objectives

- ► **Create a new table**
- ► **Convert text to a table**
- ► **Insert and delete rows and columns**
- ► **Calculate data in a table**
- ► **Sort information in a table**
- ► **Format a table**
- ► **Use the Draw Table button**
- ► **Modify a table with the Tables and Borders toolbar**

In this unit you'll learn how to format text in a table. A **table** is text arranged in a grid of rows and columns. With Word, you can add or delete information in a table without having to manually reformat the entire table. You can sort and calculate information that appears in a table and quickly make attractive tables using preset table formats. You can also customize your tables to fit your exact needs by drawing rows and columns exactly where you would like them. Tables are an excellent tool for displaying data normally found in lists or columns. ◢ Nomad Ltd has acquired an adventure travel company called Alpine Adventures. With the acquisition, Angela would like to improve the appearance of Alpine's newsletter. Because the newsletter includes pricing information, Angela uses tables to present this information to readers.

Creating a New Table

To create a blank table, you can use the Insert Table button on the Standard toolbar. Or you can use the Insert Table command on the Table menu. Angela thinks it might help potential customers decide which tour to take if they know the number of participants and general age group for each tour. She will present this information in a table.

Steps

1. Launch Word

2. Open the document named WD D-1 and save it as **Package Tours 1998**
   Begin by placing the insertion point near the end of the document.

3. Scroll to the end of the document and place the insertion point in front of the paragraph mark above the heading **Time to Leave?**
   Now you can create your table.

4. Click the **Insert Table button** ▦ on the Standard toolbar, then drag in the grid to select three rows and five columns, as shown in Figure D-1, and then click the mouse
   A blank table appears in the document. To see the entire width of the table, you might need to adjust the magnification.

5. Click in the **Zoom box** on the Standard toolbar, type **95** and then press **[Enter]**
   Compare your table to Figure D-2. A **cell** is the intersection of a row and column. Inside each cell is a **cell marker**, which identifies the end of the contents in the cell. The end of each row is identified with an **end-of-row marker**. **Borders** surround each cell so you can see the structure of the table. Neither the cell markers nor the end-of-row markers appear when you print the document. Next, you enter the information you want in the table.

6. In the first cell, type **Tour**, then press **[Tab]**
   Pressing [Tab] selects the next cell in a table. Pressing [Shift][Tab] selects the previous cell. You continue entering text in the table.

7. Type **Under 20**, press **[Tab]**, type **20-34**, press **[Tab]**, type **35-50**, press **[Tab]**, type **Over 50** and press **[Tab]**
   Pressing [Tab] at the end of a row selects the first cell in the next row. You continue entering text in the table, pressing [Tab] after each cell.

8. Type the following text in the table as indicated below (for now, *do not press [Tab] at the end of the last row*)

   | Country Culture | 15 | 20 | 25 | 45 |
   | Pastoral Idyll | 20 | 35 | 30 | 15 |

   At the end of the last row, you decide to add a new row to the bottom of the table.

Time To
✔ Save

9. Press **[Tab]** to create a new row, and type the following text in the table as indicated below *(do not press [Tab] at the end of the last row)*

   | Mountain Top | 45 | 35 | 15 | 5 |

   Compare your table to Figure D-3.

FIGURE D-1: Dragging to specify rows and columns

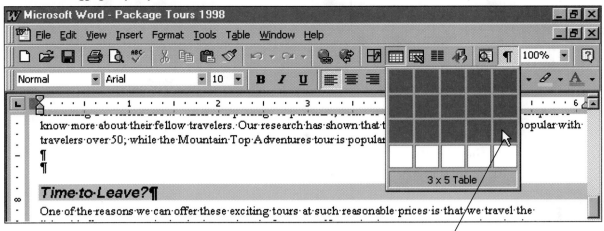

Drag to specify
rows and columns

FIGURE D-2: New table in a document

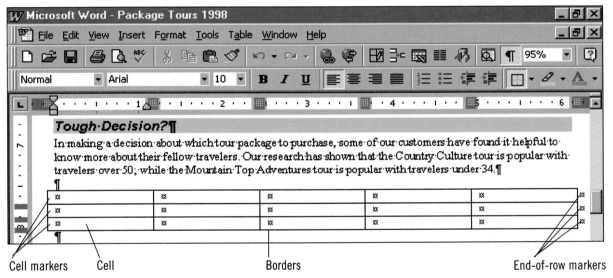

Cell markers   Cell   Borders   End-of-row markers

FIGURE D-3: Completed table

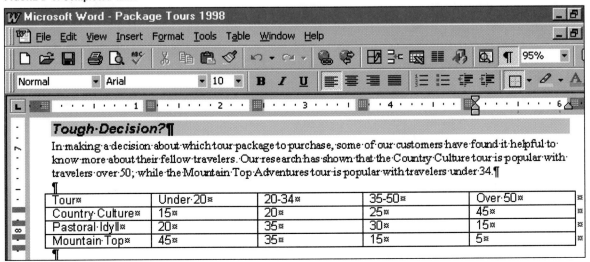

Tour	Under 20	20-34	35-50	Over 50	
Country Culture	15	20	25	45	
Pastoral Idyll	20	35	30	15	
Mountain Top	45	35	15	5	

Word 97

Converting Text to a Table

You can convert existing text into a table by selecting the text and then using the Insert Table button on the Standard toolbar. The text you are converting to a table must be formatted with tabs, commas, or paragraph marks so that Word can interpret the formatting and create the table.  Angela wants to convert the text about tour prices to a table so that readers will be able to quickly identify pricing information.

Steps123 4

1. **Scroll to the top of the document, and select the four lines that begin with Tour and end with Country Culture**
   Because this text is already formatted with tabs, you can convert it to a table.

2. **Click the Insert Table button ▦ on the Standard toolbar**
   Clicking this button is the same as choosing Insert Table from the Table menu or the Convert Text to Table command on the Table menu.

3. **Deselect the highlighted table**
   The selected text appears in a table format, as shown in Figure D-4. Because one column is too narrow for the text to fit appropriately, you need to adjust the column width.

4. **Position the pointer over the border to the right of the column heading Lodging until the pointer changes to ‹|›, then drag to the right slightly so that the heading appears on one line**
   Notice how the height of the row automatically adjusts to accommodate the amount of text that is in the tallest cell in the row. You can also customize the size of the row to a specific height.

5. **Select the text Tour in the first cell of the first row, then type Twelve-day Package Tour**
   The row height adjusts to accommodate the text you type, but notice that the column width does not adjust automatically.

6. **Place the insertion point in the empty cell below Trains and type 50**
   The last price in this column is also missing, so you move to the last cell and enter the new price.

7. **Press [Alt][PgDn] to move to the last cell in the fourth column, then type 75**
   This keyboard shortcut moves you quickly to the last cell in a column. Your table is revised, as shown in Figure D-5, so you save your work.

Trouble?

If the width of only one cell in the column changes when you adjust the column width, deselect the cell, then click the Undo button ↶ on the Standard toolbar. You must deselect the cell before adjusting the column width, if you want to adjust the width of the entire column.

Time To

☑ Save

FIGURE D-4: Text converted to a table

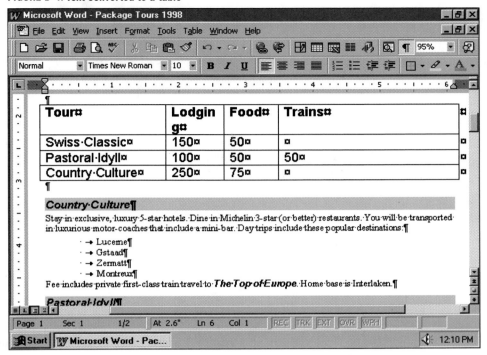

FIGURE D-5: Completed table

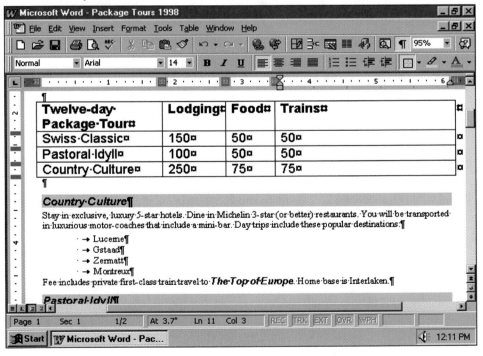

Adjusting row height

To establish a specific row height you can use the Cell Height and Width command on the Table menu. This command displays a dialog box in which you can specify a fixed height for rows. Use this feature when you want to make all the rows in a table the same height. You may also use the Cell Height and Width command to make all columns in a table the same width.

Inserting and Deleting Rows and Columns

You often need to change the number of rows or columns so that you can add or remove information. You can quickly add or delete rows and columns using the commands on the Table menu or use the commands on the pop-up menu for tables. Nomad Ltd has determined that Alpine Adventures should discontinue the Swiss Classic tour and add a new budget-oriented tour. Angela will delete the row containing the Swiss Classic information, add a row for the new tour, and also add a Total column that displays the total price of each tour.

1. **Place the insertion point in the Swiss Classic row of the first table, then click the right mouse button**
The pop-up menu for tables appears. This menu contains the commands you are most likely to use when working in a table.

QuickTip

To quickly delete an entire row or column using the keyboard, select the row or column, then press [Shift][Delete] or [Ctrl][X]. To remove only the text from a selected row or column, press [Delete].

2. **Click Delete Cells...**
The Delete Cells dialog box opens. In this dialog box, you can specify the cells you want to remove from the table. Delete the row for the discontinued tour.

3. **Click Delete Entire Row, then click OK**
This command deletes the row containing the insertion point. Now, add a new row.

4. **Click the Insert Rows button [⊟◄] on the Standard toolbar**
Notice that the Insert Table button and name changes based on what is currently selected. Next enter the information for the new tour.

5. **Type Mountain Top, press [Tab], then type the following numbers in the cells in the new row: 75   0   20**
Before adding a new column to the end of the table, you must adjust the width of the last column so that the new column will fit on the page.

6. **Position the pointer over the border to the right of the last column until the pointer changes to ◄‖►, drag to the left to the 5" mark on the horizontal ruler**
Next, you create a new column at the end of the table for the total price of each tour. To do so, you must first select the end-of-row markers to the right of the last column in the table.

7. **At the top-right of the table, position the pointer above the end-of-row marker, and when the pointer changes to ↓, click the left mouse button as shown in Figure D-6**
This selects the column of end-of-row markers.

8. **Click Table on the menu bar, then click Insert Columns**
A new blank column appears at the right end of the table. You can also click the Insert Columns button [⊞] on the Standard toolbar to insert a new column (again the Insert Table button will change based on what is selected). Word places the insertion point in the first cell of the new column when you begin typing.

Time To

✔ Save

9. **Leaving the column selected, type Total**
Compare your document to Figure D-7.

FIGURE D-6: Adding a column to the end of the table

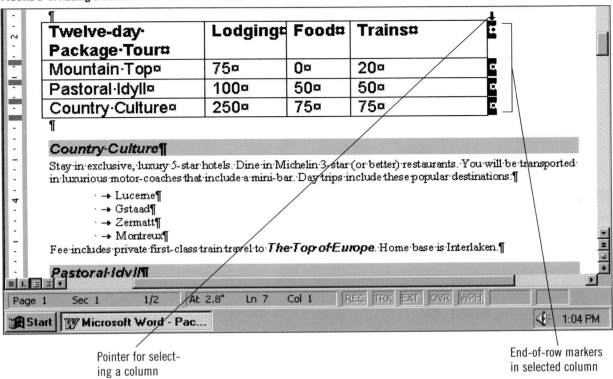

Pointer for select-
ing a column

End-of-row markers
in selected column

FIGURE D-7: Completed table

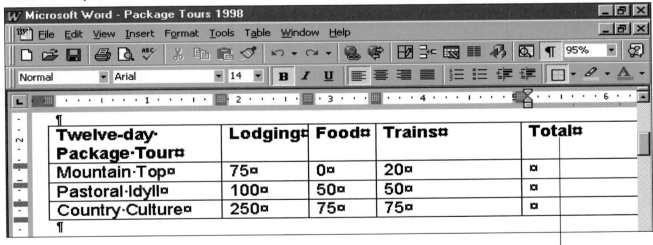

New column and text

Using the selection bar in tables

The area to the left of each row in a table contains the selection bar. Clicking in the selection bar to the left of a row selects that row in the same way clicking in the selection bar to the left of a line of text selects the entire line. In addition, each cell in the table contains its own selection bar. You can click the selection bar to the left of text in a cell to select an individual cell.

Calculating Data in a Table

Your table can include calculations based on the numbers in rows and columns. The Formula command allows you to perform calculations on data in a table. Built-in formulas make it easy to quickly perform standard calculations (such as totals or averages). Using formulas prevents mathematical errors and helps you work more quickly. You can also enter your own formulas. In addition, you can also change data in a table and update calculations. ✐ To provide the tour price for each tour, Angela uses the Formula command and a built-in formula to calculate the total cost per day for each tour.

Steps

1. **Place the insertion point in the cell below the Total cell in the first table of the document, click Table on the menu bar, then click Formula**
   The Formula dialog box opens, as shown in Figure D-8. Based on the location of the insertion point in the table, Word suggests a formula in the Formula box—in this case, the built-in SUM formula—and suggests which cells to use in the calculation, the columns to the left. Because these are the values you want to use in this calculation, accept the suggested formula.

2. **Click OK**
   The dialog box closes and the sum of the values in the row appears in the current cell. To calculate the other total values in this column, repeat the last command by pressing [F4].

3. **Press [↓] to move the insertion point to the next cell in the Total column, then press [F4]**
   [F4] is a function key located at the top of your keyboard that repeats the action you just performed. Function keys are used for shortcut commands. After you press [F4], the sum of the values in this row appears in the cell.

4. **Press [↓] to move the insertion point to the last cell in the Total column, then press [F4]**
   The sum of the values in this row appears in the cell. Next, update the cost of lodging for the Country Culture tour to reflect a new lower rate of 200.

5. **Select the last value in the Lodging column, 250, then type 200**
   The new value, 200, replaces the previous value of 250. When you change values used in a calculation, Word does not automatically update the total to reflect a new value, so you need to recalculate the values in the table.

Time To
✔ Save

6. **Select the last value in the Total column, 400, press [F9] and then deselect the cell**
   Word recalculates the total, and "350" appears in the cell, as shown in Figure D-9. Pressing [F9] updates calculations in a table.

FIGURE D-8: **Formula dialog box**

Formula ? ✕

Formula:
=SUM(LEFT)

Number format:

Paste function:

Paste bookmark:

OK   Cancel

Suggested formula

FIGURE D-9: **Completed table**

Microsoft Word - Package Tours 1998

File Edit View Insert Format Tools Table Window Help

Normal   Arial   14   B I U   ☰ ☰ ☰ ☰   95%

Twelve-day Package Tour¤	Lodging¤	Food¤	Trains¤	Total¤
Mountain·Top¤	75¤	0¤	20¤	95¤
Pastoral·Idyll¤	100¤	50¤	50¤	200¤
Country·Culture¤	200¤	75¤	75¤	350¤

Recalculated total

Creating your own calculations

To enter your own calculation in the Formula dialog box, you refer to cells in the table using cell references. A cell reference identifies a cell's position in the table. Each cell reference contains a letter (A, B, C and so on) to identify its column and a number (1, 2, 3 and so on) to identify its row. For example, the first cell in the first row is A1, and the second cell in the first row is B1, as you can see in Figure D-10. You can create a formula to multiply, divide, add, and subtract the values of individual cells. Multiplication is represented by an asterisk (*); division is represented by a slash (/). For example, the formula to determine the total price for twelve days of the Country Culture tour would be =E4*12.

FIGURE D-10: **Cell references**

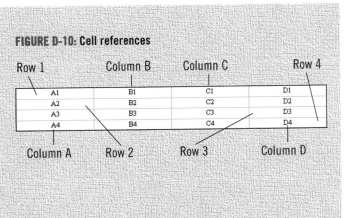

Row 1   Column B   Column C   Row 4

A1	B1	C1	D1
A2	B2	C2	D2
A3	B3	C3	D3
A4	B4	C4	D4

Column A   Row 2   Row 3   Column D

Sorting Information in a Table

Sometimes the information in a table is easier to interpret if the rows are sorted to appear in a particular order. For example, you might sort a department telephone directory by name, or a project plan by date. You can sort by a single column or by multiple columns. For each column, you can sort in **ascending** or **descending** order. Ascending order (the default) arranges rows from smallest to largest for numbers and from A to Z for text. Descending order arranges rows from largest to smallest for numbers and from Z to A for text. ◢▬▬ To arrange the rows in a logical order, Angela sorts the table so that the most expensive tour appears first and the least expensive tour appears last.

Steps

1. **Place the insertion point anywhere in the table**
   You do not need to select the entire table to perform a sort.

2. **Click Table on the menu bar, then click Sort**
   The Sort dialog box opens, as shown in Figure D-11. In this dialog box, you can specify how you want your table sorted. The Sort by list contains the headings for all the columns in the table and displays the heading for the first column by default. Instead, sort the table by the information in the Total column.

3. **Click the Sort by list arrow, then click Total in the list of columns**
   Choose the option to display the tours starting with the most expensive and ending with the least expensive.

4. **Click the Descending radio button in the Sort by section**
   This button sorts rows from the largest value to the smallest value. Next, indicate that you do not want the first row (the column headings) included in the sort.

5. **In the My list has section, make sure the Header row option button is selected**
   This button ensures that the first row of the table (containing the column headings) is not sorted along with the other rows in the table.

6. **Click OK**
   The dialog box closes, and the table is sorted based on the values in the Total column. Deselect the text and compare your document to Figure D-12.

7. **Save the document**

FIGURE D-11: Sort dialog box

First column heading appears by default

Click to display list of column headings in table

Sorts information from smallest to largest value

Sorts information from largest to smallest value

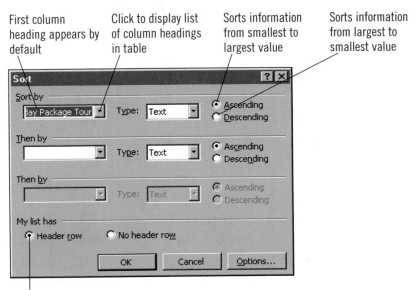

Specifies that first row is not included in the sort

FIGURE D-12: Sorted table

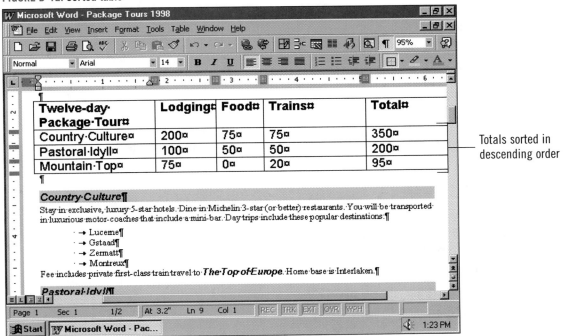

Twelve-day Package Tour¤	Lodging¤	Food¤	Trains¤	Total¤
Country·Culture¤	200¤	75¤	75¤	350¤
Pastoral·Idyll¤	100¤	50¤	50¤	200¤
Mountain·Top¤	75¤	0¤	20¤	95¤

Totals sorted in descending order

Country·Culture¶

Stay in exclusive, luxury 5-star hotels. Dine in Michelin 3-star (or better) restaurants. You will be transported in luxurious motor-coaches that include a mini-bar. Day trips include these popular destinations:¶

· → Lucerne¶
· → Gstaad¶
· → Zermatt¶
· → Montreux¶

Fee includes private first-class train travel to ***The·Top·of·Europe***. Home base is Interlaken.¶

Pastoral·Idyll¶

Sorting by more than one column

By sorting your table by more than one column, you can better organize information. For example, if you sort a table by a column containing last names, the rows containing the same last name are grouped together. To sort the rows within each group, select a second column by which to sort, such as one containing first names. You can sort by values in up to three different columns using the Sort by box and the two Then by boxes.

Formatting a Table

In the same way you can add borders and shading to paragraphs, you can improve the appearance of a table by adding borders and shading to rows and columns. Although you can use the buttons on the Tables and Borders toolbar to apply shading and borders to individual rows and columns, Word's Table AutoFormat command provides a variety of preset table formats from which you can choose. ◄══════ Now Angela will use the Table AutoFormat command to apply attractive borders and shading to the table she created.

Steps

QuickTip

For best results, you should always sort a table before formatting it with Table AutoFormat because the borders applied to a row also move when the position of a row changes after sorting. This could cause the table to be formatted inappropriately.

1. With the insertion point in the table, click **Table** on the menu bar, then click **Table AutoFormat**

The Table AutoFormat dialog box opens, as shown in Figure D-13. In this dialog box, you can preview different preset table format settings. You can also identify the parts of the table to which you want to apply specific formatting. For example, use a simple grid format for your table.

2. In the Formats list, scroll the list of formats, then click **Grid 3**

The Preview box shows how the Grid 3 option formats a table. To emphasize the information in the Total column, apply special formatting to the last column.

3. In the Apply special formats to section, click the **Last Column check box**

In the Preview box, notice that the last column of the sample table appears in bold.

4. Click **OK**

The dialog box closes and the table appears with new formatting. Notice that the Table AutoFormat command also adjusted the columns so that the table fits attractively between the margins. Next, you would like to emphasize the column headings.

5. Select the first row (the column headings), then click the **Bold button** [B] on the Formatting toolbar

The column headings appear in bold. Next, center the numbers in the table for easier reading.

6. Select the cells that contain numbers, then click the **Center button** [≣] on the Formatting toolbar

The numbers in these cells appear centered in the columns.

7. Deselect the table, then save the document

Compare your table to Figure D-14.

FIGURE D-13: Table AutoFormat dialog box

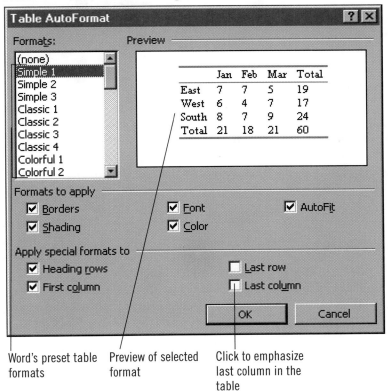

Word's preset table formats   Preview of selected format   Click to emphasize last column in the table

FIGURE D-14: Completed table

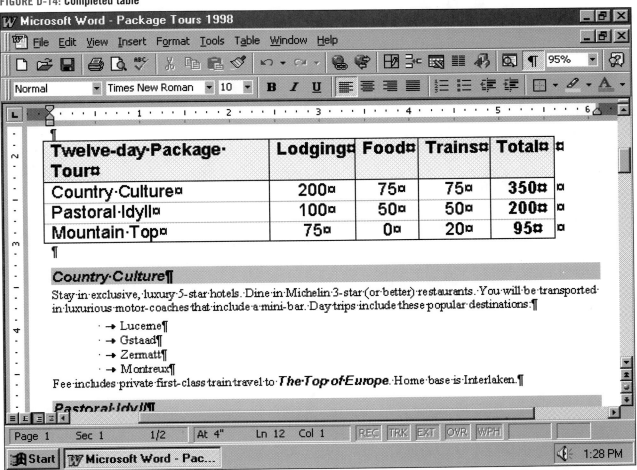

Using the Draw Table Button

Sometimes you may not want a simple table with the same number of cells in each row or column. For example, you might want a table with only one cell in the header row or an extra cell in the last column to display an emphasized total. Word's Draw Table button allows you to customize your tables by drawing the cells exactly where you want them. 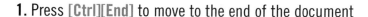 Angela would like to add a table displaying the best airfares to Switzerland. She would like the top row of the table to contain only the name of the airline. To accomplish this, she will customize her table to contain only one cell in the first row.

Steps

1. Press [Ctrl][End] to move to the end of the document

Trouble?

If you see the Office Assistant to create a table with a demonstration, click Cancel.

2. Click the **Tables and Borders button** 🔲 on the Standard toolbar
   The Tables and Borders toolbar is displayed, as shown in Figure D-15. Notice that the Draw Table button 🖉 on the Tables and Borders toolbar is automatically depressed and the Draw Table pointer 🖉 is displayed.

3. With the table pointer near the last paragraph mark of the document, click while dragging down and to the right, creating a cell about 4" wide and 1" tall
   Use the rulers as a guide for determining the size of the cell. The first cell you draw using the Draw Table button represents the outside border of the entire table. Next create smaller cells within the first one.

4. Click on the left side of the cell about ¼" below the top line and drag the pointer straight across to the right side of the cell, and then release the mouse
   Notice as you drag the pointer across the table, you can see a dotted line representing a cell border. Next you create a column in the table.

QuickTip

If you do not like the placement of a line in your table, you can erase the line using the Eraser button 🔲 on the Tables and Borders toolbar. Just click the Eraser button and then click the line you want to erase.

5. Click the bottom of the new line about 1¼" from the left edge of the table and drag down to the bottom line of the table
   Compare your table to Figure D-16. Next, you add more rows to the table.

6. Click on the left side of the table about ¼" under the top cell and then drag across to the right side of the table
   A new row is added to the table. Add another column that divides the right column.

7. Create another line that splits the right column at 2¼", then click the **Draw Table button** 🖉 on the Tables and Borders toolbar
   Clicking the Draw Table button deactivates the table pointer. After customizing your table you are ready to add text.

Time To

✔ Save

8. Place the insertion point in the first cell of the table, then type **World Travel Airlines**, as shown in Figure D-17
   In the next lesson, you will modify your table to make it more attractive.

FIGURE D-15: **Tables and Borders toolbar**

Eraser button
removes lines
between cells

Line Style

Line Weight

Borders

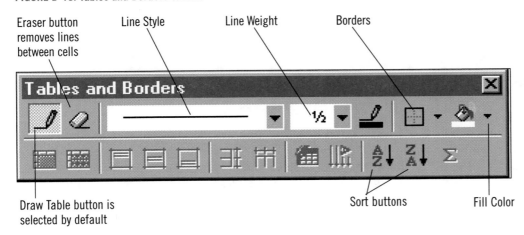

Draw Table button is
selected by default

Sort buttons

Fill Color

FIGURE D-16: **Adding a row to a custom table**

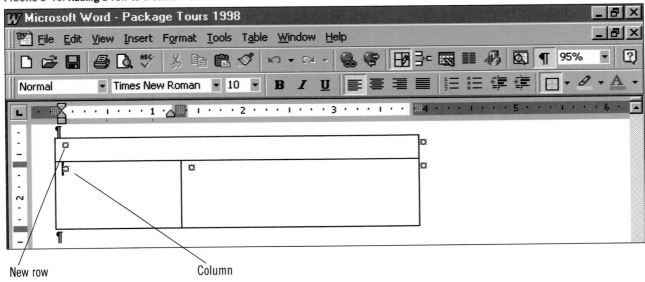

New row

Column

FIGURE D-17: **Completed table**

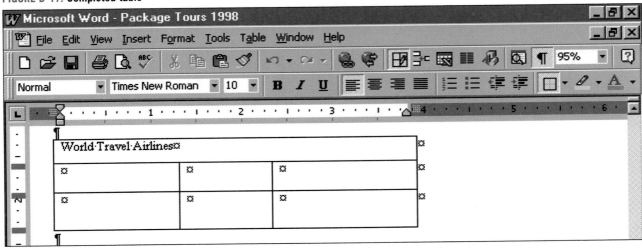

Modifying a Table with the Tables and Borders Toolbar

You can also use the Tables and Borders toolbar to improve the appearance of your tables. This toolbar contains various buttons that can be used to format the table itself or arrange the text within the table. For example, the Distribute Columns button automatically makes selected columns equal widths. Angela will use the Tables and Borders toolbar to improve the appearance of her table. She will begin by splitting the cells in the table to add another column to the end of the table.

1. Select the last column of the second and third rows, and then click the Split Cells button 🎛 on the Tables and Borders toolbar
   The Split Cells dialog box opens, as shown in Figure D-18. In this dialog box, you can choose to split the selected cells into additional rows or additional columns or both. In this case, split these cells into 2 rows and 2 columns.

2. Verify that the Number of rows and Number of columns boxes both display 2, then click OK
   The original cells are divided into 4 smaller cells, as shown in Figure D-19. Next, you make the width of all the columns equal.

3. Select the entire table, then click the Distribute Columns Evenly button 🎚 on the Tables and Borders toolbar
   All the columns are now the same width. Now you are ready to enter text.

4. In the new cells, type the text shown in Figure D-20 and be sure to press [Tab] at the end of the last row to create a new row of cells
   Next, center the text in the columns.

QuickTip

To select the table without selecting the end-of-row markers, select the text in the first row, then drag down and to the right.

5. Select the entire table (do *not* select the end-of-row markers), then click the Center button ≣ on the Formatting toolbar
   To improve the appearance of the table, make all the rows the same height.

6. Select all the rows in the table, if necessary, and click the Distribute Rows Evenly button 🎚 on the Tables and Borders toolbar
   Now all the rows are the same height. Next you can give the table a more elegant appearance.

7. Click anywhere in the table, click the Table AutoFormat button 📇 on the Tables and Borders toolbar, and then scroll to and double-click the Elegant preset format

8. Click Table on the menu bar, and then click Cell Height and Width, and on the Row tab, click the Center option button, and then click OK
   Your table is centered on the page. Compare your table to Figure D-20.

9. Click the Tables and Borders button 🖽 on the Standard toolbar
   The Tables and Borders toolbar is hidden. Angela has finished working with the document for now.

Time To

✔ Save
✔ Preview
✔ Print
✔ Exit

FIGURE D-18: Split Cells dialog box

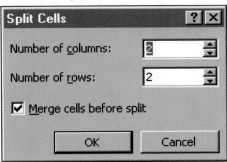

FIGURE D-19: New cells

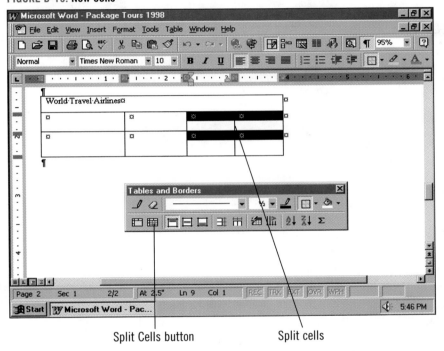

Split Cells button   Split cells

FIGURE D-20: Completed table

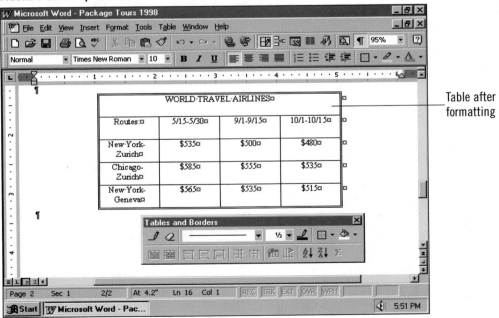

Table after formatting

Practice

► Concepts Review

Label each of the elements in Figure D-21.

FIGURE D-21

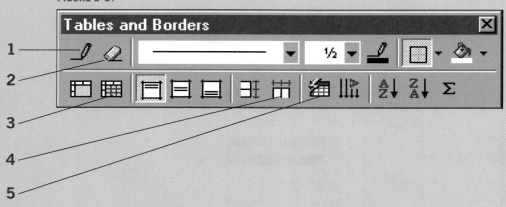

Match the number of each of the following terms with the statement that best describes its function.

6. Insert Table button
7. Table AutoFormat
8. = SUM
9. Gridlines
10. Descending order

a. Sorting from largest to smallest or from Z to A
b. Allows you to choose from preset tables
c. Creates a table from existing text
d. The built-in formula provided by Word in the Formula dialog box
e. Printing lines separating cells in a table

Select the best answer from the list of choices.

11. Which of the following statements is **NOT** a major benefit of using tables (rather than tabs) to align text in rows and columns?
    a. You can add and delete information without reformatting the entire table.
    b. You can format the table using the Table AutoFormat command.
    c. The status bar displays the cell reference to identify your location in the table.
    d. You can sort and calculate information in a table.

12. Which statement best describes the commands available on the pop-up menu for working in a table?
    a. The pop-up menu contains only the commands found on the Table menu.
    b. The pop-up menu contains the commands you are likely to use most often when working in a table.
    c. The pop-up menu contains Table AutoFormat settings from which you can choose.
    d. The pop-up menu contains the Formula command to insert calculations in a table.

13. Which of the following statements best describes how to delete only the text inside a row?
    a. Select the row, then press [Delete].
    b. With the insertion point in the row, click Table then click Delete Cells. Then click Delete Entire Row.

c. Select the row, then click the Cut button.

d. Select the row, click Edit, then click Cut.

14. To insert a column at the end of a table, you must first:

a. Select the last column.

b. Place the insertion point in the last column.

c. Select the last cell in the table.

d. Select the end-of-row markers at the right end of the table.

15. To add a new blank row to the bottom of a table, you:

a. Place the insertion point in the last row, click Table, then click Insert Rows.

b. Select the last row, click Table, then click Insert Rows.

c. Place the insertion point in the last cell of the last row, then press [Tab].

d. Select the end-of-row markers at the right end of the table, then press [Tab].

16. In which one of the following instances does the row height in a table NOT adjust?

a. When the amount of text in a cell fits on more than one line.

b. When you click Table, then click Cell Height and Width.

c. When you drag a horizontal gridline between rows.

d. When you click Cell Height and Width on the table pop-up menu.

17. When sorting a table, what is the easiest way to ensure that the header row is NOT sorted along with the other rows?

a. In the Sort dialog box, click the Header row radio button in the My list has section.

b. Sort the table before adding the header row.

c. Split the table before sorting it.

d. Use the Table AutoFormat command first.

18. Which of the following statements is NOT true of the Table AutoFormat command?

a. You can apply special formatting to the last column.

b. You can apply special formatting to the last row.

c. You can see an example of the format in the Table AutoFormat dialog box.

d. You can see an example of your table with new formatting in the Table AutoFormat dialog box.

19. Which of the following is a valid cell reference for the first cell in the third column?

a. C1

b. ROW1COL3

c. 1C

d. 3A

20. Which of the following is NOT true about sorting rows in a table?

a. The Sort command always sorts all the rows in a table.

b. You can sort a table by more than one column.

c. You can specify not to sort the header row.

d. You can choose the order in which you want rows sorted.

▶ Skills Review

1. Create a table and convert text to a table
  a. Launch Word, then open the document named WD D-2 and save it as "Travel Expenses".
  b. Select all six lines of text.
  c. Click the Insert Table button on the Standard toolbar.
  d. Select the text "Taxis", then press [Delete].
  e. Type "Transportation", then click Bold if necessary.
  f. Type "January" in the empty cell in the first row.
  g. Click the Save button on the Standard toolbar.

2. Insert and delete rows and columns.
  a. With the insertion point in the third row, click Table on the menu bar, then click Delete Cells, click Delete Entire Row, then click OK.
  b. Place the insertion point in the last cell of the last row of the table, then press [Tab].
  c. Type "Misc.", press [Tab], then type "54.88" [Tab] "73.65" [Tab] "63.49".
  d. Select the end-of-row markers at the right end of the table, then click the Insert Columns button on the Standard toolbar.
  e. In the first cell of the new column, type "Expense Total".
  f. Click the Save button on the Standard toolbar.

3. Calculate data in a table.
  a. Place the insertion point in the second cell in the Expense Total column, click Table on the menu bar, click Formula, then click OK.
  b. Press [↓] to move the insertion point to the next cell in the Expense Total column and press [F4].
  c. Repeat Step 3b for the remaining cells in the Expense Total column.
  d. Select the Transportation value in the January column, then type "123.50".
  e. Select the Transportation value in the Expense Total column, then press [F9] to update the total.
  f. Click the Save button on the Standard toolbar.

4. Sort information in a table.
  a. Place the insertion point anywhere in the table.
  b. Click Table on the menu bar, then click Sort.
  c. In the Sort by section, select Expense Total in the columns list.
  d. Click the Descending radio button.
  e. In the My list has section, make sure the Header row radio button is selected, then click OK.
  f. Click the Save button on the Standard toolbar.

5. Format a table.
  a. If the table is not already selected, click Table on the menu bar, then click Select Table.
  b. Click the Tables and Borders button on the Standard toolbar.
  c. Click the Table AutoFormat button on the Tables and Borders toolbar.
  d. In the Formats list, review different formats by selecting each and viewing it in the Preview section.
  e. In the Formats list, click Columns 5.
  f. In the Apply special formats to section, click the Last column check box, then click OK.
  g. Select all the cells that contain numbers and click the Align Right button on the Formatting toolbar.
  h. Add "0" to the cents place of any value that is missing the final zero.

   i. Click the Save button on the Standard toolbar.
   j. Click the Print button on the Standard toolbar, then close the document.

6. **Use the Draw Table button.**
   a. Open a new document and save it as "Agenda".
   b. Drag and draw a cell 2" high and 3" wide.
   c. Drag a line below the top line of the table creating a cell about .25" high.
   d. Repeat Step 6c creating a table with four cells total.
   e. Add a vertical line in the middle of the last three cells to make two columns.
   f. Enter the text below.
   Agenda
   8:30   Opening Ceremonies
   10:00
   12:00   Group Luncheon
   g. Click the Save button on the Standard toolbar.

7. **Modify a table with the Tables and Borders toolbar.**
   a. Select the empty cell in the third row.
   b. Click the Split Cells button.
   c. Be sure that the Number of columns box contains 2, and that the Number of rows box contains 1, then click OK.
   d. Enter the text below.
   Meeting A for Advisors
   Meeting B for Committee Members
   e. Select the first column in the table and position the pointer over the border between the first and second columns. Drag the pointer to the left until the column is about ¾" wide.
   f. Select the third row and position the pointer over the border between the second and third columns. Drag the pointer to the left until the two cells are about the same size.
   g. Select the table, then click the Center button on the Formatting toolbar.
   h. Use the Colorful 2 format in Table AutoFormat.
   i. Save, print, and close the document. Then hide the Tables and Borders toolbar and exit Word.

Independent Challenges

1. As the director of marketing for ReadersPlus publishing company, you are responsible for sales projections for the new beginners reading series called "Everyone Is A Reader." You have been asked to present these projections at the upcoming sales kickoff meeting. Begin by creating a new document and saving it as "Projected Sales". Then format the document with the following changes, using Figure D-22 as a guide for how the completed document should look.

To complete this independent challenge:

1. Create a table with 5 rows and 5 columns.
2. Enter the following text:

Everyone is a Reader	West	East	Midwest	South
Anthologies Only	5000	7000	5800	7200
Supplements Only	2400	3500	4000	1100
Anthologies with guides	6800	6700	9400	8200
Complete Package	6500	7500	6300	7700

3. Adjust the last column width to be about 1".
4. Add a Total column to the right side of the chart.
5. Calculate the total for each row.
6. Format the table with the Grid 3 preset format.
7. Preview, save, print, then close the document.

FIGURE D-22

Everyone is a Reader	West	East	Midwest	South	Total
Anthologies Only	5000	7000	5800	7200	25000
Supplements Only	2400	3500	4000	1100	11000
Anthologies with guides	6800	6700	9400	8200	31100
Complete Package	6500	7500	6300	7700	28000

2. As the conference coordinator for Educational Consultants, Inc., you are in charge of tracking the costs for an upcoming Creativity Conference. You want to compare this year's conference costs with those of last year's conference. Create a new document and save it as "Conference Costs". Complete the following formatting.

To complete this independent challenge:

1. Create a table with 7 rows and 3 columns.
2. Enter the following text:

Conference Costs	1997	1998
Dinner	740	1300
Audio/video rental	270	425
Presenter fees	300	550
Decorations	500	800
Printing fees	300	420
Hall rental	800	1100

3. Adjust the last column width to be about 1".
4. Add a column to the right side of the chart.
5. Add the column heading "Difference" to the new column.
6. In the Difference column, calculate the difference between 1998 versus 1997 costs for each row. Hint: For the first row, type "=C2-B2" in the Formula dialog box. Using the [F4] key to repeat a command copies the previous formula so you cannot use [F4] to insert formulas with varying cell references.
7. Sort the table by 1997 costs, from highest to lowest.
8. Format the table with the List 5 preset format.
9. Center the columns so that they contain fee values.
10. Preview, save, print, then close the document.

3. Task References are documents which summarize commands, buttons, and keystroke shortcuts for the features you learn about in each unit. Log on to the Internet and use your browser to go to http://www.course.com. From there, click Student On Line Companions, and then click on the link to go to the Microsoft Office 97 Professional Edition-Illustrated: A First Course page, then click on the Word link for Unit D. Download the Unit D Task Reference. Although this document is already formatted as a table, you decide to customize the table. Save the final table as "Table Task Reference".

1. Sort the by the text in the first column.
2. Sort the table again, this time by the text in the third column and the first column.
3. Improve the table's appearance by applying the preset format setting.
4. Preview, save, print, then close the document.

4. As a co-chairman of the entertainment committee for the Lake City 1998 class reunion, you are responsible for calculating attendance fees for the planned events. You want to create a table showing the distribution of attendees among all the events. Another member of the committee has provided you with the number of classmates who have responded for specific events. Open the document named WD D-3 and save it as "Reunion Costs".

To complete this independent challenge:

1. Convert the tabbed text to a table.
2. Add a row to the end of the table, specifying "Variety Show" as the event with 120 attendees at $7 per person.
3. Calculate the total for each row, using a multiplication formula. (Hint: For the first row, type "=B2*C2" in the Formula dialog box. Using the [F4] key to repeat a command copies the previous formula so you cannot use [F4] to insert formulas with varying cell references.)
4. Format the table with the List 8 preset format.
5. Right align the columns that contain numerical values.
6. Preview, save, print, then close the document.

Visual Workshop

As part of your responsibilities as the director of the Extreme Fitness health club, you must prepare a price list for club activities. Use the Draw Table button and other features on the Tables and Borders toolbar to create a table that identifies activities such as basketball, racquetball, aerobics classes, etc., and enter a price for each activity. Use Figure D-23 as a guide for creating your table. Use the Eraser button to delete any border lines you don't want in your table. (Hint: Use the Distribute Columns Evenly button and the Distribute Rows Evenly button to make your columns and rows even.) Format the table in any preset format desired. Save the document as "Activity Prices".

FIGURE D-23

Activity	Price	Sales	Total
Aerobics classes	$15.00	89	$1335.00
Basketball	$7.00	152	$1064.00
Raquetball	$10.00	214	$2140.00
Swimming	$10.00	345	$3450.00
Total for 1997		**800**	**$7989.00**

Formatting
Pages

Objectives

► **Control text flow between pages**
► **Adjust document margins**
► **Insert headers**
► **Insert footers**
► **Modify text in a footer**
► **Change page orientation**
► **Change formatting in multiple sections**
► **Create headers for specific pages**

In addition to formatting text and paragraphs, you can format the pages of your documents. **Page formatting** includes determining the margins between the text and the edge of the page. It also includes the size and orientation of a page. Additional formatting options allow you to specify the text flow on and between pages. Another feature allows you to add text that will appear at the top or bottom of each page in the document, in the form of headers and footers. To complete the formatting in her financial summary for Nomad Ltd, Angela Pacheco needs to adjust the document's margins, change the orientation for an additional page, and add headers and footers to her document.

Controlling Text Flow between Pages

When the amount of text in a document fills a page, Word automatically creates a page break, which places any remaining text at the start of the next new page. Sometimes this break results in a line or two appearing alone at the bottom of the page with the rest of the paragraph continuing on the next page, giving the document an awkward appearance. Using text flow features, you can control how text flows on and between pages. 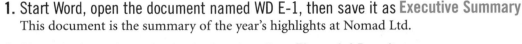 Angela would like to have the Financial Results heading appear with the paragraph that follows it.

QuickTip

Turn off spelling and grammar checking. Display paragraph marks.

1. **Start Word, open the document named WD E-1, then save it as Executive Summary**
   This document is the summary of the year's highlights at Nomad Ltd.

2. **Place the insertion point in the last heading, Financial Results**
   To control the flow of text affecting this heading and the next paragraph, you can use the Paragraph command.

3. **Click Format on the menu bar, then click Paragraph**
   The Line and Page Breaks tab contains the formatting option you want to use.

QuickTip

You can quickly insert your own page break anywhere in a document by pressing **[Ctrl][Enter]**. In normal view, this kind of break (sometimes called a hard page break) appears as a light gray line labeled "Page Break" in your document.

4. **Click the Line and Page Breaks tab**
   The Line and Page Breaks tab appears foremost in the dialog box. The Pagination area contains the options that affect the flow of text over the pages of the document. Table E-1 describes the text flow options. Choose the option to always keep this heading with the following paragraph.

5. **Click the Keep with next check box, then click OK**
   The heading (and the text that follows it) appears on the next page. To get a better picture of the flow of the document, preview it.

6. **Click the Print Preview button 🔍 on the Standard toolbar**
   The document appears in the Preview window. Next, preview all the pages of the document.

Trouble?

Do not be concerned if the amount of text you see in your own document does not match the amount of text shown in the figure. The exact amount of text you see can depend on the resolution of your monitor, or the type of printer connected to your computer.

7. **Click the Multiple Pages button 🖼 on the Preview toolbar and click the second box in the first row of the grid to see the entire document**
   Compare your document to Figure E-1. The text in the legend that appears to run off the second page will be addressed later in this unit. If you see only one page of the document, click the Multiple Pages button again, and this time click to the first box in the second row. Click the Multiple Pages button one more time, and click to the second box in the first row.

8. **Click File on the menu bar, then click Save**
   The document is saved. Notice that several lines of text appear on the second page. Because you want all the headings in the summary document to appear on the first page, you will adjust the margins so that the text will appear on the first page.

FIGURE E-1: **New text flow in document**

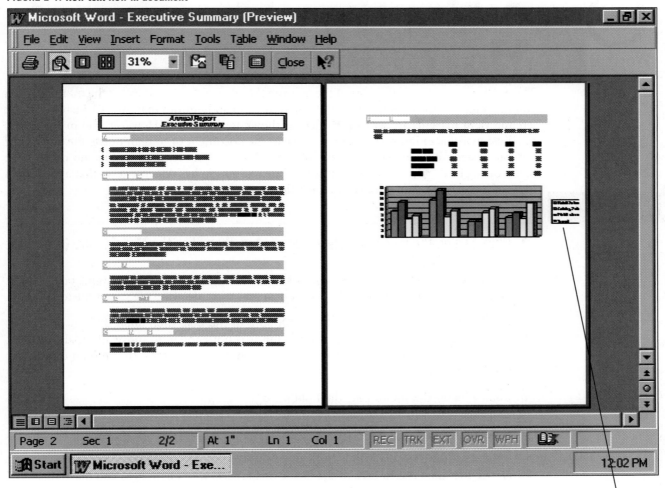

This problem will be corrected later in this lesson.

TABLE E-1: **Pagination text flow options**

choose this option	to
Widow/Orphan control	Prevent the last line of a paragraph from printing at the top of a page (widow), and the first line of a paragraph from printing at the bottom of a page (orphan)
Keep lines together	Prevent a page break within a paragraph
Keep with next	Prevent a page break between the selected paragraph and the paragraph after it
Page break before	Position the selected text at the top of the next page

Adjusting Document Margins

The white space between the edge of the text and the edge of the page is called the margin. When you first create a document, the default size of the top and bottom margins is 1 inch, while the left and right margins are set to 1.25 inch, as shown in Figure E-2. However, you might decide to adjust margins to improve the appearance of the document or to manipulate the amount of text on a page. You can adjust the size of individual margins on the Margins tab of the Page Setup dialog box. ✎ Angela will adjust the margins in her document, so that all the main ideas of her summary document fit on the first page.

1. **Click File on the menu bar, click Page Setup, then click the Margins tab (if it is not already foremost)**
   The Page Setup dialog box appears, as shown in Figure E-3. On the Margins tab, you can determine the size of the margins for a document. First, decrease the size of the top margin.

2. **Click the Top down arrow until .8" appears in the box, then click OK**
   This reduces the size of the top margin, but it is not enough to move all the desired text from page 2 to the first page. Change the other margins to increase the amount of text that will fit on the first page.

3. **Click File on the menu bar, then click Page Setup**
   The Page Setup dialog box opens with the Margins tab displayed.

4. **Click the Bottom down arrow until .7" appears, click the Left down arrow until 1" appears, and then click the Right down arrow until 1" appears**
   Notice that the Preview area of the dialog box reflects your changes as you make them.

5. **Click OK**
   Adjusting the margins causes Word to move the text that previously appeared on the second page onto the bottom of the first page. The part of the chart that appears to run off the second page will be addressed later in this unit. To have the entire table appear on the next page with the chart, you can apply additional text flow formatting.

6. **Click Close on the Preview toolbar**
   The document appears in the normal view; you can now apply formatting to have all the lines of the entire table stay together on the same page.

7. **Select all five lines of the table under the Financial Results heading, then click Format from the menu bar, then click Paragraph**

8. **On the Line and Page Breaks tab, click the Keep with next check box, then click OK**

9. **Click the Print Preview button 🔍 on the Standard toolbar**
   The document appears in the Preview window, as shown in Figure E-4.

10. **Click Close on the Preview toolbar**
    The document appears in the normal view.

Trouble?

Different screens at different resolutions might display the flow of text differently.

Time To

✔ Save

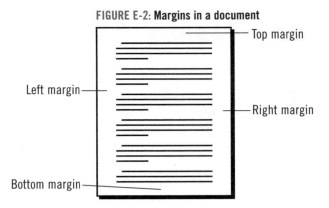

Top margin

Left margin

Right margin

Bottom margin

FIGURE E-3: Margins tab in Page Setup dialog box

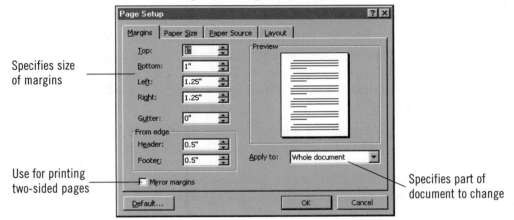

Specifies size
of margins

Use for printing
two-sided pages

Specifies part of
document to change

FIGURE E-4: Preview of highlights document

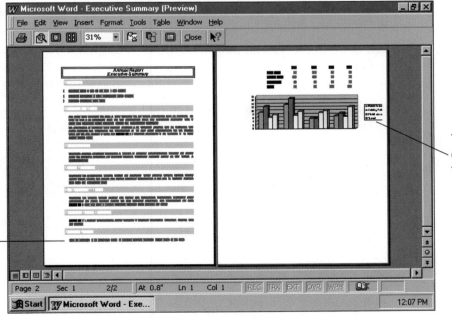

This problem will be
corrected later in
this lesson.

Text previously on
second page

CLUES TO USE

Adjusting the Margins with the Ruler

You can adjust document margins in the page layout view or in the Preview window (if the ruler is displayed) by dragging the edges of the rulers. Position the pointer at an edge of a ruler until the pointer changes to ↔, and then drag to the size you want. If you hold down [Alt] as you drag, you can see the exact margin size.

Inserting Headers

In multiple page documents the top or bottom of every page typically contains information such as the page number, title, author's name, or date. Text that appears at the top of every page is called a **header**, while text appearing at the bottom of every page is called a **footer**, which you will learn about in the next lesson. You can use both headers and footers in your document. Angela would like the title of the Executive Summary to appear at the top of every page, so she begins by selecting and cutting the text she wants to use as a header.

Steps

1. **Select the first two lines in the document including the paragraph marks (enclosed in the double-box border) and click the Cut button ✄ on the Standard toolbar**
   Cutting this text removes the bordered title from the document and places it on the Clipboard. Because this is the text you want to appear at the top of every page, open the Header area of the document.

2. **Click View on the menu bar, then click Header and Footer**
   The document appears in Page Layout view but the text is dimmed. You cannot edit the body of the document while the Header or Footer area is displayed. This command also displays the Header and Footer toolbar, as shown in Figure E-5. In the Header area, you can type the text you want to appear at the top of every page, or you can paste the text you placed on the Clipboard.

3. **Click the Paste button 📋 on the Standard toolbar**
   Clicking the Paste button inserts the text from the Clipboard into the Header area. You can drag the Header and Footer toolbar to another area of the window if it obscures your view.

4. **Scroll down to the second page**
   The header also appears on the next page of the document. Compare your document to Figure E-6. You are now ready to create a footer, but save your work first before continuing.

5. **Click the Save button 💾 on the Standard toolbar**

FIGURE E-5: Inserting headers

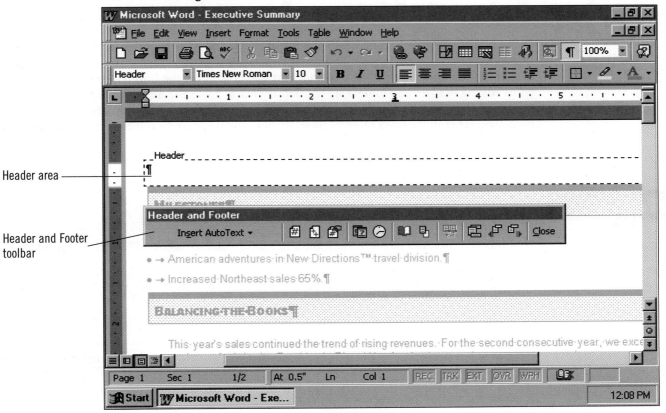

Header area

Header and Footer toolbar

FIGURE E-6: Text in a header area

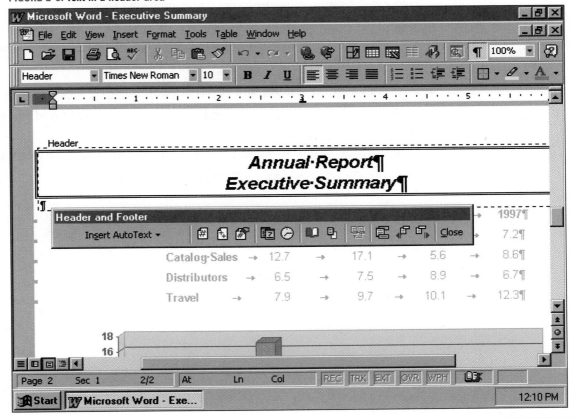

Inserting Footers

In the same way headers display information at the top of every page, footers display information at the bottom of every page. You use the Header and Footer toolbar to switch between the header and footer areas. With the Header and Footer toolbar, the features you use most often when editing headers and footers are within easy reach. Table E-2 describes each of the buttons available on the Header and Footer toolbar. ✐ Angela would like the date and page number to appear at the bottom of every page. Because she is currently working in the header area, she begins by switching to the footer area.

Steps 1 2 3 4

1. **Click the Switch Between Header and Footer button 🔲 on the Header and Footer toolbar**
   Clicking this button displays the Footer area, in which you can type or insert the information you want to appear at the bottom of every page.

2. **Click the Insert Date button 🔲 on the Header and Footer toolbar**
   The current date appears in the footer. Use the preset tab stops already defined in the footer area to position text. You can also insert text that you want to precede the page number.

3. **Press [Tab] twice, type Page, then press [Spacebar]**
   With the text in the footer, you are ready to insert the page number.

4. **Click the Insert Page Number button 🔲 on the Header and Footer toolbar**
   Clicking the Insert Page Number button inserts an instruction so that Word automatically supplies the correct page number on each page. Compare your footer to the one shown in Figure E-7. Now examine the footer on the following page.

5. **Scroll to the next page**
   The footer also appears on the next page of the document. You have finished working with headers and footers for now, so you can close the footer area.

6. **Click Close on the Header and Footer toolbar**

7. **Click Page Layout View button 🔲 and scroll to the bottom of the page to see the footer in the document**
   Compare your document with Figure E-8. Notice that the text in the footer appears dimmed.

8. **Click the Save button 🔲 on the Standard toolbar**

FIGURE E-7: **Page numbers in a footer area**

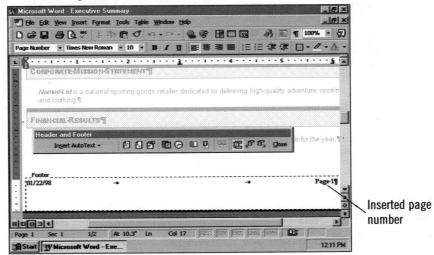

Inserted page number

FIGURE E-8: **Text in a footer**

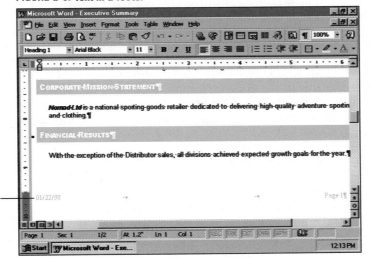

New text in the footer

TABLE E-2: **Buttons on the Header and Footer toolbar**

click	to
🔲	Move the insertion point between the header and footer areas
🔲	Move the insertion point to the previous header or footer area, when the document is divided into sections
🔲	Move the insertion point to the next header or footer area, when the document is divided into sections
🔲	Insert the header or footer from the previous section in the current section OR break the connection between sections, allowing different headers or footers to be created
🔲	Insert a field for sequential page numbers, starting with 1, that is updated when pages are added or deleted
🔲	Insert a field for the current date, based on the computer's clock, that is updated when the document is opened or printed
🔲	Insert a field for the current time, based on the computer's clock, that is updated when the document is opened or printed
🔲	Display the Page Setup dialog box, where you can modify the margins, paper source, paper size, and page orientation
🔲	Display or hide the document text while working in headers and footers

Modifying Text in a Footer

When you need to edit the text in a header or footer, you simply display the header or footer area again. Although you can use the Header and Footer command on the View menu, when you are in page layout view, it is quicker to double-click in the area you want to edit. For example, to edit the footer in your document (which is displayed in page layout view), double-click the footer part of the document. Next, Angela decides to display the document name along with the page number. She uses a built-in AutoText entry to accomplish this.

Steps 1 2 3 4

1. **Scroll to display the footer in the document window, then double-click anywhere in the footer**
   The footer area opens. Now, you are ready to edit the footer.

2. **Place the insertion point in front of the word Page**
   Next, insert the document name using the AutoText feature.

3. **Click Insert AutoText on the Header and Footer toolbar, as shown in Figure E-9**

4. **Click Filename, type a comma, and press [Spacebar]**
   The filename of the document appears in the footer. If you change the name of the document, Word automatically updates this information in the footer. Because it is useful to know the total number of pages in a document, you can supply this information at the end of the footer.

5. **Place the insertion point after the page number, press [Spacebar], type of, then press [Spacebar] again**

6. **Click the Insert Number of Pages button ⊞ on the Header and Footer toolbar**
   The total number of pages in the document appears in the footer, as shown in Figure E-10.

7. **Click Close on the Header and Footer toolbar**
   The Header and Footer toolbar closes. Compare your document to Figure E-11.

8. **Click the Save button ⊟ on the Standard toolbar**

FIGURE E-9: Insert AutoText button

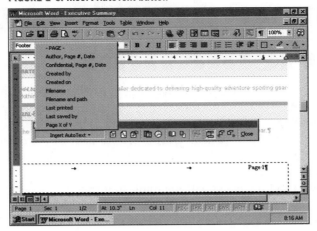

FIGURE E-10: Number of pages in footer

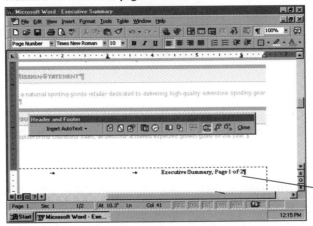

New information in footer

FIGURE E-11: Completed footer

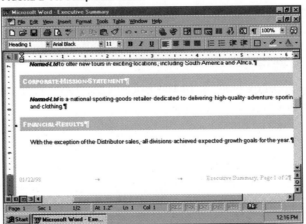

CLUES TO USE

Using fields

You can use fields to insert and update information that Word retrieves from your document and your computer. A **field** is an instruction or code that tells Word what you want to insert. Word offers hundreds of fields, each inserting very specific information in the document. Some of the more common fields you might insert in a document include the document name, revision number, the date that the document was saved or printed, and information that appears in the Properties dialog box (available with the Properties command on the File menu).

Changing Page Orientation

In most of the documents you create, the page itself is oriented such that it is taller than it is wide. This orientation is called **portrait**. When you arrange text on a page that is wider than it is tall, this orientation is called **landscape**. Figure E-12 illustrates the difference between portrait and landscape orientation. ◆━━━ On the second page of the document, Angela noticed that the legend in the chart is too close to the edge of the page. She would like to change the orientation for the second page. She starts by displaying the document in normal view, so she can better locate the part of the document she wants to format.

Steps 123 4

1. Click the **Normal View button** 🔳

2. Scroll to and place the insertion point at the beginning of the text **Financial Results**
   Only the text from this point forward will be formatted with a new orientation.

3. Click **File** on the menu bar, then click **Page Setup**
   This command displays the Page Setup dialog box. The orientation settings are on the Paper Size tab.

4. Click the **Paper Size tab**
   Clicking this tab displays the Paper Size options in the Page Setup dialog box, as shown in Figure E-13. You can display the second page of the document in landscape orientation so that all of the chart appears when it is printed.

5. In the Orientation area, click the **Landscape option button**, click the **Apply to list arrow**, then click **This point forward**
   Clicking this button formats the contents of the second page in landscape orientation. Next, check the margins for this part of the document.

6. Click the **Margins tab**
   Notice that the previous settings for the top and bottom margins are now the settings for the left and right margins. You can change the margins so that they are consistent throughout the document.

7. In the Top box type **.8**, in the Bottom box type **.7**, in the Left box type **1**, and in the Right box type **1**
   Notice that the Preview area of the dialog box reflects your changes as you make them. Next, specify the part of the document you want formatted.

8. Click the **Apply To list arrow** and click **This point forward**
   This selection ensures that only this part (page two and after) of the document is affected by these changes.

9. Click **OK**, then click the **Save button** 💾 on the Standard toolbar
   Although you cannot see the changes in normal view, the second page is now formatted in landscape orientation with new margins. A double dotted line labeled "Section Break (Next Page)" was automatically inserted, as shown in Figure E-14. A section break allows you to format different parts of the same document with different page setup settings. Section breaks are inserted whenever you specify Page Setup options that affect only part of a document.

FIGURE E-12: Comparing page orientation

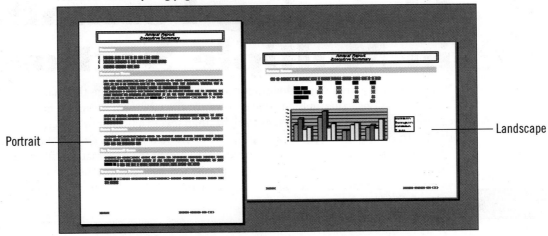

Portrait

Landscape

FIGURE E-13: Paper size options

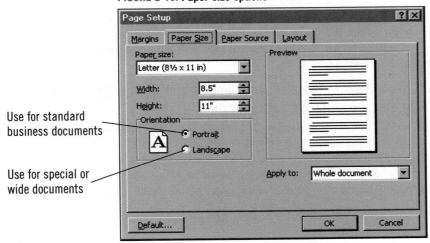

Use for standard
business documents

Use for special or
wide documents

FIGURE E-14: Section break in a document

Section break

Small squares
indicate that text
flow formatting is
applied

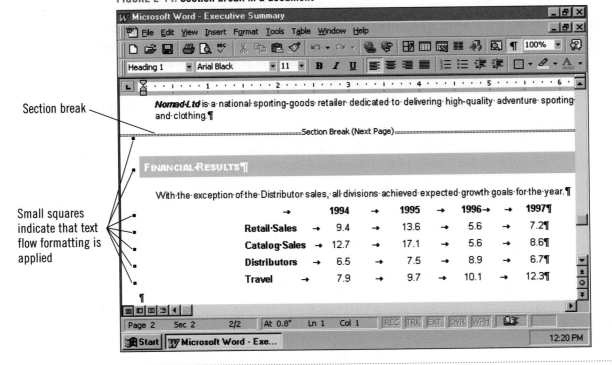

Changing Formatting in Multiple Sections

Whenever you format your document into sections and change the margins or orientation in different sections, you might also need to adjust the tab positions in the headers and footers. For example, suppose you inserted tabs to right-align text in a header or footer, and then you changed the width of the document by adjusting the document margins or orientation. You will want to adjust the tab position in the header or footer to match the new margins in the document, so that the text continues to be centered or right-aligned between the new margins. ✎ Angela wants to adjust the tab position in the footer for the second section to keep the page numbers aligned with the right margin.

Steps 1234

1. **Place the insertion point in the second page of the document, click View on the menu bar, then click Header and Footer**
   The Header area for section two appears. Because the header is centered without a tab, it is unaffected by the changes to the page orientation and requires no adjustments. But the page number in the footer was placed with tabs and needs adjustment, so you can start by displaying the footer area.

2. **Click the Switch Between Header and Footer button 🔳 on the Header and Footer toolbar, then scroll to the right margin**
   The Footer area for section two appears. Notice also that the Same as Previous button is indented on the Header and Footer toolbar, as shown in Figure E-15. By default, each section in a document uses the same footer information as the previous section. Because of the wider orientation in section two, you want to adjust the tab position for the footer in this section, so you must break this connection between the footers.

3. **Click the Same As Previous button 🔳 on the Header and Footer toolbar, then scroll to the right margin again**
   The button is no longer indented and the connection is broken between the two sections. Now, you can adjust the position of the right-aligned tab stop.

4. **Drag the right-aligned tab in the horizontal ruler to the 9-inch mark**
   The page number information appears at the right margin in the footer. You have finished formatting the document for now, so you can close the Footer area.

5. **Click Close on the Header and Footer toolbar**
   The Footer area closes and you return to the document. Before closing and printing the document, preview the document to see how it will look.

6. **Click the Print Preview button 🔳 on the Standard toolbar**
   Examine both pages of the document. Compare your document to Figure E-16.

7. **Click Close on the Preview toolbar**
   Return to the document window.

8. **Click the Save button 🔳 on the Standard toolbar, then click the Print button 🔳 on the Standard toolbar**

9. **Close the document**

FIGURE E-15: **Second section footer area**

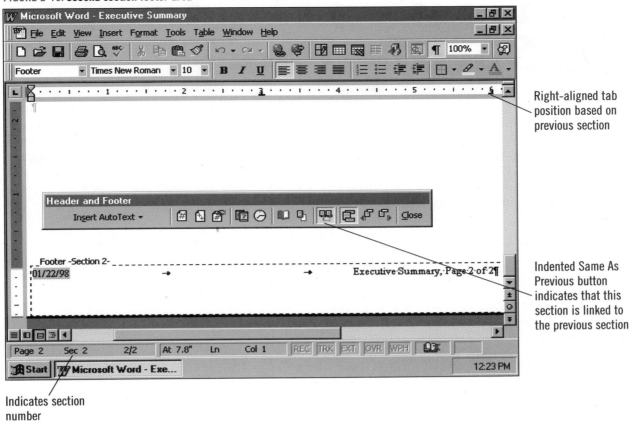

Right-aligned tab position based on previous section

Indented Same As Previous button indicates that this section is linked to the previous section

Indicates section number

FIGURE E-16: **Different footers in the same document**

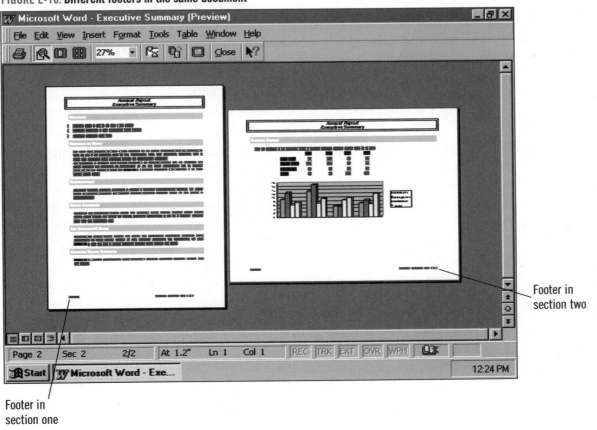

Footer in section two

Footer in section one

Creating Headers for Specific Pages

Word 97

Word also offers various header and footer formatting that is especially helpful in larger documents. Often when you create a large document, it will contain a title page on which you may not want to include the headers or footers. The Layout tab on the Page Setup command allows you to specify a different header or footer for the first page of the document. This tab also allows you to create different headers and footers for the even and odd pages of a document. Angela would like to add headers to the Nomad Annual Report. Since the report will be printed with the pages facing each other in a book format, Angela would like the page numbers to appear on the outside margin of the pages.

Steps 1 2 3 4

1. **Open the document named WD E-2, then save it as Nomad 1998**
   This document contains a more in-depth report of activities occurring at Nomad Ltd throughout the past year. You will add to the document headers containing the page numbers.

2. **Click File on the menu bar, then click Page Setup**
   The Page Setup dialog box opens. On the Layout tab, you can specify the header and footer options you want for the document.

3. **Click the Layout tab, then click the Different first page check box in the Headers and Footers box**
   Choosing this option will allow you to exclude the page number on the title page of your document. Since the page numbers always appear on the outside of facing pages, you will need to align the numbers on the even and odd pages differently.

4. **Click the Different odd and even check box, then click OK**
   The Page Setup dialog box closes. You are now ready to enter the page numbers in the headers.

5. **Place the insertion point in the second page, click View on the menu bar, then click Header and Footer**
   The Header and Footer areas and the Header and Footer toolbar are displayed in the document window. Notice the Header area is labeled Even Page Header. All the headers and footers are now labeled Even, Odd, or First Page. You will use Insert AutoText on the Header and Footer toolbar to insert page numbering information.

6. **With the insertion point left-aligned, click Insert AutoText on the Header and Footer toolbar, click Page X of Y, select the text, then press [F9]**
   Page X of Y AutoText entry automatically inserts the page number and the total number of pages in the document, as shown in Figure E-17. You need to press [F9] to update the header to reflect the number of pages in the document. Next insert this same information for the odd pages of your document.

7. **Scroll to the third page, with the insertion point in the Odd Page Header box, click the Align Right button ▤ on the Formatting toolbar, and then repeat step 6**

8. **Click Close on the Header and Footer toolbar**

9. **Click the Print Preview button 🔍 on the Standard toolbar and display all four pages of the document, as shown Figure E-18. Then click Close on the Preview toolbar**

Time To
- ✔ Save
- ✔ Print the document
- ✔ Exit Word

FIGURE E-17: **Page X of Y AutoText entry**

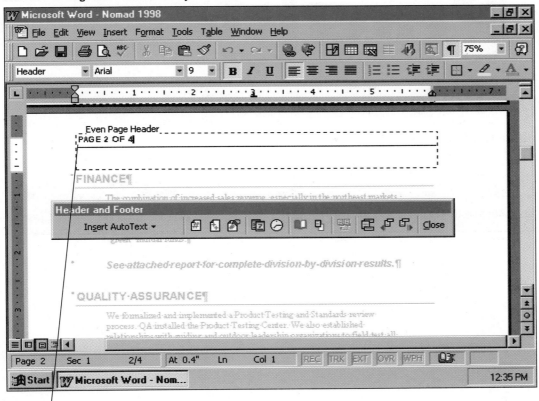

Page number and
number of pages in
document

FIGURE E-18: **Entire document in Print Preview**

No header on
first page

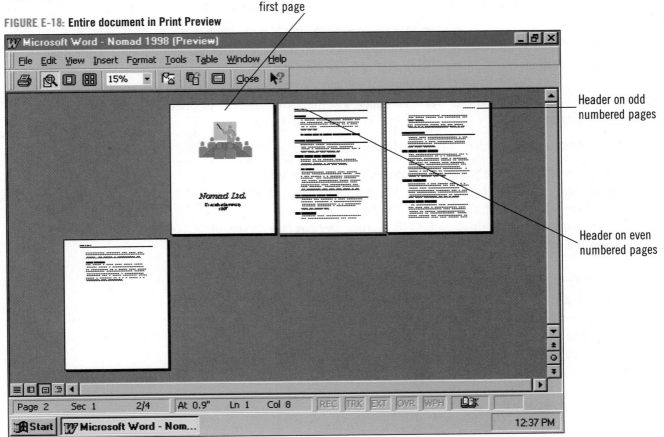

Header on odd
numbered pages

Header on even
numbered pages

Practice

► Concepts Review

Label each of the elements in Figure E-19.

FIGURE E-19

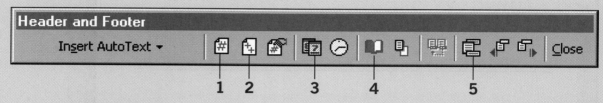

Match each of the following terms with the statement that best describes its function.

6. **Footer**
7. **Header**
8. **Portrait orientation**
9. **Field**
10. **Margin**
11. **Landscape orientation**

a. Text that appears at the top of every page in a document
b. The white space between the edge of the text and the edge of the page
c. A page that is wider than it is tall
d. A special instruction or code for information that Word automatically updates
e. Text that appears at the bottom of every page in a document
f. A page that is taller than it is wide

Select the best answer from the list of choices.

12. **Which of the following can you NOT accomplish in the Page Setup dialog box?**
    a. Adjust the margins for the top, bottom, left, and right edges of a document.
    b. Adjust the tab settings for a header and footer.
    c. Apply unique page formatting options to multiple sections of a document.
    d. Select the page orientation.

13. **When you decrease the size of all margins in a document:**
    a. You increase the amount of text that will fit on the page.
    b. You decrease the amount of text that will fit on the page.
    c. The amount of text that will fit on the page does not change.
    d. You are not able to add headers and footers to the document.

14. **Which of the following is NOT true about headers and footers?**
    a. Clicking View, Header and Footer displays the Header and Footer toolbar.
    b. You can insert fields in a header or footer.
    c. You can paste existing information into a header or footer without having to retype it.
    d. You can edit document text while you are working in headers and footers.

15. **Which of the following is NOT an example of a field you can enter in a header or footer?**
    a. Document name
    b. Current date
    c. Total number of pages in the document
    d. Right-aligned tab stop

16. **Which of the following is true when you create a new section with modified orientation and margin settings?**
    a. Any existing tab settings in the header and footer areas are automatically adjusted to match the new margin settings.
    b. In normal view, there is no visible indication in the document that a new section has been created.
    c. You cannot create a new section with both modified orientation and margin settings.
    d. You may have to manually adjust headers and footers so that they align properly with the new margin settings.

17. **To break the connection between a header or footer in multiple sections of a document, you:**
    a. Click the Switch Between Header and Footer button on the Header and Footer toolbar.
    b. Double-click one of the headers with the right mouse button.
    c. Click the Same As Previous button on the Header and Footer toolbar.
    d. Click the New Section button on the Header and Footer toolbar.

18. **Which of the following is a good reason to use landscape orientation in a document?**
    a. You are formatting a long document.
    b. You are creating a document with unusually wide margins.
    c. A document requires that it is printed on a page that is wider than it is tall.
    d. Landscape orientation is useful only when creating graphics.

19. **Which of the following is NOT a way to display the number of pages in a document?**
    a. Numbering button on the formatting toolbar.
    b. Insert Page Number button on the Header and Footer toolbar.
    c. NumPages field using Field command on the Insert menu.
    d. Insert Number of Pages button on the Header and Footer toolbar.

20. **Which of the following is NOT true when you format part of a document in landscape orientation?**
    a. You must change the position of the printer paper before printing the landscape page.
    b. After changing the orientation, you might need to adjust the width of the header and/or footer areas.
    c. You can see the different orientation in the print preview window.
    d. The landscape orientation option appears on the Paper Size tab in the Page Setup dialog box.

▶ Skills Review

1. Control text flow between pages.
   a. Start Word and open the document named WD E-3. Save the document as "Software Letter".
   b. Place the insertion point in the heading "Reference Card..."
   c. Click Format on the menu bar, then click Paragraph.
   d. Click the Line and Page Breaks tab to bring it forward.
   e. Click the Page break before check box and click OK.

2. Adjust document margins.
   a. Click the Print Preview button on the Standard toolbar and examine all pages of the document.
   b. Click File on the menu bar, click Page Setup, then click the Margin tab.
   c. In the Top box, click the down arrow until .7 appears in the box. In the Bottom box, click the down arrow until .7 appears. In the Left box click the down arrow until 1 appears, and in the Right box click the down arrow until 1 appears. In the Header box, click the up arrow until .8 appears. Then click OK.
   d. Click Close on the Preview toolbar.

3. Insert a header.
   a. Select the first line in the document (the date), be sure to include the paragraph mark, and click the Cut button on the Standard toolbar.
   b. Click View on the menu bar, then click Header and Footer.
   c. Click the Paste button on the Standard toolbar.
   d. Scroll through the document to review your changes and save the document.

4. Insert a footer.
   a. Click the Switch Between Header and Footer button on the Header and Footer toolbar.
   b. Type "Page", press [Spacebar], then click the Insert Page Number button on the Header and Footer toolbar.
   c. Press[Spacebar], type "of", then press [Spacebar].
   d. Click the Insert Number of Pages button on the Header and Footer toolbar.
   e. Click Close on the Header and Footer toolbar, then save your work.

5. Modify a footer.
   a. Click the Page Layout View button, if not already in Page Layout view.
   b. Double-click the footer.
   c. Press [End], then press [Tab] twice and type "Continued on Next Page".
   d. Drag the right-aligned tab marker to the right, to the 6.5" mark.
   e. Scroll through the document to review your changes.
   f. Click Close on the Header and Footer toolbar, then save your work.

6. **Change page orientation.**
   a. Scroll to and place the insertion point at the top of the second page.
   b. Click File on the menu bar, then click Page Setup.
   c. Click the Paper Size tab.
   d. In the Orientation area, click the Landscape radio button.
   e. Click the Apply To list arrow and click This point forward.
   f. Click the Margins tab.
   g. In the Top box, type ".7", in the Bottom box, type ".5", in the Left box type "1", and in the Right box type "1".
   h. Click the Apply To List arrow and click This point forward.
   i. Click the Layout tab.
   j. Click the Section Start arrow and choose New Page, if it is not already selected.
   k. Click OK and save your changes.

7. **Use different footers in the same document.**
   a. Place the insertion point in the second page of the document, click View on the menu bar, then click Header and Footer.
   b. With the insertion point in the Header area, click the Same as Previous button on the Header and Footer toolbar (to deselect it).
   c. Select the date and press [Delete].
   d. Click the Switch Between Header and Footer button on the Header and Footer toolbar.
   e. Click the Same as Previous button.
   f. Drag the right-aligned tab in the horizontal ruler to the 9" mark.
   g. Delete the text "Continued on Next Page".
   h. Type "Transport Express Inc., 1998".
   i. Click the Close button on the Header and Footer toolbar.
   j. Click the Print Preview button on the Standard toolbar and review your changes.
   k. Click Close on the Preview toolbar.
   l. Save your document and print it.
   m. Close the document and exit Word.

► Independent Challenges

1. The Mountain Top Tours travel company would like to create a more dramatic format to announce their upcoming tours in Switzerland. As their in-house publishing expert, you have been asked to create a new look for their brochure. Open the document WD E-4 and save it as "Mountain Landscape".

To complete this independent challenge:

1. Format the entire document in landscape orientation.
2. Adjust the top margin to be .4" and the footer margin to .3".
3. Insert a left-aligned header with the text "DRAFT 1.0"
4. Adjust the right-aligned tab in the footer so that it is even with the new right margin.
5. Preview, save, and print the document, then close it.

2. As co-chair for the Lake City High School Reunion entertainment committee, you want to help golfers attending the golf tournament find their way to the golf course. Add a map as a second page to a draft version of the golf announcement. Open the document WD E-5 and save it as "Golf Map". Make the following changes in the document. To complete this independent challenge:

1. Format the second page in landscape orientation.

2. Adjust the top and bottom margins to be .7 inch each for the second page only.

3. Adjust the header margin to be .4 inch and the footer margin to be .3 inch for the second page only.

4. Create a footer in each section that includes a field for the name of the file at the left margin and the date at the right margin. Adjust the right-aligned tab in the footer in the second section.

5. Preview, save, and print the document, then close it.

3. As an intern in the Communications Department for a large manufacturer of microprocessors, you have been asked to improve the appearance of the analysis document of the company's financial statement. For quick access to this information, the company has placed an electronic version of the annual report on its Web site. After exploring the report highlights, you obtain a copy of the text (much of which is already complete) and add a few finishing touches to prepare the document for printing. Because this document will be printed on two sides of each page (to save paper), you will need to create different footers for odd and even numbered pages. To complete this independent challenge:

1. Create a new blank document in Word and save it with the name "Financial Summary".

2. Log on to the Internet and use your browser to go to http://www.course.com. From there, click Student Online Companions, then click the link for this textbook, click the Word link for Unit E, then locate the 1995 Highlights page.

3. Click the Financial Statements link and finally click the link Managements Discussion and Analysis.

4. Select all the text in the document and copy it to the Clipboard. Paste it into the new blank document. Format the entire document in 12pts and 1.5 line spacing.

5. Add a title to the top of the document and add headings (use whatever text you wish) before every second paragraph. Format each of the headings so that they are never separated from the body of the following paragraph.

6. Adjust the top and bottom margins to be 1.25".

7. Specify different headers/footers for odd and even numbered pages.

8. Center the company name in the header for all pages. For odd numbered pages create a footer that contains the name of the document at the left margin, the date in the center, and page numbering information (use the Page X of Y format) at the right margin. Reverse this order for the footers in even numbered pages.

9. Preview, save, and print the document, then close it.

4. Your company has recently created a program to help the local food pantry collect food. Through this program employees are given longer lunch hours to volunteer at the food pantry, sorting donations and stocking shelves. You would like to give a certificate to all the employees who have volunteered over the past year. Using Figure E-20 as a guideline for formatting, create a new document and save it as "Volunteer Certificate". To complete this independent challenge:

1. Use a border and indentation to create a signature line.

2. Experiment with different fonts, font sizes, and alignment.

3. Create a new first page by inserting a hard page break. On the new first page, create a cover memo to accompany the award.

4. Change the orientation of the last page of the memo (for the certificate) to print in landscape orientation.

5. Adjust the margins as necessary.

FIGURE E-20

MEMO

DATE: 06/23/97

TO: ANDRA CARSON, VICE PRESIDENT

FROM: YOUR NAME

RE: ATTACHED CERTIFICATE

Here is my first attempt at creating an certificate that goes to all of the employees who have volunteered at the food shelf over the past year. Please share any comments or suggestions you have about the certificate. I would like to have the certificate printed and distributed by the end of the month

Enc. 1

IN APPRECIATION OF YOUR EFFORTS

Awarded to

Recipient

Food Shelf Volunteer

Presented by

Carson Associates

Wednesday, June 24, 1997

_____

Your Name

▶ Visual Workshop

As the conference coordinator for the upcoming Decorative Ideas Conference, you have been assigned the task of finalizing the conference menu. The caterer has supplied a menu for your approval. Open the document named WD E-6 and save it as "Final Menu". Using Figure E-21 as a guide, format the document so that the menu appears on a separate page and in landscape orientation. The letter should appear in portrait orientation. Also add a header containing the date, and a footer containing the document name and a page number. Adjust margins as necessary.

FIGURE E-21

Mr. Archibald Ryden
Banquet Caterer
Pinewood Center
Grande Point, MN 55509

Dear Mr. Ryden:

Your ideas for the menu at our creativity conference are exactly what we had in mind. I took the liberty of preparing a menu card that will accompany the meal. Because I need to give the printers at least two weeks lead time, please try to get in touch by the end of the week.

Please feel free to comment on any changes made to the menu and offer suggestions as you feel necessary.

Thanks again for your prompt and attentive service.

Sincerely,

[your name]
Conference Coordinator
Decorative Consultants, Inc.

9/05/98

Decorative Conference Cuisine Menu

Hors D'Ouevres	*A savory collection of herbs and flavors on focaccia*
First Course	*Pasta with Fresh Tomato and Basil Sauce*
Main Course	*Curried Salmon with Fresh Vegetables*

Dessert	*Tarte tatin*

Bon Appetite!

Final Menu   Page 2 of 2

Word 97

Formatting
with AutoFormat and Styles

Objectives

► **Create and apply character styles**
► **Use AutoFormat and the Style Gallery**
► **Modify styles**
► **Create and apply new paragraph styles**
► **Display style names in a document**
► **Move around with styles**
► **Replace styles**
► **Format as you type**

There are many formatting features available in Word that provide a variety of ways to quickly format a document the way you want. By using **styles**, which are collections of format settings you store together, you can apply combinations of format settings quickly. And with the AutoFormat feature, Word automatically applies styles and improves formatting in an entire document for you. You can also use the Style Gallery to format a document, choosing from many built-in, professionally designed business documents provided with Word. You can even opt to format as you type. ✒️ Angela will use a variety of techniques to improve the appearance of a cover letter to shareholders and an executive summary for the annual report.

Creating and Applying Character Styles

Using styles can save a lot of time and reduce formatting errors. A **character style** is a stored set of font format settings. When you create a character style, you store the font format settings so that you can apply them quickly in one step, rather than applying each setting to each occurrence you want to format. Using character styles to format text ensures consistent formatting. For example, if you use bold, small caps, and italics formatting for product names in a brochure, you want all the product names to be formatted the same way. ✎ In the summary document, Angela would like to format *all* occurrences of the company name with identical format settings.

1. **Start Word 97, open the document named WD F-1 and save it as Nomad Report**
   Because the first occurrence of the company name, Nomad Ltd, is already formatted with the settings you want to use, you can create a style based on an example of existing character formatting.

2. **Select the first occurrence of the company name Nomad Ltd, click Format on the menu bar, then click Style**
   The Style dialog box opens in which you can view, modify, and create new character and paragraph styles. Here, you can create a new character style.

3. **Click New**
   The New Style dialog box opens, as shown in Figure F-1. In this dialog box, provide a name for the new style and specify the type of style you want to create.

4. **In the Name box, type CompanyName**
   This stores the format settings of the selected text in a style called "CompanyName." You can use uppercase or lowercase characters, punctuation, and spaces in a style name. Next, indicate that you are creating a character style rather than a paragraph style.

5. **Click the Style type list arrow, then click Character**
   Note that the Preview area shows how text will appear with the format settings, and the Description area lists the settings.

6. **Click OK to close the New Style dialog box, then click Apply in the Style dialog box**
   The dialog box closes. You won't see any change in the selected text, because it is already correctly formatted. The CompanyName character style is applied to the text. Now you can apply this style to other occurrences of the company name in the document.

7. **In the second-to-last body paragraph, select the company name, click the Style list arrow on the Formatting toolbar, then click CompanyName**
   The style list contains all the styles you can apply to text, including the new style you created, as shown in Figure F-2. In addition, character styles are followed by the **a** icon to distinguish them from paragraph styles, which are followed by a **¶**.

8. **Repeat Step 7 for the next occurrence of Nomad Ltd**
   Compare your document to Figure F-3.

9. **Click the Save button 🖫 on the Standard toolbar**

FIGURE F-1: New Style dialog box

Enter a new style name

Select the style type

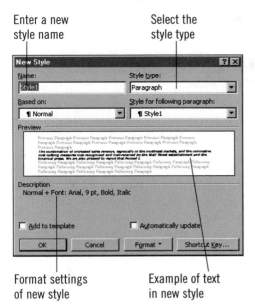

Format settings of new style

Example of text in new style

FIGURE F-2: Style list

Current style

Style arrow

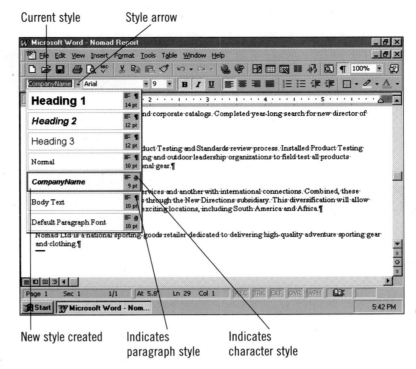

New style created

Indicates paragraph style

Indicates character style

FIGURE F-3: Character styles applied

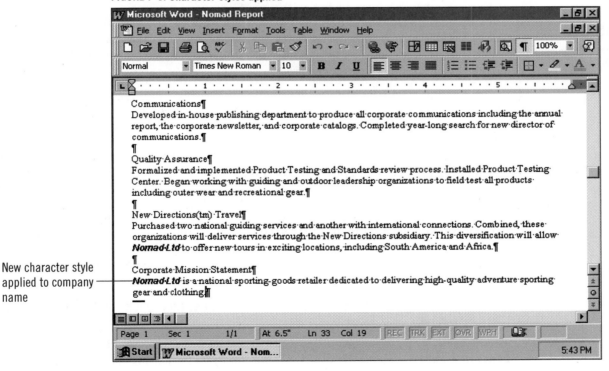

New character style applied to company name

Applying styles when creating them

When you create a style based on selected text, it is important to click Apply in the Style dialog box. By clicking Apply, you apply the style name to the text, so that this text is also updated if you later decide to change characteristics of the style.

Using AutoFormat and the Style Gallery

With the AutoFormat feature, Word makes a number of changes, described in Table F-1, that improve the appearance of a document. In addition, certain paragraph styles found in the default template, Normal, are applied automatically. A **paragraph style** is similar to a character style, except that it contains format settings you can apply to paragraphs, rather than to selected words. Once styles are established in a document, you can use the Style Gallery to format your document in styles from the different templates provided. A **template** is a special document containing styles and other options you want to use in specific kinds of documents. Angela wants to add attractive formatting and paragraph styles to the summary document.

1. **Press [Ctrl][Home], click Format on the menu bar, then click AutoFormat**
The AutoFormat dialog box opens. This dialog box offers the option of accepting or rejecting changes after the document has been formatted (you won't use that option now) or of formatting the document without first reviewing each change. This default option is a fast way to format a document.

2. **Select the Auto Format now option button, if necessary, then click OK**
AutoFormat enhances the appearance of the document, as shown in Figure F-4. Styles are applied throughout the document. To give the document a more professional look, choose a template from the Style Gallery.

3. **Click Format on the menu bar, then click Style Gallery**
The Style Gallery dialog box opens. In this dialog box, you can choose from the list of templates and preview your document with styles from the selected template. Select a professional template and preview the document.

> **Trouble?**
> Do not be concerned if this step takes a few minutes.

4. **In the Template list box, scroll down, then click Professional Memo**
The Preview of box displays the document in styles from the Professional Memo template.

5. **Click OK**
Word applies the styles defined in the template as shown in Figure F-5. To see which style was applied to the headings, place the insertion point in a heading.

6. **Place the insertion point in the heading Balancing the Books**
Notice the style name that appears in the Style list box on the Formatting toolbar indicates that the Heading 1 style is applied to this paragraph. Because of its location under the large bold title, the text "Milestones" was not correctly analyzed as a heading during the AutoFormat process. You can format it with the same style as the other headings by applying the Heading 1 style.

7. **Place the insertion point in the heading Milestones, then click the Style list arrow on the Formatting toolbar**
The Style list box now displays the styles available in the Professional Memo template. Notice that the style names are displayed with the style's formatting characteristics.

8. **Scroll the Style list box, then click Heading 1 (the first style displayed in the Style list)**
Compare your document to Figure F-6.

9. **Click the Save button 💾 on the Standard toolbar**

FIGURE F-4: Document formatted with AutoFormat

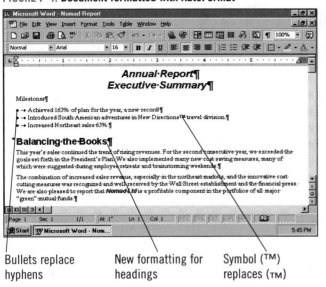

Bullets replace hyphens   New formatting for headings   Symbol (™) replaces (TM)

FIGURE F-5: Reformatted document with PROFESSIONAL MEMO styles

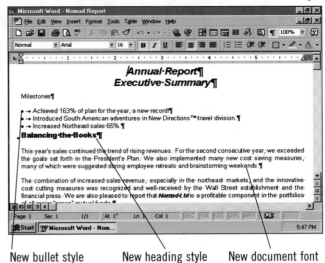

New bullet style   New heading style   New document font

FIGURE F-6: Updated style

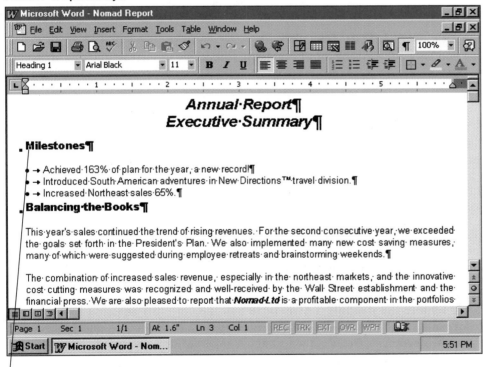

Updated Heading 1 style

TABLE F-1: Changes made by AutoFormat

change	description
Applies styles	Applies paragraph styles to all paragraphs in a document, including headings, lists, body text, salutations, addresses, etc.
Adjusts spacing	Adds and removes extra paragraph marks as needed and replaces spaces and tabs with proper indentation
Replaces symbols and characters	Replaces hyphens and other symbols used to denote a list with bullets and replaces fractions entered as "1/2" with ½ symbol and inserts the trademark, registered trademark, and copyright symbols where indicated

Modifying Styles

When you use styles to format text, you can change format settings quickly and consistently for every occurrence of the style in the document. Modifying a style changes the appearance of all text formatted in that style. You save time and make fewer mistakes because you don't need to search for each occurrence of text that has formatting you want to change. The fastest way to modify a style is to change the formatting in a selected example and reapply the style. After reviewing the style of the Milestones heading, Angela decides to change the style of the font to small caps. After modifying the font style for the first heading, she'll update the Heading 1 style to change all the text formatted with this style.

Steps 1234

1. Select the Milestones heading

2. Click Format on the menu bar, then click Font
   The Font dialog box opens. To make the heading text more distinctive, use the font effect called "small caps".

3. Click the Small caps checkbox

4. Click the Shadow checkbox, then click OK
   Now that you have adjusted the font formatting, you decide to increase the spacing before each heading.

5. Click Format on the menu bar, then click Paragraph

6. On the Indents and Spacing tab, click the Spacing before up arrow once to 6 pts, then click OK
   The space before this paragraph is increased. Now that this heading contains the formatting you want, modify the Heading 1 style, based on the modified "Milestones" heading, to format all the headings in the document in the same way. After changing the formatting, you can update a style by reapplying it to the same text.

7. Click the Style list arrow on the Formatting toolbar, then click Heading 1
   The Modify Style dialog box opens, as shown in Figure F-7. You can either update the style based on the selected text, or reformat the selected text with the original attributes of the style. In this case, modify the style based on the currently selected text.

8. Click OK to update the Heading 1 style based on the currently selected text
   All text formatted with the Heading 1 style now appears in small caps and is shadowed throughout the document. Deselect the text and compare your document to Figure F-8.

9. Click the Save button on the Standard toolbar

QuickTip

A fast way to apply a built-in heading style is to press [Alt][Ctrl] and the corresponding heading level. For example, to apply a Heading 1 style, press [Alt][Ctrl][1]. To apply a Heading 2 style, press [Alt][Ctrl][2], and so on.

FIGURE F-7: Modify Style dialog box

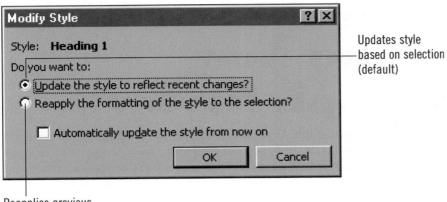

Updates style based on selection (default)

Reapplies previous style to selection

FIGURE F-8: Updated style

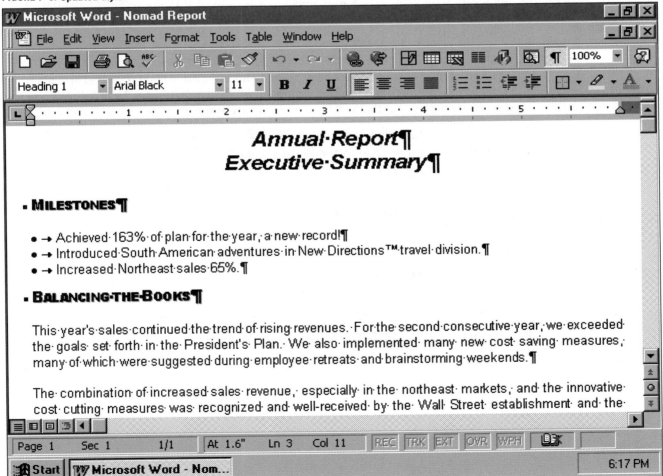

Creating and Applying New Paragraph Styles

You are not limited to using the paragraph styles provided by Word templates. In the same way you created a character style earlier in this unit, you can create your own customized paragraph styles. You can create a new style based on an example of selected text or you can specify the paragraph formatting you want in the Style dialog box. You can even assign a keyboard shortcut to a style. Angela would like to create a style to format the title of the Executive Summary so that it is distinctive.

QuickTip

You can quickly apply a style by pressing [Ctrl][Shift][S] to select the Style list on the Formatting toolbar. Type the name of the style in the Style list, then press [Enter].

1. Select the first line of the document, click Format on the menu bar, then click Style
With the Style dialog box open, you are ready to create a new style.

2. Click New, and in the Style Name box type NewTitle
The name "NewTitle" is the name of the new style. Next, identify that you want to create a paragraph style.

3. Click the Style Type arrow and select Paragraph, if it is not already selected
To use a border as part of the NewTitle style, you need to specify additional format characteristics next.

4. Click Format, then click Border on the list
The Borders and Shading dialog box appears. This is the same dialog box that appears when you select the Borders and Shading command on the Format menu. In this dialog box you can specify the settings that will be applied as part of the new style you are creating.

5. From the Style list, click the double line, click the Width list arrow, click 3 pt, then click the Box border style in the Setting area on the left side of the dialog box, if it is not already selected
A preview of the border appears in the Preview area.

6. Click OK until you return to the Style dialog box, then click Apply
The first line of the title appears with a border around it. Now, you can apply the NewTitle style to the next line of the title.

7. Place the insertion point in the next line, click the Style arrow on the Formatting toolbar and click NewTitle
The next line of the title appears in the NewTitle style, as shown in Figure F-9.

8. Click the Save button 💾 on the Standard toolbar

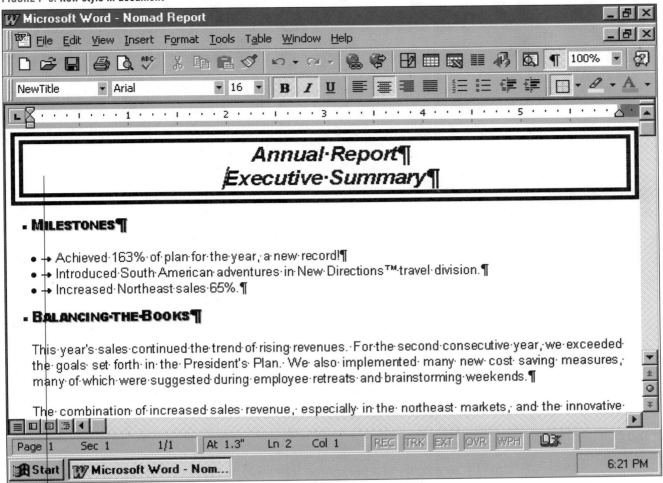

Title in new style

Assigning keyboard shortcuts to styles

To apply styles even faster, you can assign a keyboard shortcut to a style. In the Style dialog box you choose the style to which you want to assign a keyboard shortcut. Then click the Modify button. Then click the Shortcut key button. Press the combination of keys you want to use as a shortcut and click Assign. Take care not to assign a keyboard shortcut that has already been assigned to another command. If you share a computer with others, click the Save Changes in arrow and select the document you are currently editing.

Displaying Style Names in a Document

When formatting with styles it is often useful to see the name of the style applied to a paragraph. In the document's normal view, you can display the style names in the Style area at the left side of the window. You can also modify a style by double-clicking the style name in the Style area. These style names do not appear in the printed document, but you do have the option to print a separate document describing all the styles that are used. ✎ Angela would like to see the names of all the paragraph styles she is using in her document.

Steps

1. **Click Tools on the menu bar, click Options, then click the View tab**
   The View tab appears foremost in the dialog box, as shown in Figure F-10. On this tab, you can specify the width of the Style area in the document window.

2. **Click the Style area width up arrow until you see 1", then click OK**
   When you return to the document window, you see the names of the styles at the left edge of the window, as shown in Figure F-11. So that the Style area takes no more space than necessary, adjust the width of it.

3. **Position the pointer over the vertical line that separates the Style area from the rest of the document, and when the pointer changes to ╫, drag the line so that the Style area is no wider than the longest style name**
   Depending on your computer system, you might need to increase or decrease the Style area. Next, make one last change to the Body Text style.

4. **Scroll (if necessary) to a paragraph formatted in the Body Text style and double-click the style name in the Style area**
   The paragraph that is formatted in Body Text style is selected. The Style dialog box opens, so you can now modify the style.

5. **Click Modify, click Format, then click Paragraph from the list**
   In the Paragraph dialog box, decrease the spacing after each body paragraph.

6. **In the Spacing After box, click the down arrow once, changing the spacing to 6 pt, then click OK until you return to the Style dialog box**
   Continue by applying these changes.

7. **Click Apply, then deselect the text**
   Clicking Apply closes the dialog box and updates the style throughout the document. Because you no longer need the Style area displayed, you can hide it.

8. **Position the pointer over the vertical line that separates the Style area from the rest of the document, and when the pointer changes to ╫, drag to the left until the Style area disappears**
   Compare your document to Figure F-12. You have completed modifying your document for now, so you can save it.

9. **Click the Save button 🖫 on the Standard toolbar**

FIGURE F-10: **View tab in Options dialog box**

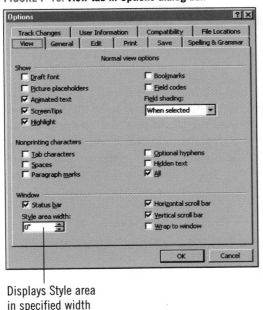

Displays Style area
in specified width

FIGURE F-11: **Style area in document**

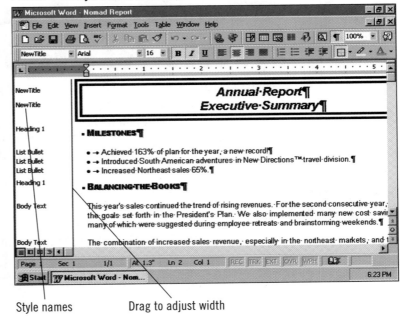

Style names

Drag to adjust width

FIGURE F-12: **Completed document**

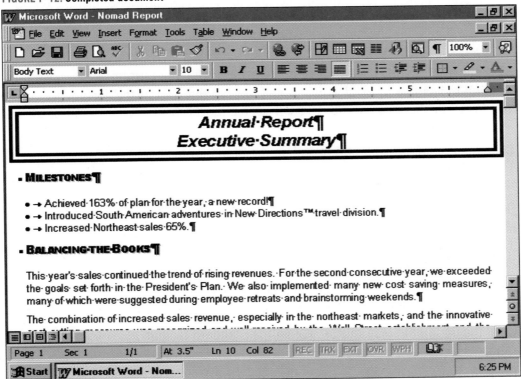

Printing styles

You can get a hard copy document that contains a description of the formatting used in each of the styles in a document. When you print a document using the Print command, click the Print What arrow in the Print dialog box, then choose Styles from the list. This feature prints a list of styles and a description of each one. Use this feature when you want to keep track of the styles in your document.

Moving Around with Styles

Styles can also play a valuable role as you move around in a longer document, because you can use styles to move to different parts of a document. For example, you can scroll through a document by "paging" through its headings. You can also use the Document Map to display headings on the left half of the window and the document text on the right half. By clicking a heading on the left, you can move the insertion point to the heading on the right. ✐ Angela wants to review each of the headings in the document, so will take advantage of the styles in the document to move to the locations she wants.

Steps 1 2 3 4

1. **Press [Ctrl] [Home] to place the insertion point at the beginning of the document**

2. **Click the Select Browse Object button ⊙ at the bottom of the vertical scroll bar**
   This button displays a menu of items you can use to scroll through a document, as shown in Figure F-13. You want to scroll through the headings.

3. **Click the Browse by Heading button ▤**
   The insertion point moves to the first heading in the document. Notice that the Previous and Next Page buttons in the scroll bar change color. The color indicates that clicking these buttons will move the insertion point from item to item, not from page to page as they normally do.

4. **Click the Next Heading button ▼ and Previous Heading button ▲ to move from heading to heading in the document, and back to the start of the document**
   To view all the headings at once and still see the text of the document, you can use the Document Map feature.

5. **Click the Document Map button ▧ on the Standard toolbar**
   The window splits into two parts. On the left side you see the headings in the document. On the right side is the document text, as shown in Figure F-14.

6. **On the left side of the window, click the last heading in the document, Corporate Mission Statement**
   The insertion point moves to that heading on the right side of the window. You can now edit the text in this heading.

7. **Select the text Mission Statement and type Vision**
   Notice that the heading on the left is also updated. Turn off the Document Map feature.

8. **Click the Document Map button ▧ on the Standard toolbar**
   Compare your document to Figure F-15.

9. **Click the Save button ▤ on the Standard toolbar**

FIGURE F-13: Search Items box

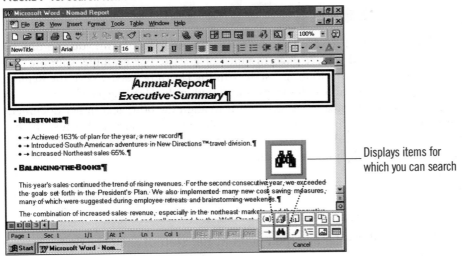

Displays items for
which you can search

FIGURE F-14: Document Map

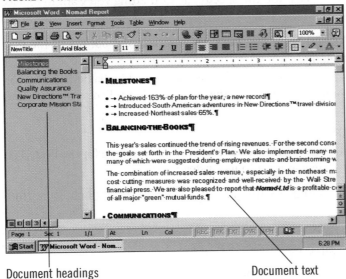

Document headings

Document text

FIGURE F-15: Completed document

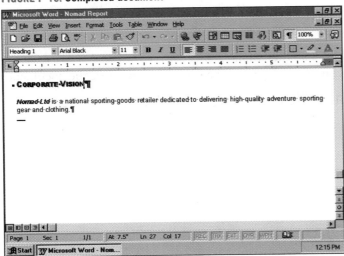

Replacing Styles

The same way you search for and replace text and formatting in a document, you can use the Replace command to locate and replace each instance of a style. For example, suppose you decide to change all instances of the Heading 3 style with the Heading 2 style. With the Replace command you can instruct Word to search for text formatted in the Heading 3 style and format it in the Heading 2 style instead. ◆ Angela wants to align the body text in her document with the text (after the bullets) in the bulleted list at the start of the document. Because there is a Body Text Indent style available, she will use the Replace command to substitute this style for the current Body Text style throughout the document.

Steps 1 2 3 4

1. **Press [Ctrl][Home] to place the insertion point at the start of the document**

2. **Click Edit on the menu bar, click Replace, then click More to extend the dialog box if all the options are not displayed**
   The Find and Replace dialog box opens. You can specify the formatting you want to replace by clicking the Format button.

3. **With the insertion point in the Find What box, click Format near the bottom of the dialog box, then click Style from the list**
   The Find Style dialog box opens, as shown in Figure F-16. From this dialog box you can select the style for which you want to search. Select the current style applied to the body text in your document.

4. **Click Body Text, then click OK**
   The Format area below the Find What box indicates that you are searching for the Body Text style. Next, you can specify the style you want to use instead.

5. **With the insertion point in the Replace With box, click Format, then click Style from the list**
   You can select a new body text style.

6. **Click Body Text Indent, then click OK**
   The Format area below the Replace With box indicates that the text should be formatted in the Body Text Indent style, as shown in Figure F-17. You are now ready to replace the styles.

7. **Click Replace All**
   A message indicates the number of changes made.

8. **Click OK to return to the dialog box, then click Close**
   Compare your document to Figure F-18. Then save your changes and close the document.

9. **Click the Save button 🖫 on the Standard toolbar, then close the document**

FIGURE F-16: Find Style dialog box

Find Style

Find what style:

```
(no style)
¶ Block Text
¶ Body Text
¶ Body Text 2
¶ Body Text 3
¶ Body Text First Indent
```

Description

OK   Cancel

FIGURE F-17: Find and Replace dialog box

Find and Replace

| Find | Replace | Go To |

Find what: _____ Find Next

Format: Style: Body Text Cancel

Replace with: _____ Replace

Format: Style: Body Text Indent Replace All

Less ±

Search: All

☐ Match case
☐ Find whole words only
☐ Use wildcards
☐ Sounds like
☐ Find all word forms

Replace

No Formatting   Format ▾   Special ▾

FIGURE F-18: Body Text Indent style in document

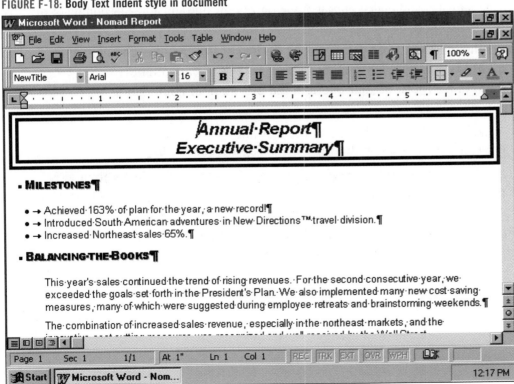

Microsoft Word - Nomad Report

File Edit View Insert Format Tools Table Window Help

NewTitle   Arial   16   B I U   100%

Annual·Report¶
Executive·Summary¶

▪ **MILESTONES¶**

• → Achieved·163%·of·plan·for·the·year,·a·new·record!¶
• → Introduced·South·American·adventures·in·New·Directions™·travel·division.¶
• → Increased·Northeast·sales·65%.¶

▪ **BALANCING·THE·BOOKS¶**

This·year's·sales·continued·the·trend·of·rising·revenues.·For·the·second·consecutive·year,·we·exceeded·the·goals·set·forth·in·the·President's·Plan.·We·also·implemented·many·new·cost·saving·measures,·many·of·which·were·suggested·during·employee·retreats·and·brainstorming·weekends.¶

The·combination·of·increased·sales·revenue,·especially·in·the·northeast·markets,·and·the·

Page 1   Sec 1   1/1   At 1"   Ln 1   Col 1   REC TRK EXT OVR WPH

Start   Microsoft Word - Nom...   12:17 PM

Formatting as You Type

Formatting a new document in Word can be as easy as typing. When you type certain combinations of text and formatting, Word formats the text as you type. For example, when you type a hyphen and then press the [Tab] key, Word formats the line with a bullet. ✎ The next document Angela would like to create is a draft document describing a new promotion. As she types the document, Word applies the appropriate formatting.

Steps 1234

1. Click the New button 🗋 on the Standard toolbar

2. Click Tools on the menu bar, click AutoCorrect
   In this case, verify the options for the AutoFormat As You Type feature.

3. Click the AutoFormat As You Type tab and compare the dialog box to Figure F-19, clicking any options not already enabled, then click OK
   The dialog box closes, and you are now ready to type the text of your document.

4. Type Announcing new discount pricing for our "favorite" retailers and press [Enter] twice
   When you press [Enter] twice after entering a line of text (that does not end in a punctuation mark), Word formats the line in the Heading 1 style.

5. Type o (a lowercase "o"), press [Tab], then type Sell at least 1/2 of your quota in the 1st week of each month and press [Enter]
   Notice that as you type, the fraction "1/2" changes to a fraction symbol "½," the text "1st" changes to "1st" and bullets appear at the start of the line and at the beginning of the new line. Continue typing the document.

6. Type the following two lines, pressing [Enter] at the end of each line:
   Sell at least 3/4 of your quota in the 2nd week of each month
   Sell at least 100% of your quota in the 3rd week of each month
   Next, add a blank line.

7. Press [Enter] again at the end of the last line
   Pressing [Enter] twice stops the AutoFormatting in a bulleted list.

8. Type Your store needs to meet only two of the above milestones to qualify
   Compare your document to Figure F-20. You have completed typing and formatting your document for now, so print and save your work and close the document.

Time To
✔ Save

9. Print the document, click File on the menu bar, click Close, then click Yes and save the file with the name Promotion, then exit Word

FIGURE F-19: AutoFormat As You Type tab

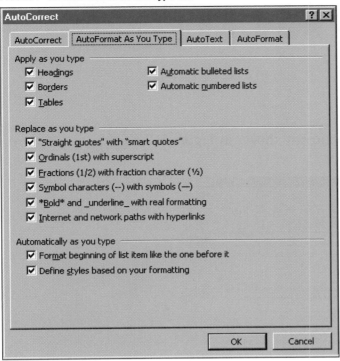

FIGURE F-20: Document formatted as you type

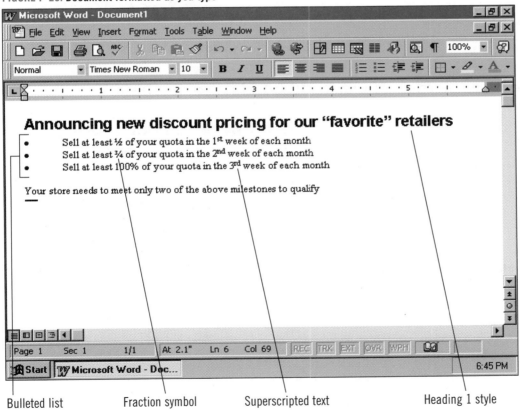

Bulleted list   Fraction symbol   Superscripted text   Heading 1 style

▶ Concepts Review

Label and describe each of the parts of the document shown in Figure F-21.

FIGURE F-21

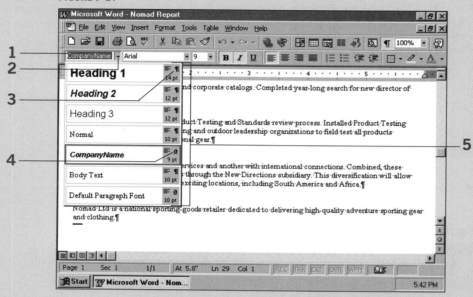

Match each of the following descriptions with the term that it describes best.

6. AutoFormat
7. Paragraph style
8. Templates
9. Style Gallery
10. Character style

a. A named set of paragraph format settings
b. Displays document in another set of styles
c. A named set of character format settings
d. Special documents containing styles and other options specific to different kinds of documents
e. Improves a document's appearance by applying styles and inserting symbols

Select the best answer from the list of choices.

11. Which of the following is true about replacing formatting in the Replace dialog box?
    a. You can click Replace All to review each occurrence of replaced formatting.
    b. To remove formatting from the search or replacement text, you click the Clear button.
    c. You can use buttons on the Formatting toolbar to select formatting options.
    d. You cannot use the Font or Paragraph dialog boxes to select formatting options.

12. To create a character style, you
    a. Type a name in the Style box on the Formatting toolbar and press [Enter].
    b. Click Format on the menu bar, then click Style.
    c. Click Format on the menu bar, then click Style Gallery.
    d. Select a style from the Style list on the Formatting toolbar.

13. **Which of the following is not a benefit of using styles?**
    a. Checks your document for proper grammar and word usage so it is appropriate for the kind of document you are creating
    b. Quickly applies format settings in one step
    c. Modifies style characteristics and reapply to all occurrences
    d. Previews a document in styles from other templates

14. **Which statement is not true about character styles?**
    a. You can create a character style using the Style dialog box.
    b. You can create a character style by using selected text as an example.
    c. Character styles affect the entire current paragraph.
    d. You can redefine a character style based on a selected example.

15. **Which statement best describes when to use styles in a document?**
    a. When text or paragraphs scattered throughout a document require similar and consistent formatting
    b. When text or paragraphs on the same page require the same format settings
    c. When text or paragraph formatting is not likely to change
    d. When text or paragraphs do not require many different format settings

16. **Which statement best describes the AutoFormat feature?**
    a. The AutoFormat command allows you to review changes before accepting them.
    b. AutoFormat corrects grammatical and spelling errors in a document.
    c. AutoFormat sorts items in a list for you.
    d. The AutoFormat command allows you to apply and reject formatting changes to improve the appearance of your document in one step.

17. **Which of the following changes is not made by AutoFormat?**
    a. Applies paragraph styles to all paragraphs in the document
    b. Adjusts spacing and inserts appropriate indentation
    c. Applies character styles to appropriate text
    d. Inserts appropriate symbols and characters

18. **Which of the following statements is NOT true about modifying styles?**
    a. You can modify a style based on the formatting in the current selection.
    b. You must open the Style dialog box and click the Modify button, and then open the dialog boxes for the type of formatting you want to use in the style.
    c. The Reapply Style dialog box gives you the option to redefine the style or apply original formatting.
    d. Redefining the style based on the current selection is the default option in the Reapply Style dialog box.

▶ Skills Review

1. **Format text with AutoFormat.**
   a. Start Word and open the document named WD F-2. Save the document as "Healthy Home".
   b. Click Format on the menu bar, then click AutoFormat to apply standard styles and formatting to your document.
   c. Click OK.
   d. Scroll through the document and review the changes.

2. **Use the Style Gallery.**
   a. Click Format on the menu bar, then click Style Gallery.
   b. Select different templates and examine your document as it would appear with these templates.
   c. Click Elegant Memo in the list of templates.
   d. Click OK.
   e. Save your changes.

3. Apply paragraph formatting and styles.

a. With the insertion point in the first paragraph in the body of the document, click Paragraph on the Format menu. In the Line spacing list, select 1.5 Lines, then click OK.

b. Select the Body Text style from the Style list box on the Formatting toolbar.

c. Make sure the first option for updating the style is selected in the Modify Style dialog box, then click OK.

d. In the first list in the document (near the top of page 3, depending on your monitor), select the first line (yoga).

e. Click Paragraph on the Format menu. Change the Spacing After to 3 pt. Click OK to close the dialog box.

f. With the same line still selected, click Bullets and Numbering on the Format menu. On the Bulleted tab, change the bullet style to a diamond. Click OK to return to the document.

4. Create and apply new styles.

a. Select the text "EnviroTech" near the beginning of the second page. Change the formatting of the text by choosing Arial from the Font box and 9 pt from the Font Size box then click the Bold button.

b. Click Format on the menu bar, then click Style. Click New. In the Name box, type "EnviroTech" and from the Style Type list choose Character. Then click OK and in the Style dialog box, click Apply.

c. Apply the EnviroTech character style to each occurrence of the company name "EnviroTech".

d. Select the heading "Introduction" and apply the Document Label style.

e. With the heading still selected, click Format on the menu bar, click Paragraph, then apply 18 pts of spacing after.

f. Click the Lines and Page Breaks tab, then click the Keep with next checkbox. Click OK.

g. Reapply the Document Label style and update the style to reflect these changes in formatting.

h. Deselect the heading.

5. Replace styles in a document.

a. Click Edit on the menu bar, then click Replace. Click Format and then click Style.

b. Choose Heading 1 from the list of styles, click OK.

c. Click in the Replace with box, then click the Format button and then click Style.

d. Choose Document Label from the list of styles, click OK.

e. Click Replace All. There were two replacements made.

f. Close the dialog box and save the document.

6. Display style names in the document.

a. Click Tools on the menu bar, click Options, then click the View tab.

b. Click the up arrow in the Style area width box until you see 1", then click OK.

c. Position the pointer over the vertical line that separates the Style area from the rest of the document and, when the pointer changes shape, drag the line so that the Style area is no wider than the longest style name.

d. Scroll (if necessary) to a paragraph formatted in the List Bullet style and double-click the style name.

e. Click Modify, click Format, then click Paragraph from the list.

f. On the Indents and Spacing tab, type "6" in the Spacing After box, to change the spacing to 6 pt, then click OK until you return to the Style dialog box.

g. Click Apply.

h. Position the pointer over the vertical line that separates the Style area from the rest of the document and, when the pointer changes shape, drag to the left until the Style area disappears.

i. Preview then print your document.

j. Save your changes.

7. Format text as you type.

a. Click the New button on the Standard toolbar.

b. Click Format on the menu bar, click AutoFormat, then click the Options button.

c. Click the AutoFormat As You Type tab, clicking any options not already enabled, then click OK twice.

d. Type "Customer Satisfaction Survey Results" and press [Enter] twice.

e. Type at least six hyphens in a row and press [Enter] (this creates a line border).

f. Type o (an "o"), press [Tab], then type "More than 1/2 of catalog customers received their orders within the 1st week of placing their order" and press [Enter].

g. Type the following two lines, pressing [Enter] at the end of each line:
Just under 3/4 of retail customers returned to make 2nd and 3rd purchases
Over 1/2 of the customers surveyed expressed positive comments regarding their 1st purchase experience

h. Press [Enter] again at the end of the last line.

i. Type "These survey results mean that while generally positive, we must continue to pursue even higher customer satisfaction results. Let's all strive to ship orders within the 1st week for 1/2 of our customers, and increase positive purchase experiences to at least 3/4 of the customers."

j. Save your document as "Sales Promotion" and print it.

k. Close both documents, saving any changes.

l. Exit Word.

▶ Independent Challenges

1. As a member of the acquisitions team for an investment research company called Expansion Inc., you have been asked to improve the formatting of a summary analysis prepared by a colleague. Open the document named "WD F-3" and save it as "New Growth". Using Figure F-22 as a guide, apply the following formatting.

To complete this independent challenge:

1. Use the AutoFormat command to apply styles.
2. Use the Style Gallery to apply styles from the Professional Memo template.
3. Apply Heading 2 style to the six sub-headings "The Benefits of Growth", "Future Expansion", "Initial Expansion", etc.
4. Use the Replace command to format all occurrences of the name "World Travel Airlines" in bold italics.
5. Change the formatting for the Heading 1 style so that it appears with a bottom border and in 18 pts. Reapply and update the style.
6. Apply the Heading 2 style to the text "Cruise Lines Offer Opportunity for Growth" and the next two headings.
7. Preview, save, and print the document before closing it.

FIGURE F-22A

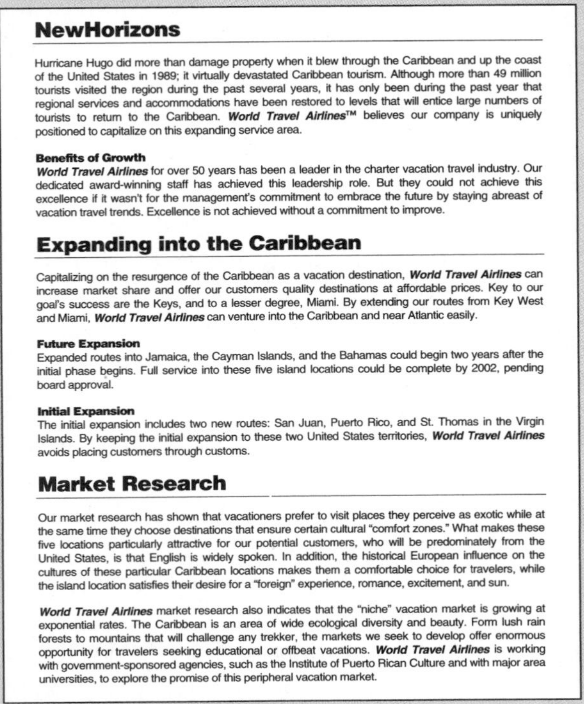

NewHorizons

Hurricane Hugo did more than damage property when it blew through the Caribbean and up the coast of the United States in 1989; it virtually devastated Caribbean tourism. Although more than 49 million tourists visited the region during the past several years, it has only been during the past year that regional services and accommodations have been restored to levels that will entice large numbers of tourists to return to the Caribbean. *World Travel Airlines*™ believes our company is uniquely positioned to capitalize on this expanding service area.

Benefits of Growth
World Travel Airlines for over 50 years has been a leader in the charter vacation travel industry. Our dedicated award-winning staff has achieved this leadership role. But they could not achieve this excellence if it wasn't for the management's commitment to embrace the future by staying abreast of vacation travel trends. Excellence is not achieved without a commitment to improve.

Expanding into the Caribbean

Capitalizing on the resurgence of the Caribbean as a vacation destination, *World Travel Airlines* can increase market share and offer our customers quality destinations at affordable prices. Key to our goal's success are the Keys, and to a lesser degree, Miami. By extending our routes from Key West and Miami, *World Travel Airlines* can venture into the Caribbean and near Atlantic easily.

Future Expansion
Expanded routes into Jamaica, the Cayman Islands, and the Bahamas could begin two years after the initial phase begins. Full service into these five island locations could be complete by 2002, pending board approval.

Initial Expansion
The initial expansion includes two new routes: San Juan, Puerto Rico, and St. Thomas in the Virgin Islands. By keeping the initial expansion to these two United States territories, *World Travel Airlines* avoids placing customers through customs.

Market Research

Our market research has shown that vacationers prefer to visit places they perceive as exotic while at the same time they choose destinations that ensure certain cultural "comfort zones." What makes these five locations particularly attractive for our potential customers, who will be predominately from the United States, is that English is widely spoken. In addition, the historical European influence on the cultures of these particular Caribbean locations makes them a comfortable choice for travelers, while the island location satisfies their desire for a "foreign" experience, romance, excitement, and sun.

World Travel Airlines market research also indicates that the "niche" vacation market is growing at exponential rates. The Caribbean is an area of wide ecological diversity and beauty. Form lush rain forests to mountains that will challenge any trekker, the markets we seek to develop offer enormous opportunity for travelers seeking educational or offbeat vacations. *World Travel Airlines* is working with government-sponsored agencies, such as the Institute of Puerto Rican Culture and with major area universities, to explore the promise of this peripheral vacation market.

FIGURE F-22B

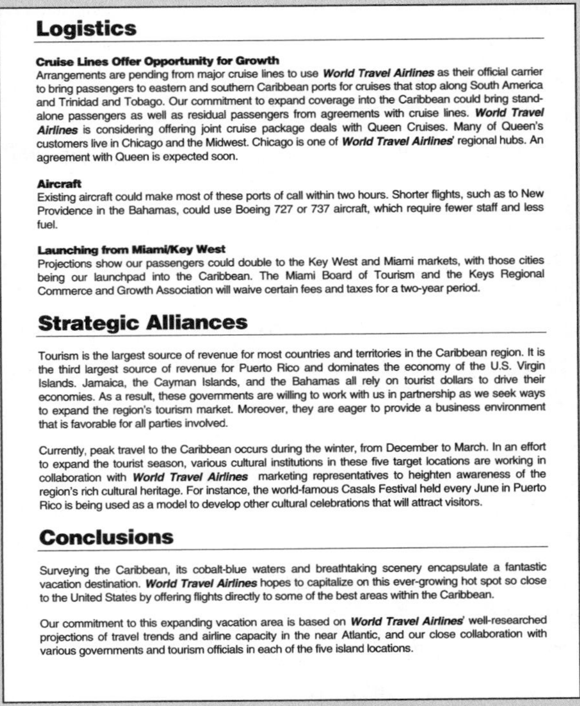

Logistics

Cruise Lines Offer Opportunity for Growth
Arrangements are pending from major cruise lines to use *World Travel Airlines* as their official carrier to bring passengers to eastern and southern Caribbean ports for cruises that stop along South America and Trinidad and Tobago. Our commitment to expand coverage into the Caribbean could bring stand-alone passengers as well as residual passengers from agreements with cruise lines. *World Travel Airlines* is considering offering joint cruise package deals with Queen Cruises. Many of Queen's customers live in Chicago and the Midwest. Chicago is one of *World Travel Airlines*' regional hubs. An agreement with Queen is expected soon.

Aircraft
Existing aircraft could make most of these ports of call within two hours. Shorter flights, such as to New Providence in the Bahamas, could use Boeing 727 or 737 aircraft, which require fewer staff and less fuel.

Launching from Miami/Key West
Projections show our passengers could double to the Key West and Miami markets, with those cities being our launchpad into the Caribbean. The Miami Board of Tourism and the Keys Regional Commerce and Growth Association will waive certain fees and taxes for a two-year period.

Strategic Alliances

Tourism is the largest source of revenue for most countries and territories in the Caribbean region. It is the third largest source of revenue for Puerto Rico and dominates the economy of the U.S. Virgin Islands. Jamaica, the Cayman Islands, and the Bahamas all rely on tourist dollars to drive their economies. As a result, these governments are willing to work with us in partnership as we seek ways to expand the region's tourism market. Moreover, they are eager to provide a business environment that is favorable for all parties involved.

Currently, peak travel to the Caribbean occurs during the winter, from December to March. In an effort to expand the tourist season, various cultural institutions in these five target locations are working in collaboration with *World Travel Airlines* marketing representatives to heighten awareness of the region's rich cultural heritage. For instance, the world-famous Casals Festival held every June in Puerto Rico is being used as a model to develop other cultural celebrations that will attract visitors.

Conclusions

Surveying the Caribbean, its cobalt-blue waters and breathtaking scenery encapsulate a fantastic vacation destination. *World Travel Airlines* hopes to capitalize on this ever-growing hot spot so close to the United States by offering flights directly to some of the best areas within the Caribbean.

Our commitment to this expanding vacation area is based on *World Travel Airlines*' well-researched projections of travel trends and airline capacity in the near Atlantic, and our close collaboration with various governments and tourism officials in each of the five island locations.

2. As an executive member of an organization dedicated to the improvement of media services called "Communication for the Future", you are in charge of planning the upcoming 1998 convention. While in town, many of your members will want the opportunity to explore the Boston area. You have contracted with a travel agency to prepare a visitor's guide. The travel agency has prepared a draft, and you have decided to make the document more attractive. Open document named WD F-4 and save it as "Tourist Info".

To complete this independent challenge:

1. Use the AutoFormat command to apply styles.
2. Change the formatting for the Heading 1 style so that the text is 18 pt and italics. Reapply and update the style.
3. Change the formatting for the Heading 2 style so that the text is 14 pt and 4 pts of spacing after. Reapply and update the style.
4. Change the List Bullet style so that it is formatted with the left indent of 0.50 inches, a hanging indent of 0.50 inches, and 2 pt spacing before and after. Reapply and update the style.
5. Create a character style called Highlight that is 9 pt, bold, Arial. When you create this style, assign a keyboard shortcut to the Highlight style, [Alt] + [Shift] + [H]. Apply this style (using the keyboard shortcut) to the first few words or phrase in each paragraph formatted in the List Bullet style. Be sure to save the shortcut in the document and not in the template.
6. Preview, save, and print the document before closing it.

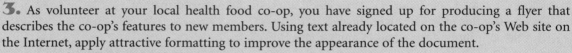

3. As volunteer at your local health food co-op, you have signed up for producing a flyer that describes the co-op's features to new members. Using text already located on the co-op's Web site on the Internet, apply attractive formatting to improve the appearance of the document.

To complete this independent challenge:

1. Log on to the Internet and use your browser to find a Web page of a co-op in your area or of special interest to you. If you can't find one, go to http://www.course.com. From there, click Student Online Companions, click the link for this textbook, then click the Word link for Unit F. Click on one of the links provided, then copy all the text in the document that appears. Paste the contents of the clipboard into a new blank document. Save the document with the name Co-op Flyer.
2. First improve the appearance of the document using AutoFormat (in the AutoFormat dialog box, choose Letter as the document type), then apply the styles in the Contemporary Memo template in the Style Gallery.
3. Edit the list of items in the store's inventory so that each group of items appears on a separate line. Apply the List 2 style to the first list. Then change the Spacing after to 6 pts, click the Increase Indent button three times, apply bullets, then redefine the List 2 style. If your document does not have a list of products, format the second, third, and fourth paragraphs. Create a List Number style that is similar to the List 2 style, but formatted with numbers.
4. Apply the List Number style to another list in the document. Or apply it to the first list if your document has only one.
5. Apply text flow formatting so that the lines of the store's address are never separated by a page break. Then create a new paragraph style called StoreAddress based on this formatting. Apply the StoreAddress style to the list of the hours at the end of the document.
6. Delete any extra paragraph marks that were used for spacing between paragraphs, and spell check the document.
7. Preview, save, and print the document before closing it.

4. As the marketing director for a small adventure travel agency, Majica Tours, you would like to announce a new tour offering. Using the AutoFormat As You Type in Word, create an attractive document that describes the tour features. Use Figure F-23 as a guide to complete this independent challenge:

1. Create a new blank document and save it as Majica Sea Tours. On the AutoFormat As You Type tab in the AutoCorrect dialog box, verify that all check boxes are checked.
2. Type "Announcing Seabreeze Sailing Adventures" and then press [Enter] twice to create a heading formatted in the Heading 1 style.
3. Change the Heading 1 style so that the font size is 18pts, and the paragraph formatting is 10 pts before and 18 points after, and centered.

4. Type ">" followed by a tab and then type the text shown in Figure F-23. Press [Enter] after each line.
5. Press [Enter] twice to stop bulleted formatting.
6. Under the heading, type 5 hyphens and then press [Enter] to create a solid line.
7. Change the formatting of the text in the bulleted list, so that it is formatted in Arial, 14 pts and 1.5 Line Spacing. Create a new paragraph style based on this formatting, name it Arrow List, and apply it to the bulleted list.
8. At the end of the document, type another set of hyphens and then press [Enter].
9. Type "Majica SeaTours Offices:" and apply the modified Heading 1 style to this text. Press [Enter] to create a new line.
10. Type the names of three cities (each on a separate line) and apply the Arrow List style to the list.
11. Preview, save, and print the document before closing it.

FIGURE F-23

Announcing Seabreeze Sailing Adventures

➢ Small groups, 8-10 guests

➢ Low cost, only $599 complete

➢ Gourmet meals, crew includes a gourmet chef

➢ Expert crew, 5 members with over 50 years of guiding and sailing experience

Majica SeaTours Offices:

➢ Lake of the Woods

➢ Big Mountain

➢ Lake Pacifica

▶ Visual Workshop

As conference coordinator for Creative Consultants, Inc.'s 1998 Creativity Conference, you are in charge of developing an attractive document that describes the conference seminars to interested participants. A draft document contains the text you want to include. Open the document WD F-5 and save it as "Conference Overview". Figure F-24 serves as a guide for what your completed document should look like. Begin by using AutoFormat to apply consistent styles to the document. Then use the Style Gallery to apply the styles contained in the Contemporary Memo template. Create and apply a character style named "Planners" to the text "Artistic Planners." Continue formatting the document using the features you have learned in previous units, such as borders and shading, modifying bullets, and paragraph alignment. Remember to modify and reapply styles to quickly and consistently make changes throughout the document.

FIGURE F-24

Artistic Planners'
Creativity Conference
1998

Welcome to *Artistic Planners'* 1998 Creativity Conference™! This year's conference combines traditional creativity enhancing techniques with new methods tested in a variety of human endeavors. Learn how to become a more creative individual no matter what your field or interests. Today's sessions will help you:

❖ Learn to use guided imagery to focus your creative energies.

❖ Apply creativity enhancing techniques in everyday problem solving.

❖ Learn how to find your creative "zone" and stay in the zone through to the completion of a project.

❖ Discover how massage and relaxation techniques can enhance creativity.

Guided Imagination
Learn new techniques for finding the images that guide you towards your goals. Not all images work in every situation, so in this session you learn how to clarify your objectives to select the appropriate images. *Artistic Planners'* presenters will provide structures for inter-weaving images are also identified for gaining heightened integration.

Creativity Every Day
Creativity is not just for the traditional "artists" or traditional "artistic" endeavors. Employing creative thinking and creative problem-solving can help us achieve success in everyday activities at work, at home, and even at play. In this session, learn how to think "outside of the lines" no matter what you do.

The "Zone"
Sometimes our creativity comes unbidden, and if we are fortunate enough to take the time and energy to act on it, we are satisfied. But what to do when you "have" to be creative and your muse has abandoned you? In this session, we explore writer's block (and similar disabilities) in an effort to understand and triumph over them. Learn how to call up hidden stores of creativity, even when you feel dull and uninspired.

Enlightened Massage
View demonstrations of deep breathing, massage, and creative visualization exercises. Learn how various relaxation techniques can enhance your creative abilities. An informal dinner and discussion (with *Artistic Planners'* panel of experts) is scheduled after this final session.

Merging
Word Documents

Objectives

► **Create a main document**
► **Create a data source**
► **Enter records in a data source**
► **Insert merge fields**
► **Work with merged documents**
► **Create a label main document**
► **Merge selected records**
► **Format labels**

Mail merge is widely used by companies who need to send similar documents to many individuals at once. The recipient's name and other personal information are often added to a document to create a more personal impression. The Word Mail Merge Helper guides you step-by-step through the **mail merge process**, which combines a standard document with customized information. ◢━━ Angela wants to respond to several customers' requests for information about upcoming alpine adventure tours. She'll use the Mail Merge Helper to create a form letter, enter names in a mailing list, and generate a mailing label for each envelope.

Creating a Main Document

In the mail merge process, the **main document** contains **boilerplate text**, basic text that is common to all the versions of the merged document. The Mail Merge command on the Tools menu makes it easy to create and edit each of the merge elements. Table G-1 defines the basic elements of the mail merge process. Be sure to view the CourseHelp "Understanding Mail Merge" before completing this lesson. ✎━━ Instead of retyping each letter to each customer, Angela will use the Mail Merge Helper to modify a standard cover letter and merge it with a mailing list of customers, creating a personalized letter for each customer. First, she'll open the document that contains the boilerplate text for the letter.

Steps 1 2 3 4

CourseHelp

To view the CourseHelp for this lesson, click the Start button, point to Programs, point to CourseHelp, then click Microsoft Word 97 Illustrated. Choose the Understanding Mail Merge CourseHelp.

1. Start Word, open the student file WD G-1, then save it as Response Letter Main
This document contains the boilerplate text for the main document. First you will insert today's date.

2. With the insertion point at the beginning of the document, click Insert on the menu bar, then click Date and Time
The Date and Time dialog box opens.

3. Verify that the Update Automatically check box is cleared, click the fourth option in Available Formats list box, and then click OK
The current date appears in the format you specified. Clearing the Update Automatically check box ensures that the date will not be updated each time you save or print the document. Now you are ready to start the Mail Merge Helper.

4. Click Tools on the menu bar, then click Mail Merge
The Mail Merge Helper dialog box opens. Helpful instructions regarding the next step in the merge process appear at the top of the dialog box.

5. In the Main Document section, click Create, then click Form Letters
You will create a form letter using Letter Main as the main document, which is already open and is the active window.

6. Click Active Window
The merge type and main document name appear in the Main Document section of the Mail Merge Helper dialog box, as shown in Figure G-1.

TABLE G-1: Definition of mail merge elements

term	definition
Main document	The document containing the standard information that is the same for each merged document. It also contains the field names that represent the variable information to be inserted during the merge
Data source	The document containing the personalized information that varies for each merged document, such as name and address, payment due amount, appointment date and time, etc.
Data field	An attribute that describes an item or individual. A group of data fields that relate to a specific item is called a record
Merge field	The merge fields you insert in a mail merge main document instruct Word where to insert unique information from the selected data source. These fields appear with chevrons («») around the name
Record	The entire collection of fields related to an item or individual, contained in the data source
Header row	The field names, which appear in the first row of the data source
Boilerplate text	The text in the main document that is the same for each version of a merged document

FIGURE G-1: **Mail Merge Helper dialog box**

Watch this area for instructions

Click to create a main document

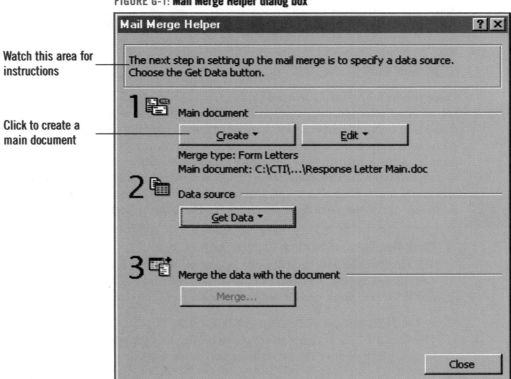

CLUES TO USE

Viewing CourseHelp

The camera icon on the opposite page indicates there is a CourseHelp available for this lesson. CourseHelps are on-screen "movies" that bring difficult concepts to life, to help you understand the material in this book. Your instructor received a CourseHelp disk and should have installed it on the machine you are using. To start CourseHelp, click the Start button, point to Programs, point to CourseHelp, then click Microsoft Word 97 Illustrated. In the main CourseHelp window, click the topic that corresponds to this lesson. Because CourseHelp runs in a separate window, you can start and view a movie even if you're in the middle of completing a lesson. Once the movie is finished, you can click the Word program button on the taskbar and continue with the lesson, right where you left off.

Creating a Data Source

Once you have specified a main document, you are ready to create the data source, which will contain the information that differs in each version of the merged document. The data source consists of fields related to an item or individual. A field is a specific item of data (such as a first name or a zip code) for a product or individual. A group of data fields that relate to a specific item is called a record. You can create a new data source, or specify an existing source that already contains the fields and information you would like in your form letter. ✎ Angela will create a new data source and specify the fields it will contain—in this case, the names and addresses of the Nomad customers to whom she wants to send the letter.

1. **Click Get Data, then click Create Data Source**
   The Create Data Source dialog box opens, as shown in Figure G-2. Several commonly used field names appear, and you can also create your own field names. First, you must remove any fields you don't need to use in the letter from the data source.

2. **In the Field names in header row box, click JobTitle, then click Remove Field Name**
   The JobTitle field is removed from the header row list and will not be included in the data source. Next, remove the other fields you don't need.

🔦 Trouble?

If you accidentally remove
a field name from the
data source in the Create
Data Source dialog box
while the field name still
appears in the Field
name box, just click the
Add Field Name button. If
the Field name box shows
a different name, type the
name of the field you
accidentally removed in
the Field Name box, and
then click the Add Field
Name button.

3. **Repeat Step 2 to remove the following field names: Company, Address2, Country, HomePhone, and WorkPhone**
   These fields are removed from the header row list. After removing or adding fields to the data source, you can close the Create Data Source dialog box.

4. **Click OK**
   The Save As dialog box opens. When you save your data source (which is a Word document) and give it a name, the data source becomes attached to the main document. Next, enter a name for the data source so that it is attached to the main document.

5. **Type Response Letter Data in the File name box, then click Save**
   Be sure to save the document in the same drive and folder as your other practice documents. After you click Save, the dialog box shown in Figure G-3 appears, indicating that there are currently no records in the data source. In the next lesson, you will add individual customer records to the data source.

FIGURE G-2: **Create Data Source dialog box**

Helpful information and instructions

Type new field name here

Click to add field name specified in Field name box

Click to remove a selected field name

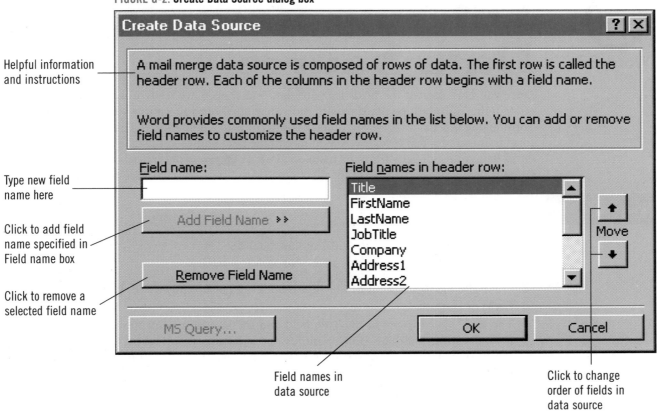

Field names in data source

Click to change order of fields in data source

FIGURE G-3: **Mail Merge dialog box**

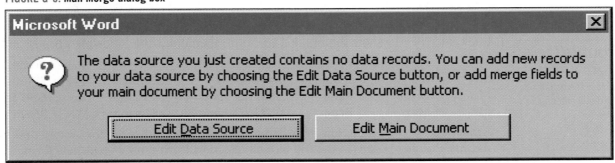

Entering Records in a Data Source

Once you have created the fields for your data source, you are ready to add records. **Records** contain the information related to each individual to whom you want to send a letter. The Data Form dialog box makes it easy to quickly add records to a data source. This dialog box shows a form that includes text boxes corresponding to the field names in the data source. You can also edit a data source directly from the main document. ▰▰▰ Angela needs to enter records that contain the names and addresses of the Nomad customers who have requested alpine expedition information.

Steps 1234

1. **Click Edit Data Source to add the new records**
   The Data Form dialog box opens, as shown in Figure G-4.

2. **Place the insertion point in the Title field if it's not already there, type Ms., then press [Tab] or [Enter]**
   The text "Ms." appears in the Title field and the insertion point moves to the FirstName field. Pressing [Tab] or [Enter] moves the insertion point to the next field. Pressing [Shift][Tab] returns the insertion point to the previous field. You are now ready to enter more records.

3. **Enter the following for the fields in the first record:**

Title	FirstName	LastName	Address1	City	State	PostalCode
Ms.	Lilly	Thomas	346 Lake St.	Cooper	MN	55321

   Remember to press [Tab] or [Enter] to move to the next field.

4. **Click OK**
   Clicking OK closes the Data Form dialog box. You can always return to this dialog box.

5. **Click Tools on the menu bar, click Mail Merge, then click Edit in the Data Source area**

6. **Choose Response Letter Data**
   When you click Edit then Response Letter Data in the Data Source area, the Data Form dialog box opens.

Trouble?

Take care not to press [Esc] or you will lose the record you are currently entering.

7. **Click Add New to show the blank data form, then enter the following data records:**

Title	FirstName	LastName	Address1	City	State	PostalCode
Mr.	Joe	Blondel	843 2nd St.	Midtown	TX	75150
Ms.	Leslie	Rauh	56311 S. Main Rd.	Canton	IL	60072
Mr.	Max	Bruni	358 Park Lane	Northport	WA	98023

   Remember to click Add New after completing the data forms for the second and third records. Pressing [Enter] at the end of each record will also show a blank data form.

8. **Click OK after completing the data form for the last record, then click Save 🖫 on the Standard toolbar**
   All records and changes to the data source are saved, and the dialog box closes. You return to the main document. Note that the Mail Merge toolbar appears in the document window, as shown in Figure G-5. This toolbar offers easy access to the commands you need when merging documents.

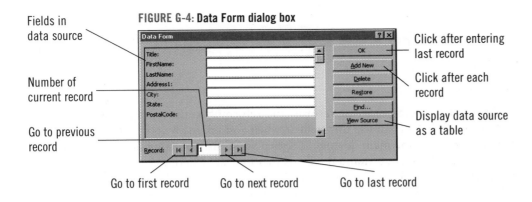

FIGURE G-4: Data Form dialog box

Fields in data source

Number of current record

Go to previous record

Click after entering last record

Click after each record

Display data source as a table

Go to first record

Go to next record

Go to last record

FIGURE G-5: Mail Merge Toolbar

Click to choose a field from attached data source

Choose fields to insert Word information

Click to return to Mail Merge Helper

FIGURE G-6: Data records displayed in table format

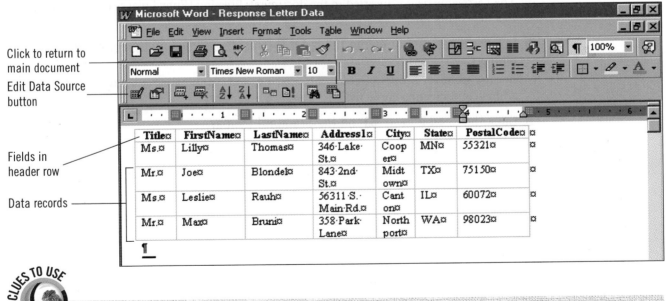

Click to return to main document

Edit Data Source button

Fields in header row

Data records

Title¤	FirstName¤	LastName¤	Address1¤	City¤	State¤	PostalCode¤	¤
Ms.¤	Lilly¤	Thomas¤	346·Lake·St.¤	Coop er¤	MN¤	55321¤	¤
Mr.¤	Joe¤	Blondel¤	843·2nd·St.¤	Midt own¤	TX¤	75150¤	¤
Ms.¤	Leslie¤	Rauh¤	56311·S.·Main·Rd.¤	Cant on¤	IL¤	60072¤	¤
Mr.¤	Max¤	Bruni¤	358·Park·Lane¤	North port¤	WA¤	98023¤	¤

CLUES TO USE

Editing the data source

It is easy to make changes to your data source. The Edit Data Source button 📝 on the Mail Merge toolbar opens the Data Form dialog box, as shown in Figure G-4. Here you can click the View Source button to show the data records in table format, as shown in Figure G-6. Each field in the Data Form dialog box corresponds to a cell in the header row of the table. You can click the Manage Fields button in this view to add new fields or delete those you no longer need. Click the Mail Merge Main Document button when you are ready to return to the main document.

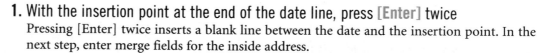

Inserting Merge Fields

After specifying a data source, entering records, and returning to the main document, you see the Mail Merge toolbar. You can use this toolbar when you are ready to insert the field names from the data source into the main document. When you finish inserting fields, the main document will contain boilerplate text and the fields that indicate where variable information will be inserted during the merge. This is the last step before performing the actual merge. To merge her main document and the data source, Angela will insert the merge fields that make up the inside address and greeting of the letter to Nomad's customers.

1. **With the insertion point at the end of the date line, press [Enter] twice**
   Pressing [Enter] twice inserts a blank line between the date and the insertion point. In the next step, enter merge fields for the inside address.

2. **Click Insert Merge Field on the Mail Merge toolbar, click Title in the list of fields, then press [Spacebar]**
   The Title field is inserted in the document, surrounded by chevrons (« »). The chevrons distinguish merge fields from the rest of the text in the main document. The space separates the Title field from the next field you enter.

3. **Click Insert Merge Field, click FirstName, then press [Spacebar]**
   The FirstName field is inserted in the document, followed by a space.

4. **Click Insert Merge Field, click LastName, then press [Enter]**
   The LastName field is inserted in the document. Pressing [Enter] places the insertion point in a new blank line.

5. **Insert the remaining merge fields for the inside address and greeting, as shown in Figure G-7**
   Be sure to insert proper punctuation, spacing, and blank paragraphs to format the inside address and greeting correctly.

6. **Click the Save button on the Standard toolbar**

Go to previous record   Current record   Check main document for errors   Click to merge documents to another document   Click to merge documents to the printer   Merge options

FIGURE G-7: **Main document with merge fields**

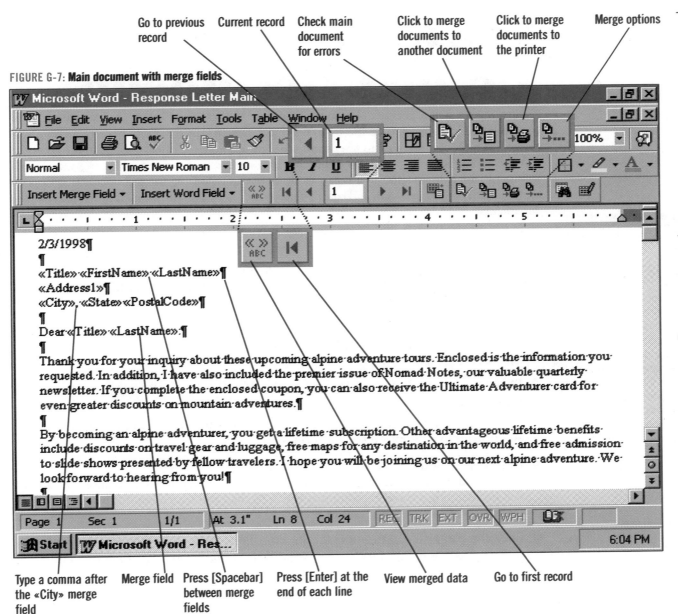

Type a comma after the «City» merge field   Merge field   Press [Spacebar] between merge fields   Press [Enter] at the end of each line   View merged data   Go to first record

Working with Merged Documents

Performing the actual merge operation is as simple as clicking a button. You can merge all of your documents to a separate file or to a printer, or you can specify only certain records to merge. Even though merging to a separate file requires more disk space, you gain the ability to edit and review before printing. See Table G-2 for a summary of merge options. ✐ Angela will merge the Nomad letter to a separate file so she can view the merged documents in print preview, verify the page layout, and complete any necessary customization for individual merged documents.

Steps

QuickTip

You can save space on your hard disk by merging a large main document or many records directly to a printer rather than saving the merge in a new document. It is quick and easy to recreate the same merge at any time with the click of a button in the Mail Merge Helper dialog box.

1. Click the Merge To New Document button 🔲 on the Mail Merge toolbar
   The main document and data source are merged to a new document called "Form Letters1". Each merged letter is separated with a section break, which you can see by scrolling through the document.

2. Click the Print Preview button 🔍 on the Standard toolbar
   The document appears in print preview.

3. Click the Multiple Pages button 🔳 on the Print Preview toolbar, then drag to select four pages
   You see all of the merged letters. In the Print Preview window, you can make last minute adjustments to customize a specific form letter.

4. Double-click in the body text in the second page
   The second merged letter appears close-up, as shown in Figure G-8. Because Mr. Blondel will be attending a travel exposition at which Nomad will have a booth, customize the last sentence of the letter to this customer.

5. Click the Magnifier button 🔍 on the Print Preview toolbar, then edit the last sentence to read: We look forward to seeing you at the Adventures Plus Convention in Dallas!

6. Click File on the menu bar, then click Save
   The Save As dialog box opens.

7. In the File name box, type Response Letter Merge, then click Save
   The document containing all the merged letters (and the changes) is saved with the name Response Letter Merge. You can now print the letters.

8. Click the Print button 🖨 on the Print Preview toolbar, then click Close on the Print Preview toolbar after printing the documents
   All the merged letters print on the printer connected to your computer. You can close all open documents.

9. Hold down [Shift] while you click File on the menu bar, then click Close All
   Click Yes in response to any messages asking you to save your changes.

Text insert from
data source

FIGURE G-8: **Close-up of merged letter in print preview**

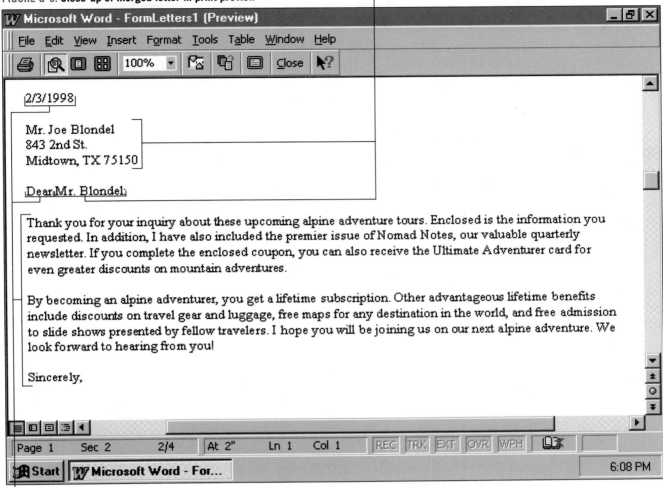

Boilerplate text

TABLE G-2: **Merge options**

click this button	or press	to
	[Alt][Shift][N]	Merge the main document and all records of the data source to a new file
	[Alt][Shift][M]	Send the merged main document and data source to the printer; does not create a new file
		Specify a range of records to include in the merge; also shows the Query options dialog box

Creating a Label Main Document

Using the data source you created earlier in this unit, you can easily print envelopes or labels for mailing the letters. Simply specify a new main document, attach the existing data source, and select a setup format. You will learn about many standard formats that correspond to name brand business labels and envelopes, including index cards, postcards, name tags, and disk labels. You can also customize labels and envelope sizes. ✍ Angela will use a data source that her assistant has already created.

Steps 1234

1. Click the New button ▭ on the Standard toolbar to create a new document

2. Click Tools on the menu bar, then click Mail Merge
   The Mail Merge Helper dialog box opens. Now create a new main document for the mailing labels.

3. Click Create, click Mailing Labels, then click New Main Document
   A temporary name for the main document appears in the Mail Merge Helper dialog box.

4. Click Get Data, then click Open Data Source
   The Open Data Source dialog box opens. You will use a data source that has already been created.

5. Click WD G-2, then click Open
   A message box appears, prompting you to finish setting up your main document.

6. Click Set Up Main Document
   The Label Options dialog box appears. In this dialog box, you need to select the appropriate type of label. The default brand name Avery standard appears in the Label Products box. You need to select the product number for the label.

7. In the Product number box, scroll to and click 5161 - Address, then click OK
   The Create Labels dialog box opens. Here, you can enter the field names for the labels.

8. Click Insert Merge Field, click Title, press [Spacebar], then continue entering the remaining merge fields and appropriate punctuation, as shown in Figure G-9
   Note that nonprinting characters (spaces and paragraph marks) are not visible in the Sample Label box.

9. Click OK to return to the Mail Merge Helper dialog box, as shown in Figure G-10
   In the next lesson, you will specify only selected records for the labels merge.

FIGURE G-9: **Create Labels dialog box**

Read this area for instructions

Click to choose a field you want to insert

Insert a space after the merge field

Type a comma and space after the «City» merge field

Press [Enter] at the end of each line

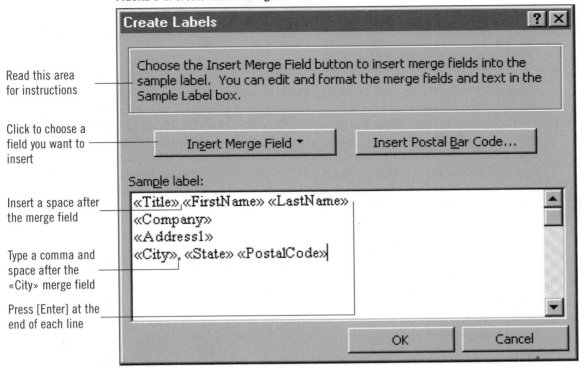

Create Labels

Choose the Insert Merge Field button to insert merge fields into the sample label. You can edit and format the merge fields and text in the Sample Label box.

Insert Merge Field ▾   Insert Postal Bar Code...

Sample label:

«Title», «FirstName» «LastName»
«Company»
«Address1»
«City», «State» «PostalCode»

OK   Cancel

FIGURE G-10: **Mail Merge Helper dialog box**

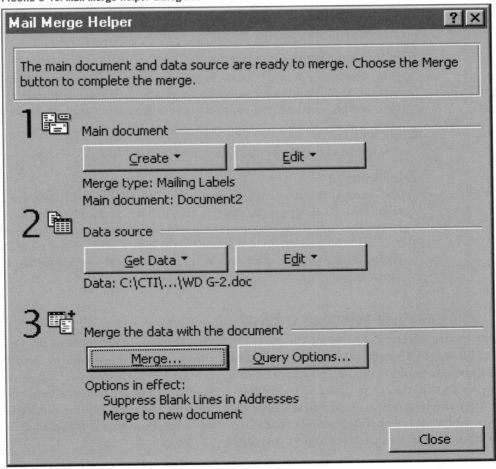

Mail Merge Helper

The main document and data source are ready to merge. Choose the Merge button to complete the merge.

1 Main document

Create ▾   Edit ▾

Merge type: Mailing Labels
Main document: Document2

2 Data source

Get Data ▾   Edit ▾

Data: C:\CTI\...\WD G-2.doc

3 Merge the data with the document

Merge...   Query Options...

Options in effect:
    Suppress Blank Lines in Addresses
    Merge to new document

Close

Merging Selected Records

Sometimes you do not want to send a document to all the individuals in a data source. For example, you might want one group of individuals to receive one kind of document, and another group of individuals to receive another. With the Mail Merge Query Options feature, you can specify the criteria for choosing which records in a data source should be merged with a main document. When you use Query Options, you can identify the fields and their contents that each record must match to be included in the merge. ✏ Angela is sending letters to Nomad customers in Massachusetts. She will only need labels for customers living in this state. In the Query Options dialog box, Angela puts MA in the state field to be included in this merge.

Steps 1234

1. **In the Mail Merge Helper click Merge**
   The Merge dialog box opens. In this dialog box, indicate that you want to use Query Options to select records to merge.

2. **Click Query Options**
   The Query Options dialog box opens. In this dialog box, describe the criteria to use when selecting records to merge.

3. **In the Field column, click the fields list arrow and scroll down to select State**
   This is the field you want to include when selecting records. Next, verify how the field should be evaluated.

4. **In the Comparison column, be sure Equal to appears in the first box**
   This selection specifies that the contents of the State field in a record must exactly match the contents you will specify.

5. **In the Compare to column, type MA**
   Your selection criterion appears in the column. Compare your dialog box to Figure G-11. You can specify additional selection criteria in the subsequent rows of the dialog box. You have completed specifying your selection criteria, so continue with the merge process.

6. **Click OK**
   You return to the Merge dialog box, as shown in Figure G-12 so you can merge the records.

7. **Click Merge**
   The selected records are merged to a new document. The labels are arranged in a Word table. Each label appears in separate cells that are divided by grey (non-printing) gridlines. Notice that only those customers with an address in Massachusetts are merged on the labels. You have finished merging documents for now. Compare the merged label document to Figure G-13. With the labels in a Word table, you can quickly format the labels so they are easier to read.

Using multiple selection criteria

When you specify selection criteria for the data records to include in a merge, you are not limited to specifying a single field's contents. In fact, you can specify up to six criteria in the Query Options dialog box. After entering criteria in the first line of the dialog box, you click the operator arrow at the start of the next line. When you click the arrow, you can choose the And operator or the Or operator. Choose the And operator to identify additional required criteria that a record must match so that it is included in the merge. Choose the Or operator to identify additional optional criteria that a record can contain so that it is included in the merge.

FIGURE G-11: **Query Options dialog box**

Specify contents or value

Specify fields

Specify conditions

Specify comparison

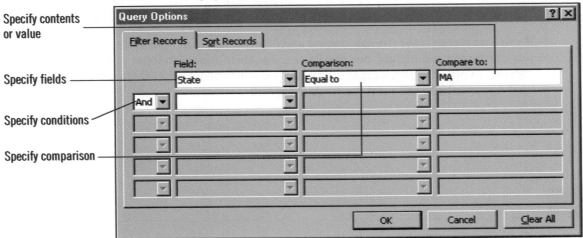

FIGURE G-12: **Merge dialog box**

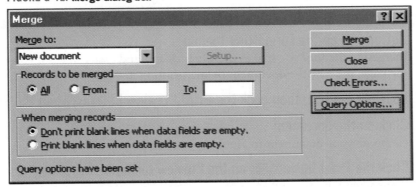

FIGURE G-13: **Merged label document**

Merged records in label format

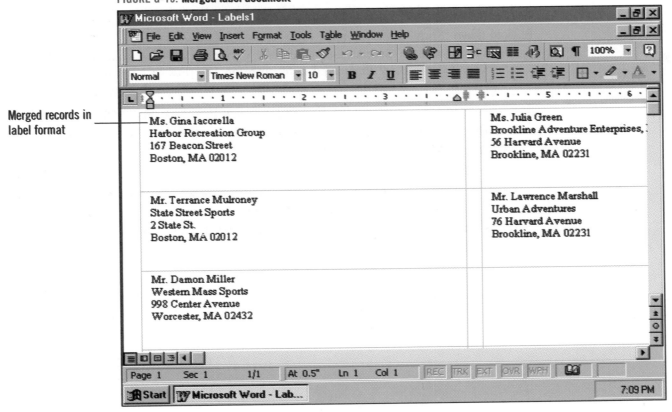

Formatting Labels

If you have merged your main document and data source to a new file (rather than to a printer), you can format the merged documents to make them more attractive before printing them. To make her labels easier to read, Angela will format the label. After editing the merged label document, she will print the labels using ordinary paper in her printer.

Steps

1. Click Edit on the menu bar, then click Select All

This command selects all the text in the merged label document.

2. Click the Font Size arrow on the Formatting toolbar, then click 14, and click the Bold button ⓑ on the Formatting toolbar

Increasing the font size makes the labels clearer and easier to read. To get an overall view of the page, preview the document before printing it.

3. Deselect the text, then click the Print Preview button 🔍 on the Standard toolbar

4. Click on the document

Compare your document to Figure G-14.

5. Click the Print button 🖨 on the Preview toolbar

Remember you can print from print preview. Next, close all open documents. To choose this command, press and hold down [Shift] (otherwise, the Close command will appear on the File menu instead of Close All).

6. Hold down [Shift] while you click File, then click Close All

When you choose the Close All command, you are prompted to save changes to any open documents and to name any unnamed documents before you close each file. Be sure to carefully watch for the message box that indicates which document is currently being closed and saved.

7. Click Yes in each message box that prompts you to save a document, save the files with the file names listed below, click No if you are asked to save any changes in the data source WD G-2, then Exit Word

Save this file	With this content	With this filename
Labels merged document	the final merge product, labels with customer information	**MA Only Labels Merge**
Labels main document	the document with the merge fields	**Labels Main**

The changes to each document are saved and all open documents are closed.

FIGURE G-14: Merged label document in print preview

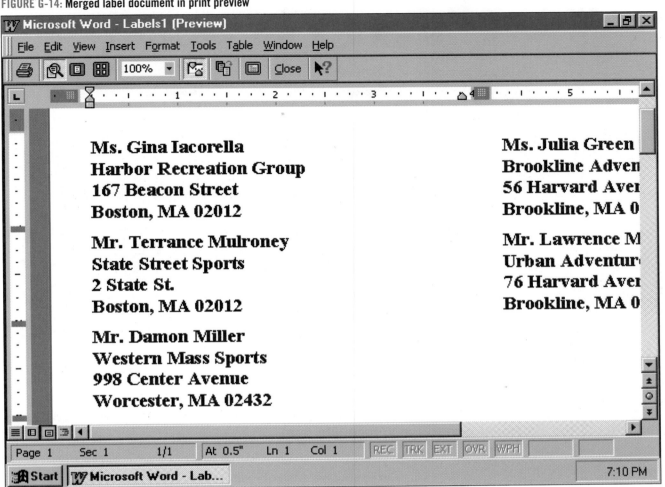

Practice

► Concepts Review

Label each part of Figure G-15

FIGURE G-15

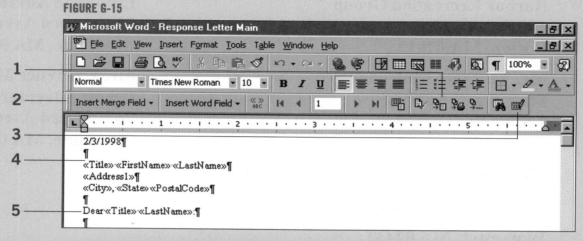

Match each of the following terms with the statement that best describes its function. Write the letter of the statement next to the appropriate term.

6. Data source
7. Data record
8. Boilerplate text
9. Main document
10. Field
11. View Source
12. Merge Field button
13. Mail Merge Helper
14. Data records

a. A piece of information specific to an item or individual
b. The entire collection of fields related to an item or individual
c. Contains the customized information that differs in each merged document
d. The text that is the same for each version of a merged document
e. Contains the common text for all versions of the merged document
f. Shows data records in table format
g. Are added to the data source in the Data Form dialog box
h. The Mail Merge command on the Tools menu shows this dialog box
i. Shows the list of fields to be entered in the main document

Select the best answer from the list of choices.

15. Which of the following is NOT a benefit of merging to a new file, rather than to a printer?
    a. You can format the merged documents to enhance their appearance.
    b. You can view the layout of merged documents in print preview.
    c. You save space on your hard disk.
    d. You can edit individual documents.

16. Which of the following statements best describes what you can accomplish when you show data records in table format?
    a. Add merge fields to the main document
    b. View one data record at a time
    c. Edit the merged document
    d. Add or delete fields from the data source

17. **Which of the following tasks cannot be accomplished in the Query Options dialog box?**
    a. Sort records by fields in ascending or descending order
    b. Save query specifications for future merge operations
    c. Select fields to be included in the data source
    d. Select records to be included in the merge operation

▶ Skills Review

1. **Create a main document.**
   a. Start Word, open the document named WD G-3, then save it as "Ideas Main".
   b. Select the text "[your name]" and replace it with your own name, then select the text "[Click here and type subject]" and replace it with "Ideas Wanted".
   c. Open the Mail Merge Helper dialog box using Tools, then Mail Merge, and choose the Form Letters option to create a form letter main document based on the memo document in the active window.

2. **Create a data source.**
   a. Click Get Data then click Create Data Source.
   b. In the Field Names in Header Row box, remove all the fields except FirstName, LastName, and JobTitle.
   c. In the Field Name box, type "Mailstation", click Add Field Name, then click OK.
   d. Type "Ideas Data" in the File name box, then click Save.

3. **Enter records in a data source.**
   a. Click Edit Data Source to add new records.
   b. Enter the following information in the appropriate fields to complete the data form for each of the recipients of this memo.

	FirstName	LastName	JobTitle	Mailstation
Record 1	Jules	Martinez	Marketing Manager	34
Record 2	Carl	Ortez	Customer Service Manager	18
Record 3	Sandy	Woodward	Vice President of Sales	48
Record 4	Elizabeth	Lewis	Charter Sales Division	45

   c. Click OK after completing the data form for the last record.
   d. Click the Save button on the Standard toolbar.

4. **Insert merge fields.**
   a. Place the insertion point after the tab character that follows the heading TO:.
   b. Click Insert Merge Field on the Mail Merge toolbar and click FirstName, then press [Spacebar].
   c. Click Insert Merge Field and click LastName. Then type a comma and press [Spacebar].
   d. Click Insert Merge Field and click JobTitle.
   e. Place the insertion point after the tab character that follows the Mailstation: heading.
   f. Click Insert Merge Field and click Mailstation.
   g. Click the Save button on the Standard toolbar.

5. **Preview and edit merged documents.**
   a. Click the Merge To New Document button on the Mail Merge toolbar.
   b. Click the Print Preview button on the Standard toolbar.
   c. Click the Multiple Pages button on the Print Preview toolbar, and select four pages.
   d. Click the magnifier pointer anywhere in the first page.

e. Click the Magnifier button on the Print Preview toolbar.

f. Select the last sentence of the letter and type "Please begin design for tour brochures". Close print preview, then print the first page.

g. Click File on the menu bar, click Close then click Yes.

h. In the File name box, type "Ideas Merge" and save the file.

i. Press and hold [Shift], click File on the menu bar, click Close All, then click Yes to save all versions.

6. **Create a label main document.**

a. Click the New button on the Standard toolbar, creating a new blank document.

b. Click Tools on the menu bar, then click Mail Merge.

c. Click Create, click Mailing Labels, then click Active Document Window.

d. Click Get Data, then click Open Data Source.

e. Click Ideas Data, then click Open.

f. Click Set Up Main Document.

g. In the Product Number box, click 5161-Address, then click OK.

h. Click Insert Merge Field, click FirstName, press [Spacebar], insert the LastName field, then press [Enter].

i. Click Insert Merge Field and click JobTitle. Press [Enter].

j. Click Insert Merge Field and click Mailstation.

k. Click OK to return to the Mail Merge Helper dialog box, then click Close.

l. Save the document as "Ideas Labels Main".

7. **Merge and format labels.**

a. Click the Merge to New Document button on the Mail Merge toolbar.

b. Click Edit on the menu bar, then click Select All.

c. Click the Font Size list arrow on the Formatting toolbar, then click 14.

d. Click the Bold button on the Formatting toolbar.

e. Preview the labels.

f. Close Print Preview.

8. **Merge selected records.**

a. Click Window on the menu bar, then click the Ideas Labels Main document.

b. On the Mail Merge toolbar, click the Mail Merge Helper button to show the Mail Merge Helper dialog box.

c. Click Query Options.

d. In the Field column, click the arrow and scroll down to choose Mailstation.

e. In the Comparison column, be sure "Equal to" appears in the first box, then in the Compare to column, type "45".

f. In the next line, click the operator arrow and choose Or.

g. In the Field column, click the fields list arrow and scroll down to choose Mailstation.

h. In the Comparison column, be sure "Equal to" appears in the first box, then in the Compare to column, type "34", then click OK.

i. Click Merge twice (be sure New Document is selected).

j. Click Edit on the menu bar, then click Select All.

k. Click the Font Size list arrow on the Formatting toolbar, then click 14. Click the Bold button on the Formatting toolbar.

l. Hold down [Shift] while you click File, then click Close All.

m. Click Yes and save your merged query label document with the name "Ideas Label Merge". You do not need to save the first merged document.

n. Click Yes to save changes to Ideas Label Main.

o. Click File on the menu bar, then click Exit.

► Independent Challenges

1. As an account representative for Lease For Less, a company that rents office equipment such as fax machines and large copiers, you previously drafted a letter describing the corporate discount program to a current customer. Open the document named WD G-4 and save it as "Discount Main" and save WD G-5 as "Discount Data", then close "Discount Data". Complete the following steps to edit a main document, attach an existing data source, and create and edit a merged document.

To complete this independent challenge:

1. Open the Mail Merge Helper and specify Discount Main as the form letter main document.
2. Attach the existing data source Discount Data to the main document.
3. Insert today's date at the top of the main document, adding a blank line after the date. Edit the signature block to show your name.
4. In the main document, replace the placeholder text enclosed in brackets with the merge fields in the data source.
5. Merge the documents to a new file named "Discount Merge".
6. Preview the documents. Add the following sentence to the end of the last letter, "P.S. I hope the above information has answered your questions about Lease For Less services. If you have any further questions, please contact me at 666-2345".
7. Print the merged documents. Compare the later letter to Figure G-16. Save any changes to all open files before closing them.

FIGURE G-16

March 15, 1998

Ms. Brittany Brinig
Independent School Dist. 667
200 Gervais Pkwy.
Plains, NY 54012

Dear Ms. Brinig:

Thank you for your inquiry about a corporate discount for our copier rentals. Enclosed is the information you requested. In addition, I have also included the premier issue of WorkADay, our exclusive management newsletter.

To be eligible for a corporate discount, you must contact to rent 2 or more of our fax or copier machines for at least six months. Of course all of our machines come with unlimited service by our highly trained technicians. As a corporate customer, you will receive a 20% discount on general office rentals and a 30% discount for our industrial copiers including color copy machines. As your account representative, I would be pleased to discuss your office requirements with you. I will call you to arrange a time when we can meet.

Sincerely,

[your name]
Lease for Less
Account Representative

P.S. I hope the above information has answered your questions about Lease for Less services. If you have any further questions, please contact me at 666-2345.

2. As an executive assistant, you are responsible for the distribution of your company's newsletter to consultants at various other companies. Your company has just purchased a new printer that can print address labels. Using the printer for labels will save time when distributing the newsletter. Newsletter recipients in New York City will receive their documents via a hand-delivered courier (who has already provided the required labels), while the remaining companies will receive their documents via U.S. Mail and will require printed labels. Use the Mail Merge Helper to create a label main document named "Newsletter Main". You can also choose to create envelopes instead of labels if your printer has this option.

To complete this independent challenge:

1. Open the document WD G-6 and save it with the name "Newsletter Data" and close the document.
2. Use the Mail Merge Helper to attach the existing data source Newsletter Data to the label document.
3. If you are using labels, use the Avery label 5161-Address. If you are merging to envelopes, use the default envelope style. Insert the merge fields in the main document and save it as "Newsletter Main".
4. Enter your own address in the Return Address area (if you are creating envelopes, not labels).
5. Add an additional record to the data source using any name and address you wish.
6. Use the Query Options feature to specify a selection criterion. Use the "Not Equal To" comparison operator in your selection criterion to select records that do not contain "New York City" in the City field.
7. Merge the label (or envelope) and data source to another document named "Newsletter Merge".
8. Print your labels(or envelopes), then save any changes to all open files before closing them.

3. You are the fundraising coordinator for Companies for Kids, a non-profit organization that collects money and materials for children housed in local shelters. In response to requests for information from potential corporate sponsors, you previously drafted a short letter describing the benefits of being a sponsor. Open the letter named WD G-7 and save it as "Children Main". Complete the following steps to edit a main document, and create a data source and a merged document.

To complete this independent challenge:

1. Open the Mail Merge Helper and specify "Children Main" as the form letter main document.
2. Insert today's date at the top of the main document, adding a blank line after the date. Edit the signature block to show your name.
3. Create a new data source with the following merge fields: Title, FirstName, LastName, Company, Address1, City, State, PostalCode. Save the data source with the name "Children Data".
4. Add at least three records to the Data Form dialog box using any contact names, company names, and addresses you wish.
5. In the main document, replace the placeholder text (enclosed in brackets) with the merge fields created in Children Data.
6. Merge the documents to a new file named "Children Merge".
7. Preview and print the merged documents.
8. Create and print labels (or envelopes) to send with the letters, you do not need to save the labels. Use any label type you wish. Save any changes to all open files before closing them.

4. As a recent college graduate, you have just begun your search for a position requiring a background in business administration. Complete the following steps to edit a main document, create a new data source, and create a merged document.

To complete this independent challenge:

1. Create a new document that is a generic letter of inquiry. Leave blanks (or some other indicator) for where variable information (such as names, addresses, company names, and area of companies' specialization) belongs. Use Figure G-17 as a guide for inserting variable information that will be provided by your data source. Save the letter as "Inquiry Main".
2. Open the Mail Merge Helper and specify "Inquiry Main" as the form letter main document.

3. Use your Web browser to search for financial or investment companies and note their names and mailing addresses. Create a data source using the names and addresses of at least five companies for whom you would like to work. Be sure to include a field for an area of specialization to which you would refer in your letter.

4. For an example of a good web source for locating companies, log on to the Internet and use your browser to go to http://www.course.com. From there, click Student Online Companions, click the link for this textbook, then click Word for unit G. Follow the link to the Business BigBook.

5. Save the new data source as "Inquiry Data".

6. Attach the data source to the main document.

7. In the main document, replace the placeholder text with the merge fields in the data source.

8. Merge the documents to a new file named "Inquiry Merge".

9. Perform a second merge, this time generate letters for only those companies in your home state (or some other state in which you might wish to live). Use the Query feature to specify the criteria. Save this second merged document as "Home State Inquiry Merge".

10. Print the merged documents. Save any changes to all files before closing them.

FIGURE G-17

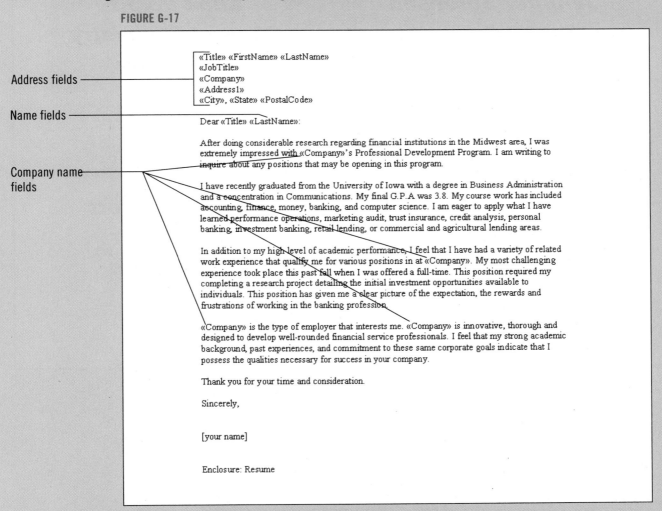

Address fields

Name fields

Company name fields

«Title» «FirstName» «LastName»
«JobTitle»
«Company»
«Address1»
«City», «State» «PostalCode»

Dear «Title» «LastName»:

After doing considerable research regarding financial institutions in the Midwest area, I was extremely impressed with «Company»'s Professional Development Program. I am writing to inquire about any positions that may be opening in this program.

I have recently graduated from the University of Iowa with a degree in Business Administration and a concentration in Communications. My final G.P.A was 3.8. My course work has included accounting, finance, money, banking, and computer science. I am eager to apply what I have learned performance operations, marketing audit, trust insurance, credit analysis, personal banking, investment banking, retail lending, or commercial and agricultural lending areas.

In addition to my high level of academic performance, I feel that I have had a variety of related work experience that qualify me for various positions in at «Company». My most challenging experience took place this past fall when I was offered a full-time. This position required my completing a research project detailing the initial investment opportunities available to individuals. This position has given me a clear picture of the expectation, the rewards and frustrations of working in the banking profession.

«Company» is the type of employer that interests me. «Company» is innovative, thorough and designed to develop well-rounded financial service professionals. I feel that my strong academic background, past experiences, and commitment to these same corporate goals indicate that I possess the qualities necessary for success in your company.

Thank you for your time and consideration.

Sincerely,

[your name]

Enclosure: Resume

▶ Visual Workshop

As the conference coordinator for the annual Texas Educators Convention, you are in charge of creating nametags for conference attendees. Using the Mail Merge feature in Word, create a mailing labels main document named "Conference Main". Then create a data source with the following merge fields: FirstName, LastName, Grade/Subject, and District. Save the data source with the name "Conference Data". Add at least four records in the Data Form dialog box. Using Figure G-18 as your guide, set up the main document by selecting the product 5095-Name Badge in the Label Options dialog box and inserting the merge fields in the Create Labels dialog box. Merge the labels to a new document named "Conference Labels". Use formatting to enhance the appearance of your nametags. Preview and print the labels on plain paper. Save any changes to all files, then exit Word.

FIGURE G-18

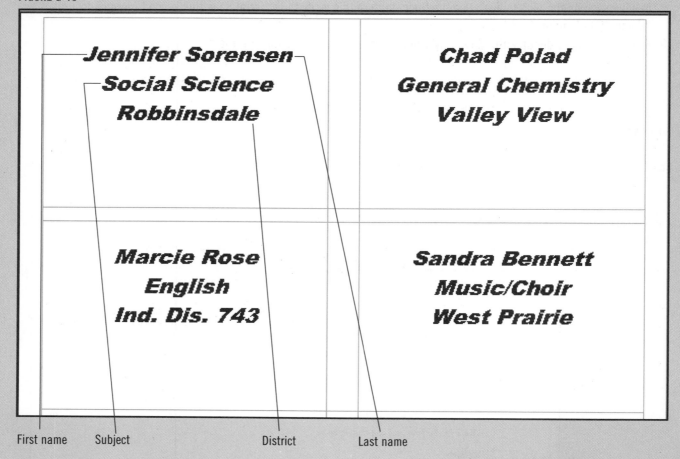

First name   Subject   District   Last name

Working
with Graphics

► **Insert clip art graphics**
► **Modify clip art graphics**
► **Create custom graphics**
► **Modify custom graphics**
► **Apply special effects to graphics**
► **Position graphics and AutoShapes**
► **Insert a graphic from another program**
► **Create a callout**

By adding and positioning graphics in a document, you can achieve dramatic effects. Graphics break up the monotony of large blocks of text and reinforce ideas presented in the text. Word provides many built-in graphics files (called **clip art**) covering a wide variety of topics, as well as decorative elements such as borders, bullets, and backgrounds. If the clip art collection provided with Word does not meet your needs, you can use the Drawing feature in Word to create your own graphics. Also, with the aid of the Drawing feature, you can create callouts, which draw your reader's attention to specific parts of a document. Angela has produced a simple report summarizing the year's highlights. Now she would like to spice up the text by inserting graphics and borders to create a flyer for Nomad Ltd senior management called *NomadNotes*.

Inserting Clip Art Graphics

In Word you can insert pictures (in the form of graphics files, many of which are provided with the Word program) to better illustrate ideas and enhance your document. With Microsoft Clip Gallery 3.0, you can view available clip art graphics side-by-side. In addition, the Clip Gallery gives you easy access to recorded sound and video clips that you can insert in a document. After you insert a graphic, you can size and position it to fit where you want on the page. ✎━━ In the NomadNotes flyer, Angela wants to insert a graphic in the article about the new travel division. She would also like to insert a border under the name of the flyer.

1. Start Word

2. Open the document named **WD H-1** and save it as **Flyer Graphics**
   The document opens in page layout view.

3. Scroll to the top of the document and place the insertion point in front of the title **NomadNotes**, click **Insert** on the menu bar, click **Picture**, then click **Clip Art**
   The Microsoft Clip Gallery dialog box opens, as shown in Figure H-1. The pictures you see in this dialog box are the figures available in the currently selected category. If you see different pictures, it could be because another category is already selected on the left side of the dialog box. You can choose a category to view a collection of related pictures.

4. From the Categories list, click **Signs**, select a graphic that looks like a sign post with arrows pointing in several directions, and then click **Insert**
   The selected graphic appears in the document at the insertion point. After inserting a graphic, you often need to resize it to fit in the document. You can size a graphic object by dragging its sizing handles, which appear on all four sides and corners of a graphic.

5. Select the graphic (if necessary), position the pointer over the lower-right sizing handle, when the pointer changes shape ↖ then drag up and to the left until the graphic is about **1" wide** and **1.5" tall**
   The Picture toolbar appears when a picture is selected. Compare your document to Figure H-2. In addition to the pictures shown in Clip Gallery, you can also insert lines, backgrounds, and bullets. To better separate the title from the rest of the document, insert a decorative border.

6. Place the insertion point in front of the heading **Corporate Vision**, click **Insert** on the menu bar, click **Picture**, and then click **From File**
   The clip art folders include various folders with graphics and other decorative elements. Next locate the Lines folder.

7. Click the **Up One Level button** 🔼 if necessary, then double-click the **Lines folder**

8. Select **Green and Black Stripe**, then click **Insert**
   Compare your document to Figure H-3. For now, don't be concerned about the position of your graphics in the document. You will learn how to position graphics later in this unit. For now save your changes to the document.

9. Click the **Save button** 💾 on the Standard toolbar

Trouble?

If you do not see the Clip Art command, click the From File command. Double-click the Popular folder.

Trouble?

If the Picture toolbar doesn't appear when the graphic is selected, click View on the menu bar, click Toolbars, then click Picture. If you accidentally moved the graphic, click Undo and be sure to drag the sizing handles, not the figure.

Trouble?

If you do not see the file in the Lines folder, it means that the correct graphics filters were not installed on your computer. You can continue working in this unit but your document will not contain the line shown in the figures.

FIGURE H-1: Clip Gallery dialog box

FIGURE H-2: Sized graphic

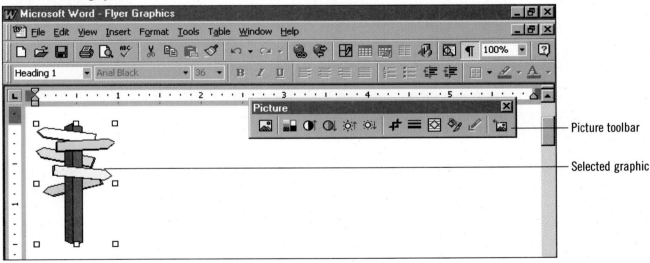

Picture toolbar

Selected graphic

FIGURE H-3: Border graphic inserted

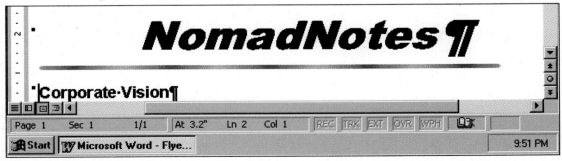

Modifying Clip Art Graphics

In Word you can modify clip art graphics to meet your needs. You might decide to change the color of the graphic or add a border around the picture. The Picture toolbar, as shown in Figure H-4, contains the buttons that provide easy access to the commands you need to modify clip art graphics. For example, with the Format Picture command on the Picture toolbar, you can specify color, line, position, and text wrapping options. ✦ Angela would like to modify the arrows sign graphic. Along with changing the color and adding a border, she would also like to modify the picture so that the text will wrap around the graphic instead of displacing the text.

Steps 123 4

1. **Select the arrows sign graphic you inserted in the previous lesson**
   The Picture toolbar appears in the document window. Because the document might not be printed on a color printer, change the image color.

2. **Click the Image Control button** 🖼️ **on the Picture toolbar, then click Grayscale**
   The color in the graphic changes to shades of gray. This option can be helpful if your printer does not print in color.

3. **Click the Text Wrapping button** 🔲 **on the Picture toolbar, then click Square**
   The text wrapping feature allows you to specify how you would like the text to be arranged around the picture. Some text wrapping options include text being placed only above or below the picture, text going through or behind the picture, and text arranged tight against all sides of the graphic. With square text wrapping, the text will flow around all sides of the graphic evenly. You can add a border around a graphic to enhance its appearance.

4. **Click the Line Style button** ▤ **on the Picture toolbar, then select the 3 pt double line**
   A double line border appears around the graphic. You can also change the color of a graphic.

5. **Click the Format Picture button** 🖌️ **on the Picture toolbar**
   The Format Picture dialog box opens. In this dialog box you can specify a variety of colors, patterns, and other characteristics for your picture. Next, you will change the background color of the graphic.

6. **Click the Colors and Lines tab**
   On the Colors and Lines tab, you can specify fill color, line style, and arrow styles as shown in Figure H-5.

7. **In the Fill area, click the Color list arrow**
   A color palette appears, allowing you to choose from a variety of colors. At the bottom of the palette, you see the More Colors and Fill Effects options. These options allow you to choose from a larger variety of colors or create your own hue and apply texture to your fill.

8. **Choose the last color in the fourth row, then click OK**
   The graphic now has a gray background. You have finished modifying this graphic for now. Compare your graphic to Figure H-6.

9. **Click the Save button** 💾 **on the Standard toolbar**

FIGURE H-4: Picture toolbar

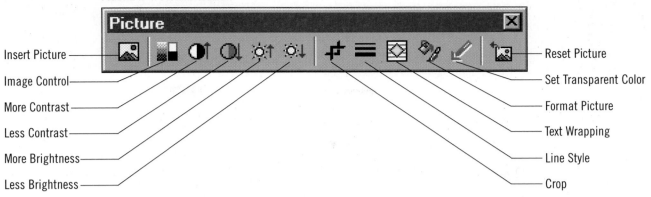

Insert Picture

Image Control

More Contrast

Less Contrast

More Brightness

Less Brightness

Reset Picture

Set Transparent Color

Format Picture

Text Wrapping

Line Style

Crop

FIGURE H-5: Format Picture dialog box

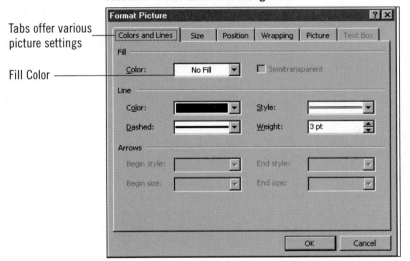

Tabs offer various picture settings

Fill Color

FIGURE H-6: Modified graphic

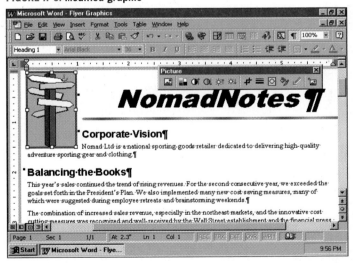

Using the cropping tool to modify a graphic

Occasionally you will want to use only a small part of a graphic offered by Word. In this case you can use the cropping tool on the Picture toolbar to crop or cut away the undesired parts. To crop a picture, first select the graphic, then click the Crop button on the Picture toolbar. After clicking the Crop button the pointer will change to . Click this pointer on any of the sizing handles and drag over the areas you wish to crop.

Creating Custom Graphics

When you want to insert graphics in your document, you are not limited to the clip art files provided by Word. In Word, you have the ability to create your own custom graphics using simple (but powerful) drawing tools on the Drawing toolbar. You can create lines and shapes, and apply colors to them. With the AutoShapes button on the Drawing toolbar you can create simple shapes quickly without having to draw them from scratch. AutoShapes include squares, triangles, lightning bolts, block arrows, and stars and banners. ✎ Angela would like to use a graphic to accompany the article about environmental relations in her newsletter. Because Word does not provide a graphic that she feels is relevant, she creates her own.

Steps 1 2 3 4

1. Click the **Drawing button** 🖉 on the Standard toolbar
   The Drawing toolbar appears at the bottom of the Word document window, as shown in Figure H-7. You use the buttons on this toolbar to create your own graphics in your Word documents.

2. Click **AutoShapes** on the Drawing toolbar, click **Basic Shapes**, then click the **Isosceles Triangle** in the second row
   When you click an AutoShape feature, the pointer changes shape to ┼ . With this pointer, you can drag and draw the selected shape to a desired size. The AutoShape option on the Drawing toolbar offers a variety of presets you can draw.

3. Scroll to the end of the document, click the pointer in a blank area (below the text) at the bottom of the page, then drag the pointer down and to the right until you have a triangle with a **1" base** and **1" tall** (you do not need to be very exact).
   Compare your shape to Figure H-8. Just as you can copy and paste text, you can also copy and paste selected graphics and AutoShapes.

4. Select the triangle shape, if it is not already selected, click the **Copy button** 🗐 on the Standard toolbar, then click the **Paste button** 📋 on the Standard toolbar
   Another triangle shape appears near the original shape.

5. With the second shape selected, drag the bottom right sizing handle up and to the left so the new shape is just slightly smaller than the first shape
   With the shape selected you can drag it to a new position.

6. With the second shape still selected, position the pointer near the shape until the pointer changes to ✛, then drag the second shape so that it overlaps the first shape, as shown in Figure H-9
   The overlapping triangles will represent the mountains in the graphic.

7. Click the **Oval button** ⬭ on the Drawing toolbar
   You can use this tool to draw circles, as well as ovals.

8. Press and hold down **[Shift]** and, near the top of the triangle shapes, drag a circle that is about one-half inch across
   Holding down the [Shift] key as you drag with the Ellipse tool creates a perfect circle. Compare your document to Figure H-10.

9. Click the **Save button** 🖫 on the Standard toolbar

Trouble?

If you don't see the second shape, it is because Word pasted it exactly on top of the first shape. Click the shape and then drag it to the right, so you can work with the new one.

FIGURE H-7: **Drawing toolbar**

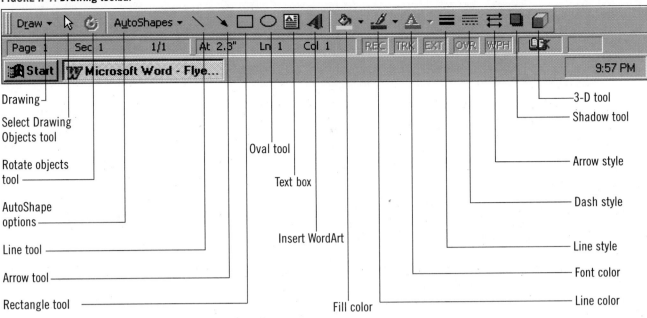

Drawing
Select Drawing Objects tool
Rotate objects tool
AutoShape options
Line tool
Arrow tool
Rectangle tool

Oval tool
Text box
Insert WordArt
Fill color

3-D tool
Shadow tool
Arrow style
Dash style
Line style
Font color
Line color

FIGURE H-8: **AutoShape**

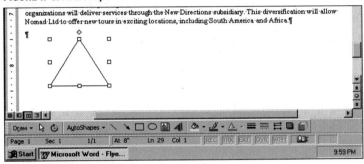

FIGURE H-9: **Overlapping shapes**

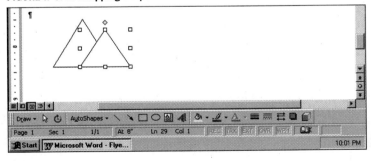

FIGURE H-10: **Completed custom graphic**

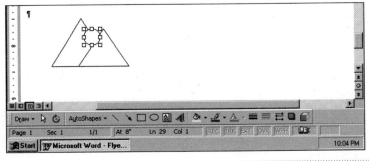

Modifying Custom Graphics

You are not limited to only drawing lines and shapes in your custom graphics. You can also fill your shapes with colors and rearrange shapes (as well as make many other modifications) to make your creations look the way you want. Angela's drawing needs color to make it look more realistic. Angela adds color to her shapes and makes other changes to her graphic to achieve the effect she wants. First, she adds color to the circle shape.

Steps 1 2 3 4

1. **Select the circle in the drawing, then click the Fill Color list arrow 🎨 ▾ on the Drawing toolbar**
   Clicking the Fill Color button shows a palette of colors from which you can choose to fill the selected shape, as shown in Figure H-11.

2. **Click the Yellow color on the Palette**
   The circle is filled with the yellow color, as shown in Figure H-12. Only the circle will be filled with yellow because this is the selected shape.

3. **Select the larger triangle and click the Fill Color list arrow 🎨 ▾ on the Drawing toolbar, then click a Dark Blue color on the Palette**
   The triangle is filled with dark blue. Now, fill the other triangle with another color.

4. **Repeat step 3 for the other triangle, this time choosing the Dark Green color**
   The second triangle is filled with dark green. Objects you draw appear in layers, one on top of another. The sequence in which you draw a shape determines the order in which the shapes are layered. For example, because the circle is the last object you drew, the circle appears on top of the other shapes. The Drawing button on the Drawing toolbar offers options for placing shapes in relation to each other and to text.

5. **Click the circle shape, click Draw on the Drawing toolbar, click Order, then click Send to Back**
   The circle appears behind the triangle, giving the appearance of a sun setting between two mountains.

6. **Adjust the position of each of the shapes (as necessary) by clicking and dragging them so that your picture approximates the illustration in Figure H-13**
   Do not be concerned if the colors for your two mountains are reversed. What is important is that your mountains are different colors from the sun shape and from each other. After you have finished modifying the various shapes in a custom graphic, you can group the shapes together, so that you can work a group of objects as a single shape.

7. **Click the Select Objects button ⯈ on the Drawing toolbar, then drag a rectangle to surround all the objects**
   With all the shapes selected, you see the sizing handles for each of the objects. So that you can work with the objects as a single item, you group the objects together.

8. **Click Draw on the Drawing toolbar, then click Group**
   With the objects grouped, you see only one set of sizing handles as shown in Figure H-14. Grouping the shapes makes a single drawing object, so you can now select the entire arrangement by clicking only one shape. Having the shapes grouped together will make it easier to move the graphic in the document.

9. **Click the Save button 💾 on the Standard toolbar**

FIGURE H-11: Fill Color palette

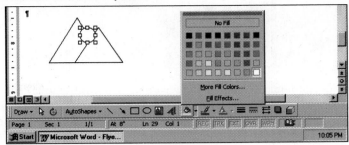

FIGURE H-12: Filled circle

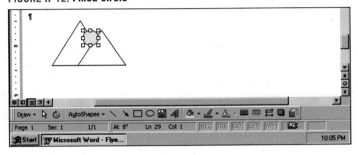

FIGURE H-13: Circle object sent to back

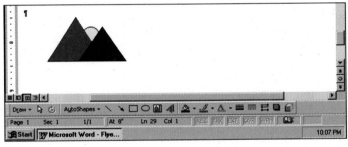

FIGURE H-14: Grouped drawing objects

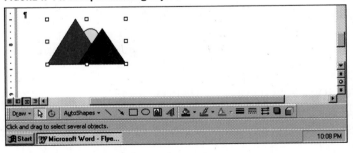

CLUES TO USE

Sizing shapes with precision

As you size shapes, you might have noticed that the lines in the shapes appear to "jump" as your pointer moves. This is because the shapes are automatically aligned to an invisible grid. The Snap to Grid, which is turned on by default, aligns shapes along a very tightly spaced grid. This feature makes it easier to align shapes with one another. If you want more flexibility to create and drag shapes exactly where you wish, you can turn off the Snap to Grid feature. Click the Draw button on the Drawing toolbar and then click Grid. Clear the Snap to Grid check box and click OK.

Applying Special Effects to Graphics

The Drawing toolbar contains many features you can use to enhance the shapes you insert in a document. For example, you can give a shape a unique appearance by adding special fill patterns, such as gradient. You can display a shape in three-dimensions. You can even rotate the shape to an exact angle you choose. Angela would like to add a block arrow to emphasize the section on Balancing the Books. She would also like to experiment with some of the more dramatic fill effects found in the Fill Effects Dialog box.

Steps

1. Click AutoShapes on the Drawing toolbar, click Block Arrows, then select the Down Arrow

   After selecting an AutoShape, the pointer will change to $+$. With this pointer, you can click and drag the selected shape to any size and anywhere in the document.

2. In the white space at the end of the document, click and drag down 1" and to the right .5"

   Just as you modify custom graphics, you can modify AutoShapes using the Drawing toolbar.

3. Click the Fill Color list arrow on the Drawing toolbar, then click Fill Effects

   The Fill Effects dialog box opens as shown in Figure H-15.

4. Select the Gradient tab if it is not already selected, then click the Preset option button in the Color area

   Notice the Variants and Shading styles at the bottom of the dialog box. You can also preview the fill effects in the sample box in the lower right corner. You can choose from a list of preset color options.

5. Click the Preset colors list arrow, select Desert, then click OK

   The arrow is filled with the Desert fill effect.

6. Click the Line Color list arrow on the Drawing toolbar, choose Red

   You can use the Line Style arrow to choose new colors and patterns for the lines outlining your AutoShapes. The 3-D feature can add an even greater dramatic effect to AutoShapes.

7. Click the 3-D button on the Drawing toolbar, then select 3-D Style 1

   The arrow appears with a 3-D effect. With the Free Rotate feature, you can rotate your figure to point in any direction that you choose.

QuickTip

Drag when the green dot appears in the center of the pointer.

8. Click the Free Rotate button on the Drawing toolbar, click any rotate handle, drag the arrow around until it points up, then click the Free Rotate button again to turn it off

   You can also change the size of the pointed part of the arrow. For example, you can squeeze down the top part of the arrow. (You need to turn off the Free Rotate feature to see the yellow sizing diamond you use in the next step.)

Time To

✔ Save

9. Position the pointer over the yellow diamond under the pointed part of the arrow and drag up a short distance

   Compare your document to Figure H-16.

FIGURE H-15: Fill Effects dialog box

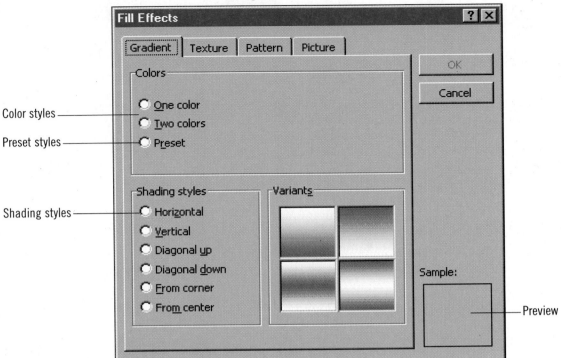

Color styles ———

Preset styles ———

Shading styles ———

— Preview

FIGURE H-16: Modified AutoShape

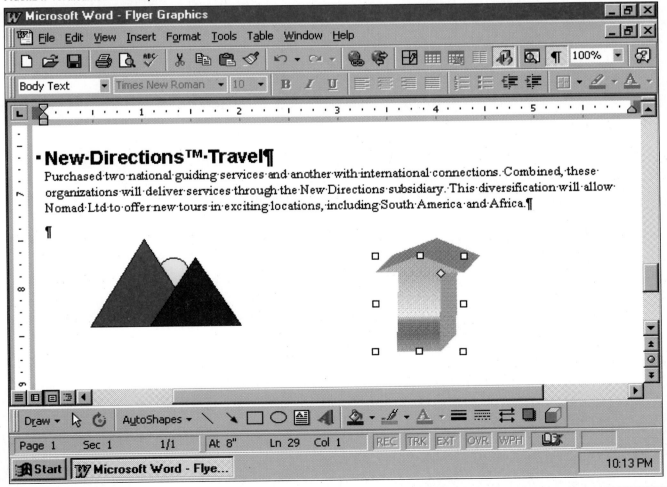

Positioning Graphics and AutoShapes

Word offers various options when positioning graphics. To move a graphic, you simply select the graphic and drag it to the desired location. When positioning a graphic near text, you can specify how you would like the text to wrap around the graphic. The Format AutoShapes and Format Object dialog boxes contain options for positioning, text wrapping, and other types of formatting for graphics. You can open these dialog boxes by double-clicking the graphic.  Angela has finished modifying her graphics and would like to position them throughout the document. She will specify how she would like the text to wrap before moving the graphics.

Steps

1. **Select the border graphic and drag it so it appears under the paragraph below the heading Corporate Vision**
   You will need to position the border about .25" below the paragraph. Placing graphics can often require several attempts before you get the results you want. Keep positioning it by releasing the mouse and re-selecting the graphic until it appears in the proper location. If text is misplaced, simply reselect and position the graphic again.

2. **Double-click the Up Arrow graphic, then click the Wrapping tab (if it is not already in front)**
   Double-clicking an AutoShape opens the Format AutoShape dialog box, as shown in Figure H-17. The Format AutoShape dialog box offers various formatting options such as positioning, text wrapping, and size.

3. **Select Tight in the Wrapping Style area and Right in the Wrap to area, then click OK**
   After you have specified the text wrapping style, you can move the graphic to the desired position.

4. **Click inside the Up Arrow graphic, drag the graphic and place it under the heading Balancing the Books**
   Make sure the heading is above the graphic with the paragraph text to the side of the graphic, as shown in Figure H-18. Notice the text wraps to the shape of the AutoShape.

QuickTip

You do not need to be concerned if your text does not wrap exactly the same as shown in the figure. You can adjust the size of the arrow, if you wish.

5. **Double-click the custom mountain graphic**
   Double-clicking a custom graphic opens the Format Object dialog box. The Format Object dialog box offers the same options as the Format AutoShape dialog box.

6. **Select Tight in the Text Wrapping area, select Left in the Wrap To area, then click OK**
   With the wrapping options specified, you can position the custom graphic.

7. **Drag the graphic to the right of the paragraph below the Environmental Relations heading**
   The text flows to the left of the mountain graphic. To enhance the effect, format the paragraph so that both left and right edges of the paragraph are even.

8. **Click anywhere in the paragraph below the Environmental Relations heading, then click the Justify button ▤ on the Formatting toolbar**
   Compare your document to the illustration shown in Figure H-19.

Time To

✔ Save

9. **Scroll to the top of the page, then select and drag the arrow signs graphic so that it is to the left of the heading New Directions Travel**
   Compare your document to Figure H-20.

FIGURE H-17: Format AutoShape dialog box

Text wrapping options

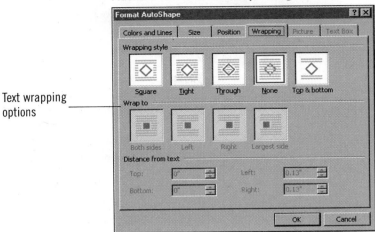

FIGURE H-18: Positioned graphic

Text wraps tight and to the right

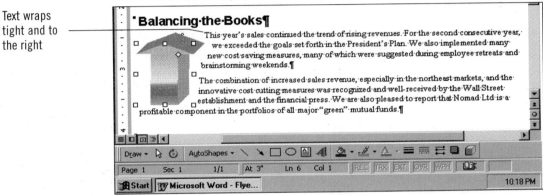

FIGURE H-19: Custom graphic positioned

Justified paragraph

Text wraps tight and to the left

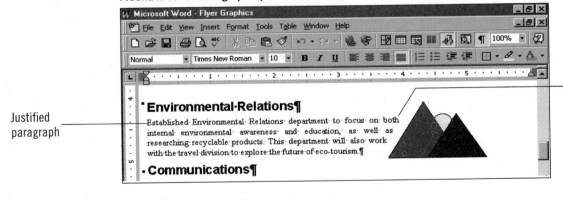

FIGURE H-20: Clip art positioned in document

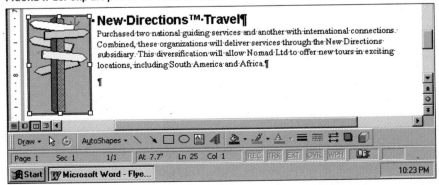

Inserting a Graphic from Another Program

You are not limited to working with graphics either provided in Word's clip art collection or those you create with the Drawing toolbar. There are many drawing programs on the market with which you can create sophisticated graphics, and you can insert graphics created in these programs into your Word documents. The advertising department at Nomad has been busy creating a new logo in a graphics program called Paint, which is provided with Microsoft Windows 95. Michael Belmont has created a new graphic to use as a logo for Nomad Ltd, which Angela would like to insert in the newsletter.

Steps 1234

1. Place the insertion point at the end of the title NomadNotes

2. Click Insert on the menu bar, then click Object

   The Object dialog box opens. You can click the Create from File tab to help locate a file. The Nomad logo file is located on your Student Disk.

3. Click the Create from File tab

   The Create from File tab is now foremost in the dialog box, as shown in Figure H-21. On this tab you can locate the Paint file.

4. Click Browse, then locate and double-click the drive that contains your student files

   With the appropriate drive selected, you can select the file you want to insert.

5. Click the Preview button 🗒 (if it's not already selected), scroll to and select the file WD Logo, click OK in the Browse dialog box

   The logo filename appears in the File Name dialog box.

6. Click OK in the Object dialog box

   The picture appears in the document.

7. Select the Paint object, click the Text Wrapping button 🔲 on the Picture toolbar, then click Square

   The Picture toolbar appears when you select an object, as it does when you select a picture.

8. Drag the object to the right of the title NomadNotes

   Compare your document to Figure H-22.

9. Click the Save button 💾 on the Standard toolbar

CLUES TO USE

Modifying a Paint object

When you insert an object that was created in another program, you can edit the object in the original program (provided that the program is installed on your computer). For example, if you insert a Paint file as an object, you can modify the graphic using Paint without actually leaving Word. To edit an object, you simply double-click the object to display the object's original program environment. You will still be able to see the Word document in the original program window. To move back to the Word program simply click outside the object.

FIGURE H-21: **Create from File tab in Object dialog box**

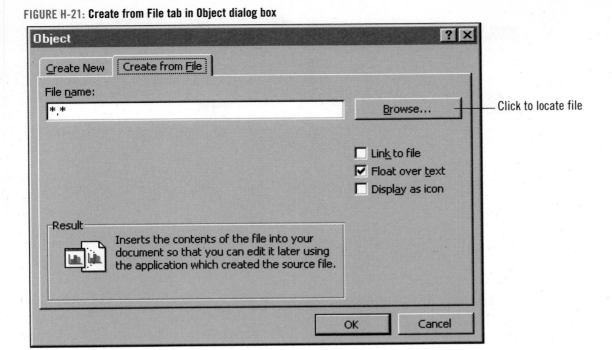

Click to locate file

FIGURE H-22: **New picture in document**

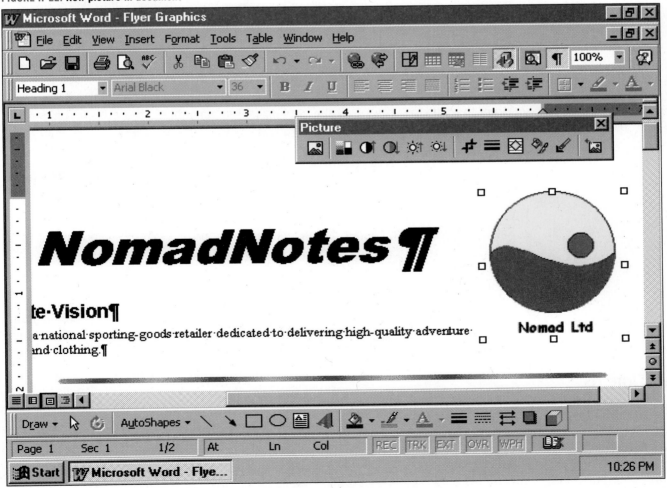

Creating a Callout

When you want to draw your reader's attention to a specific item in a document, you can create a callout to that item. A **callout** is a graphic object containing text and a line pointing to a location in a document. You can enter any text you want in a callout. In addition, you can position it exactly where you wish. Angela would like to make sure her readers notice the new tour destinations available in the upcoming year, so she creates a callout to this part of the document.

Steps

1. Click **AutoShapes** on the Drawing toolbar, click **Callouts**, then select **Line Callout 2**
   With the Callout tool selected, you can drag your callout anywhere in the document.

2. Click the pointer near the end of the **New Directions** paragraph, and drag down and to the right about one-half inch
   A callout appears next to the text, as shown in Figure H-23. Immediately after you insert a callout, you can enter text.

3. Type **New for 1998!**
   You can use the yellow sizing handles to adjust the callout position.

4. Click the **callout frame** to select it and display its sizing handles, then drag the yellow sizing handle connected to the text box and pull down and to the left
   Notice that the first yellow sizing handle stays anchored.

5. Click the callout and drag the bottom sizing handle up so that the callout box is not larger than the text, then drag the right sizing handle until the text appears on one line
   With the callout still selected you can use the buttons on the Drawing toolbar to modify the text box itself.

6. Click the **Dash Style button** 🔲 on the Drawing toolbar, and select the **Round Dot line**
   The callout appears with dashed lines.

7. Select the text in the callout, then click the **Bold button** 🄱 on the Formatting toolbar, then click the **Font list arrow** on the Formatting toolbar and click **Arial**
   To display the callout more clearly without the paragraph marks, you can hide the nonprinting characters.

8. Click the **Show/Hide button** ¶ on the Standard toolbar, then deselect the callout
   Compare your document to Figure H-24. You have finished working with graphics in your document, so you can hide the Drawing toolbar and save your changes.

9. Click the **Drawing button** 🎨 on the Standard toolbar and save your changes
   The Drawing toolbar is hidden.

Time To

- ↳ Save
- ↳ Print the document
- ↳ Close
- ↳ Exit Word

FIGURE H-23: Creating a callout

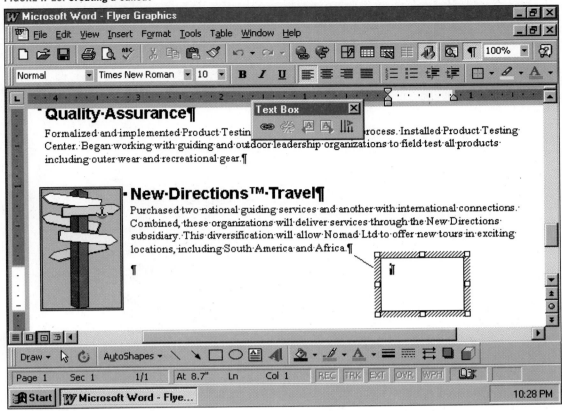

FIGURE H-24: Completed callout

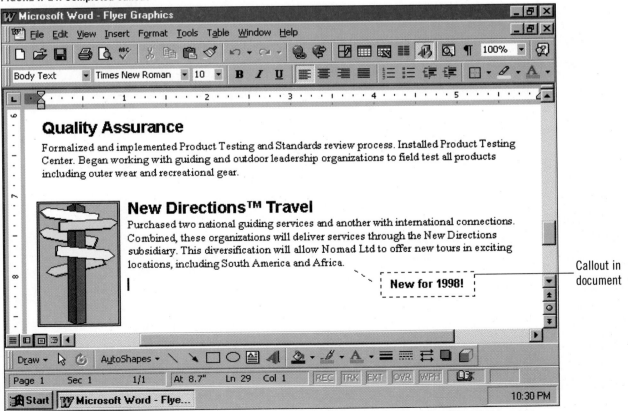

Word 97

Practice

► Concepts Review

Label each of the elements in Figure H-25.

FIGURE H-25

Match each of the following features with the correct descriptions.

9. Callout
10. Oval button
11. Select Objects button
12. Sizing handle
13. Drawing toolbar

a. Allows you to draw a circle or oval shape
b. Allows you to group custom shapes or AutoShapes into one graphic
c. Contains buttons you can use to create custom graphics
d. Framed text pointing to an area in a document
e. Allows you to size an object

Select the best answer from the list of choices.

14. **To insert a graphic provided by Word, you**
    a. Click Insert, then click Picture.
    b. Click the Drawing button on the Standard toolbar.
    c. Click the Picture button on the Drawing toolbar.
    d. Click View, then click Picture.

15. **To draw your own custom graphic, you must first**
    a. Click Insert, then click Picture and select the picture you want.
    b. Click the Drawing button on the Standard toolbar.
    c. Click the Picture button on the Drawing toolbar.
    d. Click View, then click Picture.

16. **Which of the following is NOT true about using graphics in Word?**
    a. You can create your own graphics in another program and insert them in Word.
    b. You can select graphics from Word's collection of clip art.
    c. You cannot modify graphics you insert in Word.
    d. You can edit graphics created in another program.

17. **To modify a graphic, you need to**
    a. Click Edit, then click Graphic.
    b. Exit Word and start the program that was used to create the graphic.
    c. Select the graphic and use the Picture toolbar.
    d. Triple-click the graphic.

18. **To change the color of a shape, you**
    a. Select the Fill Color button on the Drawing toolbar.
    b. Select the shape then click the Fill Color button.
    c. Delete the shape, click the Fill Color button and redraw the shape.
    d. Select the shape, click the Fill Color button, then select a new color.

19. **To draw a perfect circle, you**
    a. Click the Circle button and drag a circle.
    b. Click the Oval button and press [Ctrl] as you drag a circle.
    c. Click the Freeform button and carefully draw a circle.
    d. Click the Oval button and press [Shift] as you drag a circle.

20. **To insert an AutoShape, you**
    a. Click Insert, then click AutoShapes.
    b. Click AutoShapes on the Drawing toolbar.
    c. Click Tools, then click AutoShapes.
    d. Choose AutoShapes in the Picture dialog box.

► Skills Review

1. Insert a graphic.
  a. Start Word.
  b. Open the document named WD H-2 and save it as "Theatre Graphics".
  c. Place the insertion point at the beginning of the document.
  d. Click Insert, click Picture, then click Clip Art.
  e. In the Screen Bean category, select the graphic that looks like someone scratching his head, then click Insert.

2. Modify a graphic.
  a. Select the graphic and drag individual sizing handles until it is .75" wide and 1.25" tall.
  b. Click the Line Style button on the Picture toolbar, then select a 1 ½ pt line.
  c. Click the Format Picture button on the Picture toolbar.
  d. Click the Wrapping tab, click the Tight option, then Wrap to the Right option.
  e. In the Distance form text area, click the down arrow until 0" is shown in the Right box.
  f. Click the Color and Lines tab, click the Fill Color list arrow, select Lavender.
  g. Click OK.
  h. Position the graphic to the left of the bulleted list under the heading Still Can't Decide?

3. Create a custom graphic using AutoShapes.
  a. Click the Drawing button to display the drawing toolbar, if necessary, click Rectangle tool, and on the blank area of the document (if needed, create a blank page), draw a square by holding down [Shift] as you draw. The square should be about two inches on each side.
  b. Click the Fill Color list arrow and select a dark blue color.
  c. Click the Oval tool, and below the square, draw a circle by holding down [Shift] as you draw. The circle should be about two inches in diameter.
  d. Click the Fill Color list arrow and select a bright pink color.
  e. With the circle selected, drag it to place it over the square.
  f. Click AutoShapes on the Drawing toolbar, click Basic Shapes, then select the Diamond.
  g. Holding down [Shift] drag a diamond 2" by 2".
  h. Click the Fill Color list arrow and select a dark green color.
  i. Position the diamond over the circle.
  j. Click the Select Objects button and drag a rectangle around all three objects (if you cannot drag a rectangle around all of the objects, hold down [Shift] as you click each shape).
  k. Click Draw on the Drawing toolbar, then click Group.
  l. Hold down [Shift] and drag a corner sizing handle so that the graphic is about 1.5" on all sides.
  m. Double-click the graphic, click the Wrapping tab, click Tight, then click OK.
  n. Position the graphic to the left of the title.

4. Insert a Paint object.
  a. Place the insertion point near the middle of the page and click Insert on the menu bar, then click Object.
  b. Click the Create from File tab.
  c. Click the Browse button.
  d. Locate the student file called WD LOGO2, then click OK until you return to the document.
  e. Position the graphic to the left of the paragraph that is under the heading Othello, then size it attractively.
  f. Click the Text Wrapping button on the Picture toolbar, then click Tight.

5. Create a callout.

    a. Click the AutoShapes button on the Drawing toolbar, then click Callouts.

    b. Select Line Callout 3 (No Border), the third callout in the fourth row.

    c. Drag the callout down and to the right just under the shaded paragraph at the end of the document.

    d. Enter the text "Experience the classics in a modern setting!"

    e. Drag the sizing handles on the callout to fit just the text.

    f. Preview, save, and print the document, then close it.

▶ Independent Challenges

1. As the communications coordinator for the annual Students for Peace Conference, you are responsible for designing attractive note paper for the staff. Begin by creating a new document and save it as "Peace Paper". Use Figure H-26 as a guide for how the completed note paper should look.

To complete this independent challenge:

1. Draw a rounded-rectangle 1.5" high and about 7" wide. (Hint: Use the Rounded Rectangle AutoShape found under Basic Shapes.) Position the rectangle just below the top of the page. Fill the rectangle with the sky blue color.
2. Insert the Dove graphic in the Animals category.
3. Size the graphic and position it so that it fits in the left side of the rectangle.
4. Using the Lines Autoshape, draw a long line down the left edge of the page. Format the line so it is 6 pts thick. Apply the sky blue color to the line.
5. Draw two horizontal lines near the bottom of the vertical line. Apply the color yellow to both these lines. Format them so that they are 6 pts thick. Send the upper yellow line behind the other lines.
6. Select all three lines and group them. Copy the grouped shapes and paste the graphic near the right edge of the page.
7. Select the second group of lines, click the Rotate or Flip command on the Draw button, then click Flip Horizontal. Position the lines so that the vertical line is aligned with right edge of the rectangle.
8. Preview, save, and print the document, then close it.

FIGURE H-26

2. As marketing communications specialist for The Magic Shop, a chain of stores selling magic supplies and costumes, you have decided to create your business card. Begin by creating a new document and saving it as "Magic Card". Use Figure H-27 as a guide for how the completed card should look.

To complete this independent challenge:

1. Type the company name, your name, an address, and a phone number, each on a separate line.
2. Format the text in the font you wish. Size the name of the shop at 14 pt. Right-align all the text.
3. Insert the graphic that looks like a magic hat in the Entertainment category.
4. Size the graphic to be about 1" by 1".
5. Apply tight and wrap to the right text wrapping. (Hint: Use the Format Picture dialog box, not the toolbar.)
6. Position the graphic to the right of the text so that the magic wand extends over the store name slightly.
7. Create a border around the graphic and text using the Rectangle tool. Modify the Rectangle so that it has no fill and 3 pt double-lines.
8. Preview, save, and print the document, then close it.

FIGURE H-27

The Magic Shop
444 Moonlight Lane
Minneapolis, MN 55555
Steven Lee (612) 555-1234

3. As the marketing communications specialist at Sunset Travel, an international travel agency, you have been asked to design a new company logo that will adorn all company documents. You can begin your design using the Drawing toolbar. Create a new document and save it as "Sunset Logo". Use Figure H-28 as a guide for how the completed logo should look.

To complete this independent challenge:

1. Draw a rectangle 2" wide and 1" high.
2. Copy the rectangle and position it directly under the first shape.
3. Fill the bottom rectangle with the dark blue color.
4. Size the bottom rectangle so that it is only ¾" high. The top edge of the bottom rectangle should still be touching the bottom edge of the top rectangle.
5. Fill the top rectangle with the preset Late Sunset fill Effect. (Hint: Use the Gradient tab in the Fill Effects dialog box.)
6. Draw an oval about .5" across and fill it with the gold color.
7. Position the oval over the two rectangles.
8. Select the bottom rectangle and choose the Bring to Front option.
9. Group the three objects together.
10. Preview, save, and print the document, then close it.

FIGURE H-28

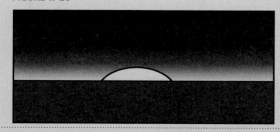

WEB WORK

4. As communications director of the City of Boston's tourism department, you have recently written the text for a flyer for city visitors. Now you would like to add graphics to make the document look more attractive. Open the document called WD H-3 and save it as "Boston Graphics".

To complete this independent challenge:

1. Insert the graphic line Neighborhood. Size the graphic so that it is the width of the text on the page, not including margins, and position it above the title.
2. Insert the champagne bottle graphic, size it so that it is about 1" by 1".
3. Adjust the text wrapping around this graphic to be tight and to the right.
4. Position the graphic next to the heading Night Life.
5. Log on to the Internet and use your browser to search for information about Boston. Search for museums in the Boston area and add at least one name to the bulleted list in your document. If you can't locate a Boston museum, use your browser to go to http://www.course.com. From there, click Student Online Companions, click the link for this textbook, then click the Word link for Unit H. Insert another graphic of your choice (preferably a graphic that reflects the name of a museum you've identified). Size the graphic so that it is about one inch on each side and position it near the bulleted list.
6. Preview, save, and print the document, then close it.

▶ Visual Workshop

Your work at the local state tourism office has taught you a great deal about what your state has to offer in the area of tourism and outdoor recreation. Every quarter you print a newsletter to promote exploration of your state. It's time to publish the Spring/Summer Issue. Use the draft document WD H-4 and save it as "Tourism Graphics". Figure H-29 serves as a guide for how your completed document should look. Use AutoShapes to create the triangle and sun graphics. You'll also insert the sailboat graphic from the transportation category.

FIGURE H-29

Spring/Summer Issue

EXPLORER

State Office of Tourism

Don't let summer pass you by without experiencing some of the special times only this season can bring. Set some time aside out of your busy schedule and give yourself a week or two to do some of these things you like to do best, or to explore someplace new. Plan a real vacation. Squeeze in a few long weekends of fun as well. It's never too early to make a few plans.

This issue or the Outdoor Explorer is full of ideas to help you on your way to a great vacation. For additional information to plan your trip or getaway. See the article on page 6 for details on the kinds of travel information services available in the north woods.

So put on those sandals, grab that oil, and kick back. Let the warmth of the summer sun melt away that tension and stress. Let this be one summer you'll never forget!

The first half of the newsletter features stories on what's new in the state, plus ideas on where to stay when you're traveling. On page 10 is a comprehensive, statewide Calendar of Events for April through August.

What's Inside

4   From Blues to Bach, the summer air swells to the sweet strains of music
6-7   Explore the lakes and woods of the local forests
8-9   Latest outdoor theater
9   Hit the garden highlights tour
10   Spring/Summer Calendar of Events

800-999-9999

In the local Metro Area

800-999-9000

From USA and Canada

For the most up to date info

Sharing
Information with Other Programs

Objectives

- ► **Understand linking and embedding objects**
- ► **Attach an Access data source**
- ► **Select records to merge**
- ► **Create a PowerPoint presentation from a Word outline**
- ► **Insert a PowerPoint object**
- ► **Insert an Excel object**
- ► **Modify an Excel object**
- ► **Send a fax**

Sometimes the information you want to include in a Word document is actually stored in a file that was created in another Office 97 program. For example, a list of names to whom you want to send a form letter might already exist in an Access database. Or perhaps you want your financial summary document to include financial information that has already been entered in an Excel spreadsheet. Most Office 97 programs can include information created in other programs from within the Word program, and without retyping information that already exists in other files. This ability to share information with other programs is called Object Linking and Embedding (or simply "OLE"). Angela wants to create a proposal to combine the many publications produced at Nomad Ltd into a single document. She will save time and effort by taking advantage of OLE features to include information already created by others at Nomad Ltd.

Understanding Linking and Embedding Objects

There are a variety of ways you can use information that is stored in files created in other Office 97 programs. In addition, Microsoft Office programs have the ability to convert information into a format that you can use in Word. For example, you can use the OfficeLinks button on the Database toolbar in Access to transfer database information to another Microsoft Office program, such as Excel. In addition, the Send to command on the File menu in each program displays a list of programs to which you can convert your data. The method you choose depends on what you want to accomplish and the programs you have installed on your computer. Figure I-1 illustrates some of your options. Angela is working on a presentation in which she proposes to combine different publications produced at Nomad Ltd. She wants to use information and features in other programs in her documents.

 You can copy and paste information from another program into a Word document
If the information you want to include in your document is not being continually edited and does not need to be kept up to date, you can open the other program, open the file you want, and copy the information to the clipboard. You can then return to the Word document and paste in the contents of the clipboard. The information becomes part of the Word document, and you can use Word commands to edit the information. For example, spreadsheet information you copy and paste into a Word document appears as a Word table, which you can edit using table commands and features. Any changes you make to this information in your document are not reflected in the original file. If you want to create a connection between files using the copy and paste method, you can use the Paste Link command on the Edit menu when you first paste the information in your document.

 You can insert information as an object from another program
An **object** is any information (such as text, graphics, database information, spreadsheet data, or a presentation slide) created in another program. When you insert an object (not copy it), you can edit the object using the original program's commands and features from within the Word program window. For example, if you insert Excel spreadsheet information as an object, the Excel program window appears, and you can edit the data using Excel commands and features without ever leaving Word. Using this method can significantly increase the size of your document, so don't use it if you are short of disk space.

 You can link information from another program
Similar to inserting an object, creating a link provides the added ability to automatically update the object each time you open the document with the object in it. Use this method when information in another file is maintained separately, and you want to ensure that the object in your document reflects the latest changes. You can also edit the object in its original program (provided that the original file is not already open by another user), and your changes will also be reflected in the original file. Use this method when you are inserting files that are maintained by others.

You can create a hyperlink to other files
Creating a hyperlink gives an online reader of your document the ability to view the contents of another file (even one created in another program) without leaving the Word document. With a hyperlink connection between your document and the file, you can view the file by clicking the hyperlink icon in the document. Neither you nor the reader can edit the information directly from the Word document, but you can view the information. Use this method to give the reader quick access to another file without actually storing the information in your Word document. In addition, your reader can open this other file without knowing the file name or where the file is stored on the computer.

FIGURE I-1: Sharing information with other programs

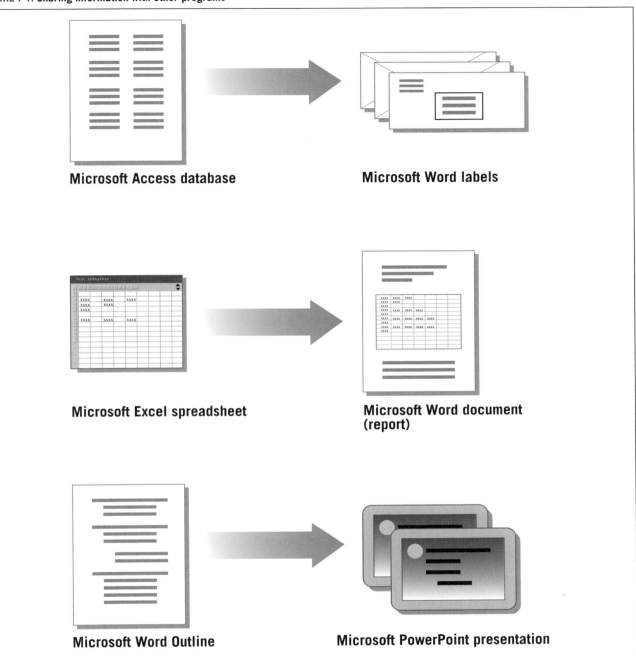

Microsoft Access database   Microsoft Word labels

Microsoft Excel spreadsheet   Microsoft Word document (report)

Microsoft Word Outline   Microsoft PowerPoint presentation

CLUES TO USE

Understanding the difference between linking and embedding

When you insert a link to another Office program, Word creates a **dynamic data exchange** (DDE) link with a file created in another program. When new information becomes available in a linked document, the object you inserted is updated to reflect the new information when you open or save the document. You can also update the linked object, by clicking the object and pressing [F9]. An embedded object is not updated if the original file is changed. You can, however, edit an embedded object by double-clicking it.

Attaching an Access Data Source

The Mail Merge feature in Word is a great way to create mailing labels for many individuals at one time. When you create a labels main document, you also attach it to a data source that contains the name and address information for each recipient. If you don't wish to create a new data source in Word, you can use an existing file from another program as a data source. For example, if a mailing list that is being maintained in Access already contains the name and address information you want to use, you can specify the Access database as your data source. ✏️ Angela plans to send the draft presentation to all of the department heads at Nomad Ltd. Because the name and internal mailing address information for the department heads is already stored in an Access database, Angela uses this file as the data source.

Steps 1 2 3 4

1. **Start Word**

2. **Click Tools on the menu bar, then click Mail Merge**
   The Mail Merge Helper dialog box opens. Now create a main document for the mailing labels.

3. **Click Create, click Mailing Labels, then click Active Window**
   A temporary name for the main document appears in the Mail Merge Helper dialog box. Next, specify the data source that has already been created in Access.

4. **Click Get Data, click Open Data Source, click the Files of type list arrow, then click MS Access Databases**
   Access database files appear in the dialog box. Choose the name of the file you want to use.

5. **Click WD I-1, then click Open**
   After a moment, you see a Microsoft Access dialog box that shows the names of the tables available in the database, as shown in Figure I-2. Database information is usually stored in tables within a database. You need to specify the table that contains the data you want to use.

6. **Click the Tables tab (if it is not already displayed in the dialog box), click Department Heads, then click OK**
   A message in the status bar indicates that a DDE link with Microsoft Access is being created. In the next dialog box, indicate that you want to set up the main document. Depending on your computer, this step could take a few minutes.

7. **Click Set Up Main Document**
   The Label Options dialog box appears. In this dialog box, you need to select the appropriate type of label. The default brand name Avery Standard appears in the Label Products box. You need to select the product number for the label.

8. **In the Product number box, scroll to and click 5161 - Address, then click OK**
   The Create Labels dialog box opens. In this dialog box, you can enter the field names for the labels.

9. **Click Insert Merge Field, click First_Name, press [Spacebar], then continue entering the remaining merge fields, as shown in Figure I-3**
   Note that nonprinting characters (spaces and paragraph marks) are not visible in the Sample Label box.

10. **Click OK to return to the Mail Merge Helper dialog box, as shown in Figure I-4**

FIGURE I-2: Tables in an Access database

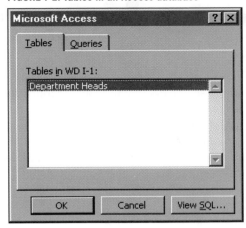

FIGURE I-3: Inserting merge fields in a label

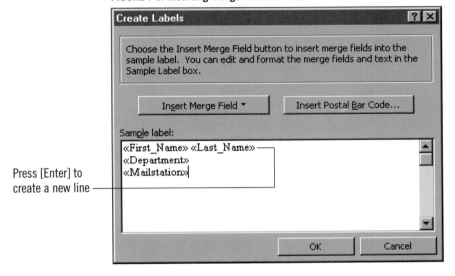

Press [Enter] to
create a new line

FIGURE I-4: Mail Merge Helper dialog box

Main document
with merge fields

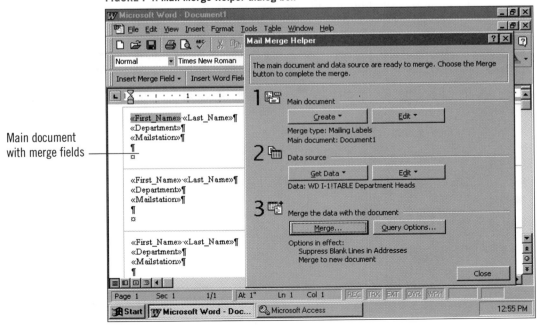

Selecting Records to Merge

Sometimes you do not want to send a document to all the individuals in a data source. With the Mail Merge Query Options feature, you can specify the criteria for choosing which records in a data source should be merged with a main document. When you use Query Options you can identify the fields and their contents that each record must match to be included in the merge. ✎ Angela does not need to send a document to herself, so she will specify criteria to exclude her name from this merge.

Steps

1. In the Mail Merge Helper dialog box, click Merge

The Merge dialog box opens. In this dialog box, indicate that you want to use Query Options to select records to merge.

2. Click Query Options

The Query Options dialog box opens. In this dialog box, describe the criteria to use when selecting records to merge.

3. In the Field column, click the Field list arrow and select Last name

This is the field that contains the data you want to evaluate when selecting records. Next, verify how the field should be evaluated.

4. In the Comparison column, click the Comparison list arrow and select Not equal to

This selection specifies that the contents of the Last Name field in a record must not match the contents you will specify.

5. In the Compare to column, type Pacheco

Your selection criterion appears in the column. Compare your dialog box to Figure I-5. You can specify additional selection criteria in the subsequent rows of the dialog box. You have completed specifying your selection criteria, so you can continue with the merge process.

6. Click OK, then click Merge

The selected records are merged to a new document. The labels are arranged in a Word table. Each label appears in separate cells, which are divided by gray (nonprinting) gridlines. Notice that all the department heads (except Angela) have labels. You have finished merging documents for now. Compare the merged label document to Figure I-6.

7. Click the Save button 🖫 on the Standard toolbar in the File name box, type Proposal Merge, click Save, click the Print button 🖨, then click the Close button ✖ in the document window

After you close the Proposal Merge document, the main document appears in the document window.

8. Click 🖫, in the File name box, type Proposal Main, click Save, then click ✖ in the document window

FIGURE I-5: Query Options dialog box

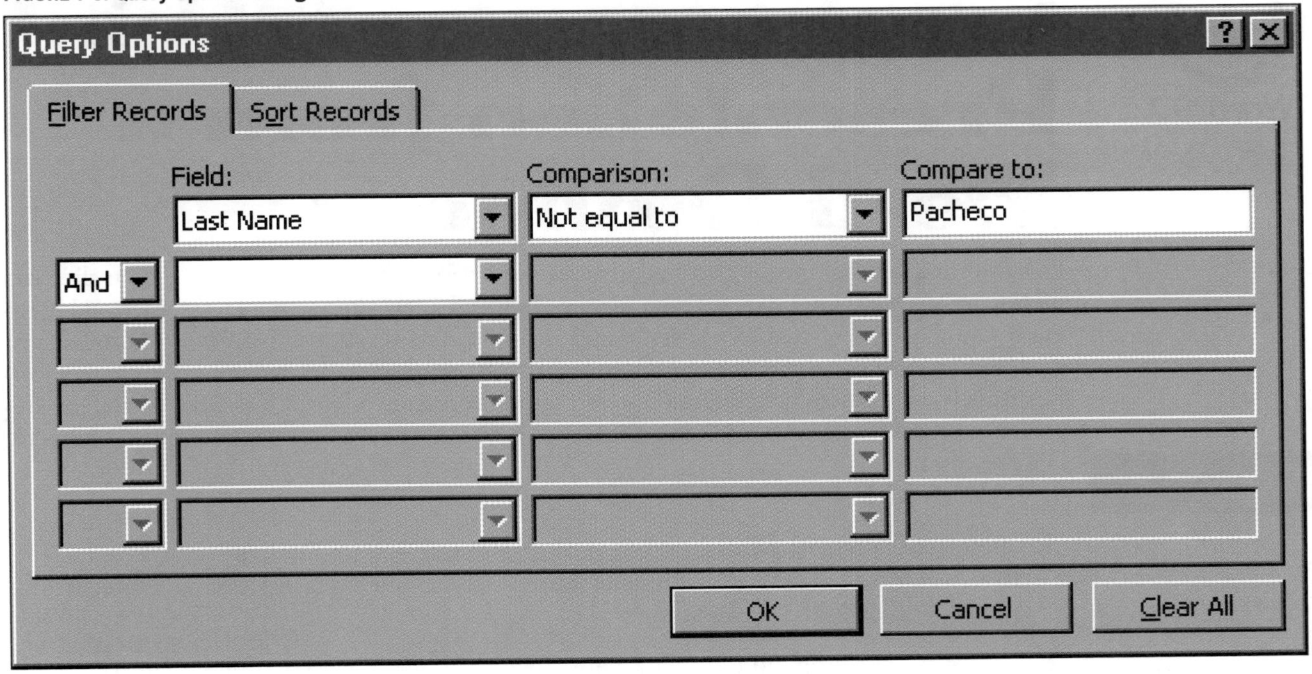

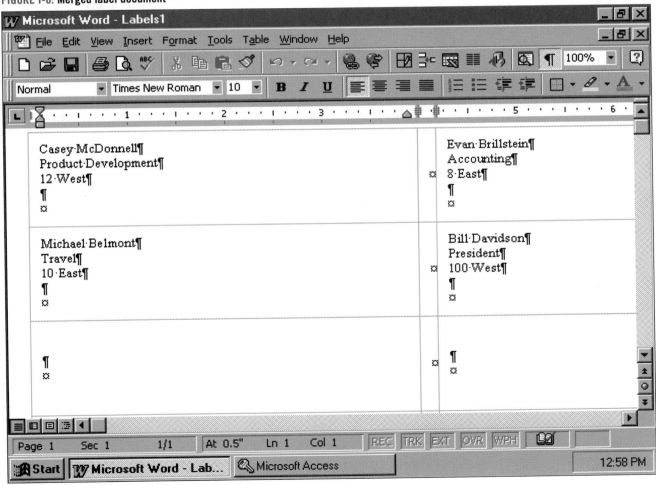

FIGURE I-6: Merged label document

Creating a PowerPoint Presentation from a Word Outline

PowerPoint is a program for creating attractive slides for presentations. Because each slide can display only several lines of text (such as a heading and a few supporting ideas), each slide generally contains text related to a specific idea or topic. As a result, using a Word outline can be great way to start creating a PowerPoint presentation. 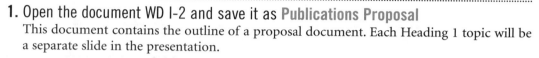 At an upcoming company meeting, Angela will present her proposal for combining company publications. She has already created an outline for her proposal document, but now she wants to use the outline as a basis for her presentation.

1. **Open the document WD I-2 and save it as Publications Proposal**
   This document contains the outline of a proposal document. Each Heading 1 topic will be a separate slide in the presentation.

2. **Click File on the menu bar, click Send To, then click Microsoft PowerPoint**
   After a moment the outline document appears in the PowerPoint program window, as shown in Figure I-7. In this window, you can edit text and modify the appearance of the slide presentation. Begin by creating a new slide.

3. **With the insertion point at the top of the presentation, next to the first slide icon, type Nomad Ltd Integrated Product Catalog and Magazine**
   Notice that the text appears in the Color window. You can also change the formatting of the slide presentation.

4. **On the Common Tasks toolbar in the program window, click Apply Design**
   The Apply Design dialog box appears, as shown in Figure I-8. In this dialog box you can select and preview different color and formatting schemes for a slide presentation.

5. **Scroll through the list of designs, click Professional, then click Apply**
   The Color window displays a thumbnail picture of the first slide. You can also change the format of an individual slide.

6. **On the Common Tasks toolbar, click Slide Layout**
   The Slide Layout dialog box appears. In this dialog box, you can change the layout of the selected slide.

7. **Click the first slide in the first row, then click Apply**
   The title layout is applied to the first slide. With the presentation complete, you can view all the slides at once.

8. **Click the Slide Sorter View button on the horizontal scroll bar**
   All the slides appear in the program window, as shown in Figure I-9. With the presentation complete, save your changes.

9. **Click the Save button 💾 on the Standard toolbar, in the File name box type Proposal, then click Save**

FIGURE I-7: **PowerPoint program window**

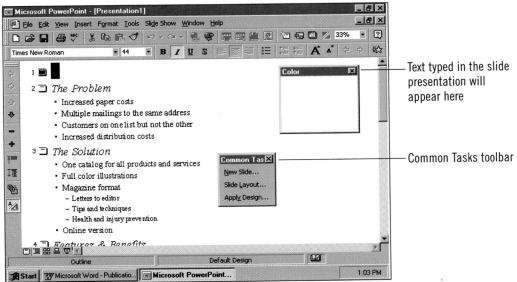

Text typed in the slide presentation will appear here

Common Tasks toolbar

FIGURE I-8: **Apply Design dialog box**

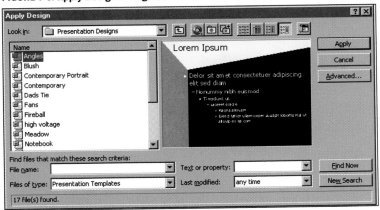

FIGURE I-9: **All slides in the program window**

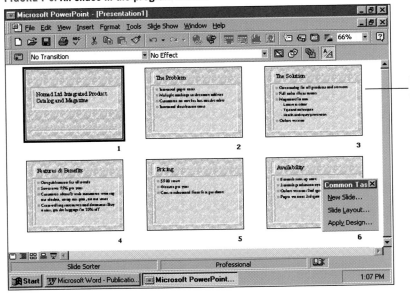

Depending on the resolution of your monitor and your printer, the arrangement of slides on your computer may be different

Inserting a PowerPoint Object

To insert the text of a PowerPoint presentation in a Word document, you use the Send to command in the PowerPoint program window. In PowerPoint this command gives you the option of specifying how you want the slides and accompanying lecture notes to be laid out in your document. Once the presentation is in a Word document, you can use the familiar editing and formatting tools you already know in Word. 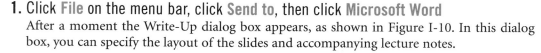 Angela would like to add text to the presentation. Because Angela is not as comfortable using PowerPoint as she is using Word, she will convert her slides to a Word document and write her lecture notes using Word.

1. **Click File on the menu bar, click Send to, then click Microsoft Word**
   After a moment the Write-Up dialog box appears, as shown in Figure I-10. In this dialog box, you can specify the layout of the slides and accompanying lecture notes.

2. **Be sure the Notes next to slides option button is selected**
   You can create a link between the Word document you are about to create and the original slide presentation file.

3. **Click the Paste link option button, then click OK**
   This option creates a link so that the lecture notes you create in Word are also stored as lecture notes in the presentation file. After a moment, the presentation appears as a table in a new Word document, as shown in Figure I-11. The blank column is where you can type the lecture notes next to each slide.

4. **Press [Ctrl][Home] to move to the top of the document**

5. **Place the insertion point in the cell to the right of the second slide, then type After several years of moderately increasing prices, the cost of paper has skyrocketed by 67% in the last year. There have been smaller, yet significant increases in labor, fleet maintenance and fuel costs. Press [Enter]**
   You can save your lecture notes document.

6. **Click the Save button 🖫 on the Standard toolbar**

7. **In the File name box, type Proposal Lecture Notes, then click Save**
   Your document is saved. Compare your document to Figure I-12. Because you no longer need to use PowerPoint, you can close the PowerPoint program window.

8. **Right-click the Microsoft PowerPoint button in the task bar of your desktop, click Close on the pop-up menu, then click Yes to save the changes to the presentation**
   The PowerPoint program window closes.

QuickTip

You can also choose to display blank lines instead of lecture notes so that you can use the printed document as a handout for the audience.

Trouble?

PowerPoint presentations that you send to Word documents create very large files that do not fit on a floppy disk. If you are saving your work on a floppy disk you will not be able to complete steps 6 and 7. Click the Print button and proceed with step 8.

Inserting a presentation with the Object command on the Insert menu

If you click Insert on the menu bar, then click Object to insert a PowerPoint object in your document, only the first slide is inserted as a graphic in your document. Use this feature when you wish to create a cover page for a document and would like to use the first slide from a PowerPoint presentation as a graphic. You can use the Object command on the Insert menu, click the Create from File tab, and specify the name of the presentation you want to use.

FIGURE I-10: Write-Up dialog box

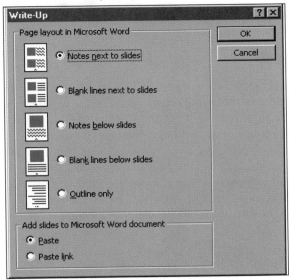

FIGURE I-11: Presentation in Word document

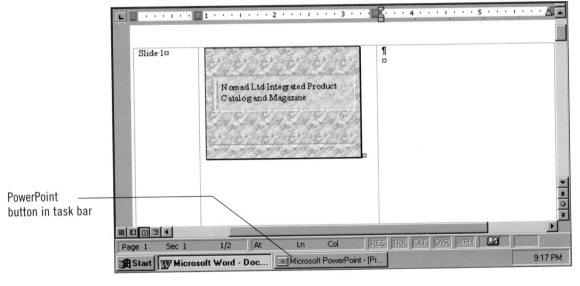

PowerPoint button in task bar

FIGURE I-12: Lecture notes in document

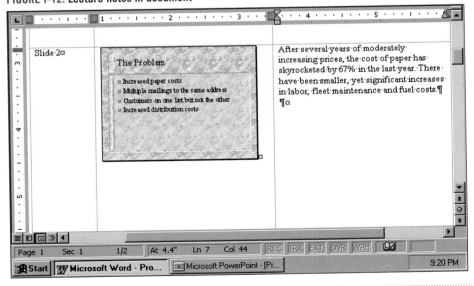

Inserting an Excel Object

Although tables in Word provide basic mathematical operations suitable for simple calculations, Excel is a full-featured **spreadsheet** program, for performing sophisticated numerical analysis. Data entry features and extensive built-in calculations and functions make working with numerical information fast and easy. If the data you want to include in a Word document is already stored in an Excel file, you can insert the spreadsheet. If this file is continuously updated to reflect new information, you can create a link to the file so that the spreadsheet in your document is always up to date. ➤ Nomad Ltd's accounting department stores the cost of the catalog and other publications the company sends to its customers in an Excel spreadsheet. Angela will create a link to this information in her presentation document. First, she makes room in the table for the spreadsheet.

Steps 1 2 3 4

1. **Select the third row of cells in the table, click the Insert Rows button ▤ on the Standard toolbar, click Table on the menu bar, then click Merge cells**
   The spreadsheet you insert will appear at the insertion point in this part of the document.

2. **Click Insert on the menu bar, then click Object**
   The Object dialog box opens. In this dialog box you can create a new object in another program (on the Create New tab). You can also insert an existing object from another file that was created in another program.

3. **Click the Create from File tab, then click Browse**
   When you click the Browse button you can locate and select the file you want to insert. To make it easier to identify the file you want, you can specify the file extension for Excel spreadsheet files.

4. **In the File name box, type *.xls, then press [Enter]**
   The asterisk (*) is called a wildcard. It represents the first part of the file name. "xls" is the file extension for Excel spreadsheet files. The names of the Excel files you can insert appear in the Browse dialog box.

5. **Click WD I-3, then click OK**
   You return to the Create from File tab in the Object dialog box, as shown in Figure I-13. With the file name specified, you can indicate how you want the file inserted in the document.

6. **Click the Link to file checkbox, then clear the Float over text checkbox**
   Clicking Link to file ensures that the spreadsheet in the document is automatically updated every time you open the document. Any changes that were made to the spreadsheet since the last time you opened the document are reflected in the spreadsheet inside the document. Clearing the Float over text checkbox ensures the spreadsheet is inserted in the table as a text object that you can format, rather than a graphic object.

7. **Click OK**
   After a moment, the spreadsheet appears in the file, as shown in Figure I-14.

8. **Click the Save button ▤ on the Standard toolbar**

Trouble?

If you are saving your work on floppy disk, you will not be able to complete step 8. Click the Print button and proceed to the next lesson.

FIGURE I-13: **Create from File tab in the Object dialog box**

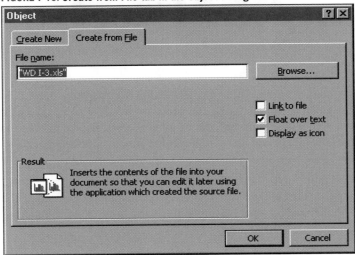

FIGURE I-14: **Spreadsheet object inserted in a document**

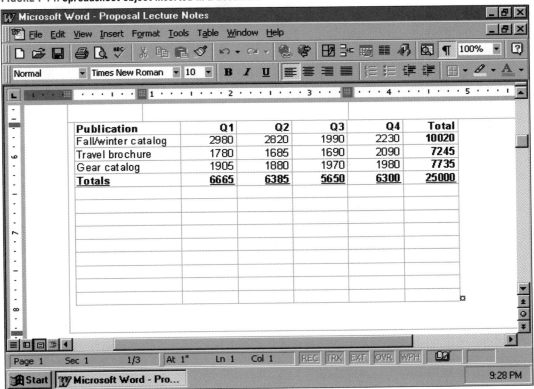

TABLE I-1: **Object options**

option	description
Link to file	Creates a DDE link to the file so that whenever you open or save this document, the object you inserted is updated to reflect the latest changes. Clearing this option simply inserts the object without linking it.
Float over text	Inserts the object such that you can position it in the same way you position a graphic. For example, you can drag the object anywhere in the document and can apply text flow formatting around the object. Clearing this option inserts the object such that you can apply alignment and other types of paragraph formatting to the object.
Display as icon	Inserts an icon that represents the object. Double-clicking the icon opens the object.

Modifying an Excel Object

After inserting an object in a document, you can edit the object inside the Word document. By double-clicking the object, you can open the object's original program window and make your changes. If you have linked the object in your document, the original file will also be updated to reflect your changes. ✐ Angela wants to add an item that is missing from the spreadsheet.

1. **Double-click the spreadsheet object in the document**
   The Excel program window opens from within Word, as shown in Figure I-15. So that the original student file remains unchanged by your editing and to have your changes reflected in a new file, save the spreadsheet with a new name.

2. **Click File on the Excel menu bar, then click Save As, in the File name box, type Publication Costs, then click Save**
   With the spreadsheet saved to a new file, you need to establish a link to the new file you just saved.

3. **Click in the Word document, and with the linked object still selected, click Edit on the menu bar, click Links, click Change Source, double-click Publication Costs, then click OK**
   The Word document is linked to the new file. You can now take advantage of the data editing and formatting features available in Excel. You can edit the data and change the appearance of the spreadsheet object. For example, you can add another row to the spreadsheet.

4. **Double-click the spreadsheet object, select the second row in the spreadsheet, then click Insert on the menu bar and click Rows**
   A new row appears in the spreadsheet. You can enter data for the new row.

5. **Select the first cell in the new row, then type Spring/summer, press [Tab] to move to the next cell, then type the following, pressing [Tab] after each entry as indicated:**
   2820   [Tab]   3035   [Tab]   2690   [Tab]   2990   [Tab]
   You can calculate the total for this row.

6. **With the insertion point in the last column, click the AutoSum button Σ on the Standard toolbar, then press [Enter]**
   When you click the AutoSum button, the values to be added to compute a total are highlighted. When you press Enter, you accept the values in this highlighted area and Excel supplies the correct value in the cell. Compare your spreadsheet to Figure I-16. Now you can change the formatting of the data.

7. **Select all the rows in the spreadsheet, click the Currency Style button $ on the Formatting toolbar, then click the Bold button twice B on the Formatting toolbar**

8. **Right-click the Microsoft Excel button in the task bar of your desktop, click Close on the pop-up menu, then click Yes to save the changes**
   The Excel program closes.

9. **Click anywhere outside of the spreadsheet object, click the Save button 🖫 on the Standard toolbar, then click the Print button 🖨 on the Standard toolbar**
   Clicking outside of the object closes the object's original program and returns you to your Word document in the Word program. Compare your spreadsheet to Figure I-17. Clicking Save saves your changes in both the document and in the Excel file, Publication Costs.

Trouble?
If you are saving your work on a floppy disk, you will not be able to complete step 9. Click the Print button and proceed to the next lesson.

FIGURE I-15: Excel program window

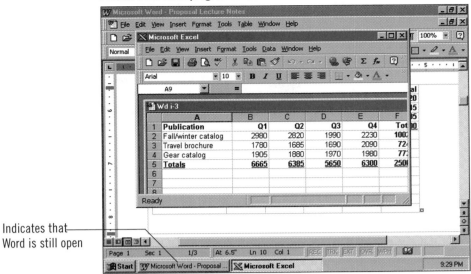

Indicates that
Word is still open

FIGURE I-16: New row in spreadsheet

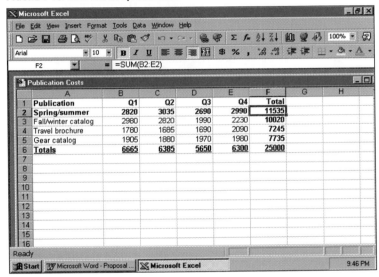

FIGURE I-17: Updated spreadsheet object

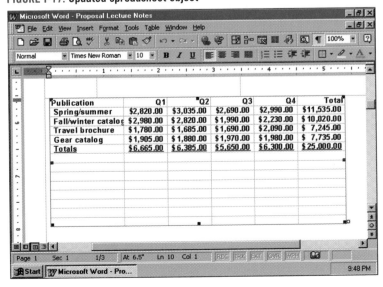

Sending a Fax

Instead of sending paper documents using mail or courier services, you can send a fax. A **fax** is an electronic image of a document that is transmitted over the telephone. Even if you do not have a fax machine, you can still send a fax over the telephone using a modem and fax software on your computer. Word includes a Fax Wizard, which helps guide you through the process of creating the fax cover page and sending the fax. Angela would like to send a draft of her outline to a colleague in the product development department. She will use the Fax Wizard to get started.

Steps 1234

1. **Click File on the menu bar, click Send to, then click Fax Recipient**
   The Fax Wizard starts, as shown in Figure I-18. After you respond to the prompts on each Fax Wizard dialog box, click Next to continue. The icons on the left side of the page indicate your progress as you move through the Wizard.

2. **Click Next to display the next Fax Wizard dialog box, then verify that the current document name appears in the box and that the With a cover sheet option button is selected, then click Next**
   In the next dialog box you identify the fax software you wish to use. In this case, indicate that you want to print this document.

3. **Click the last option button in the dialog box, then click Next**
   If you had your own computer with its own modem and were sending a real fax to a real fax recipient, you would choose the first option button. In the next Fax Wizard dialog box, you identify the name and fax number of the recipient of your fax.

4. **Place the insertion point in the first box, type Casey McDonnell, press [Tab], type 818-282-0990, then click Next**
   On the next Fax Wizard dialog box, choose the style you want for the fax cover sheet.

5. **Click the Professional option button (if it is not already selected), then click Next**
   On the next Fax Wizard dialog box, you can identify yourself as the sender of the fax.

6. **Complete the page as follows, then click Next to continue**

In this box	Type
Name	Angela Pacheco
Company	Nomad Limited
Phone	818-282-2282
Fax	818-282-2323

7. **On the final Fax Wizard dialog box, click Finish to complete the fax**
   The fax cover page appears in a new document window.

8. **Click each of the areas indicated at the top of the cover page and type the text shown in Figure I-19**
   You have finished editing the fax cover page, so you can save the cover page document.

Time To

✓ Print
✓ Close all documents
✓ Exit Word

9. **Click the Save button 🖫 on the Standard toolbar, in the File name box, type Fax Cover for Proposal, then click Save**

FIGURE I-18: Fax Wizard dialog box

FIGURE I-19: Completed fax cover page

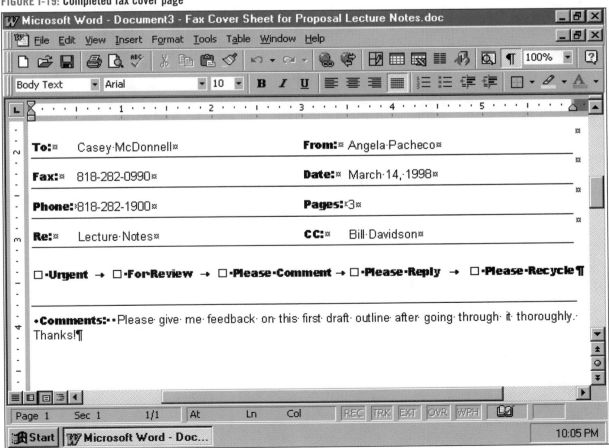

Practice

► Concepts Review

Label each of the elements of the Object dialog box in Figure I-20.

FIGURE I-20

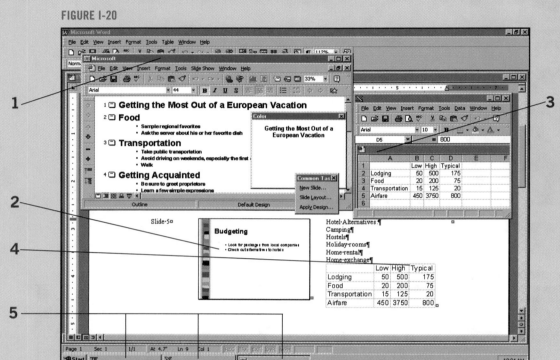

Match each of the following terms with the statement that best describes it.

6. OLE
7. PowerPoint
8. Excel
9. Access
10. Link

a. Updates the inserted object each time you open the document
b. Program in which you can create slide presentations
c. Program in which you can store and manage information in a database
d. Provides the ability to insert information from another file created in another program
e. Spreadsheet program for performing numerical analysis

Select the best answer from the list of choices.

11. **If you want to use information from another program, which statement best describes this capability in Word?**
   a. Copying and pasting information from the other file is the only way to accomplish this.
   b. You can insert objects created in other programs or create new objects from within Word.
   c. You must retype the information you want to use in your document.
   d. You must coordinate your efforts with others if you want to ensure the information you insert is up to date.

12. **What is a fax?**
   a. A paper version of a document sent by U.S. Mail or by courier
   b. An outline of a document
   c. An electronic image of a document that is transmitted over the telephone
   d. A spreadsheet object

13. **In Excel you can**
    a. Edit data and change the appearance of a spreadsheet object.
    b. Create a Word outline.
    c. Create a mail merge document.
    d. Create a PowerPoint presentation.

14. **What is true about the Mail Merge feature?**
    a. There is only one type of label you can use.
    b. You can create many mailing labels at one time.
    c. You cannot use a file from another program as a data source.
    d. You must re-create the data source each time you merge.

15. **Presentation slides in PowerPoint**
    a. Can display as many lines of text as you choose.
    b. Cannot be edited nor their appearance modified.
    c. Contain text related to a specific idea or topic.
    d. Contain labels with names and addresses.

16. **Which program features a spreadsheet program?**
    a. Access
    b. PowerPoint
    c. Mail Merge Query Options
    d. Excel

17. **Which of the following groups represent objects you can insert?**
    a. A link, an icon, and a hyperlink
    b. Text, spreadsheets, graphics, and database information
    c. Labels, mail merge, and address information
    d. Commands, features, and dialog boxes

18. **What best describes a Fax Wizard?**
    a. A Fax Wizard guides a user through the process of sending a fax.
    b. A Fax Wizard transmits a fax cover page.
    c. A Fax Wizard uses one kind of software.
    d. A Fax Wizard has no option for printing a document.

▶ Skills Review

1. **Attach an Access data source.**
   a. Start Word.
   b. Click Tools on the menu bar, then click Mail Merge.
   c. Click Create, click Mailing Labels, then click Active Window.
   d. Click Get Data, click Open Data Source, click the Files of type list arrow, then click MS Access Databases.
   e. Click WD I-4, then click Open.
   f. Click the Tables tab (if it is not already displayed in the dialog box), click "Attendees", then click OK.
   g. Click Set Up Main Document.
   h. In the Product number box, scroll to and click "5161 - Address", then click OK.
   i. Click Insert Merge Field, click Prefix, press [Spacebar], then continue entering the remaining merge fields so that the name information appears on the first line, the address appears on the second line, and the city, state, and zip code appear on the third line. Remember to put a comma after the city.
   j. Click OK to return to the Mail Merge Helper dialog box.

2. **Select records to merge.**
   a. In the Mail Merge Helper, click Merge.
   b. Click Query Options.
   c. In the Field column, click the fields list arrow and select State.
   d. In the Comparison column, click the Comparison list arrow and select Not equal to in the first box.
   e. In the Compare to column, type "CA".
   f. Click OK.
   g. Click Merge. Notice that no attendees from California are listed among the five labels.
   h. Click the Save button and save the merged labels document with the name "No CA Labels". Print and close the merged labels document.
   i. Click the Save button and save the main document with the name "Telecommuting Main". Close the document after you save it.

3. **Create a PowerPoint presentation from a Word outline.**
   a. Open the document WD I-5 and save it as "Telecommuting Lecture".
   b. Click File menu bar, click Send to, then click Microsoft PowerPoint.
   c. With the insertion point at the top of the presentation, next to the first blank slide icon, type "Getting Telecommuting to Work".
   d. On the Common Tasks toolbar in the program window, click Apply Design.
   e. Scroll through the list of designs, clicking the different designs available to preview them in the dialog box, click Professional, then click Apply.
   f. On the Common Tasks toolbar in the program window, click Slide Layout.
   g. Click the first slide in the first row, then click Apply.
   h. Click the Slide Sorter View button on the horizontal scroll bar.
   i. Click the Save button, in the File name box, type "Telecommuting Slides", then click Save.

4. **Insert a PowerPoint object in Word.**
   a. Click File menu bar, click Send to, then click Microsoft Word.
   b. Be sure the Notes next to slides option button is selected.
   c. Click the Paste link option button, then click OK.
   d. Scroll near the top of the document, place the insertion point in the cell to the right of the second slide, then type "Depending on circumstances workers value flexibility and choice over modest salary increases."
   e. Click the Save button on the Standard toolbar, if you are not saving on a floppy disk.
   f. In the File name box, type "Telecommuting Lecture Notes", then click Save.
   g. Right-click the PowerPoint button in the task bar of your desktop, then click Close on the pop-up menu.

5. **Insert an Excel object.**
   a. Scroll the outline and place the insertion point in the column to the right of the "Telecommuting Costs" slide.
   b. Click Insert on the menu bar, then click Object.
   c. Click the Create from File tab, then click Browse.
   d. In the File name box, type "*.xls", then press [Enter].
   e. Click WD I-6, then click OK.
   f. Click Link to file checkbox, then clear the Float over text checkbox.
   g. Click OK.
   h. Click the Save button on the Standard toolbar, if you are not saving on a floppy disk.

6. **Modify an Excel object.**

   a. Double-click the spreadsheet object in the document.

   b. Click File on the menu bar, then click Save As, in the File name box, type "Telecommuting Costs", then click Save.

   c. Click the Word document, and with the linked object still selected, click Edit on the menu bar, click Links, click Change Source, double-click "Telecommuting Costs", then click OK.

   d. Double-click the Excel object, select the row labeled "Phone" in the spreadsheet, click Insert on the menu bar, then click Rows.

   e. Select the first cell in the new row, then type "Internet".

   f. Press [Tab] to move to the next cell, then type the following:

   0   [Tab]   20

   g. Select the cells in the spreadsheet.

   h. Click the Currency style button on the Formatting toolbar.

   i. Click the Word document outside of the spreadsheet object.

   j. Click the Save button on the Standard toolbar, if you are not saving on a floppy disk.

   k. Click the Print button on the Standard toolbar.

   l. Right-click the Microsoft Excel button on the task bar, then click Close and save your changes.

7. **Send a fax.**

   a. Click File on the menu bar, click Send To, then click Fax Recipient.

   b. Click Next, then verify that the current document name appears in the box and that the With the cover sheet option button is selected, then click Next.

   c. Click the last option button in the dialog box, then click Next.

   d. Place the insertion point in the first box, type "Alexa Mikapolis", press [Tab], type "213-290-1220", then click Next.

   e. Click the Professional option button (if it is not already selected), then click Next.

   f. On the next Fax Wizard dialog box, identify yourself as the sender of the fax.

   g. Complete the dialog box as follows, then click Next to continue.

In this box	Type
Company	Nomad Limited
Phone	214-370-1880
Fax	214-370-1881

   h. On the final Fax Wizard dialog box, click Finish to complete the fax.

   i. Click each of the areas indicated at the top of the cover page and type appropriate business related text.

   j. Click the Save button on the Standard toolbar, in the File name box type "Telecommuting Fax Cover", then click Save.

   k. Print the document, close all the documents, then exit Word.

▶ Independent Challenges

1. As the marketing coordinator for Going Wild, a wildflower seed company, you would like to offer a promotion for your customers living in milder climates. Because the company already maintains a list of customer names and addresses, you decide to save time by creating mailing labels using this database as your mail merge data source.

To complete this independent challenge:

1. In Word, open the Mail Merge Helper by clicking Mail Merge on the Tools menu.

2. Create a new main mailing labels document based on the active window.

3. Get an existing data source, called WD I-7. In the Access dialog box, specify that you want to use the table called Customers.

4. Set up the labels main document by inserting name and address merge fields in the Create Labels dialog box. Place the company name on the first line, the name fields on the second line, address fields on the third line, and the remaining fields on the fourth line. Be sure to include proper spacing and punctuation between fields.

5. When you return to Mail Merge Helper, click the Query Options button in the dialog box, and specify that you want to exclude records where the State field contains "MN".

6. Merge the records and save the merge labels with the file name "Mild Climate Seeds".

7. Print the labels. There should be 4 labels.

8. Close all open files, saving the main document with the name "Seeds Main".

2. As a motivational speaker and representative for a local health care center, you've been asked to speak at a health fair. The event coordinator would like to see an outline of your remarks. To make a good impression, you've decided to supply a complete slide presentation. You will use Word to type the text of the presentation, and then convert the Word document to a PowerPoint presentation.

To complete this independent challenge:

FIGURE I-21

1. Open a new Word document and type the text shown in Figure I-21. Indent the supporting ideas and apply bullets to them as shown. Save your document with the name "Health Fair Outline".

2. Use the Send to command on the File menu to convert the document to a PowerPoint presentation.

3. In PowerPoint, select a presentation style of your choice. Save the presentation with the file name "Health Fair Slides".

4. Use the Send to command to convert the slides back to a Word document. Choose the first layout option so that the lecture notes appear next to each slide.

5. In the cell next to a slide of your choice, type any text that is related to the topics mentioned in the slide.

6. Save this document with the name "Health Fair Presentation" if you are not saving to a floppy disk.

7. Preview, print, save, and close your documents. Close the PowerPoint program.

Keys to Fitness
- Eating right
- Staying active
- Reducing stress

Eating Right
- Eat less fat
- Avoid salt and highly processed foods
- Enjoy fruits, vegetables, and grains

Staying Active
- Exercise daily
- Introduce extra steps
- Walk, bike, run, row
- Enjoy active play with friends and family

Reducing Stress
- Don't let work pile up
- Set and achieve small goals
- Stay "in the moment"
- Meditate, listen to music, develop spirituality
- Enjoy regular quiet times

3. As an accounting analyst for Valley Sports Center, you've been asked to provide a description of the Center's services to the chairman of the facilities board, accompanied by an up to date report of the revenues these services have generated in the last quarter. You've developed a draft document describing the services, but now you'd like to insert a spreadsheet already developed in Excel that contains the most recent revenue figures.

To complete this independent challenge:

1. Open the document called WD I-8 and save it with the name "Center Services".

2. Place the insertion point at the end of the document, then use the Object command on the Insert menu to insert the existing Excel file called WD I-9.

3. After you specify the file you want to insert, specify that you want to create a link to this Excel file and not float the object over text.

4. Save the spreadsheet with the name "Center Revenue".

5. Click the Word document, and with the linked object still selected, click Change the source object to be the new file, "Center Revenue".

6. Double-click the object, change the third quarter value for the "A la Carte" to 1250.

7. Select all the numeric values in the spreadsheet and format them with dollar signs.

8. When you return to your document, save your changes.

9. Create a professional-style fax cover page for your document, using names, phone numbers, and text of your own choosing.

10. Save the fax document with the name "Revenue Summary Fax".

11. Preview, print, save, and close your documents.

4. Your company, Green Press, is a publisher of gardening magazines. As the marketing coordinator, you've been asked to help prepare a proposal to introduce a new magazine for children, called Kids Garden. Another member of the marketing team has already drafted an outline that you will use to convert to a PowerPoint presentation. After finalizing the presentation, you will create a cover page for a fax so that you can send the proposal to your supervisor who is speaking at a home and garden show in another state.

To complete this independent challenge:

1. Open the document WD I-10 and save it with the name "Kids Garden Outline".

2. Convert the document to a PowerPoint presentation in any design you wish. Format the first slide as a title slide. Save the presentation as "Garden Slides".

3. Convert the presentation back to a Word document, such that you can add lecture notes to the right of each slide.

4. Use your Web browser to locate a website related to gardening and supply its address and a brief description in the lecture notes cell next to the CyberGardens topic. If you can't locate a related site, use your browser to go to http://www.course.com. From there, click Student Online Companions, click the link for this textbook, then click the Word link for Unit I.

5. In Word, add a new row under the Current Offerings slide, then merge the cells to create one wide cell in this row.

6. Create a link to the Excel file called WD I-11 next to the Current Offerings slide. Open the Excel object and save it as "Current Subscriptions". With the linked object still selected, click Change the source object to be the new file, "Current Subscriptions".

7. Select the values in the Total row and apply bold and currency formatting. Return to the Word document.

8. Save the document as "Garden Proposal".

9. Create a contemporary-style fax cover page, using whatever names and numbers you wish. Save the document as "Garden Fax".

10. Preview, print, save, and close your documents.

▶ Visual Workshop

After a recent speaking engagement on European vacations, you entered the names and addresses of individuals who gave you their business cards into an Access database. You would like to send all but your New York contacts an updated version of your presentation. For the individuals in New York, you decide to fax a copy of the presentation. Create mailing labels using WD I-13 as a data source, omitting any New York contacts. Save the labels as "No NY labels" and the main document as "Vacation Main". Create a new document with the headings and indentations shown in Figure I-22. Save your document with the name "Vacation Tips". Convert the outline to a slide presentation, and then convert the presentation back to a Word document so that you can add lecture notes in Word. Add any related text next to each slide. Next to the indicated slide, insert the Excel file named WD I-12. Save the spreadsheet with the name "Vacation Costs". Change the link to the new source file. Change a few values in the spreadsheet and save your changes. Save the Word document as "European Vacation Presentation". Create a contemporary fax cover page using any name and number you wish. Save the fax as "Vacation Fax". Note: The text in your slides might wrap differently than the slides in the figure.

FIGURE I-22

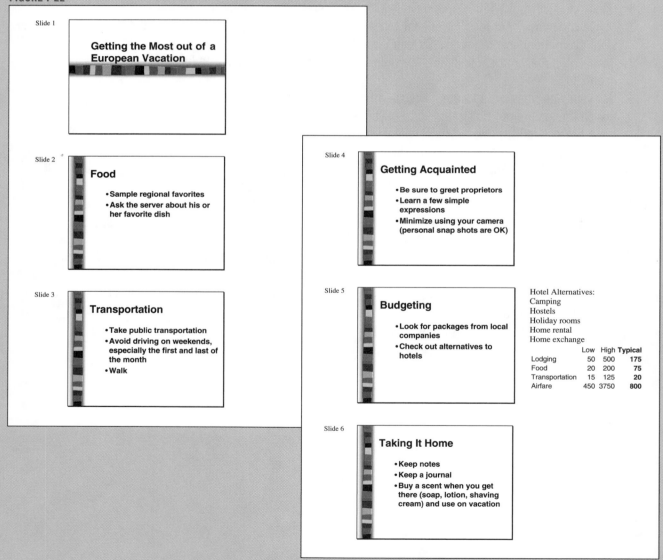

Creating
a Web Site with Word

Objectives

- ► **Plan a Web site**
- ► **Create a simple Web page with a wizard**
- ► **Create a form Web page**
- ► **Modify Web pages**
- ► **Convert a Word document to a Web page**
- ► **Add scrolling text to a Web page**
- ► **Add hyperlinks**
- ► **View a Web page online**

The Internet is a worldwide network of computers that serves as a vast warehouse of diverse information. In the same way a public library contains information from many sources, the Internet contains information from research facilities, libraries, museums, educational institutions, governments, and non-profit organizations. Increasingly, businesses use the Internet as a form of advertising. With thousands of people using the Internet every minute, Web pages are a convenient way to communicate to potential customers. By creating Web pages in Microsoft Word, you can create online documents that others can read over the Internet. As head of the marketing division at Nomad Ltd, Angela would like to reach new customers by creating a Web site for Nomad Ltd's products and services.

Planning a Web Site

A **Web page** is a document that is stored on the World Wide Web. You can view a Web page on your computer or you can download (copy) a Web page to your computer, so you can edit the page if you wish. A **Web site** is a collection of Web pages linked together with hyperlinks. Before you create Web pages, it is important to consider how you expect to use the site and what you want to accomplish. Depending on your purposes, you can use Word templates and wizards to help you create individual Web pages. Angela begins to design her Web site by evaluating her requirements and reviewing the process of creating a Web site.

Details

 Determine the purpose of the Web site.
You can use a Web site to accomplish a variety of objectives. For example, you could use the Web site to communicate information about a company, inform customers about products and services, obtain information from potential customers, or make sales.

 To make your Web site easy to use, create a new page for each specific objective.
For example, you can create a Web page that is mostly text to provide general information. You can create another page that is a form to gather information from customers online. See Figure J-1 for a conceptual view of the way pages relate to each other.

 Use the templates or wizards provided with the Word program to create Web pages for each objective.
If you installed Word with HTML features, you can choose from many standard Web pages.

 After creating a Web page, you save the Web page document.
Web pages are saved in a special language so that the document can be stored and read on the Internet. You will learn more about this language later in this unit.

 Specify the relationship between Web pages to link them.
With multiple pages in your Web site, you need to determine how a reader will progress from one page to another. When you create a **hyperlink** you connect one page to another. By clicking hyperlinks, a reader can jump from page to page. The first page, called the **home page**, serves as a table of contents page from which a reader can jump to most or all of the other pages.

 Post your Web pages on the World Wide Web by sending your files to an Internet service provider.

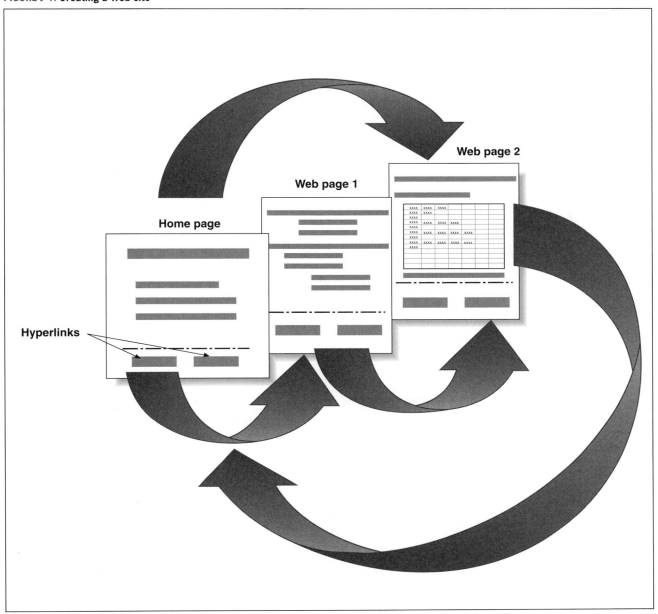

Word 97

Creating a Simple Web Page with a Wizard

The Web Page Wizard makes it easy to create your own Web pages. After you start the wizard you can choose the type of Web page you want to create. For example, you can create a Web page that you plan to use as a survey form, or a page that displays text in columns. You can also specify the visual style of the page that affects the page's layout and design.  Angela wants to create a simple Web page, so she will use the Web Page Wizard to get started.

QuickTip

The Web authoring tools must be installed on your computer to complete this unit.

Trouble?

Click No if you see a message about accessing the newest Web page authoring tools.

1. Start Word

2. Click File on the menu bar, click New, then click the Web Pages tab
The Web Pages tab in the New dialog box provides several ways to create a Web page. Using the Web wizard is a fast way to create a variety of Web pages for different purposes.

3. Double-click the Web Page Wizard icon
The first Web Page Wizard dialog box contains selections for the types of Web pages you can create.

4. In the first Web Page Wizard dialog box, click Simple Layout, if necessary
The Web page behind the dialog box appears in the Simple Layout format you selected, as shown in Figure J-2. After you make a selection you can continue using the wizard. In the next dialog box, you can choose the overall appearance of the Web page.

5. Click Next, then click Outdoors
Each style applies a consistent and cohesive set of colors, formatting, and backgrounds. After you make a selection, the wizard displays the sample page behind the dialog box in the visual style you selected. Next, complete the Web Page Wizard.

6. Click Finish
The completed page appears, as shown in Figure J-3. You can save your document as a Web page rather than as a Word document.

7. Click the Save button 🔲 on the Standard toolbar
In the Save As dialog box, you give your Web page a name and save it in a file format suitable for posting on the Internet.

8. In the File name box, type Nomad Home Page, as shown in Figure J-4, verify that the file type is HTML Document, then click Save
The HTML file format ensures that Web browsers can read your Web page document.

FIGURE J-2: Types of Web pages

Displays/hides Web toolbar

Creates a hyperlink

Previews Web page

Switches between design mode and normal view

Specify a type of Web page

Currently selected Web page

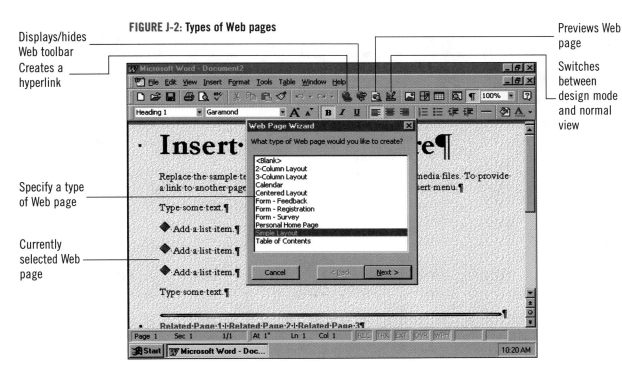

FIGURE J-3: A simple Web page created by the Web Page Wizard

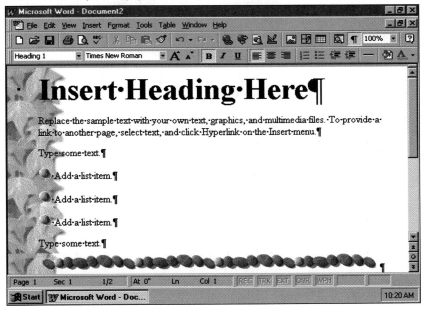

FIGURE J-4: Saving a Web page

Web page file type

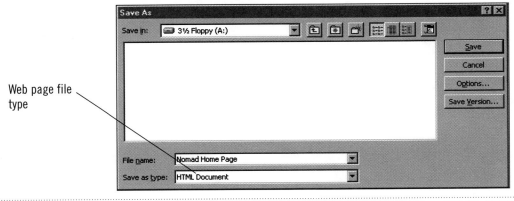

Creating a Form Web Page

When you want to collect information on the Web, you can create a form Web page. The Web Page Wizard provides several Web page forms you can use. These forms contain buttons and built-in commands that submit the information entered in the form to a Web address you specify. They also allow the user to clear the completed fields, if necessary. ✐━━ Angela wants to create a form to allow potential customers to request information about specific tours. She will use the Web Page Wizard to start creating a registration form.

Trouble?

Click No if you see a message about accessing the newest Web page authoring tools.

1. **Click File on the menu bar, click New, then click the Web Pages tab, if necessary**
   You can choose a form that already includes fields for entering name and address information.

2. **Double-click the Web Page Wizard icon**
   The first Web Page Wizard dialog box contains selections for the types of Web pages you can create.

3. **In the first Web Page Wizard dialog box, click Form – Registration**
   The Web page behind the dialog box appears in the registration form layout. After you make a selection you can continue using the wizard. In the next dialog box, choose the overall appearance of the Web page that matches the previous page you created.

4. **Click Next, then click Outdoors**
   The wizard displays the sample page behind the dialog box in the visual style you selected. Next, complete the Web Page Wizard.

5. **Click Finish**
   The completed form appears, as shown in Figure J-5. You must save your document as a Web page rather than as a Word document.

6. **Click the Save button 🖫 on the Standard toolbar**
   In the Save As dialog box you give your Web page a name, and save it in a file format suitable for posting on the Internet.

7. **In the File name box, type Nomad Request Form, then click Save**
   The HTML file format ensures that Web browsers can read your Web page document. You modify the text in this form later.

Word 97

Modifying Web Pages

With the basic layout of the Web page established, you can replace the text provided by the wizard with your own text. You can also change the appearance of a Web page by modifying the formatting or adding pictures. ✐▬▬ Angela would like to add her own text to her Web pages. She begins by editing the form page.

Steps

1. **Select the text Insert Heading Here, then type Nomad Info Request**
   The form title appears in the first cell, as shown in Figure J-6. You can leave the rest of the form unchanged for now.

2. **Click the Save button 🖫 on the Standard toolbar**
   With the registration form complete, you can now modify the home page.

3. **Click Window on the menu bar, then click Nomad Home Page**
   The home page document is now the active document. Before you replace the placeholder text with a new title, turn on Overtype mode.

4. **Place the insertion point in front of the text Insert Heading Here, double-click the OVR box in the status bar, type the heading Welcome to Nomad Ltd!, then double-click the OVR box again to turn off Overtype mode.**

5. **Select the first body paragraph, then type:**
   Nomad Ltd is a national sporting-goods retailer dedicated to delivering high-quality adventure sporting gear and clothing. And our new travel division offers ample opportunity to field-test our products for yourself.

6. **Select the next line of text, then type Here is just a sample of what we offer:**
   Add a bulleted list when you want to provide a list of features or services.

7. **Replace the text for the three bullets with the following three lines:**
   Environment-friendly camping gear
   Attractive, yet practical, clothing systems for all climates
   Excursions to exotic locations and eco-tourism adventures

8. **Select the next line of text, then type:**
   Our sales consultants are eager to equip you for your next journey whether you are traveling across the continent or across the county. Just call 1-800-828-3454 or contact us at nomad@goes.com.

9. **Click the Save button 🖫 on the Standard toolbar**
   Compare your Web page to Figure J-7.

FIGURE J-6: **Title in form**

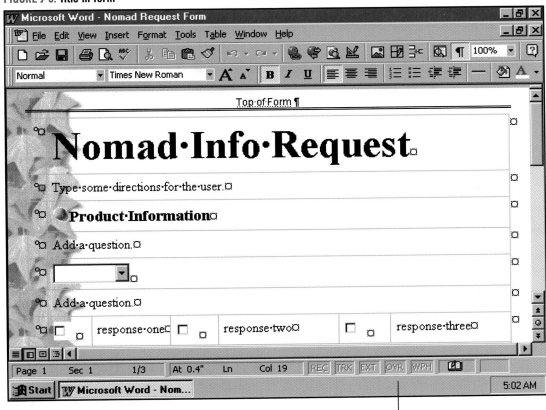

Double-click
here to turn
overtype
mode on
and off

FIGURE J-7: **Completed home page**

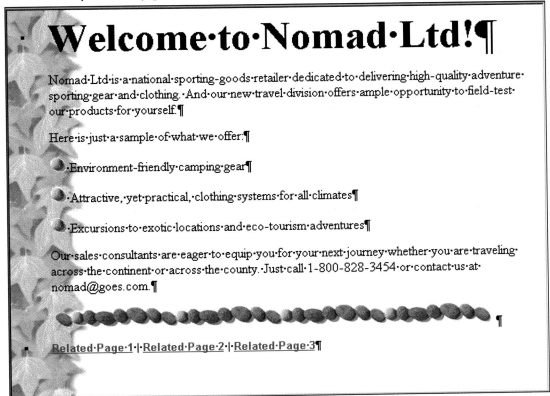

Converting a Word Document to a Web Page

If you already have a document that you would like to use as a Web page, there is no need to type the text again or even create a new document. Instead you can save a Word document in HTML format, using the Save as HTML command on the File menu. In the same way you can modify a Web page you create with a Web Page Wizard, you can modify a Web page that you have converted from a Word document. Angela would like to use a document she created for an annual report as a Web page that provides general information about Nomad Ltd.

1. **Open the document WD J-1**
   This document contains general information about Nomad Ltd.

2. **Click File on the menu bar, then click Save as HTML**
   The Save as HTML dialog box opens. This dialog box displays the names of existing files already saved in the HTML format. Here you can save the current document in HTML format.

3. **In the File name box, type Nomad Info Page, then click Save**
   Your document appears in the online view. In this view, you can edit and format your document. To give this page a look that is more consistent with the other pages you created, add a background.

4. **Click the Background button on the Formatting toolbar, then click Fill Effects**
   The Fill Effects dialog box appears. In this dialog box, you can choose a background fill effect from many different patterns and textures.

5. **In the Fill Effects dialog box, click Other Texture, locate the Microsoft Clipart folder, if necessary, click Leaves on the Side, then click OK twice to return to the document**
   The background changes to display a strip of leaves at the left edge of the page, as shown in Figure J-8. Another design element used in the Web pages that the Web Page Wizard created is a row of pebbles that serves as a horizontal line near the bottom of the page.

6. **Press [Ctrl] [End] to move to the end of the document, click Insert on the menu bar, then click Horizontal Line**
   The Horizontal Line dialog box opens, as shown in Figure J-9. You can see additional lines by clicking the More button.

7. **Click More, click Row of Pebbles, then click Insert**
   A graphic containing a row of pebbles appears centered in the document. To be consistent with the other Web pages, this graphic should not be centered.

8. **Select the graphic, then click the Align Left button on the Formatting toolbar**
   Compare your document to Figure J-10.

9. **Click the Save button on the Standard toolbar**

Trouble?

If you cannot locate the Background folder in the Clipart folder (within Microsoft Office under Program Files), close the dialog box, and click a textured background displayed in the Fill Effects dialog box.

FIGURE J-8: Leaves motif applied to background

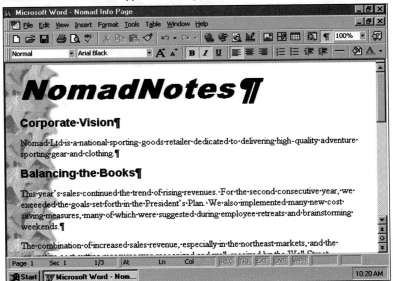

FIGURE J-9: Horizontal Line dialog box

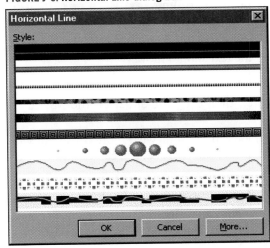

FIGURE J-10: Formatted Web page

Background

Horizontal line

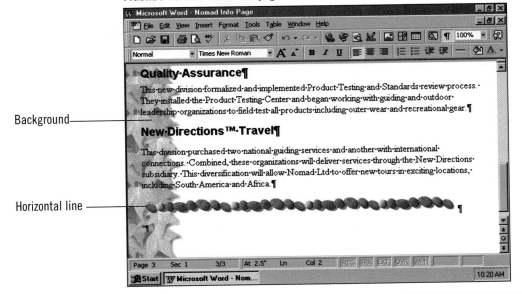

Word 97

Adding Scrolling Text to a Web Page

A dramatic way to catch your reader's attention is to display text that scrolls across the screen. This text acts as a movie marquee, constantly rolling whatever text you wish. You can also specify a background color for the area behind the scrolling text, and change the speed at which the text moves. Although you cannot add borders to scrolling text in the same way you format other text, you can use table formatting to apply a three-dimensional border to the scrolling area. Angela wants to alert her readers to watch for the completion of an exciting multimedia Web site, still-to-be-developed at Nomad Ltd. The promise of this new feature is sure to lure potential customers back to Nomad's site.

1. Press [Ctrl][Home] to place the insertion point at the top of the document

2. Click **Insert** on the menu bar, then click **Scrolling Text**
The Scrolling Text dialog box appears, as shown in Figure J-11. In this dialog box, you enter the text you want displayed.

3. Select the text in the **Type the Scrolling Text Here box**, then type **Visit the Virtual Vacation Location coming soon on the Web!**
As you type, the sample area displays your text scrolling in the dialog box. Next, you can specify the speed at which the text should move.

4. Drag the **slider bar** in the middle of the dialog box all the way to the left and observe that the text scrolls slower, then drag the slider all the way to the right and observe that it scrolls faster
To give the scrolling area a look that is somewhat more consistent with the outdoors theme you have used while developing your Web site, you can change the background color of the scrolling area.

5. Click the **Background Color list arrow**, click **Dark Yellow**, then click **OK**
A dark yellow scrolling area appears in the document. A border around the scrolling area will enhance its appearance. Before you can add a border, however, you need to insert a table around the scrolling area.

QuickTip

Do not drag to select any cells when you click the Insert Table button.

6. Click the **scrolling area** to select it, then click the **Insert Table** button 🔳 on the Standard toolbar
Clicking the Insert Table button once creates a table consisting of only one cell, which contains the scrolling text area.

7. Click **Table** on the menu bar, then click **Borders**
In the Table Borders dialog box, you can specify the borders you want to add to your scrolling text.

QuickTip

You can click the scroll text box and drag the sizing handles to adjust the width of the box, then click outside of the scrolling text box.

8. Click **Grid**, click the **Border Width list arrow**, click **1½ pt**, then click **OK**
Compare your document to Figure J-12.

9. Click the **Save button** 💾 on the Standard toolbar

FIGURE J-11: Scrolling Text dialog box

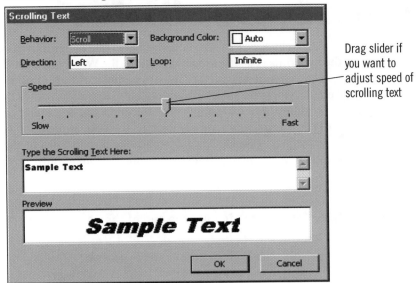

Drag slider if you want to adjust speed of scrolling text

FIGURE J-12: Scrolling text in a document

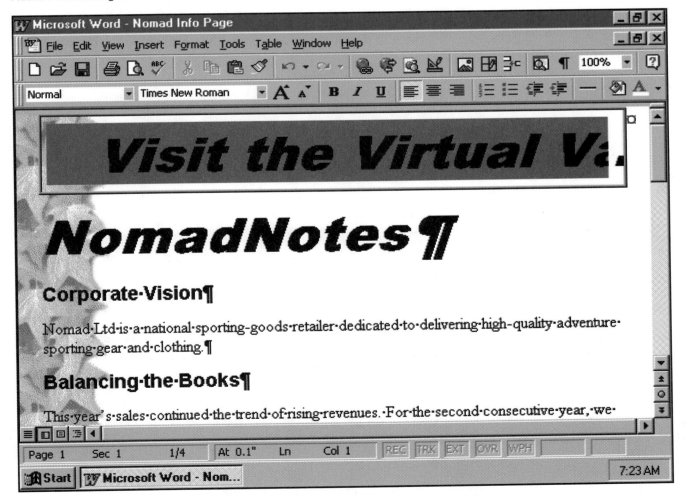

Adding Hyperlinks

If you have additional pages that you want to include in a Web site, you can create hyperlinks that display those pages when you click the hyperlink. The document created by the Web Page Wizard provides a placeholder where you can insert your hyperlinks. Your hyperlinks can also link to other Web sites. To link to another Web site, you specify the Web address (also known as the URL) in the Insert Hyperlink dialog box. In addition, you can simply type the address a document or Web page and the AutoFormat as You Type feature automatically formats the URL (which stands for Uniform Resource Locator) as a hyperlink. ✒━━ Angela would like to add links to the other Web pages she created, so that readers can get more information about Nomad Ltd.

1. Click **Window**, click **Nomad Home Page**, scroll to near the end of the page and select the text **Related Page 1**, then type **Click to display registration form**
   This new text will contain your hyperlink. Now you can create the hyperlink.

2. Select the text you just typed, then click the **Insert Hyperlink button** 🔗 on the Standard toolbar
   The Insert Hyperlink dialog box appears. In this dialog box you can specify the location of the file or Web address you want to add as a hyperlink. Although you can type the name of the document or address directly in this dialog box, you can also use the Browse button to locate the file for the form Web page you created earlier in this unit.

3. In the top part of the Insert Hyperlink dialog box, click **Browse**, click **Nomad Request Form**, click **OK** twice to return to the Web page, then click the **Save button** 💾 on the Standard toolbar
   (The list arrow in the dialog box displays a list of potential pages to which you might wish to create a link. This list changes as you continue to develop more Web pages.) The hyperlink appears on the Web page, as shown in Figure J-13. You can test the hyperlink by clicking it.

4. Click the **hyperlink**
   The form Web page appears in the document window and the Web toolbar appears. So that a reader can return to the first Web page, create a hyperlink that displays the first Web page.

5. Scroll to near the end of the page, select the text **Related Page 1**, type **Click to display the Nomad Home Page**, then delete the text **Related Page 3**
   Now you can add a hyperlink to the Nomad Home Page document.

6. Select the text you just typed, refer to steps 2–3 to add a hyperlink to the Nomad Home Page, then click 💾 on the Standard toolbar
   A hyperlink to the Nomad Home Page document appears in the document window. Now you need to add a hyperlink to the Nomad Info page on the home page.

7. Click the **hyperlink**, select the text **Related Page 2**, type **Click to display the Nomad Information Page**, select the text you just typed, refer to steps 2–3 to add a hyperlink to the Nomad Info Page, then click 💾 on the Standard toolbar

8. Click the new hyperlink to display the Nomad Info Page, place the insertion point at the end of the document below the row of pebbles, type **Click to display registration form**

9. Select the text you just typed, refer to steps 2–3 to add a hyperlink to the form page
   Compare your document to Figure J-14.

10. Click the **Save button** 💾 on the Standard toolbar.

QuickTip

If your Web page contains a graphic, you can select the graphic before clicking the Hyperlink button to create a hyperlink on the graphic itself. If you do not select text or a graphic, the name of the linked file appears in the document as a hyperlink.

Trouble?

If the Web toolbar doesn't appear, click the Web toolbar button 🌐.

FIGURE J-13: Hyperlink in a document

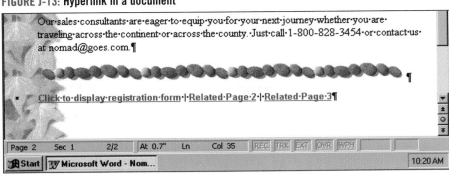

FIGURE J-14: Hyperlink in the Info Page

Web toolbar

Displays
previous page

Hyperlink to
registration
form

Displays/hides
Web toolbar

Click to see a list of
the last 10 pages
or documents you
jumped to

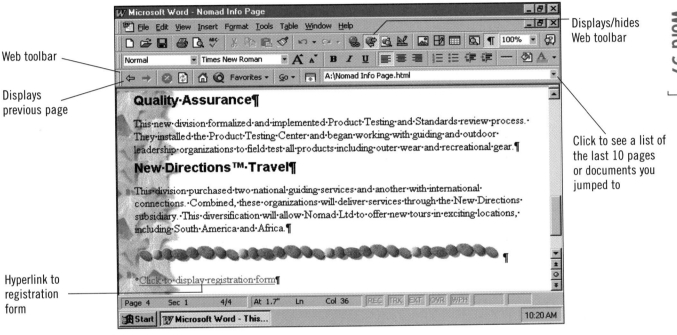

TABLE J-1: Web toolbar buttons

click this button	to
⇐	Move to previous Web page
⇒	Move to next Web page
⊗	Stop loading current page or stop current search
🔄	Refresh the current page
🏠	Return to home page
🔍	Search the Web
Favorites	Identify Web addresses you use most frequently
Go	Display a menu of Web commands that correspond to the buttons on the Web toolbar
🔲	Display/hide the other toolbars in the program window
📂	Open a file on the Internet or on your computer
Address list arrow	Display a list of the last 10 documents or Web pages you jumped to by using either the Web toolbar or a hyperlink

Viewing a Web Page Online

You can preview your Web site to simulate how a reader would see it. Viewing a Web site this way helps you identify areas you want to change and lets you test your hyperlinks. You can also view the HTML code by switching to the HTML source view, in which you can see the HTML language version of your Web page. ✐ Angela wants to see her Web site in action.

QuickTip

If you are using a browser other than Internet Explorer, your Web page might look different.

1. Click the Web Page Preview button 🔍 on the Standard toolbar
Your browser program starts, and the current Web page appears in your browser's window.

2. Scroll to the bottom of the page and click the hyperlink that takes you to the registration form, as shown in Figure J-15
The window part of your screen might look different, depending on the Web browser software you are using.

3. Click the hyperlink to display the home page

4. Click the Back button on your browser's toolbar
You return to the registration form. To leave the Web Page Preview window, you need to exit your Web browser program.

5. Click File on the menu bar, then click Close
You return to Word. After viewing a Web site as a reader would, you can also view the HTML source code for your Web page.

6. Click View on the menu bar, then click HTML Source
The HTML code for your Web page appears in the document window, as shown in Figure J-16. If you are familiar with the HTML language, you can edit your Web page directly by changing this source code. Otherwise, you can continue to edit your Web page using the Web authoring tools provided with Word.

Time To

✔ Save
✔ Print
✔ Close
✔ Exit

7. Click the Exit HTML Source button on the toolbar
You return to the online view window. You have completed your Web site, so save, print, and close your work, then exit Word. Note that the scrolling text will not print.

FIGURE J-15: Registration from hyperlink

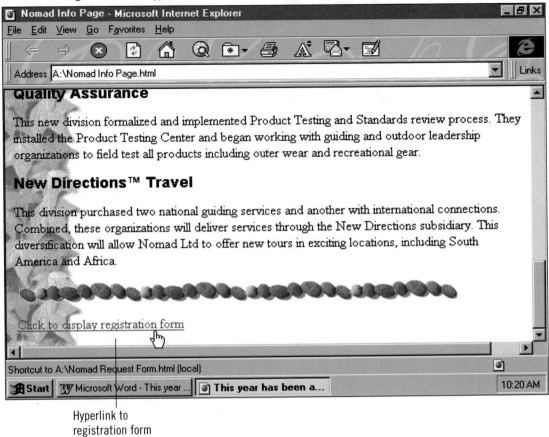

Hyperlink to
registration form

FIGURE J-16: HTML Source code

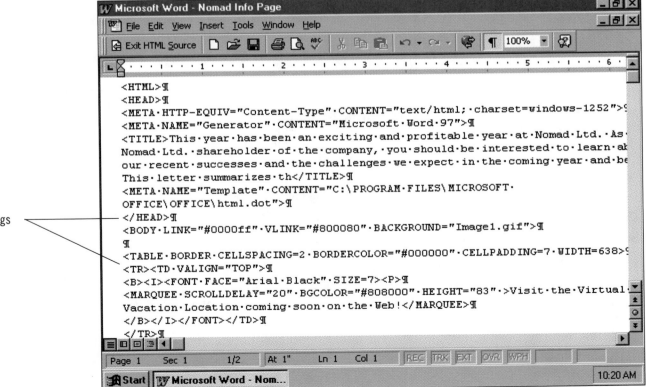

Tags

Practice

► Concepts Review

Label each of the elements in Figure J-17.

FIGURE J-17

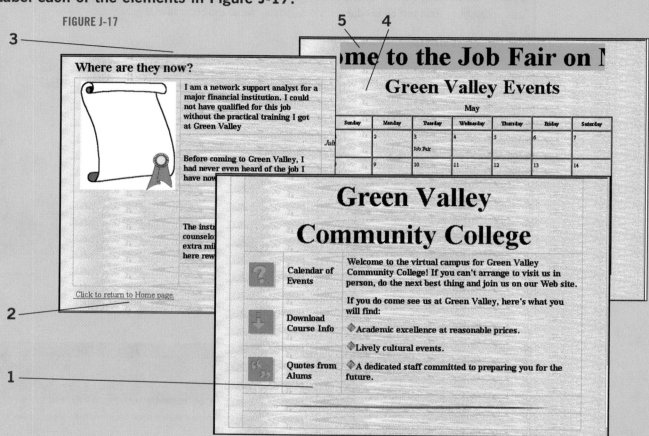

Match each of the following features with the correct descriptions.

6. Hyperlink	a. The address on the World Wide Web
7. Web page	b. Hyper Text Markup Language
8. Web site	c. A document stored on the World Wide Web that can be viewed online
9. HTML	d. Multiple Web locations linked together
10. URL	e. A live connection to another Web page

Select the best answer from the list of choices.

11. Which of the following statements is NOT true about the World Wide Web?
   a. Thousands of people use the Web every minute.
   b. No more than a few dozen people can be found on the Web at any given moment.
   c. Like a public library, the Web contains information from many sources.
   d. On the Web you can find information from research facilities, libraries, museums, educational institutions, governments, and non-profit organizations.

12. **Which of the following statements about Word is inaccurate?**
    a. Word provides templates and wizards for creating Web pages you can publish.
    b. You edit your HTML documents using Word.
    c. The Web Page Wizard helps you plan a Web page.
    d. You can convert your documents into the HTML format using Word.
13. **Which of the following options is NOT available for formatting a Web page in Word?**
    a. Scrolling text   b. Table borders   c. Paragraph borders   d. Italics
14. **When you are creating a Web page, "Outdoors" is what kind of option?**
    a. A visual style   b. A border   c. A template   d. A background

▶ Skills Review

1. **Create a simple Web page with a wizard.**
   a. Start Word.
   b. Click File on the menu bar, click New, click the Web Pages tab, then double-click the Web Page Wizard icon.
   c. In the first Web Page Wizard dialog box, click Simple Layout.
   d. Click Next, then click Community.
   e Click Finish.
   f. Click the Save button.
   g. In the File name box, type "Travel Home Page" (retain the "html" file extension), then click Save.

2. **Create a form Web page.**
   a. Click File on the menu bar, click New, then click the Web Pages tab, if necessary.
   b. Double-click the Web Page Wizard icon.
   c. In the first Web Page Wizard dialog box, click Form – Survey.
   d. Click Next, then click Community.
   e. Click Finish.
   f. Click the Save button on the Standard toolbar.
   g. In the File name box, type "Travel Survey Form", verify the file type as HTML Document, then click Save.

3. **Modify a Web page.**
   a. Select the text "Insert Heading Here", then type "Travel Survey".
   b. In the next cell of the form, replace the existing text with "Answer a few questions about your travel preferences and you could win a free first class upgrade on your next trip".
   c. In the next cell type "In the box below,+ briefly state the primary reason you travel (for example pleasure, business, family)".
   d. In the cell below the box, type "How often do you travel for the reason above?".
   e. In the next three cells next to each option button, type each of the following options: "1-2 times a year", "3-4 times a year", "More than 5 times a year".
   f. In the next cell, type "How long is your typical stay?".
   g. In the next three cells next to each option button, type each of the following options: "1-3 days", "4-7 days", "A week or more".
   h. Click the Save button on the Standard toolbar.
   i. Click Window on the menu bar, then click Travel Home Page.
   j. Turn on Overtype by double-clicking the OVR box on the status bar, place the insertion point in front of the text "Insert Heading Here", type "Welcome to the Travel Home Page", then double-click the OVR box to turn off Overtype mode.

k. Select the first body paragraph, then type "This Web site is designed to give you the latest information about the travel industry".

l. Select the next line of text, then type "Here is just a sample of what we offer:"

m. Replace the text for the three bulleted items with the following three lines:
Bargain airfare bulletins
Hotel and restaurant information
Itinerary planning

n. Select the next line of text, then press [Delete].

o. Click the Save button on the Standard toolbar.

4. **Convert a Word document to a Web page.**

a. Open the document WD J-2.

b. Click File on the menu bar, then click Save as HTML.

c. In the File name box, type "Boston Info Page", then click Save.

d. Click the Background button on the Formatting toolbar, then click Fill Effects.

e. In the Fill Effects dialog box, click Other Texture, click Brick Wall, then click OK twice to return to the document. If you do not see the Brick Wall option, locate the Microsoft Office folder on your computer. Click Clip art, and then click Backgrounds.

f. Place the insertion point in the last paragraph mark in the document, click Insert on the menu bar, then click Horizontal Line.

g. Click More, click Neighborhood, then click Insert.

h. Select the graphic, then click the Align Left button on the Formatting toolbar.

i. Click the Save button on the Standard toolbar.

5. **Add scrolling text to a Web page.**

a. Switch to the Travel Home Page, press [Ctrl] [Home] to place the insertion point at the top of the document.

b. Click Insert on the menu bar, then click Scrolling Text.

c. Select the text in the Type the Scrolling Text Here box, then type "Watch this space for weekly specials".

d. Drag the slider bar in the middle of the dialog box all the way to the left and observe that the text scrolls slower, then drag the slider all the way to the right and observe how it speeds up.

e. Click the Background Color list arrow, click Gray-25%, then click OK.

f. Click the scrolling area to select it if necessary, then click the Insert Table button on the Standard toolbar.

g. Click Table on the menu bar, then click Borders.

h. Click Grid, click the Border Width list arrow, click 1½ pt, then click OK.

i. Drag the sizing handles to adjust the size of the scrolling text object if necessary.

j. Click the Save button on the Standard toolbar.

6. **Add hyperlinks to other pages.**

a. Click View, point to Toolbars, then click Web to display the Web toolbar if necessary.

b. Click the Address list arrow on the Web toolbar, click Boston Info Page, scroll to near the end of the page and type "Click to display travel survey".

c. Select the text you just typed, then click the Insert Hyperlink button on the Standard toolbar.

d. In the top part of the Insert Hyperlink dialog box, click Browse, click Travel Survey Form, click OK twice to return to the Web page, then click the Save button on the Standard toolbar.

e. Click the hyperlink.

f. Scroll to the end of the page (after the neighborhood graphic), select the text "Related Page 1, then type "Click to display the Travel Home Page". Delete the text "Related Page 2" and "Related Page 3", then save the document.

g. Select the text you just typed, then use steps c-d, this time linking to the Travel Home Page document.

h. Click the hyperlink back to the home page.

i. Select the text "Related page 1", type "Click to display the Boston Info Page", select the text you just typed, then refer to steps b-c to add a hyperlink to the Boston Info Page document, delete the text "Related Page 2" and "Related Page 3", then click the Save button on the Standard toolbar.

j. Click the new hyperlink to display the Boston Page. Place the insertion point after "Click to display Travel Survey", press [Spacebar], then type "Click to display home page".

k. Select the text you just typed, then refer to steps b-c to add a hyperlink to the home page.

l. Save the document.

7. **View your Web page.**

a. Click the Web Page Preview button on the Standard toolbar.

b. Scroll to the bottom of the page and click the hyperlink that takes you to the survey.

c. Click the Back button on your browser's toolbar.

d. Click File on the menu bar, then click Close.

e. Click View on the menu bar, then click HTML Source.

f. Click the Exit HTML Source button on the toolbar.

g. Print and close all three documents.

▶ Independent Challenges

1. The Square Pegs Theater has engaged your marketing company to devise a way for theatergoers to make charitable donations to the theater online. Using Figure J-18 as a guide, create a Web page that is a form.

To complete this independent challenge:

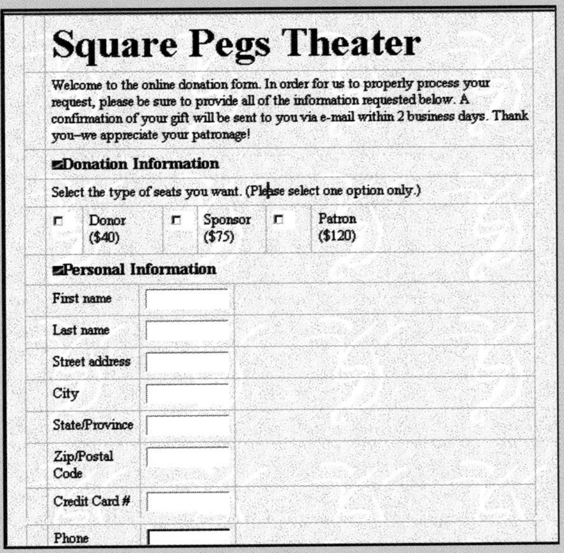

1. Create a new document using the Web Page Wizard. Select the Form-Registration option and Jazzy visual style.

2. Select the heading placeholder text and type in a title for the Web page.

3. In the next cell, replace the placeholder text with brief instructions for using the online ticket form.

4. In the next cell, replace the word "Product" with "Donation". In the cell below, type a question that asks customers the level at which they want to contribute.

5. Delete the next two rows in the form.

6. Edit the three checkboxes to identify three performance choices: Donor ($40), Sponsor ($75), Patron ($120).

7. Under Personal Information, replace the existing text "Country" with "Credit Card #".

8. Save the HTML document with the name Square Pegs Donation Form, then print and close the form.

FIGURE J-18

2. As the travel director for a small travel agency specializing in sailing trips, you have decided to create a Web page to provide information about an upcoming Hawaiian sailing package. Using text from a brochure that has already been developed, you can convert an existing Word document to a format that can be read on the Web.

1. Open the document WD J-3 and save it as an HTML file with the name Hawaiian Sail Web Page.

2. Adjust the size of the clip art so that it appears to the left of the first body paragraph.

3. Use the Background button to apply the Blue tissue background in the Fill Effects dialog box.

4. Use the Horizontal Line command to insert a horizontal red line border below and to the right of the clip art image, above the text that begins, "Here's what's included:".

5. Preview, save, and print the document, then close it.

3. As the communications coordinator for the local branch of Students for Peace, you have decided to use the power of the World Wide Web to communicate your message. Begin by creating a home page that readers can use to move to other Web pages in the site. Use Figure J-20 as a guide for how the completed home page should look.

To complete this independent challenge:

1. Create a new document using the Web Page Wizard. Select the Simple Layout option and Harvest visual style and save it as Students for Peace Home Page.

2. Select the placeholder text and type in the new text, as shown in Figure J-19.

3. To the right of the title, insert the Dove clip art.

4. Change the title font style to italics, be sure the font size is as large as possible, then change the font color to Teal.

5. Create a calendar Web page document and a registration form Web page document to serve as documents to which you can hyperlink.

6. Save the calendar page with the name Peace Calendar Page. Revise the text as you wish and enter the activity dates as shown in Figure J-19.

7. Save the registration form page with the name Peace Form Page. Revise the text as you wish.

8. Add hyperlinks in the home page to link to the two new pages. Remember to save your home page before you test the links to the other pages.

9. In the new pages add hyperlinks to return to the home page.

10. Preview, save and print the home page document, then close it.

FIGURE J-19

Students for Peace

Students for Peace is a non-profit, national consortium of secondary and college students whose mission is to raise awareness of global peace issues.

Here's an overview of upcoming local events:

⬤**March 29**–Camilla Johnston, author of "World Reconciliation," will speak at Bloom Auditorium, College of St. Therese.

⬤**May 17**–Spring fund-raising event, "Hope for Harmony." Dust off your walking shoes and join us for our march from Lincoln Parkway to Lake of the Loons.

⬤**July 9**–Annual conference, "Students for Peace 2000," at Oak Park Civic Center.

We welcome your enthusiastic participation at these events!

Event Information | Conference Registration

4. A local movie house has started a film club that caters to moviegoers in your area. As a way to keep current with the latest events in the industry, you have decided to create a Web site that will allow the film club's members quick access to movie-related sites from one location.

1. Log on to the Internet and use your browser to locate three of your favorite Web sites for movies. Then type in a topic of interest to locate a site and note the Web address. (Tip: You can select a Web address and copy it to the clipboard.) If you cannot locate a site on your own, use your browser to go to http://www.course.com. From there, click Student Online Companions, click the link for this textbook, then click the Word link for Unit J.

2. Create a home page that contains movie-related URLs and a brief description of each, similar to the one shown in Figure J-20. (Tip: Use the two-column page format in the Wizard.)

3. Add the Stationery fill effect as a background, and a green line border, as shown in Figure J-21.

4. Add the scrolling text "Club gathering this weekend at the Paramount". (*Hint*: Insert a row at the top of the table before you insert the scrolling text.)

5. Create other Web pages based on the links identified at the bottom of Figure J-20. The links on these pages should link back to the home page.

6. Preview the document and save it as Film Club. Print, then close the document.

FIGURE J-20

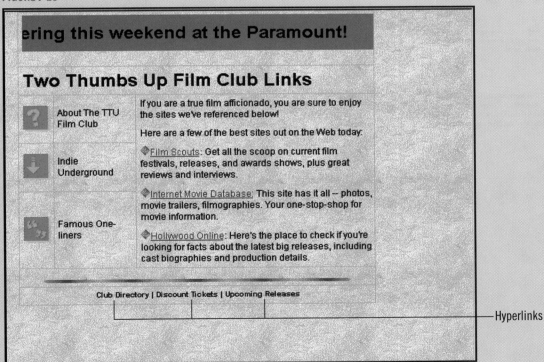

▶ Visual Workshop

As a recruiter for Green Valley community college, you've decided to create a Web site to provide information about events, alumni, and courses. Create a Web site that contains a home page, a calendar of events, and a page of testimonials from previous students. Open the document WD J-4, save it in the HTML format with the name Famous Quotes. Use the Web Page Wizard to create your pages, then save the home page as Green Valley Home Page. Save the calendar as Green Valley Calendar. Link all the pages to the home page (Tip: You can use the graphic objects in the left column as hyperlinks). Include interesting backgrounds, borders, and scrolling text for the calendar of events. Use Figure J-21 as guide for creating your home page. Preview, print, save, and close all the Web pages for this site.

FIGURE J-21

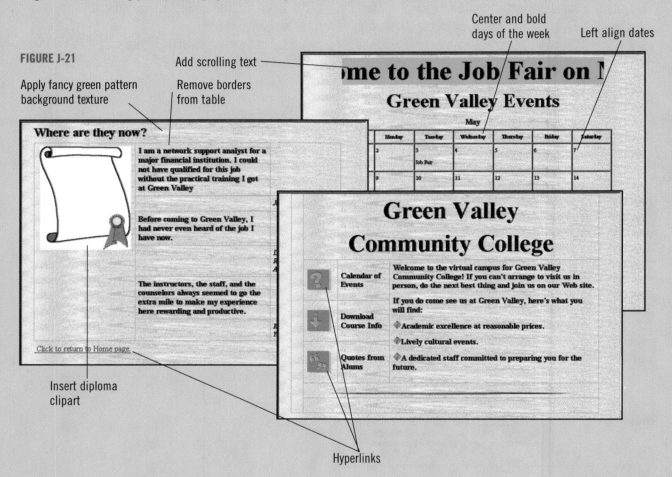

Center and bold days of the week

Left align dates

Add scrolling text

Apply fancy green pattern background texture

Remove borders from table

Insert diploma clipart

Hyperlinks

Working
with Larger Documents

Objectives

- ▶ **Create a document in outline view**
- ▶ **Edit a document in outline view**
- ▶ **Organize a document in outline view**
- ▶ **Promote and demote headings**
- ▶ **Create a table of contents**
- ▶ **Number pages in multiple sections**
- ▶ **Create an index**
- ▶ **Create master documents**

When working in large documents (longer than two or three pages) it can be a challenge to keep track of the sequence of topics. Fortunately, organizing main ideas and the text that goes with them is a lot easier when you work in the Word outline view. You can also make it easier for your readers to locate important ideas by creating a table of contents for your document. ✒ Angela creates and organizes a multiple page document that will eventually become part of the annual report. She also creates a table of contents, in which the page numbering is different from the numbering used in the rest of the document.

Creating a Document in Outline View

Outlining is a great way to organize ideas and topics in a document, especially if you plan to cover several main topics and additional subtopics. Working in outline view facilitates document outlining. You can establish the structure of a document by assigning the highest level (with a Heading 1 style) to the most important ideas in the document. Subsequent levels reflect correspondingly lower-level ideas or subtopics. Paragraphs of text not assigned a level are assigned the body text style and represent the detailed text under each heading. ✎ Angela is helping an intern, Stefan Morales, get started writing the Finance division report to be used in the Executive Bulletin. She will write the outline from which Stefan will build the rest of the document.

Steps 1 2 3 4

1. Start Word, then click the **New Document button** 🗋 on the Standard toolbar
   In a new document window, you can begin your outline in outline view.

2. On the horizontal scroll bar, click the **Outline View button** ▤
   The program window appears in outline view, as shown in Figure K-1.

3. Press **[Enter]**, then type **Financial Results 1998**
   Notice the line is assigned a Heading 1 style. The minus outline symbol ▭ indicates a line of text with no subheadings or subordinate text.

4. Press **[Enter]**, then type **Eastern Division Leads in Volume**
   This line is also assigned the default Heading 1 style. Using the Style box, you can adjust the level of your topics.

5. In the Style box, click the **Style list arrow**, then click **Heading 2**
   The new line is formatted in the Heading 2 style. It is indented to show that the idea is subordinate to the previous heading. Also note that the symbol in the previous heading changes to a plus sign, indicating that the heading contains additional subheadings or subordinate text.

6. Press **[Enter]**, then type **Catalog Sales Increase by 23%**
   Notice that the new line assumes the same Heading style as the previous line when [Enter] is pressed.

7. In the Style box, click the **Style list arrow**, then click **Heading 3**
   The new topic is assigned the Heading 3 style. Compare your document to Figure K-2.

8. Save the file as **Bulletin Outline**, print the document, then close it
   The document is now saved and closed.

FIGURE K-1: Program window in outline view

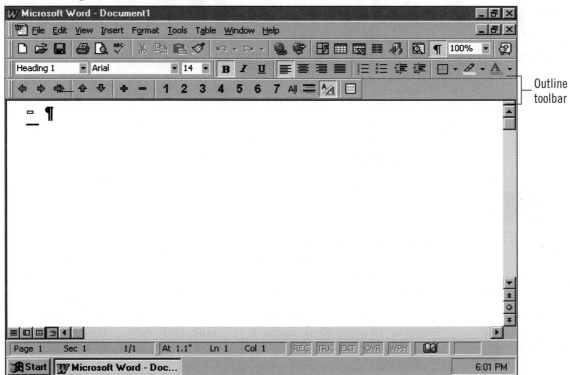

Outline toolbar

FIGURE K-2: Completed outline

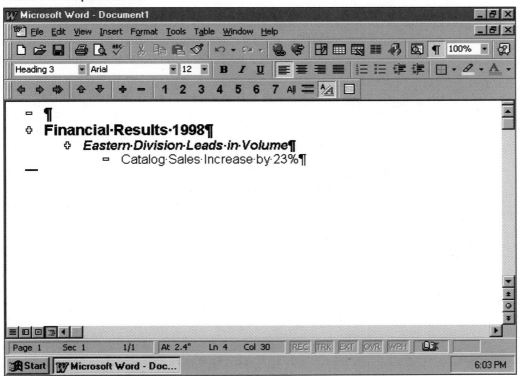

Word 97

Editing a Document in Outline View

The Word outline view displays document text based on the heading and body text styles you have applied to your document. For instance, when you want to focus on the overall organization of ideas, in outline view you can choose to view only the major headings in the document. Similarly, when you wish to focus on the detailed text under a heading, you can choose to view the text for only that heading. The Outlining toolbar contains buttons that allow you to view as much or as little information as you like. 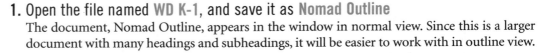 Angela begins by displaying her document in outline view, so she can examine its overall structure and organization of ideas.

1. **Open the file named WD K-1, and save it as Nomad Outline**
   The document, Nomad Outline, appears in the window in normal view. Since this is a larger document with many headings and subheadings, it will be easier to work with in outline view.

2. **On the horizontal scroll bar, click the Outline View button** ▤
   The document appears in the window in outline view, as shown in Figure K-3. (Make sure the Show First Line Only button is not indented.) Text not formatted in a heading style is called **body text** and is identified by a small square ■. Subordinate headings and text appear indented under higher-level text.

3. **On the Outlining toolbar, click the Show Heading 3 button** 3
   The first three heading levels of the document are displayed. This setting is useful when you want to see the basic structure of your document, without being distracted by all the details of the text.

4. **On the Outlining toolbar, click the Show All Headings button** All
   All heading levels and subordinate text are displayed. Often you won't need to see all the text while you are organizing the main ideas in the document, so you can display just the first line of body text under the headings.

5. **On the Outlining toolbar, click the Show First Line Only button** ☰
   Clicking this button hides all but the first line of body text. With the first line of text displayed, you can get a better idea of the content under each heading without seeing all the text. Clicking this button again, to deselect it, would show all body text again.

6. **On the Outlining toolbar, click the Show Heading 1 button** 1
   Compare your screen to Figure K-4. With only the top level displayed, you focus on just the main ideas of your document. In the next lesson, you will rearrange text in outline view.

FIGURE K-3: Document in outline view

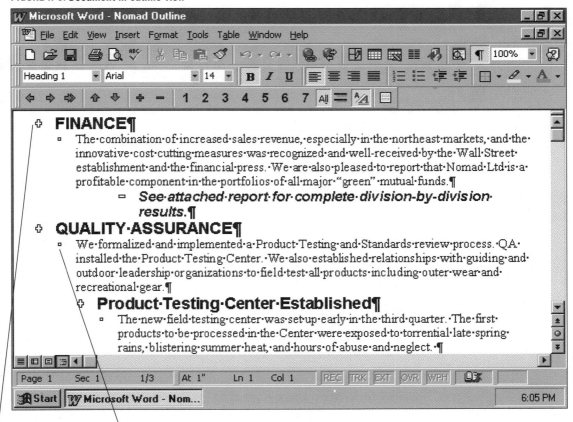

Indicates heading text   Indicates body text

FIGURE K-4: Document with only top level displayed

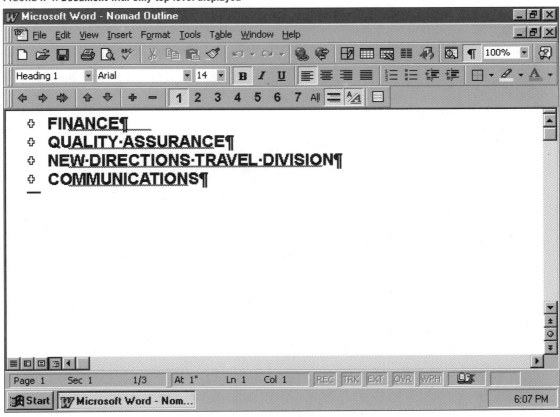

Organizing a Document in Outline View

One of the main benefits of outline view is how easily you can rearrange text. Using buttons on the Outlining toolbar or drag-and-drop mouse techniques, you can quickly move a heading, subordinate headings, and text to another location. Table K-1 includes keyboard and mouse techniques for performing these operations. Angela decides to change the order of topics in her report.

Steps

1. Place the insertion point in the heading **New Directions Travel Division**, then click the **Expand button** on the Outlining toolbar
   The next level of text, in this case Heading 2, appears for this heading only.

2. Click again
   The next level of text for this heading, and all subordinate body text, is now displayed, as shown in Figure K-5. If the subordinate text is already expanded, double-clicking the outline symbol will collapse it, and if the text is collapsed, double-clicking will expand it.

3. Position the mouse pointer over the plus outline symbol for the heading **New Directions Travel Division**, then, when the pointer changes to ✛ , double-click the mouse button
   Double-clicking a plus outline symbol **collapses** a heading by hiding subordinate headings and text. You can also click the Collapse button to hide one subordinate level at a time. With a heading completely collapsed, you can move (or delete) significant amounts of text, without selecting all the text first.

4. Select the heading **Finance**, then click the **Move Down button** on the Outlining toolbar three times
   The heading, along with all its subordinate text, moves to the end of the document.

5. Select the heading **New Directions Travel Division**, then click the **Move Up button** on the Outlining toolbar once
   The selected heading, along with all its subordinate text, moves above the previous heading in the document organization. You can also use the drag-and-drop technique to move a heading and its text throughout a document.

6. Select the line with the heading **Communications** (be sure to include the paragraph mark), then drag it to the top of the document
   The Communications heading and its subordinate text are now the first topic in the document. Be sure to drop the heading at the beginning of the line.

7. Click the **Show All Headings button** on the Outlining toolbar, then deselect the text
   Compare your document to Figure K-6. All the text under the heading Communications is displayed, showing that all subheadings and text were moved along with the heading.

8. Click the **Save button** on the Standard toolbar

FIGURE K-5: Expanded heading

Click to collapse a heading one level at a time

Click to expand a heading one level at a time

Double-click to show/hide all subordinate headings and text at once

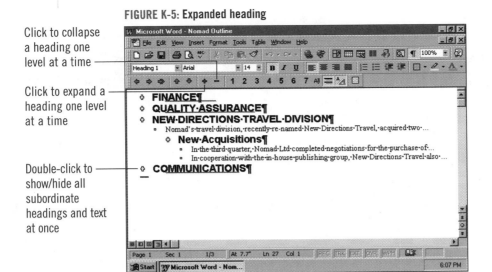

FIGURE K-6: Moved heading

Moves text down

Moves text up

Subordinate text moves along with its heading

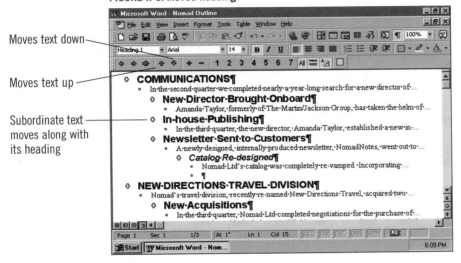

TABLE K-1: Buttons and keyboard shortcuts for viewing and moving a heading

to	click	press
Expand text under a heading one level	+	[Alt][Shift][+] (plus sign)
Collapse text under a heading one level	−	[Alt][Shift][-] (minus sign)
Display all headings and text in the document	All	[Alt][Shift][A]
Move a heading and its text up one line	⇧	[Alt] [Shift] [↑] (up arrow)
Move a heading and its text down one line	⇩	[Alt] [Shift] [↓] (down arrow)

Using the Document Map

Using the Document Map is another way to move quickly around in or view headings in a large document. The **Document Map** is a separate window that displays a document's headings. To display the Document Map, click the Document Map button [icon] on the Standard toolbar. To move to a heading, simply click on it in the Document Map. Word then displays the selected heading at the top of the document window. To close the map area, click the Document Map button or double-click the right edge of the map area.

Promoting and Demoting Headings

Another beneficial feature of working in outline view is that you can quickly modify the level assigned to a paragraph. Text at the far-left margin is assigned to level 1. Each time you indent, the level increases by one. Using the buttons on the Outlining toolbar, you promote a heading (along with its subheadings and subordinate text) to a higher level, or demote it to a lower level. Likewise, you can promote body text to a heading level. While reviewing her outline, Angela notices that some paragraphs do not have the correct level in the hierarchy. In this lesson, she changes the heading levels of text using the Outlining buttons.

Steps 1 2 3 4

QuickTip

You can also use the keyboard to promote and demote text in an outline. Press **[Alt][Shift][←]** to promote text to the next hierarchy level. Press **[Alt][Shift][→]** to demote text down one level. To demote a heading to body text, press **[Ctrl][Shift][N]**.

1. Scroll to the heading **New Alliances** under the Quality Assurance heading, select it, then click the **Promote button** ⬅ on the Outlining toolbar
   The text moves up a level. Notice that the Style box in the Formatting toolbar reflects the new heading level Heading 2.

2. Select the subheading **Newsletter Sent to Customers**, then click the **Demote button** ➡ on the Outlining toolbar
   The text moves down a level in the hierarchy, from Heading 2 to Heading 3.

3. Place the insertion point in front of the line that begins **In cooperation with...** (under New Acquisitions), then press **[Enter]**
   Pressing [Enter] creates a blank line with the same style as the previous paragraph, Body Text.

4. Place the insertion point in the blank line, then type **New Catalog Created**
   After typing a new line, you can adjust the heading level of the new text.

5. Click ⬅ on the Outlining toolbar
   Clicking the Promote button in body text promotes the text to the same level as the heading above it, in this case Heading 2, as shown in Figure K-7.

6. Place the insertion point in the last line of the document, **See attached report for complete...**, under the Finance heading, then click the **Demote to Body Text button** ➡ on the Outlining toolbar
   Notice that when you demote a heading to body text, the Normal style is applied. You will need to adjust the style of the demoted text to match the body text in the rest of document.

7. Click the **Style list arrow** on the Formatting toolbar, then scroll to and select **Body Text**
   After you have made all the structural changes, you can return to normal view to better see the formatting of your document.

Time To
✔ Save

8. Click the **Normal View button** ▤ on the horizontal scroll bar and save your changes
   Compare your document to Figure K-8.

FIGURE K-7: Promoted and demoted text in a document

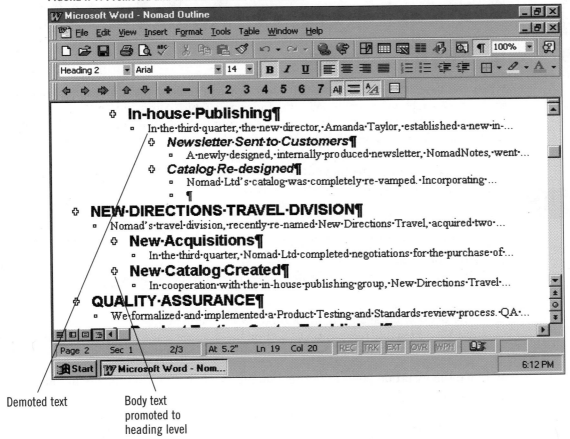

Demoted text

Body text
promoted to
heading level

FIGURE K-8: Outline in normal view

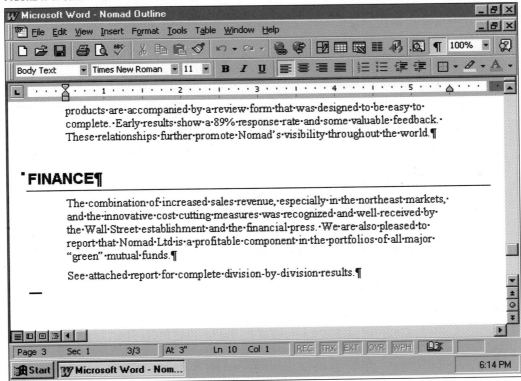

Creating a Table of Contents

When you have a large document that is divided into topics based on heading levels, you can easily create a table of contents. With the Index and Tables command on the Insert menu, you specify the heading levels you want to include in your table of contents. Because the table of contents is a unique part of your document, you may choose to create a separate section for the table of contents, so that you can apply page formatting and page numbering to the table of contents without affecting the formatting of the rest of the document. ✎ Angela wants to include a table of contents as a separate section in her report.

Steps 1 2 3 4

1. **With the insertion point at the top of the document, click Insert on the menu bar, then click Break**
   The Break dialog box opens. In this dialog box, you specify the type of break you want to insert.

2. **In the Section breaks area, click Next page, then click OK**
   A double dotted line representing a section break appears at the insertion point. The status bar displays the section number that currently contains the insertion point.

3. **Place the insertion point in the section break, click Insert on the menu bar, then click Index and Tables**
   The Index and Tables dialog box opens. This dialog box includes tabs for the four different types of indexes and tables you can insert. On the Table of Contents tab for example, you specify the kind of table of contents you want.

4. **Click the Table of Contents tab, as shown in Figure K-9, if it is not already displayed, click the Options button, verify that the Styles check box is selected, then click OK**
   Now the Table of Contents will be based on styles, not on entries that you select or add. You return to the Table of Contents tab.

5. **Click the Show page numbers check box, if it is not already selected, then verify that 3 heading levels are selected in the Show levels box**
   The Table of Contents tab also displays different formats, which can be applied. You can view a sample of the selected format in the Preview box before closing the dialog box.

6. **In the Formats box, click Formal, then click OK**
   The table of contents appears at the beginning of the document, as shown in Figure K-10. In addition to the table of contents formats available in the Table of Contents tab, you can further customize the appearance of your table of contents by changing the appearance of the tab leaders (the line or dotted line that appears in front of the page number). You can do this in the Table of Contents tab (before you create a table of contents) or in the Tabs dialog box after you create the table of contents.

7. **Select the table of contents, click Format on the menu bar, then click Tabs**
   The Tabs dialog box appears. In this dialog box you can specify the location of tab stops and the leader associated with the tab stop.

Time To
✔ Save

8. **In the Tab stop position box, type 6, click the Right option button in the Alignment area, click the 4 option button in the Leader area, then click OK**
   The page numbers continue to be right-aligned with the tab at the 6 inch mark, except now the leaders appear as lines rather than dots as shown in K-11.

FIGURE K-9: Index and Tables dialog box, Table of Contents tab

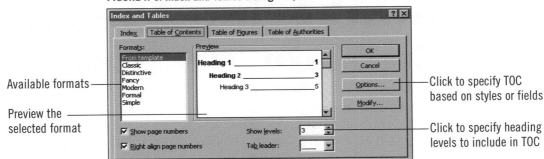

Available formats

Preview the selected format

Click to specify TOC based on styles or fields

Click to specify heading levels to include in TOC

FIGURE K-10: Table of contents based on heading styles

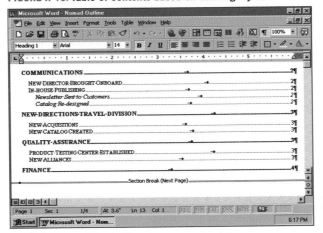

FIGURE K-11: New tab leaders in the table of contents

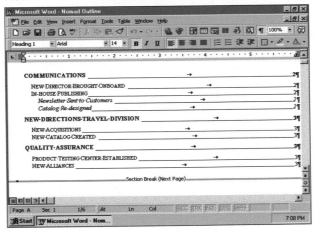

Inserting TOC fields

You can also create a table of contents based on text you select or type (rather than on heading styles). After selecting the text you want to appear in the table of contents, press [Alt][Shift][O]. In the Mark Table of Contents Entry dialog box, you can modify the text you want to appear in the table of contents and specify the level at which the text should appear. Click Mark to insert a TOC field in the document at the insertion point. Leave the dialog box open if you want to select additional text and insert more TOC fields, or click Close. When you are ready to generate a table of contents, choose the Index and Tables command and choose Options. Then check the Table entry fields check box. Click OK twice to close the dialog boxes and generate a new table of contents.

Numbering Pages in Multiple Sections

When you have multiple sections in a document, you can specify unique formatting for each section. For example, you can vary the text that appears in the headers and footers or use different page setup options in each section. ✎ So that shareholders can turn directly to the topic of interest, Angela decides to include page numbers on her report and then change the page numbering format for her table of contents.

Steps 1234

1. **Place the insertion point anywhere in the second section of the document, click** View **on the menu bar, then click** Header and Footer

   The Header and Footer command displays the document in page layout view. The Header and Footer toolbar is also displayed in the document window.

2. **On the Header and Footer toolbar, click the** Switch Between Header and Footer button ⊞**, click the** Center button ≣ **on the Formatting toolbar, then click the** Insert Page Number button ⊞ **on the Header and Footer toolbar**

   Clicking the Insert Page Number button inserts a sequential number, starting with 1, at the bottom of every page.

3. **On the Header and Footer toolbar, click** Close**, then click the** Page Layout View button ⊟ **on the horizontal scroll bar**

   It is easier to see the changes to your document in page layout view.

4. **With the insertion point anywhere in section 1 (the table of contents), click** Insert **on the menu bar, then click** Page Numbers

   The Page Numbers dialog box opens. This dialog box provides another method for inserting a page number in a header or footer.

5. **Click the** Format button**, click the** Number format list arrow**, and select the format** A, B, C...**, as shown in Figure K-12, then click** OK

   With the page number formatting set, the dialog box closes, and you return to the Page Numbers dialog box, where you can specify the position of the page numbers.

6. **Click the** Alignment list arrow **in the Page Numbers dialog box, select** Center**, then click** OK

   Section 1 now contains the newly formatted page number. So that the page numbering for section 2 begins with 1, you need to modify the page numbers for section 2.

Trouble?

If a number does not appear in the table of contents or on the first page of the report, verify that the Show number on first page check box is selected in the Page Numbers dialog box.

7. **Place the insertion point anywhere in section 2, click** Insert **on the menu bar, then click** Page Numbers

8. **Click the** Format button**, then click the** Start At option button**, verify that the starting number is 1, click** OK**, then click** Close

   Notice that you can click either Close or OK in this dialog box. Clicking OK would insert a framed page number next to the existing page number. Clicking the Close button accepts the formatting changes without inserting another page number. You are now ready to update the table of contents.

Time To

✔ Save

9. **With the insertion point anywhere in the table of contents, press** [F9]**, then in the dialog box, click** OK

   Word updates the table of contents using the default option, Update page numbers only. The table of contents now reflects the revised page number format for the report as shown in Figure K-13.

FIGURE K-12: Page Number Format dialog box

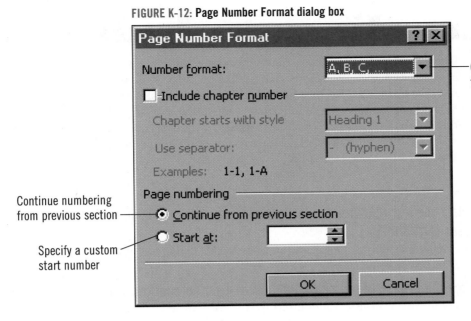

Click to display available number formats

Continue numbering from previous section

Specify a custom start number

FIGURE K-13: Updated table of contents

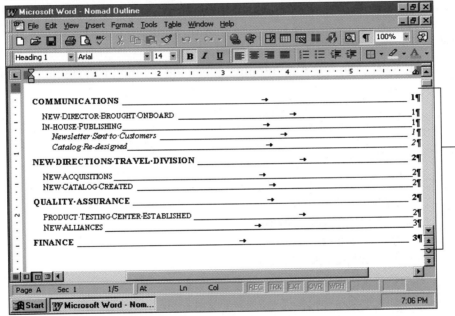

Depending on your screen resolution or current printer setting, the page numbers you see might be different

CLUES TO USE

Inserting footnotes

Another type of text that can appear at the bottom of a page is a footnote. Usually a footnote provides acknowledgment of a source of information stated in the text, or it can simply provide additional information to the reader. With the Footnote command on the Insert menu you can specify footnote options. Then Word opens a footnote pane in which you can enter the text of the footnote. When you insert new footnotes or delete existing ones, Word automatically renumbers the remaining footnotes. To edit a footnote, you simply double-click the footnote number in the document. To remove a footnote, select and delete the footnote number in the document.

Creating an Index

Like a table of contents, an index is another way to identify the page on which the major ideas or topics in a document appear. To begin building an index, you must first mark the text entries you would like included. After you have marked your entries, Word will alphabetize them and reference their page numbers. The Index tab in the Index and Tables dialog box offers many formats and options for building an index. ▄▄▄▄ Angela has decided to include an index as another way for the reader to quickly locate information in her document.

Steps

1. **Select the text publications in the body text under the heading Communications, then press [Alt][Shift][X]**
   The Mark Index Entry dialog box appears. In this dialog box, you can choose to add subentries and cross-references.

2. **Click the Cross-reference option button, type NomadNotes after See, then click Mark**
   The field code is inserted in brackets next to the selected text, as shown in Figure K-14. The entry is marked, but the dialog box stays open so you can mark other index entries.

3. **Select the name Amanda Taylor under the heading New Director, click in the Mark Index Entry dialog box, type New Director in the subentry box, then click Mark**
   The text is marked with a field code.

4. **Select the text NomadNotes under the heading Newsletter Sent to Customers, click in the Mark Index Entry dialog box, verify that the current page option button is selected in the Options area, then click Mark All**
   Clicking the Mark All button marks all text that matches the entry exactly. This feature is useful when you have a large document and do not wish to search for each occurrence of the marked text.

5. **Repeat step 4 with the following text, click Mark All after each entry**
   catalog
   New Directions Travel
   sales revenue
   Product Testing Center

6. **Click Close**
   Each entry is marked to be included in the index. Before inserting an index, you need to insert a page (or a section break) at the end of the document, so the index will appear on a separate page.

7. **Place the insertion point at the end of the document, click Insert on the menu bar, click Break, then click OK in the Break dialog box**
   A page break is inserted into the document. With all desired index entries marked and a break inserted, you are now ready to insert and format the index.

8. **Click Insert on the menu bar, click Index and Tables, click the Index tab, select Formal in the Formats list, as shown in Figure K-15, then click OK**
   Because the Mark All also marked words located in the table of contents, you can delete the page numbers labeled "A" in the index.

9. **In the Table of Contents, delete the field codes, click anywhere in the index, then press [F9]**
   The index is updated without the table of contents pages displayed as shown in Figure K-16.

FIGURE K-14: Marked index entry in the document

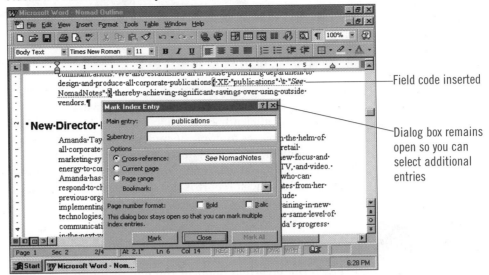

Field code inserted

Dialog box remains open so you can select additional entries

FIGURE K-15: Index tab in Index and Tables dialog box

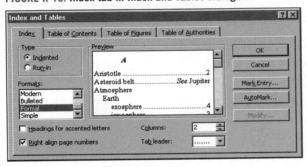

FIGURE K-16: Completed index

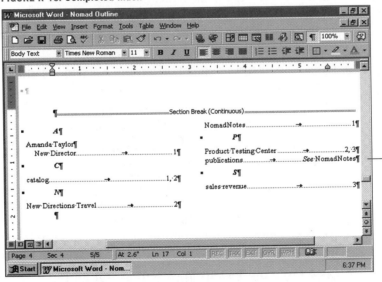

Depending on your screen resolution or current printer setting, the page numbers you see might be different

Using bookmarks in an index

By inserting a **bookmark** in a document before marking an index entry, you can show that the selected text spans over a range of pages. Begin by selecting all the text related to a certain topic that spans multiple pages. Click Insert on the menu bar, click Bookmark, type the name of your bookmark, then click Add. Press [Alt][Shift][X] to open the Mark Index Entry box. Type the index entry for the marked text, click the Page range option, select the bookmark, then click Mark.

Creating Master Documents

When you are working on several documents that you intend to produce as a single document (for example, a company report containing individual reports from separate departments), you can work more efficiently by creating a master document. A **master document** is like an outline that encompasses multiple documents, which are called **subdocuments**. When you open a master document, you see all of its subdocuments in outline view. As a result you can work in all the documents at the same time, while opening only the master document. Although the financial report is not quite complete, Angela can begin assembling her division reports document now.

Steps

1. **Place the insertion point at the end of the text before the page break, press [Enter], then click the Outline View button 🔲 on the horizontal scroll bar**
   In outline view, you can enable the master document buttons from the Outlining toolbar.

2. **Click the Master Document View button 🔲 on the Outlining toolbar**
   The Master Document toolbar opens. You can now insert a subdocument into the current document.

3. **Click the Insert Subdocument button 🔲 on the Master Document toolbar**
   The Insert Subdocument dialog box opens. In this lesson you will use the document outlined earlier.

4. **Double-click Bulletin Outline**
   After you insert the subdocument, the current document "Nomad Outline" is now a master document. Section breaks appear before and after the text of the subdocument as shown in Figure K-17. Even after creating a master document, you still have the ability to edit the inserted subdocuments.

5. **Place the insertion point after the second heading in the subdocument, press [Enter], then type Catalog Sales Soar**
   After editing the document, you will need to update the table of contents and the index to reflect the topics and pages in the subdocument.

6. **Place the insertion point in the table of contents, then press [F9], click the Update entire table option button, then click OK**
   Since both the number of pages in the document and the headings have changed, the entire table needs to be updated. The table of contents reflects the headings from the subdocument. Since you have not marked any new index entries, you do not need to update the index. After you have finished editing your document outline, it is best to switch to page layout view to review and print your document. If you print while in Outline view, only the outline prints.

Time To

✔ Save
✔ Print
✔ Close
✔ Exit Word

7. **Click the Page Layout View button 🔲 on the horizontal scrollbar and review the entire document**
   Notice that the subdocument topic appears in the table of contents, and that the page numbers reflect the addition of a new page, as shown in Figure K-18.

FIGURE K-17: Subdocument in a master document

Master document ———

Double-click to
open subdocument ———

Subdocument ———

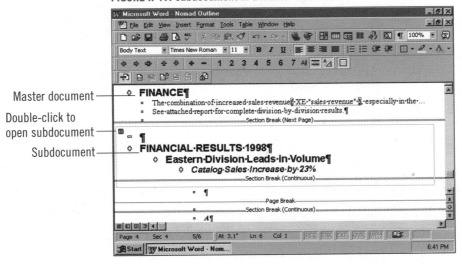

FIGURE K-18: Updated table of contents

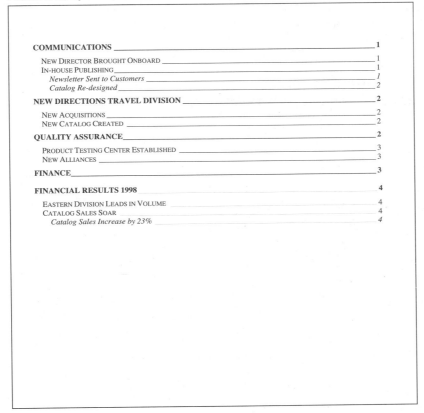

CLUES TO USE

Working with subdocuments

You might notice that when working in very large documents (more than 20 pages) or in documents containing many graphic objects, it takes longer to scroll through pages or preview a document. One solution is to divide the large document into smaller ones, called subdocuments, which you then insert in a master document. Master documents open only the subdocument you wish to edit, so your computer responds quickly to your commands and you can work more efficiently.

Practice

► Concepts Review

Label each of the elements of the Word document window in Figure K-19.

FIGURE K-19

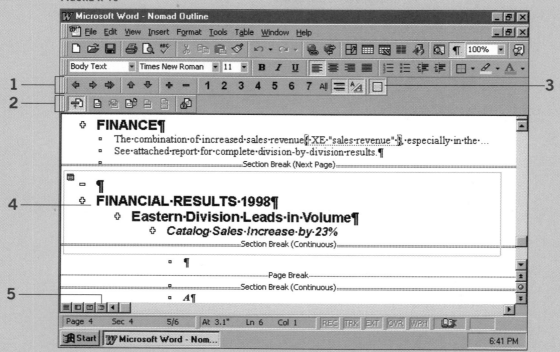

Match each of the following terms with the statement that best describes its function.

6. **Master document**
7. **Heading styles**
8. **Outline view**
9. **Sections**
10. **Promote**

a. Displays a document's hierarchical structure
b. A larger document that is organized into smaller subdocuments for easier editing
c. For formatting individual parts of a document with different settings
d. For quickly creating a table of contents based on the document's main topics
e. Increases text to a higher heading level

Select the best answer from the list of choices.

11. To create an index, you:
    a. Click Insert on the menu bar, then click Index.
    b. Click the Index button in the Table of Contents dialog box.
    c. Click Insert, Index and Tables, then click the Index tab.
    d. Click the Index button on the Outlining toolbar.

12. Which of the following is NOT a benefit of working in outline view?
    a. Allows you to quickly create a table of contents based on heading styles
    b. Only the outline view allows you to insert index entries.
    c. Allows you to reorganize the topics in a large document with minimal editing
    d. Allows you to view the main concepts of the document at a glance

13. **To create a section break that begins on a separate page, you:**
    a. Click Insert on the menu bar, click Break, then click Next Page.
    b. Click Insert on the menu bar, then click Section Break.
    c. Click the Section Break button on the Formatting toolbar.
    d. Click Insert on the menu bar, click Break, then click Continuous.

14. **When you promote a heading in an outline:**
    a. You change it to a higher level heading.
    b. Its subordinate headings and subtext remain at the previous hierarchical level.
    c. You change it to a lower level heading.
    d. You see no effect in the document.

15. **Which of the following is NOT an option on the Outlining toolbar?**
    a. Show only the first line of the text
    b. Change to Master Document View
    c. Show only Heading 1
    d. View a Document Map

16. **Which of the following statements best describes creating a table of contents in Word?**
    a. You must use the Word default heading styles as table of contents entries.
    b. You can use default heading styles, other styles, and text you choose as table of contents entries.
    c. You can create a table of contents by clicking the Tables button on the Standard toolbar.
    d. Page numbers are automatically updated when you add, remove, or move headings in a document.

17. **Which of the following statements best describes creating an index in Word?**
    a. You can specify single words or phrases as index entries.
    b. You must locate and select each occurrence of a word or phrase that you want included in the index.
    c. Page numbers in the index are automatically updated when you add, remove, or move text in a document.
    d. After creating an index, you must format the index into a two column format.

18. **Which of the following best describes the Word master document view?**
    a. You can use the master document view to outline and organize more than one document.
    b. You can use the master document view to delete and manage other documents.
    c. You can use the master document view to update a table of contents.
    d. You can use the master document view to change the Layout tab so that new sections do not begin on a new page.

▶ Skills Review

1. **Create a new document in outline view.**
    a. Click the New button on the Standard toolbar.
    b. On the horizontal scroll bar, click the Outline View button.
    c. Press [Enter] and type "INVESTMENT BASICS".
    d. Press [Enter] and type "Identify long term and short term goals".
    e. Press [Enter] and type "Identify current obligations".
    f. In the Style box, click the Style list arrow and select Heading 2.
    g. Press [Enter] and type "Identify current income".
    h. Press [Enter] and type "Identify cost saving strategies".
    i. Press [Enter] and type "Identify income enhancing strategies".
    j. Press [Enter] and type "Investing".
    k. In the Style box, click the Style list arrow and select Heading 3.

l. Press [Enter] and type "Second income strategies".

m. Print the document.

n. Click File on the menu bar, click Close, then click Yes when you see the message asking if you want to save.

o. In the File name box, type "Strategy Outline".

2. **Display a document in outline view.**

a. Open the document named WD K-2 and save it as "Investment Outline".

b. On the horizontal scroll bar, click the Outline View button.

c. On the Outlining toolbar, make sure the Show First Line Only button is indented.

d. On the Outlining toolbar, click the Show Heading 2 button.

3. **Promote and demote text in an outline.**

a. Place the insertion point in the heading "Fund Performance", then click the Promote button.

b. Place the insertion point in the heading "Windlow Stock Fund", then click the Demote button.

c. Place the insertion point in the heading "Growth Stock Fund", then click the Expand button.

d. With the insertion point in the heading "The Class B Plan provides...", click the Demote to Body Text button. Then, click the Style list arrow on the Formatting toolbar and click Body Text Ind.

e. Double-click the plus outline symbol next to the heading "Growth Stock Fund" to display all subordinate text. Then, double-click the plus symbol again to collapse the heading and hide all subordinate text.

4. **Organize text in an outline.**

a. Place the insertion point in the heading "Fund Description", then click the Collapse button.

b. Click the Move Up button once.

c. Click the Expand button.

d. Select the line with the heading "Growth Stock Fund", then drag the heading just in front of "Fund Performance".

e. On the Outlining toolbar, click the Show All Headings button to verify that all subordinate text moved along with the "Growth Stock Fund" heading.

f. On the horizontal scroll bar, click the Normal View button.

5. **Insert a table of contents.**

a. With the insertion point at the top of the document, click Insert on the menu bar, then click Break.

b. Click the Next page option button, then click OK.

c. With the insertion point in the section break, click Insert on the menu bar, then click Index and Tables.

d. Click the Table of Contents tab.

e. Click the Options button, verify the Styles check box is selected, then click OK.

f. In the Formats section, click Fancy then click OK.

6. **Reformat the page number format in sections.**

a. With the insertion point in section 1, click Insert on the menu bar, then click Page Numbers.

b. Click the Alignment list arrow, then select Center.

c. Click the Format button.

d. Click the Number format list arrow, click i, ii, iii,..., click OK twice.

e. With the insertion point in section 2, click Insert on the menu bar, then click Page Numbers.

f. Click the Format button.

g. Click the Start At option button, then verify the starting number is 1.

h. Click OK twice.

7. **Insert an index.**

a. Select the text "Omaha Investors Group" in the Introduction.

b. Press [Alt][Shift][X].

c. Click Mark All.

d. Repeat step c with the following text. Click Close when the entries are completed.

select	main entry	subentry
Fixed Income Fund	Fixed Income Fund	
Common Stock Fund	Common Stock Fund	
Windlow Stock Fund	Windlow Stock Fund	
Class A Plan	Growth Stock Plan	Class A Fund
Class B Plan	Growth Stock Plan	Class B Fund

e. Press [Ctrl][End], click Insert, then click Break.

f. Click OK.

g. Click Insert, then click Index and Tables.

h. Click the Index tab.

i. In the Formats section, select Modern, then click OK.

j. Select and delete the fields in the table of contents, place the insertion point in the index, press [F9].

8. **Create a master document.**

a. Place the insertion point before the page break at the end of the document, press [Enter], then click the Outline View button.

b. Click the Master Document View button on the Outlining toolbar.

c. Click the Insert Subdocument button on the Master Document toolbar.

d. Double-click Strategy Outline.

e. Place the insertion point in the second heading "Identify long term and short term goals", then click the Demote button.

f. Click the Page Layout View button to switch to page layout view.

g. Press [Ctrl][Home] and place the insertion point in the table of contents, then press [F9].

h. Click the Update entire table option button and click OK.

i. Save the document, then print and close the document.

► Independent Challenges

1. As the manager of The Write Staff's Catalog Division, it is your job to provide copy guidelines to the promotional copy writers in your department. You will draft a short outline of the guideline's headings for topics that you can later finalize. Create a new document, then save the document as "Guidelines Outline". Complete the following changes to your outline, using Figure K-20 as a guide.

To complete this independent challenge:

1. Switch to outline view and press [Enter].
2. Type the headings shown in Figure K-20 and promote and demote the headings to the levels indicated.
3. When you have finished making the changes to the document, save, print, and close the document.

FIGURE K-20

Promotional Text Writing Guidelines

> *Make it Brief*

> *Clarity*

> *Be Positive*

> *Standard Format*

>> *Boldface/Italic Type*

>> *Uniform Pricing*

>> *Shipping Weight*

General Style

> *Titles, Headings, and Captions*

Writing Guidelines

> *Introductory Text*

> *Pricing*

> *Origin of Product*

2. Suppose you are a freelance writer who has been hired by the City of Boston's tourism department to write the copy for a brochure for visitors to the city. Create a new document, then save the document as "Boston Outline".

To complete this independent challenge:

heading	level
Inside the Bostonian World	1
History	2
Night Life	3
Culture	2
The Streets of Boston	3
Walking Tours	2
Sightseeing by Automobile	2
Public Transportation	2
Cape Cod and the Islands	2
Nantucket	2
Martha's Vineyard	3
Boston for Kids	1
Outdoor Gardens	1
Museums	2
Ship Tours and Cruises	2

1. Add the headings shown in the first column and apply the heading level in the second column.
2. Type a few lines of text after each heading to create some text in the document.
3. Switch to outline view and view the different levels of hierarchy with the Heading buttons on the Outlining toolbar. Use the Expand and Collapse buttons to view and hide subordinate headings and text. Display three heading levels in the outline.
4. Promote the headings "Streets of Boston" and "Cape Cod and the Islands" to Heading 1.
5. Expand the Cape Cod and the Islands heading so that three heading levels are exposed. Promote the Martha's Vineyard heading to Heading 2.
6. Demote the Heading 1 "Outdoor Gardens" to Heading 2.
7. Move the Heading 3 "Night Life" below the Heading 2 "Culture". Promote the Night Life to Heading 2.
8. Add a table of contents at the beginning of the document, using any format you wish. Specify a page numbering format that uses letters not numerals. Be sure to separate the table of contents from the rest of the document with a section break that begins on the next page.
9. Add a centered title to section 2 of the document that reads "Text for Tourism Brochure".
10. Add a left-aligned footer to section 2 that contains the page number.
11. Adjust the page number format of section 2 to begin on page 1.
12. Insert a page break before each of the Heading 1 headings. Then update the table of contents.
13. When you have finished making the changes to the document, save, print, and close the document.

3. As a co-chairman for this year's national Celebrate Health Conference, you have been touring the country speaking to nutritionists and alternative health care providers. Although you have developed a draft outline to help you organize your thoughts for these local speeches, you have decided to make some changes to the structure and organization of topics. Open the document named WD K-3, then save the document as "Conference Outline".

To complete this independent challenge:

1. In outline view, display three heading levels in the outline.
2. Promote the heading "Current Topics" to Heading 1. Demote the heading "Additional Alternative Practices" to Heading 3.
3. Collapse the heading "Organically Grown Controversy", then move the heading and its subordinate text below the heading "Plants Process Nuclear Contamination". Move the entire "Research" heading above the "News Briefs..." heading.
4. Mark the text in the table to be included in the index.
5. Insert a section break that begins on a new page. In the new section add an index using the Classic format.

select	subentry	cross-reference
National Center for Health Statistics		
ToxTech Inc.	Nuclear Contamination	
Organic food		
Research		
Alternative Practices		Research
Celebrate Health Conference		

6. Use your Web browser to locate sites related to any of the following topics: organic farming, alternative medicine, or any other health and nutrition related issues or organizations. In your document, create a new heading called "Healthy Web Sites" and apply the Heading 1 level to it. In the following paragraph, create a table that includes the Web addresses for at least three different sites (in the first column) and corresponding descriptions (in the second column). If you can't locate related sites, use your browser to go to http://www.course.com. From there, click Student Online Companions, click the link for this textbook, then click the Word link for Unit K.

7. In the new text, mark index entries for any of the index entries you've already marked in other parts of the document, and then update the index.

8. When you have finished making the changes to the document, save, print, and close the document.

4. Sunset Tours and New World Airlines are promoting the upcoming season's travel bargains. You have been asked to develop the text for their sales brochure. Open the draft document named WD K-4, then save the document as "Tour Outline".

To complete this independent challenge:

1. In outline view collapse the entire outline to show only the first four heading levels.

2. Move the heading "Fly in Comfort" and its subordinate text so that it appears below the next heading in the outline.

3. Demote the heading "Paris" one level. Promote the heading "Choose from 3 exciting tour packages!" to level 3 and assign the names of the tour packages to heading level 4.

select	subentry	cross-reference
Sunset Tours		
New World Airlines	Tour Packages	
European tours		
Great Britain		European Tours
New York City		

4. Add a centered footer with the page number.

5. Mark the text in the table to be included in the index.

6. Select the three Mexican tours to be marked. Type "Mexico" as the main entry and the tour name as the subentry.

7. Create an index using the Fancy format. Insert a next page section break before the index.

8. Modify the page number in section 2 (the index) to begin at i. Compare the index to Figure K-21.

9. When you have finished making the changes to the document, save, print, and close the document.

FIGURE K-21

```
            ┌─────────────────────┐          Mazatlan, 2
            │          E          │          Puerto Vallarta, 2
            └─────────────────────┘
            European tours, 1              ┌─────────────────────┐
                                           │          N          │
            ┌─────────────────────┐        └─────────────────────┘
            │          G          │        New World Airlines
            └─────────────────────┘           Tour packages, 1, 2
            Great Britain. See European Tours   New York City, 1, 3

            ┌─────────────────────┐        ┌─────────────────────┐
            │          M          │        │          S          │
            └─────────────────────┘        └─────────────────────┘
            Mexico                         Sunset Tours, 1
               Cabo San Lucas, 2
```

► Visual Workshop

You are the marketing manager for New World Airlines. Your assistant has drafted a short proposal regarding new travel destination opportunities. It is your job to present the proposal to senior staff members at the upcoming quarterly meeting. Create an outline for marketing media strategies using the headings shown in Figure K-22 and save the document as "Media Outline". Then open the draft proposal named WD K-5 and save the document as "Airline Outline". Using Figure K-22 as a guide, apply heading styles. Insert the Media Outline subdocument and reorganize topics in the document to match the structure and organization of the table of contents. Make sure the conclusion topic appears on a separate page. Generate a table of contents, such as the one shown in Figure K-22. Include footers in the document showing the page numbers of sections. Select and mark at least five index entries of your choice and create an index at the end of the document, using Figure K-22 as a guide. Save, print, and close the document.

FIGURE K-22

C

Caribbean 1, 2

H

Hurricane Hugo
  Damage 1

M

Marketing 1

N

New World Airlines 1, 2

Q

Queen Cruises
  Official carrier 2

R

Research .... *See* Marketing

PLANNING FOR THE FUTURE **1**

NEW HORIZONS **1**

  EXPANDING INTO THE CARIBBEAN 1
    Future Expansion *1*
    Initial Expansion *1*

MARKET RESEARCH **1**

STRATEGIC ALLIANCES **2**

LOGISTICS **2**

  OFFICIAL CARRIER TO CRUISE LINES 2
  AIRCRAFT 2
  LAUNCHING FROM MIAMI/KEY WEST 2

MARKETING MEDIA STRATEGIES **3**

  PRINT ADS 3
  VIDEO 3
  OTHER 3
    CD-ROM *3*
    FAX to Agencies *3*

CONCLUSIONS **4**

Collaborating
with Documents

- ► **Insert comments in a document**
- ► **Save versions of a document**
- ► **Track changes in a document**
- ► **Compare documents**
- ► **Accept and reject changes**
- ► **Change tracking options**
- ► **Create a bookmark**
- ► **Create a hyperlink**

Sometimes you need to create documents as part of a team. For example, you might create a first draft that gets reviewed by other colleagues. You then incorporate their suggestions and revisions before submitting the final draft, which might contain additional comments of your own. To make it easier to develop documents with the collaboration of others, you can use the Compare Documents and Track Changes features to first identify changes in documents, then accept and reject individual changes. You can also save changes in separate versions within the same document, so that you can restore the document to an earlier version. In addition, you can quickly jump to different parts of a document (or even other documents) using bookmarks and hyperlinks. Angela would like to customize a standard work agreement (provided by Nomad Ltd's legal department). Because she is working with another colleague to complete this effort, she will use features in Word that make collaborating with others easier.

Inserting Comments in a Document

If you are working on a document that other people will review, you can add comments directed to your reviewer. One way to insert a comment is with the Comment feature (called Annotations in earlier versions of Word). Use it when you want to include a comment that is separate from the document text. When you insert such a comment, you enter the comment text in a separate pane. You can easily distinguish the document text from the comment itself, because the word before the comment identifier is highlighted in bright yellow. The comment text appears in a pop-up window when you move the pointer over the comment identifier. 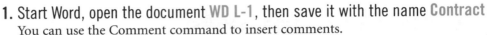 Angela starts with a standard document that was provided by Nomad Ltd's legal department. Because she would like to ask her reviewer's opinions of the changes she would like to make, she inserts comments.

Steps

1. **Start Word, open the document** WD L-1, **then save it with the name** Contract
   You can use the Comment command to insert comments.

2. **Click** Insert **on the menu bar, then click** Comment
   The Comment pane opens at the bottom of the window, as shown in Figure L-1. The letters at the start of the comment represent your initials. The number after your initials identifies the comment number. Each comment is automatically numbered sequentially as you add comments. The numbers are adjusted if you delete a comment.

3. **In the Comments pane, type** Shouldn't this document have a title?, **then click** Close
   You can read the contents of a comment by placing the pointer over a comment, which is identified by the highlighted word before the comment marker. Because comment markers are formatted in hidden text, they do not appear when you print the document.

4. **Move the pointer over the comment marker in the document until the pointer changes to** 📋
   The comment text appears as a yellow pop-up window, as shown in Figure L-2. To hide the comment, move the pointer.

5. **After you have finished reading the comment, move the pointer away from the comment identifier**
   When you need to add text to a comment, you can modify a comment.

6. **Double-click the** comment identifier **in the document**

7. **Place the insertion point at the end of the text in the comment, press** [Spacebar], **type** Please be as specific as possible., **then click** Close

8. **View the new text in the comment, as shown in Figure L-3**

9. **Click the** Save button 💾 **on the Standard toolbar**

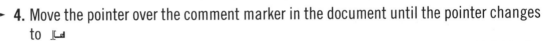

Trouble?
The initials you see will probably be different.

Trouble?
If you cannot see the comment identifier, be sure the Show/Hide button on the Standard toolbar is clicked.

QuickTip
You cannot delete the comment identifier that appears in the comment pane. To delete a comment, you must delete the comment identifier in the document. You cannot delete paragraph marks in the comment pane, either.

FIGURE L-1: **Comment pane**

Comment identifier

Writer's initials

Comment pane

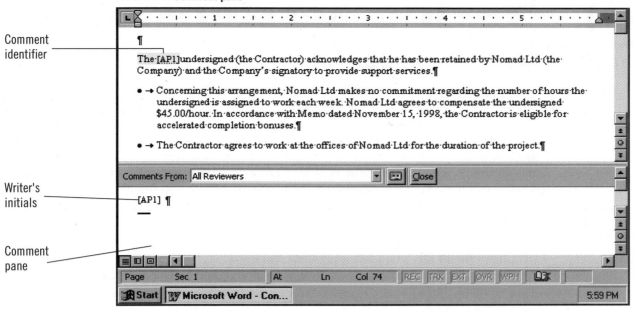

FIGURE L-2: **Comment displayed**

Move pointer near comment identifier to display comment

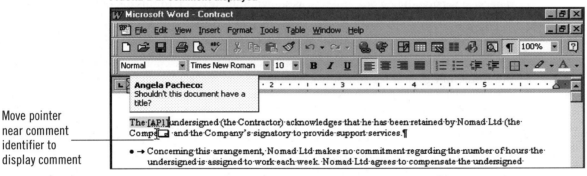

FIGURE L-3: **Modified comment**

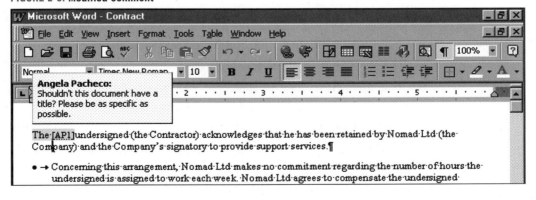

Printing comments

When you print a document that contains comments, by default the comments do not print. However, you do have the option to print the comments, either with the document or by themselves. In the Print dialog box, you can click the Print what list arrow, then click Comments to print a list of comments only. To print comments along with the document, click the Options button in the Print dialog box, in the next dialog box, click the Comments check box in the Include with document area. The comments will print after the last page of the document.

Word 97

Saving Versions of a Document

Sometimes when you are drafting a document, you might decide to pursue one line of thinking, while still retaining an earlier version of your ideas. Although you can always save the current document with a new name and make your changes in the new document, that method takes up unnecessary disk space and requires that you create and remember new file names for each separate copy. Instead, you can use the Version feature to save a version of the document within the current document. If you later need to return to an earlier version, you need only select the version you want to open. ◣━━━ Angela is investigating the possibility of lending the contractor a special scanner to use. Because she is still not certain if such a device is available, Angela wants two versions of the contract to allow for the possibility of providing it or not.

Steps 1 2 3 4

1. **Click File on the menu bar, then click Versions**
   The Versions dialog box appears. In this dialog box, you can see the versions saved in this document.

2. **Click Save Now**
   The Save Version dialog box appears, as shown in Figure L-4. In this dialog box, you can add comments or a description that will help you identify a specific version.

3. **Type Contract without scanner, then click OK**
   The Save Version and the Versions dialog boxes close. All the changes you have made so far are stored in this new version. Any new changes you make after saving a version of the document will be stored in the most recent version, which is the same as the currently open document. Now you can add text that will be saved in another version.

4. **Place the insertion point at the end of the line of the last bulleted item, press [Enter], then type For the purpose of completing tasks for current assignments, the Company will provide a flatbed scanner to be returned to the Company upon completion of the Work.**
   After this change, you can save another version of this document.

5. **Click File on the menu bar, then click Versions**
   In the Versions in Contract dialog box, you can see the versions you have saved in this document.

6. **Click Save Now, then in the Save Version dialog box, type Before legal reviewer's comments, including scanner text, then click OK**
   To view an earlier version of the document, you can open a version you saved previously.

7. **Click File on the menu bar, click Versions, the Versions in Contract dialog box appears as shown in Figure L-5, double-click the oldest version of the document (at the bottom of the list), then scroll to compare the versions**
   The earlier version of the document appears in a separate document window with the version comment, date, and time in the title. Notice that the new text appears in the most recent document, as shown in Figure L-6. Now, you can close the earlier version of the document.

8. **Click the Close button in the document window of the earlier version of the document, then click the Maximize button**

9. **Click the Save button 🖫 on the Standard toolbar**

FIGURE L-4: Save Version dialog box

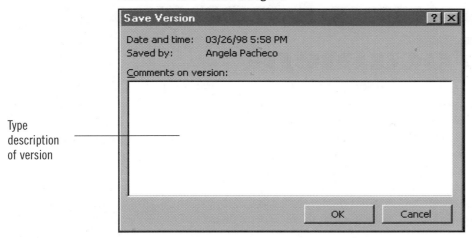

Type
description
of version

FIGURE L-5: Versions in Contract dialog box

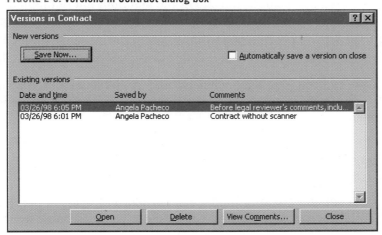

FIGURE L-6: Two versions of the same document

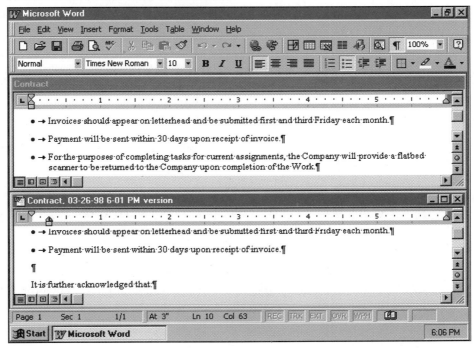

Tracking Changes in a Document

When you track the changes you make in a document, you can quickly identify the history of the modifications that you made in a document. Tracking changes is often used in legal documents, where changes made to a document must be clearly marked. For example, inserted text must be identified with an underline and deleted text must use **strikethrough** formatting. Strikethrough formatting ~~looks like this~~. You can see the deleted text, but it has a line through it, which indicates it has been deleted. You can apply this formatting yourself with options available with the Font command, or use the Highlight Changes feature to keep track of your changes automatically. Not sure of how her changes could change the legality of the document, Angela makes her changes, but leaves the original text visible so that the legal department can review her changes.

Steps

1. Place the insertion point at the end of the **last bulleted item**, press **[Enter]** to create a new line, then type **The Contractor will provide his own hardware and software. The Company will provide any proprietary material required for the final product.**
   You can apply special underline formatting to this text using options in the Font dialog box.

2. Select the text you just typed, click **Format** on the menu bar, then click **Font**
   The Font dialog box appears. From the Underline list, you can choose from nine different underlining options, which are described in Table L-1.

3. Click the **Underline list arrow**, click **Double**, click **OK**, then deselect the text
   The text is underlined with a double-underline, as shown in Figure L-7. You can show deleted text by using strikethrough formatting.

4. Select the **second bulleted item**, click **Format** on the menu bar, then click **Font**
   The Font dialog box appears. In the Effects area you can choose from two strikethrough options.

5. Click the **Strikethrough check box**, click **OK**, then deselect the text
   The text to be deleted appears formatted with strikethrough formatting, as shown in Figure L-8. You can have Word track your changes, applying the correct underlining and strikethrough formatting as you make your changes.

6. Click **Tools** on the menu bar, point to **Track Changes**, click **Highlight Changes**
   The Highlight Changes dialog box appears, as shown in Figure L-9. In this dialog box you can specify whether or not you want to see changes marked on the screen as you work in your document.

7. Click the **Track changes while editing check box**, be sure the other two check boxes are checked, then click **OK**
   Now you can make additional changes to your document.

8. Select the text **support** in the first sentence, type **web page and graphics design**, then press **[Spacebar]**
   Notice the deleted text "support" is struckthrough and the new text is underlined, as shown in Figure L-10.

9. Click the **Save button** on the Standard toolbar, then click the **Close button** in the document window to close the document

FIGURE L-7: Double-underlined text

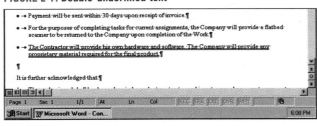

FIGURE L-8: Text with strikethrough formatting

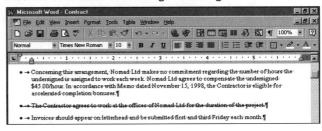

FIGURE L-9: Highlight Changes dialog box

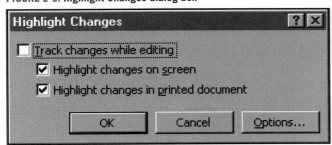

FIGURE L-10: Highlighted Changes

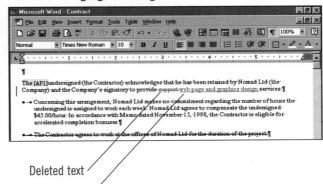

Deleted text

Inserted text

TABLE L-1: Underlining options

Single	Single, continuous underline to the selected text.
Words Only	Single underline to each word and punctuation.
Double	Double, continuous underline.
Dotted	Dotted single continuous underline.
Thick	Thick single continuous underline.
Dash	Dashed single continuous underline.
Dot Dash	Single continuous underline composed of dots and dashes.
Dot Dot Dash	Single continuous repeating underline of two dots and a dash.
Wave	Single continuous wavy underline to the selected text.

Comparing Documents

After other reviewers read your document, respond to your comments, and make changes to your document, you want to quickly identify the changes they made. Even if the reviewers did not make changes with the Highlight Changes feature turned on, you can still identify deleted and inserted text in the reviewed documents. With the Compare Documents feature, you can quickly recognize the differences between documents. As with the Track Changes feature, the Compare Documents feature uses strikethrough formatting to represent deleted text, and underlining to represent inserted text. ✐ After submitting her revised contract to the legal department, the experts there made additional changes. Angela would like to compare their completed document to hers.

Steps 1 2 3 4

1. **Open the document called WD L-2 and save it with the name Designer Contract**
   This document contains the changes made by the legal department. Before you review the changes, save the current version of the document.

2. **Click File on the menu, click Versions, then click Save Now**
   Now you can enter the comments you want to associate with this version.

3. **In the Save Version dialog box, type Contract after legal review, then click OK**
   With the version saved you are ready to compare the revised document with your original edited contract.

4. **Click Tools on the menu bar, point to Track Changes, then click Compare Documents**
   In the Compare Documents dialog box, you can specify the original document you want to compare.

5. **Click the file Contract, then click Open**
   You see a message informing you that there are already marked changes in the original document (Contract). These are the changes you highlighted earlier in this unit. It is OK to continue.

6. **Click Yes**
   After Word compares the two documents, you see the highlighted differences between the documents, as shown in Figure L-11. In the next lesson you will learn how to accept and reject individual changes. For now, save the compared document as a new version of the Designer Contract.

7. **Click File on the menu, click Versions, then click Save Now**
   Now you can enter the comments you want to associate with this version.

8. **In the Save Version dialog box, type Contract after comparison, then click OK**
   By saving the results of the comparison in a new version, you can always restore this version of the document, if you need to.

FIGURE L-11: Highlighted differences between documents

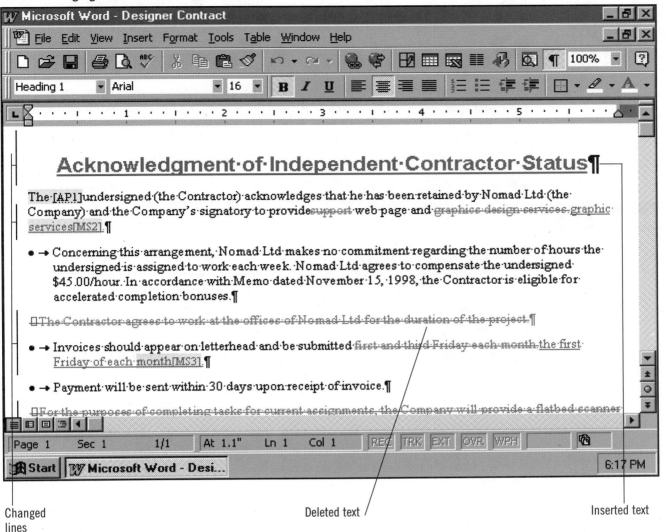

Changed lines

Deleted text

Inserted text

Why saving versions saves disk space

When you save a document with a new name, you are actually making a copy of the file. Because a file can require at least 20k per page (more if the document contains tables, graphics, comments, or charts), making many copies of a multiple-page document could take up a lot of disk space. Instead of saving each of the changes to a new copy of the file, which saves the entire contents of the file each time (even the information that is the same), you can save a version of the document. When you save a version, only the changes are saved, requiring significantly less disk space. When you open a version, the stored changes are merged with the unchanged part of the document, so that you see the entire document, change along with the unchanged parts.

Word 97

Accepting and Rejecting Changes

After comparing documents or after someone else makes changes, you can accept and reject individual changes. When you accept a change, the revised text becomes part of the document. When you reject a change, the original is restored. Using the Reviewing toolbar, as shown in Figure L-12, is an easy way to review the changes in a document. The Reviewing toolbar contains buttons for moving between changes, accepting and rejecting changes, turning on and off the Track Changes feature, saving versions, and reviewing, editing, and creating comments. ✏️ Now that Angela has compared the revised document with her original, she will accept and reject individual changes. First, she displays the Reviewing toolbar.

Steps

1. Click **View** on the menu bar, point to **Toolbars**, then click **Reviewing**
   The Reviewing toolbar appears in the document window, as shown in Figure L-12. Now you can move to and select the first change in the document.

2. Press **[Ctrl][Home]**, then click the **Next Change button** 📷 on the Reviewing toolbar
   Word selects the first change, inserted text. You can accept this change.

3. Click the **Accept Change button** 📷 on the Reviewing toolbar, then click 📷
   Word selects the first struckthrough text, indicating that it has been deleted, as shown in Figure L-13. You can read the comment at the end of the sentence, then accept the related changes.

4. Position the pointer over the comment, read the comment, click the **Accept Change button** 📷 on the Reviewing toolbar, click 📷, then click 📷
   Word makes the changes in the document. Now, move to the next change, which you can accept.

5. Click 📷, click 📷 to accept the insertion, click 📷, then click 📷 to accept the deletion

6. Position the pointer over the comment at the end of the paragraph, read the comment text, click 📷, click 📷 twice, then click 📷
   The inserted comment is accepted into the document and the next change is highlighted. You can read the next comment before rejecting the next change.

7. Place the pointer over **comment #4** and read it, click the **Reject Change button** 📷 to reject the deletion, click 📷, then click 📷
   Reapply a bullet to this paragraph.

8. Click the **Bullets button** 📷 on the Formatting toolbar
   Compare your document to Figure L-14. You can save your changes to a new version.

9. Click the **Save Version button** 📷 on the Reviewing toolbar, type **Contract after final review**, then click **OK**

FIGURE L-12: Reviewing toolbar

Insert Comment

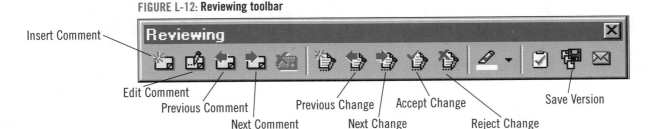

Edit Comment

Previous Comment

Next Comment

Previous Change

Next Change

Accept Change

Reject Change

Save Version

FIGURE L-13: Accepted change

Accepted change

Next change is highlighted

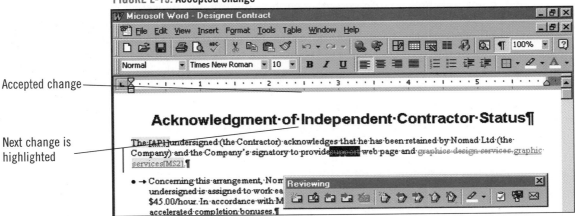

FIGURE L-14: Document after review

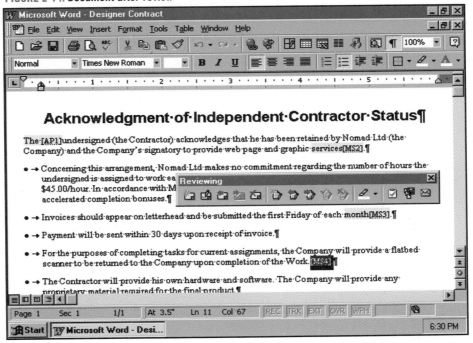

Working with multiple reviewers' comments

Each time your document is reviewed by another individual on another computer, the changes are highlighted in a different color. You can simulate multiple reviewers making changes and comments in your document by changing the User Information dialog box. Click Tools on the menu bar, then click Options. On the User Information tab, type a new name in the Name box and a different set of initials in the Initials box. When you return to your document any new changes you make will be highlighted in a different color, and the comments will be identified with a different set of initials.

Changing Tracking Options

By default, underlined text represents text that has been inserted; text that has been struck-through represents text that has been deleted. The vertical lines in the left margin identify a change of any type. By changing the tracking options, you can specify how you want each type of change formatted. For example, you might prefer double-underlining for inserted text and deleted text to simply be marked with a symbol. You can also indicate how changes in formatting should be identified. Or if you are presenting only a summary of changes, you can specify that only borders identify the parts of the document where changes have been made. ✍ Angela wants to return her revised document back to the legal department. Rather than identify each change as an insertion or deletion, she will simply identify the lines that have been revised.

Steps

1. Click **Tools** on the menu bar, click **Options**, then click the **Track Changes tab**
   The Track Changes tab in the Options dialog box displays the default highlighting options for identifying changes, as shown in Figure L-15. In this dialog box you can choose how the changes in a document are highlighted. If you want to use only borders to identify a changed line, you can remove the formatting for insertions and deletions.

2. In the Inserted text area, click the **Mark list arrow**, then click **none**
   Although inserted text will not be marked, inserted text will appear in a new color. Now you can change how deleted text is to be marked.

3. In the Deleted text area, click the **Mark list arrow**, click **Hidden**, then click **OK**
   This option indicates deleted text will be hidden. With the Track Changes options changed, you can again compare your final document to the original document.

4. Click **Tools** on the menu bar, point to **Track Changes**, then click **Compare Documents**
   Open the original document.

5. Double-click the document called **WD L-2**

6. Click **Yes** to compare the documents
   After Word compares the changes in the document, borders appear to the left of the lines that contain changes, as shown in Figure L-16. Return the Track Changes options back to the default.

7. Click **Tools** on the menu, then click **Options**, in the Inserted text area, click the **Mark list arrow**, then click **Underline**

8. In the Deleted text area, click the **Mark list arrow**, click **Strikethrough**, then click **OK**
   You can hide the Reviewing toolbar for now.

Time To

✔ Save

9. Click the **Close button** on the Reviewing toolbar
   Compare your document to Figure L-17.

FIGURE L-15: Track Changes tab in Options dialog box

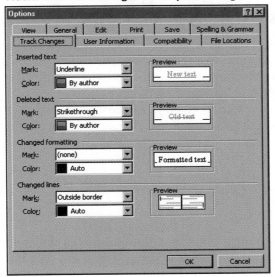

FIGURE L-16: Changed lines

Line indicates that this paragraph changed

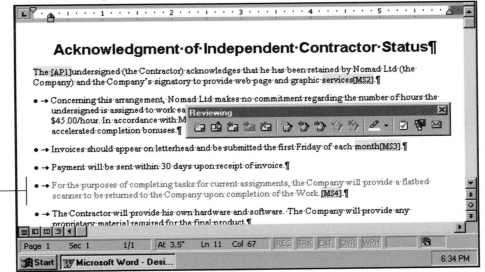

FIGURE L-17: Default highlighted changes

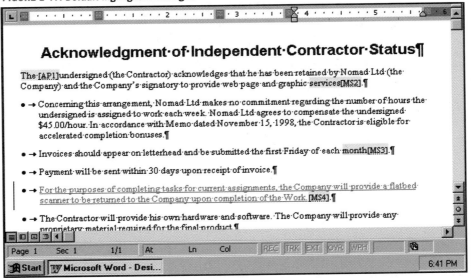

Creating a Bookmark

A **bookmark** is a location that you name and save in your document. It can be as simple as a word, phrase, heading, or paragraph, or it can be a range of text that covers many pages. By creating bookmarks in your document you can create hyperlinks that quickly move your reader to a specific location. You can also use bookmarks with the Go To feature to locate a part of the document you wish to find quickly.  To avoid having to scroll or use the keyboard to move quickly to the signature part of Angela's document, she creates a bookmark for the signature.

1. Scroll to locate the signature area near the end of the document, then place the insertion point in front of the name Maria Sanchez
   This location will become the bookmark.

2. Click Insert on the menu bar, then click Bookmark
   The Bookmark dialog box opens, as shown in Figure L-18. In this dialog box you can create and delete bookmarks that are saved in your document.

3. In the Bookmark name box, type signature, then click Add
   Your bookmark name can be up to 45 characters long, it can have no spaces, and it must begin with a letter (not a number). When you close the dialog box, you see no change in the document, but your bookmark is saved. Now you can test the bookmark.

4. Press [Ctrl] [Home] to return to the start of the document

QuickTip

You can also display the Go To dialog box by double-clicking anywhere in the left side of the status bar.

5. Click Edit on the menu bar, then click Go To
   In the Find and Replace dialog box you can specify the different ways you can move from location to location in your document (including moving from page to page, section to section, comment to comment), as shown in Figure L-19.

6. In the Go to what list, click Bookmark
   The list arrow on the right is updated to reflect the type of search. In this case, the list arrow displays the bookmark you just added. If you have more than one bookmark in a document, you can click the list arrow to display a list of bookmarks from which you can choose.

7. Click Go To, then click Close
   The insertion point moves to the signature line. The bookmark remains in the document even if you change the contents of the nearby text.

Time To

✔ Save

8. Select the name Maria Sanchez, type Angela Pacheco, then repeat steps 4-7 to test your bookmark again
   The Select Browse Object button (at the bottom of the vertical scroll bar) changes to reflect the new Go To option. Compare your screen to Figure L-20.

FIGURE L-18: Bookmark dialog box

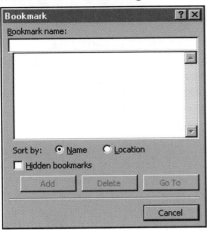

FIGURE L-19: Find and Replace dialog box

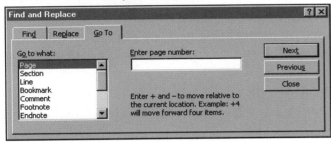

FIGURE L-20: Moving to a location with a bookmark

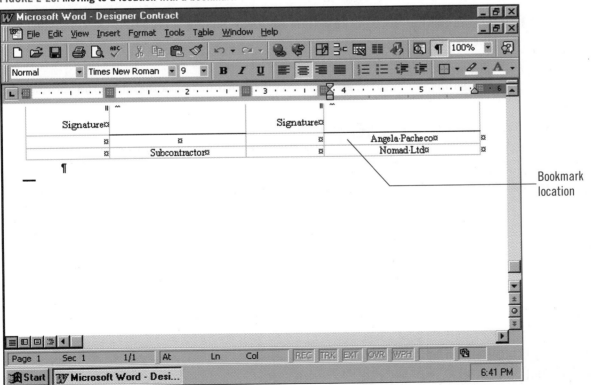

Creating a Hyperlink

To help your readers quickly locate parts of a document that require special attention, you can use hyperlinks. Hyperlinks allow you to specify the bookmark text you want displayed when you click the hyperlink. You can also create hyperlinks to other documents and to Web sites on the World Wide Web. ➤ With the bookmark to the signature created, Angela would like to ensure that her colleague can locate this important part of the document, so she creates a hyperlink to it.

Steps 1234

1. Press [Ctrl] [Home] to return to the start of the document

2. Select the text Company's signatory, click the Insert Hyperlink button 🔗 on the Standard toolbar
   The Insert Hyperlink dialog box appears, as shown in Figure L-21. In this dialog box you can specify the location of the text to which you want to link.

3. Click in the Named location in file (optional) box, then click Browse
   The Bookmark dialog box appears, in which you can specify the bookmark to which you want to create a link.

4. Be sure signature is selected, then click OK
   You return to the Insert Hyperlink dialog box. Now you can insert the hyperlink.

5. Click OK
   The hyperlink appears in the document. The text you selected is formatted in color and is underlined, as shown in Figure L-22.

6. Move the pointer over the hyperlink until the pointer changes to 🖐, as shown in Figure L-23

7. Click the hyperlink
   The hyperlink jumps to the bookmark on the signature line at the end of the document, as shown in Figure L-24.

8. Click the Save button 💾 on the Standard toolbar
   Before exiting Word, return the Go To command and the Select Browse Object button to the default "Page" setting.

9. Click the Select Browse Object button 🔘, then click the Browse by Page icon 🗋

Time To

✔ Save
✔ Print
✔ Close all documents
✔ Exit Word

CLUES TO USE

Creating hyperlinks to a Web site

The AutoFormat and AutoFormat As You Type features in Word automatically create hyperlinks whenever you type a Web address (a URL) in your document. If you do not want to show the actual URL itself as part of the hyperlink, you can specify the URL in the Link to file or URL box of the Hyperlink dialog box.

FIGURE L-21: Specifying a hyperlink

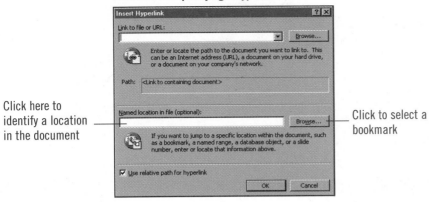

Click here to identify a location in the document

Click to select a bookmark

FIGURE L-22: Inserted hyperlink

Hyperlink is formatted in a new color and is underlined

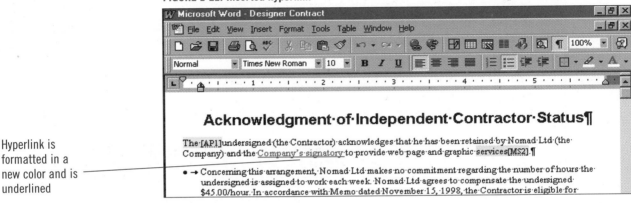

FIGURE L-23 Hyperlink pointer and screen tip

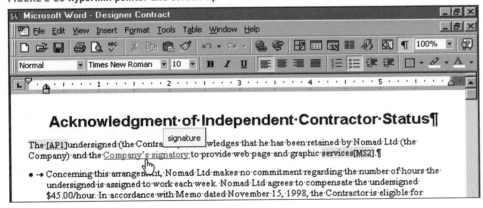

FIGURE L-24: Linked text

Bookmark location

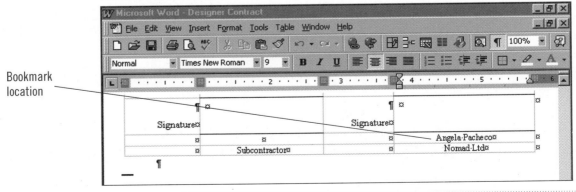

Practice

► Concepts Review

Label each of the elements in Figure L-25.

FIGURE L-25

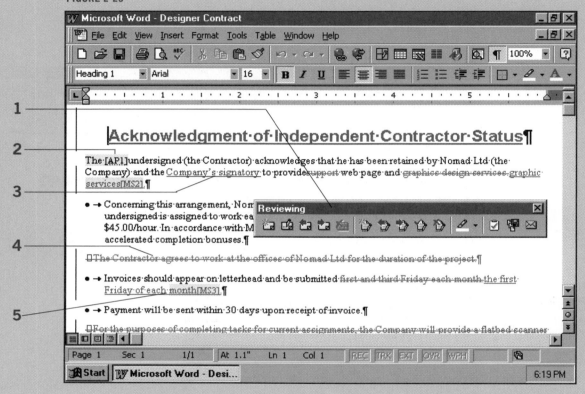

Match each of the following terms with the statement that best describes its function.

6. **Hyperlink**
7. **Bookmark**
8. **Comments**
9. **Strikethrough formatting**
10. **Versions command**

a. A location that is named and saved in a document
b. Allows you to save only the changes made to a document
c. Identifies deleted text
d. Text that is colored and underlined and when clicked moves the insertion point to a location in a file
e. A way to convey messages to the next editor through hidden text

Select the best answer from the list of choices.

11. **Which of the following statements is NOT a benefit of saving versions of a document?**
    a. Versions allow you to work in a document without seeing the comments displayed in earlier versions.
    b. Saving a document using the Version feature uses less disk space.
    c. Versions allow you to return to the original documents or track edits from previous changes.
    d. When saving a version you can add a comment or description to help you locate the version later.

12. **Which of the following statements is NOT true about using comments in a document?**
    a. Comments can be viewed by positioning the pointer over the comment marker.
    b. Comment text will be printed on a separate page at the end of a printed document.
    c. Comments can be edited by double-clicking on the comment marker.
    d. Comments are entered in a separate window pane.
13. **To delete an unwanted comment, you**
    a. Click Insert, Comments, then select the comment and press [Delete].
    b. Delete the text in the comment pane including the paragraph mark.
    c. Select the comment marker and press [Delete].
    d. You cannot delete a comment once it has been inserted.
14. **You can choose alternative formatting options for your tracked changes, using the**
    a. Options dialog box.
    b. Comments dialog box.
    c. Formatting toolbar.
    d. You cannot modify the tracking options.
15. **To accept or reject changes made to a document,**
    a. Use the Accept or Reject commands on the Edit menu.
    b. Click the Undo or Redo button on the Standard toolbar.
    c. Click the Accept or Reject buttons on the Standard toolbar.
    d. Click the Accept or Reject buttons on the Reviewing toolbar.
16. **Which of the following is NOT a way to quickly move to a location in a document?**
    a. Arrow keys
    b. Go To command on the Edit menu
    c. Bookmark
    d. Hyperlink

▶ Skills Review

1. **Insert comments in a document.**
   a. Open the document WD L-3 and save it as "Report Edits".
   b. Place the insertion point in the blank line above the table and type "Cost Comparisons".
   c. Click Insert on the menu bar, then click Comment.
   d. Type "Will this table be formatted using a preset style in the final copy?" then click Close.
   e. Position the pointer over the comment marker and double-click.
   f. Press [End] and press the spacebar and type "I added this title. Please edit as you wish".
   g. Click Close.
   h. Save your document.
2. **Save separate versions of a document.**
   a. Click File on the menu bar, then click Versions.
   b. Click Save Now, type "Publications table included", then click OK.
   c. Select and delete the entire table including the title.
   d. Click File, click Versions, then Save Now.
   e. Type "No table", then click OK.
3. **Tracking changes to a document.**
   a. Click Tools on the menu bar, point to Track Changes, then click Highlight Changes.
   b. Click the Track changes while editing check box, then click OK.

c. Scroll to the bulleted list under the heading "In-house Publishing".

d. Place the insertion point at the end of the last bulleted item and press [Enter].

e. Type "Division Reports".

f. Select the text "Newsletter" and type "NomadNotes".

g. Save your changes.

4. **Compare documents.**

   a. Open the document WD L-4 and save it as "Second Edits".

   b. Click File, click Versions, then click Save Now.

   c. Type "Second Draft", then click OK.

   d. Click Tools on the menu bar, point to Track Changes, then click Compare Documents.

   e. Double-click the file Report Edits, then click Yes to continue.

   f. Click File on the menu bar, click Versions, then click Save Now.

   g. Type "After comparisons", click OK.

5. **Accept and reject changes.**

   a. Press [Ctrl][Home].

   b. Click View on the menu bar, point to Toolbars, then click Reviewing.

   c. Click the Next Change button on the Reviewing toolbar, then click the Accept Change button.

   d. Use the Next Change and Accept Change buttons to accept the next two changes.

   e. Use the Next Change and Reject Change buttons to reject the next change.

   f. Use the Next Change and Accept Change buttons to accept the remaining changes. (Click Cancel if you are asked to review changes in the comments or to start again at the top of the document.)

   g. Click the Save version button on the Reviewing toolbar, type "Final changes", then click OK.

6. **Change tracking options.**

   a. Click Tools on the menu bar, click Options, then click the Track Changes tab.

   b. In the Insert Text area, click the Mark list arrow, then select Italic.

   c. In the Deleted text area, click the Color list arrow, then select Bright Green.

   d. Click OK.

   e. Click Tools on the menu bar, point to Track Changes, then click Compare Documents.

   f. Double-click the document WD L-4, then click Yes to continue if necessary.

   g. Scroll to and notice the changes to the edits remaining.

   h. Change the tracking options back to underlined for inserted text and By Author for deleted text.

7. **Create a bookmark and hyperlink.**

   a. Scroll to and select the heading "Shareholder Meeting".

   b. Click Insert on the menu bar, then click Bookmark.

   c. Type "meeting" and click Add.

   d. Press [Ctrl][Home] click Edit on the menu bar, then click Go To.

   e. Click Bookmark and select "meeting", click Go To, then click Close.

   f. Press [Ctrl][Home], select the last sentence of the first paragraph.

   g. Click Insert on the menu bar, then click Hyperlink.

   h. Click the Browse button next to the Name location in file area, select meeting, then click OK twice.

   i. Click the hyperlink text.

   j. Click View on the menu bar, click Toolbars, then click Reviewing to remove the toolbar.

   k. Print all the open documents.

   l. Press and hold [Shift], click File on the menu bar, then click Close All. Click Yes to save any changes, then exit Word.

▶ Independent Challenges

1. As vice president of Emerick Technologies, you need to draft a shareholder letter describing the past year's successes and detailing the upcoming shareholder meeting. After you draft the letter, you would like to add some comments for others to consider when editing the letter. You would also like to begin tracking all changes to the original letter. Begin by opening a new document and saving it as "Emerick Letter". Use Figure L-26 and L-27 as a guide for completing the letter.

To complete this independent challenge:

1. Type in the text as shown in Figure L-26.
2. After the text "Plaza Center Inn", insert the following comment: "Have we received confirmation on the conference room?"
3. Enable the Highlight changes while editing feature.
4. Change the times of the presentations to 4:00, 4:30, 5:00, and 5:30.
5. Type the following sentence at the end of the last paragraph: "Included is a reply card, which you can return to us if you plan to attend".
6. Modify the comment to include the sentence, "I prefer the River Room if it is available".
7. Compare your document to Figure L-27. Preview, save, and print the document before closing it.

FIGURE L-26

March 8, 1998

Ms. Mary Ruiz
321 Orange Way
Green Valley, CA 90272

Dear Shareholder:

This year has been an exciting and profitable one at Emerick Technologies. As a shareholder, you will want to know about recent successes and the challenges we expect in the coming year and beyond. This letter summarizes the high points of the year and provides valuable details about our work in individual areas of the organization, including finance, communications, quality assurance, and travel. I am including a complete copy of our Annual Report for the entire organization and detailed profiles for each division.

The schedule for the annual meeting is as follows:
• President's Presentation, 1:30
• Questions and answer session, 2:00
• Guest Speaker, 2:30
• Reception, 2:30

We are proud of our employees and encourage you to join us at the Emerick Technologies Annual Meeting held at the Plaza Center Inn next month.

Sincerely,

Chris Emerick
President
Emerick Technologies

FIGURE L-27

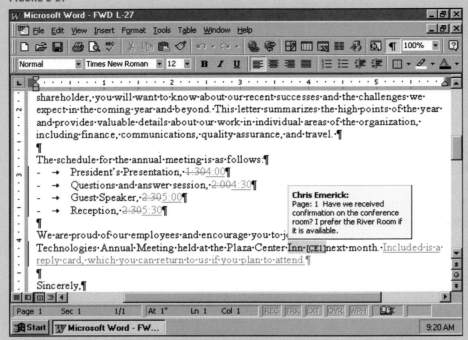

2. As co-chair for the Lake City High School class reunion, you recently drafted a letter requesting volunteers for the planning committee. Now you have decided it might be helpful to add a list of meeting dates and topics. Open the document named WD L-5 and save it as "Reunion Edits".

To complete this independent challenge:

1. Insert a comment to yourself after the first sentence in the second paragraph. Type "Must confirm location of the main reception and dinner by next month".
2. Put your name in place of [your name]. Save this version with the comment "no meeting dates".
3. Turn on the Highlight Changes feature on the Track Changes command.
4. Open the document WD L-6 and copy the table and all text. Then close the document without making changes in it.
5. Paste the table you copied after the section break at the end of the letter.
6. Add the sentence "I have enclosed a list of meeting dates and topics for your convenience." to the beginning of the last paragraph of the letter.
7. Select the date in the signature and type "1988".
8. Save the letter as a new version with the comment "with meeting dates".
9. Preview, save, and print the document, then close it.

3. As communications director of Escape Tours, you are responsible for reviewing the first draft of the new Tours brochure. You would also like to review the changes made by your assistant before accepting or rejecting them. Open the document named WD L-7 and save it as "Vacation Edits".

To complete this independent challenge:

1. Insert a comment after the first occurrence of New World Airlines stating "insert New World logo".
2. Enable the Highlight changes feature on the Track Changes command.
3. Save this version with the comment "first draft".
4. Compare the brochure to document WD L-8.
5. Using the Reviewing toolbar, review all the changes. Accept the revisions to the title and first paragraph. Reject the rest of the changes to the document.
6. Save a second version with the comment "final revisions".
7. Preview, save, and print the document, then close it.

4. As an executive member of an organization dedicated to the improvement of media services called Communication for the Future, you are in charge of planning the upcoming convention. While in town many of your members will want the opportunity to explore the Boston area. You have contracted with a travel agency to prepare a visitor's guide. The travel agency has prepared two drafts, and you would like to review the changes made and add comments for the writer. Open the document named WD L-9 and save it as "Boston Edits". Save the first version with the comment "first draft".

To complete this independent challenge:

1. Insert a comment after the first line stating "What do you think about this title?"
2. Enable the Highlight changes feature on the Track Changes command.
3. Compare the document to document WD L-10.
4. Change the tracking options to show inserted text with a double-underline and deleted text as hidden.
5. Using the Reviewing toolbar, review all the changes and comments. Reject the changes to the first paragraph and the deleted comment. Accept the paragraph mark after titles, and accept the added bullet and new phone number, then accept any other edits, including those in the comments area.
6. Save a second version with the comment "my comments".
7. Use the text "Sunset Tours" in the last paragraph to create a bookmark named "sunset".
8. Use the text "Sunset Tours" in the first paragraph to create a hyperlink to the bookmark "sunset".
9. Log on to the Internet and use your browser to locate Web sites for some of the attractions mentioned in the document in the Boston/Cambridge area. If you can't locate suitable Web sites on your own, use your browser to go to http://www.course.com. From there, click Student Online Companions, click the link for this book, then click the Word link for Unit L.
10. In your document, insert the Web addresses (the URLs) next to the topic in the document. The URLs are automatically formatted as hyperlinks to the Web site as you type them.
11. Preview, save, and print the document. Before closing the document, return the tracking options to the default settings, inserted text as underlined, and deleted text with strikethrough formatting.

► Visual Workshop

As conference coordinator for an upcoming Creativity Conference, you have final responsibility for all conference communications. Your assistant has drafted a flyer and made some revisions she would like you to approve. Open the document named WD L-11 and save it as "Conference Edits". Use the Compare Documents and Track Documents features to compare the document to the file WD L-12, then review the changes. Accept and reject changes according to the document shown in Figure L-28. Also, review and respond to the comments by inserting comments of your own. Use Figure L-28 as a guide for responding to the comments. In addition, create hyperlinks at the start of the document (and the necessary bookmarks) to locate the massage session and the Artist Planners address information at the end of the document. Don't forget to save one version before you compare documents, and one version after the revisions are approved. Preview, save, and print the document, then close it.

FIGURE L-28

Artistic Planners
Creativity Conference 1998

Welcome to <u>Artistic Planners</u> 1998 Creativity Conference™! This year's conference combines traditional creativity enhancing techniques with new methods tested in a variety of human endeavors. Learn how to become a more creative individual no matter what your field or specialty. Today's sessionswill help you:

❖ Learn to use guided imagery to focus your creative energies.

❖ Apply creativity enhancing techniques in everyday problem solving.

❖ Learn how to find your creative "zone" and stay in the zone through to the completion of a project.

❖ Discover how <u>massage</u> and relaxation techniques can enhance creativity.

GUIDED IMAGINATION

Learn new techniques for finding the images that guide you towards your goals[AP1]. Not [CE2]all images work in every situation, so in this session you learn how to clarify your objectives to select the appropriate images. Structures for inter-weaving images are also identified for gaining heightened integration.

CREATIVITY EVERY DAY

Creativity is not just for the traditional "artists" or traditional "artistic" endeavors. Employing creative thinking and creative problem-solving can help us achieve success in everyday activities at work, at home, and even at play. In this session, learn how to think "outside of the lines" no matter what you do.

HIDDEN IDEAS

Sometimes our creativity comes unbidden, and if we are fortunate enough to take the time and energy to act on it, we are satisfied. But what to do when you "have" to be creative and your muse has abandoned you? In this session, we explore writer's block (and similar ailments[AP3]) in [CE4]an effort to understand and triumph over them. Learn how to call up hidden stores of creativity, even when you feel dull and uninspired.

ENLIGHTENED MASSAGE

View demonstrations of deep breathing, massage, and creative visualization exercises. Learn how various relaxation techniques can enhance your creative abilities. An informal dinner and discussion is scheduled after this final session.

A TIME TO RELAX

This year's conference will be held in Minneapolis at the Riverside Plaza on September 18.For a complete registration packet write to: Artistic Planners; P.O. Box 12567, Minneapolis, MN 56784.

Page: 1
[AP1]This session received the most positive ratings from last year's attendees, but the session was severely under attended. Any ideas for promoting greater attendance this year?

Page: 1
[CE2]I thought we could print some of the shorter (and most exuberant) testimonials on buttons and wear them at the registration table when people sign in.

Page: 1
[AP3]The word "disabilities" might be overstating the severity of the problem. Our friends with true disabilities might be offended. Can you think of another term?

Page: 1
[CE4]Here are some other possibilities: maladies, afflictions, obstacles.

Arranging
Text and Text Objects

Objectives

► **Arrange text in columns**
► **Move and edit text in columns**
► **Modify column formatting**
► **Position text using text boxes**
► **Modify text box formatting**
► **Create a WordArt object**
► **Modify a WordArt object**
► **Add color effects to a WordArt object**

Word provides formatting techniques for arranging text on the page to give your document a polished, professional appearance. For example, by formatting text in columns, you give a document a newsletterlike appearance. By inserting and positioning text in text boxes, you create a text object, which you can place anywhere on the page. And with WordArt, you can achieve dramatic effects by formatting text in unique shapes and orientations. From a simple report she created earlier, Angela would like to apply WordArt effects in a newsletter format for the Nomad Ltd newsletter called NomadNotes.

Word 97

Arranging Text in Columns

In letters, reports, and memos you typically see text formatted in one column that spans the width of a page. In newsletters, magazines, and other forms of mass communication, it is common to see text arranged in multiple columns. Within the same document, or even on the same page, you can format text in different numbers of columns. For example, a headline or a wide table might appear in one column while the remainder of the text on the page appears in two or more columns. You can format different parts of the same document differently by separating the document into sections. Within each section you can apply column formatting without affecting other parts of the document. ✎ Angela wants to format the title and milestones in one column, while the middle part of the document will have two columns.

Steps 1 2 3 4

1. Start Word, open the document named WD M-1, and save it as Nomad Newsletter
   The document appears in normal view in the document window.

2. Click the Columns button ▦ on the Standard toolbar, then drag to select 3 columns, as shown in Figure M-1
   Your document is displayed in three columns. When you format your document in columns, the view automatically changes to page layout view so you can see the text arranged in columns.

3. With the insertion point in front of the heading Quality Assurance, click Insert on the menu bar, then click Break
   The Break dialog box opens. In this dialog box, you can specify the kind of break you want to insert.

4. In the Section breaks area, click the Continuous option button, then click OK
   A new section appears on the same page as the previous section. A section break appears as a double dotted line, as shown in Figure M-2. The status bar now indicates that the insertion point is located in section 2. With two sections in a document, you can now format the first section as one column.

5. Place the insertion point anywhere in section 1 (refer to the status bar for the location), click ▦, then drag to select 1 column
   The first section, which contains the Milestones information and the document title, now appears in one column.

QuickTip

You can also press [F4] to repeat the last command.

6. Place the insertion point in front of the paragraph mark above the heading Corporate Vision, using the same skills you used in steps 3-5, then format section 3 so it is one column
   The third section of the document is formatted in one column. To have a better view of the changes you have made to your document, you can change the magnification. You can type in a magnification value in the Zoom box.

7. Select the percentage in the Zoom box, type 70, then press [Enter]
   Now you can see more of the page. By clicking the Zoom list arrow you can see a list of preset magnifications. The magnification settings you use depend on the type of monitor you are using and your personal preferences.

Time To

✔ Save

8. Click the Zoom list arrow on the Standard toolbar, then click Page Width
   The Page Width setting displays the width of the document in the document window, as shown in Figure M-3.

FIGURE M-1: Columns button

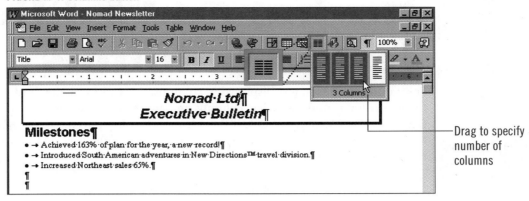

Drag to specify number of columns

FIGURE M-2: New section in document

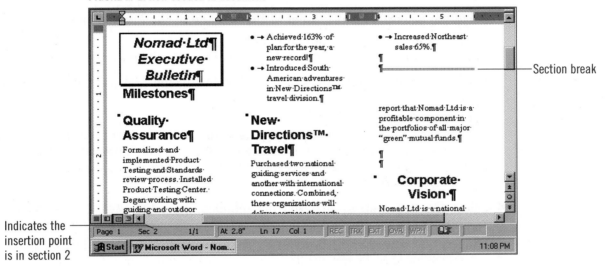

Section break

Indicates the insertion point is in section 2

FIGURE M-3: Multiple column formatting

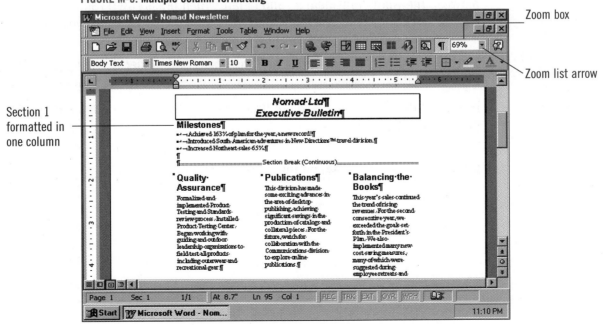

Zoom box

Zoom list arrow

Section 1 formatted in one column

Moving and Editing Text in Columns

You can rearrange the text displayed in columns. You can move the third column to appear as the first column. You can delete columns and add new text to columns. All the while, the column formatting is retained as text flows from one column to the next. 🖋 Angela would like to change the order of the columns in the middle of the page and also add text for another topic in the newsletter.

Steps 1234

1. Select all the text in the third column (in section 2), then click the Cut button ✂ on the Standard toolbar

   The selected text is removed from the document and placed on the clipboard. Now, you can paste the text in the new location.

2. Place the insertion point in front of the heading in the first column, then click the Paste button 📋 on the Standard toolbar

   The text appears in the first column. Now you can enter text for a new column.

3. Place the insertion point at the end of the text in the first column, press [Enter], then type:

   Communications [Enter]
   This division developed an in-house publishing department to produce all corporate communications including the annual report, the corporate newsletter, and corporate catalogs. They also completed a yearlong search for a new director of communications.
   Notice that the text flows to the next column as you type.

4. Select the first line of text you just entered, click the Style list arrow on the Formatting toolbar, then click Heading 1

   The text is formatted in the Heading 1 style. To ensure that the words in a specific phrase are not separated at the end of a line, you can add a nonbreaking space between words.

5. In the first paragraph under the heading Balancing the Books, select the space between the word "President's" and "Plan", then press [Ctrl] [Shift] [Spacebar]

   A small dot representing a nonbreaking space appears between the two words, and both words appear together on the same line, as shown in Figure M-4.

6. Select the heading Publications and the paragraph under it, then press [Delete]

   Now that you have deleted some of the text in this section, you can remove a column.

7. With the insertion point anywhere in section 2, click the Columns button ▦ , then drag to select 2 columns

   Compare your document to Figure M-5, then save your changes.

8. Click the Save button 💾 on the Standard toolbar

FIGURE M-4: A nonbreaking space between words

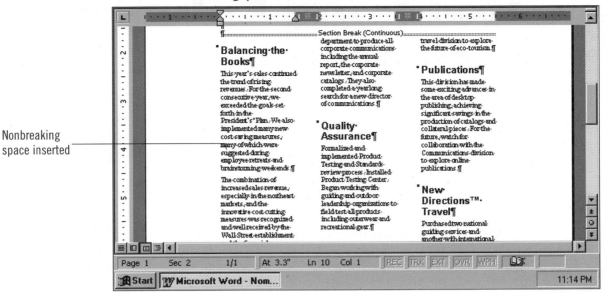

Nonbreaking space inserted

FIGURE M-5: One- and two-column formatting on the same page

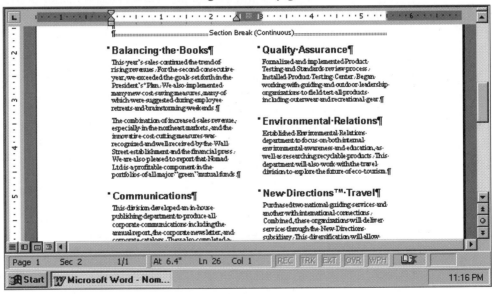

TABLE M-1: Types of breaks

break type	description
Page break	Inserts a new page. Subsequent text appears on the next page
Column break	Text after the break appears in the next column. Does not create a new column
Section break	Inserts a new section
Next page	New section (and text after the break) begins on the next page
Continuous	New section (and text after the break) begins on the same page
Even page	New section (and text after the break) begins on the next even-numbered page. If the previous section ends on an even page, this option inserts one blank page between sections
Odd page	New section (and text after the break) begins on the next odd-numbered page. If the previous section ends on an odd page, this option inserts one blank page between sections

Modifying Column Formatting

While the Columns button formats text in columns using default column settings, you can use the Columns command when you want to take advantage of special column formatting options. You can also use the Columns command to modify the column formatting for text already arranged in columns. You can choose a preset format, including uneven columns (in which one column is wider than the other). You can also specify the amount of space between columns and indicate whether or not you want a vertical line to separate columns. To create a more even right margin, you can add hyphens to longer words at the end of some of the lines. However, if you plan to make additional changes to the column formatting, consider using an **optional hyphen**. This type of hyphen breaks a word where you specify only if the word does not fit on the line. You can also create a **nonbreaking hyphen** that does not break at the end of the line. Use this type of hyphen when you use hyphenated words that you do not want separated by a line break. Angela would like to improve the appearance of the text in columns by adding hyphens to some of the words, and adding a vertical line between the two columns.

Trouble?

Depending on your monitor resolution and other factors, your text might wrap differently.

1. In the Communications paragraph, place the insertion point between the "**b**" and the "**l**" in the word "publishing", then press [**Ctrl**] [**Hyphen**]
   The word "publishing" is now broken over two lines. To prevent an already hyphenated word from breaking at the end of a line, you can insert a nonbreaking hyphen.

2. In the first paragraph under "Balancing the Books", select the **space** between the words "cost" and "savings", then press [**Ctrl**] [**Shift**] [**Hyphen**]
   This text will not break over two lines, no matter how you continue to format the columns. Now, you can continue to format your columns.

3. With the insertion point anywhere in the second section of the document, click **Format** on the menu bar, then click **Columns**
   The Columns dialog box opens, as shown in Figure M-6. In this dialog box you can add a vertical line between the columns and increase the space between the columns.

4. Click the **Line between check box**
   In the Preview area, a vertical line appears between the two columns.

5. Click the **Spacing up arrow** until **.7"** appears in the box, then click **OK**
   Notice that the width of the column changes as the spacing changes. Depending on the printer and type of monitor connected to your computer, the Quality Assurance heading might have dropped back into the previous column. Even if it did not, you can ensure that this heading always appears at the top of the second column. To do this you insert a column break.

6. Place the insertion point in front of the **Quality Assurance heading**, click **Insert** on the menu bar, then click **Break**
   The Break dialog box opens. In addition to selecting page or section breaks from this dialog box, you can also choose to insert a column break.

7. Click the **Column break option button**, then click **OK**
   Word inserts a dotted line labeled "Column Break," as shown in Figure M-7. The text after the column break appears at the top of the new column.

8. Click the **Save button** 💾 on the Standard toolbar

FIGURE M-6: Columns dialog box

Displays columns in uneven widths

Adjusts column width

Adds vertical line between columns

Adjusts width of space between columns

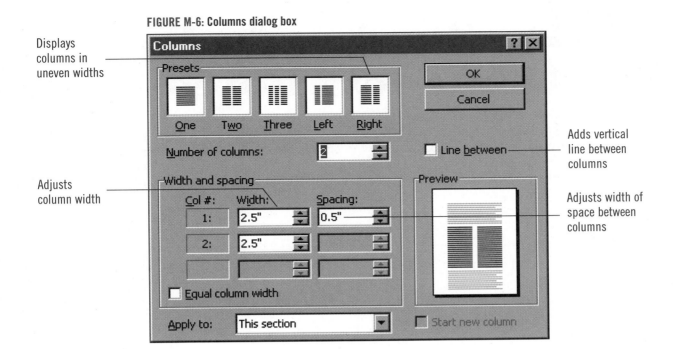

FIGURE M-7: Modified column formatting

Line between columns

Column break

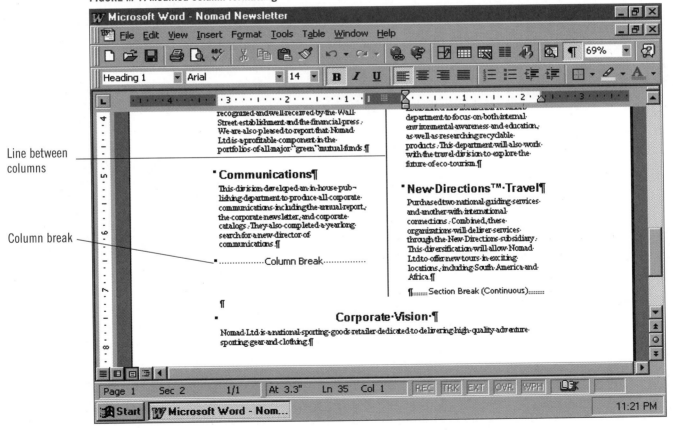

Positioning Text Using Text Boxes

The heading "Milestones" and the bulleted items in the first part of the newsletter could be presented as a **sidebar**, which is a smaller boxed section of text positioned vertically next to a main article. To create a sidebar, you need to be in page layout view to insert a text box around the appropriate text. By inserting a text box around text, you can position the text exactly where you want it on the page. ✎　Angela decides to position the Milestone topics as a sidebar to give readers an overview of the topics.

Steps 1 2 3 4

1. Select the heading **Milestones** and the **three bulleted items** in the list below the heading

   With the text selected, you can insert a text box.

2. Click **Insert** on the menu bar, then click **Text Box**

   A gray hashed border representing the text box (which does not appear in the printed document) appears around the text, as shown in Figure M-8. By default the text is also surrounded by a thin black border that does appear when you print. Notice that the frame has sizing handles—small black boxes—around it. Dragging the handles allows you to resize the frame.

3. Place the pointer over the right center sizing handle until the pointer changes to ↔, drag the **handle** to the left until the frame is about **1 ½" wide**, then release the mouse button

   The text appears in a square at the left edge of the page. Notice that an anchor icon appears next to the paragraph containing the text box. The **anchor icon** identifies the paragraph with which the text box is associated. If you move the paragraph, the text box moves with it. With the text now inserted in a text box, you can position the box anywhere in the document.

4. Position the pointer over a border of the frame until the pointer changes to ✛, then drag the framed text about **½" to the left** and about **2 ½" down** so that the anchor icon appears near the **Balancing the Books heading**, as shown in Figure M-9

   The sidebar appears outside the left margin as a box of text. You can still modify the text inside a text box after it has been inserted.

5. Click the **Font list arrow** on the Formatting toolbar, then click **Arial**

   The text inside the frame appears in the Arial font. Notice that the formatting of the surrounding text is not affected.

6. Select the **three bulleted items**, click the **Font Size list arrow** on the Formatting toolbar, then click **9**

   The font size of the bulleted items is reduced without changing the font size of the surrounding text outside the frame. To make the sidebar text even more dramatic, you can apply animated font formatting. If you have not installed the Animation effects in Word, skip the next two steps.

7. Select the heading **Milestones** in the text box, click **Format** on the menu bar, then click **Font**

8. Click the **Animation tab**, click **Sparkle Text**, then click **OK**

9. Deselect the text and compare your document to Figure M-10

Time To

✔ Save

FIGURE M-8: Inserted text box

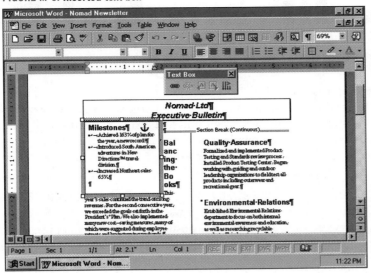

FIGURE M-9: Positioning text box

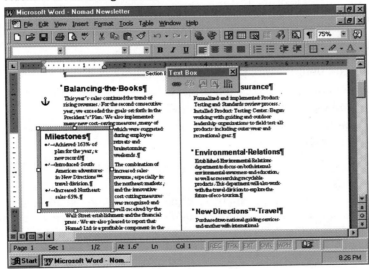

FIGURE M-10: Text box positioned as a sidebar

Anchor icon

Sizing handle

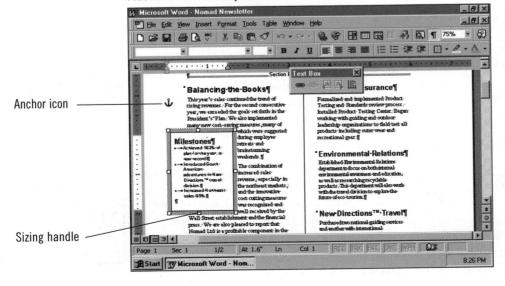

Modifying Text Box Formatting

Like other graphics and objects, you can modify a text box for more visual appeal. For example, you can change the line style of the border around the text box or choose to have no line at all. You can also adjust the color of the background in a text box to enhance it. In the same way you can adjust text wrapping around graphics, you can adjust text wrapping around a text box. 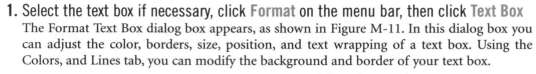 Angela would like to modify her text box to have a tan background and a different border.

Steps

1. **Select the text box if necessary, click Format on the menu bar, then click Text Box**
   The Format Text Box dialog box appears, as shown in Figure M-11. In this dialog box you can adjust the color, borders, size, position, and text wrapping of a text box. Using the Colors, and Lines tab, you can modify the background and border of your text box.

2. **Select the Colors and Lines tab, click the Color arrow in the Fill area, then click Tan**
   The text box will appear with a tan background. Before closing the dialog box, you can also adjust the line style of the text box.

3. **Click the Line Style list arrow, click the first 4½ pt double-line, then click OK**
   The fill color and line style are changed.

4. **Position the pointer over the middle sizing handle at the bottom of the text box until the pointer changes to ↕, then drag to hide the blank space at the bottom of the text without hiding the text, as shown in Figure M-12**
   Notice that the text box no longer covers the surrounding text, but instead this paragraph wraps around the text box.

5. **Select the ™ symbol in the heading "New Directions Travel", then type sm**
   "SM" stands for "Service Mark," which is similar to a registered trademark, but usually used for services rather than products. Like the trademark designation, it can be **superscripted** (positioned slightly above and to the right of the name) or it can be **subscripted** (positioned slightly below and to the right of the name).

6. **Select the text you just typed**

7. **Click Format on the menu bar, click Font, then click the Font tab if it is not already selected**
   The Font dialog box appears. Both the superscript and subscript format options are available with the Font command.

8. **Click the Subscript check box, click the All caps checkbox, then click OK**
   The service mark designation appears subscripted. Notice that subscripting the text also decreases the size of the text, but it does not change the font size.

9. **Deselect the text, then click the Save button ▣ on the Standard toolbar**
   Compare your document to Figure M-13.

Using drop caps

Another creative use of text boxes in Word is to format the first character of a paragraph as a drop cap. A **drop cap** is an initial character of a paragraph that is formatted significantly larger than the surrounding text, as shown in Figure M-14. With the Drop Cap command on the Format menu, the first character of the current paragraph is formatted to be three lines high and appears in its own text box.

FIGURE M-14: Drop cap

FIGURE M-11: **Format Text Box dialog box**

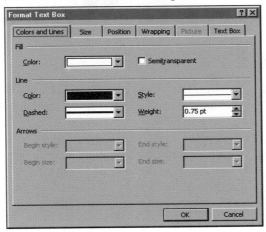

FIGURE M-12: **Completed text box**

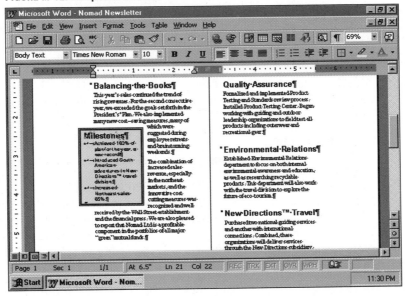

FIGURE M-13: **Subscripted text**

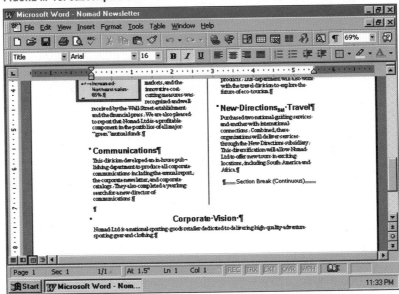

Creating a WordArt Object

WordArt is a built-in program you can use to display text in unique shapes, orientations, and patterns. For example, using WordArt you can place text in the shape of circles, triangles, and curves. You can also arrange text at an angle or around an arc pointing up or down. With WordArt, you can display text filled with interesting patterns. When you create a WordArt object, your documents take on exciting and unique qualities suitable for announcements, newsletters, brochures, and other special documents in which you want to achieve a greater visual impact. ⬥ Angela would like a more dramatic look for the title. Because she also wants to change the title, Angela begins by deleting the existing text.

Steps 1 2 3 4

1. **Select the two lines of text, Nomad Ltd and Executive Bulletin, then press [Delete]**
   After removing the existing text, you can use WordArt to create the new title.

2. **Click Insert on the menu bar, click Picture, then click WordArt**
   The WordArt Gallery dialog box opens, as shown in Figure M-15. This dialog box displays the various styles you can choose for your WordArt text.

3. **Select the fourth option in the fourth row, then click OK**
   The Edit WordArt Text dialog box opens. In this dialog box you enter the text to be used in the WordArt object.

4. **Type NomadNotes**
   In this dialog box you can also adjust the size and font style of the text.

5. **Click the Size list arrow, select 48, then click OK**
   The text in the document appears in a wave style, as shown in Figure M-16. The WordArt toolbar also appears in the document window. This toolbar contains buttons that can be used to modify a WordArt object and will appear only when a WordArt object is selected. Notice when the WordArt object is selected, you can see sizing handles to adjust the size of the object before positioning it.

6. **Drag the lower right sizing handle down and to the right until the object is about ¾" high and spans the width of both columns**
   After you have sized your WordArt object, you can position it in the document by dragging it to the desired location.

7. **Position the pointer over the WordArt object until the pointer changes to ✛, then drag the object to just above the section break at the top of the page**

8. **Click in the document anywhere outside of the object**
   The object is deselected and the WordArt toolbar is hidden. Compare your document to Figure M-17.

9. **Click the Save button 🖫 on the Standard toolbar**

FIGURE M-15: WordArt Gallery

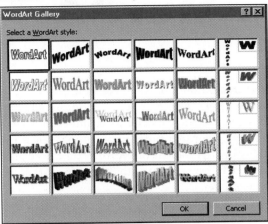

FIGURE M-16: Inserted WordArt object

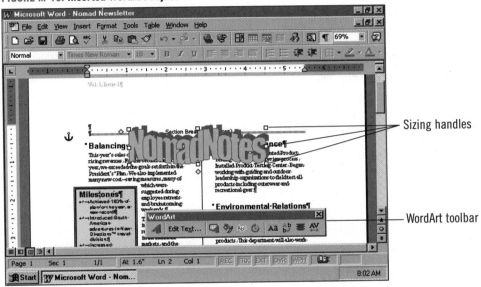

Sizing handles

WordArt toolbar

FIGURE M-17: Completed WordArt object

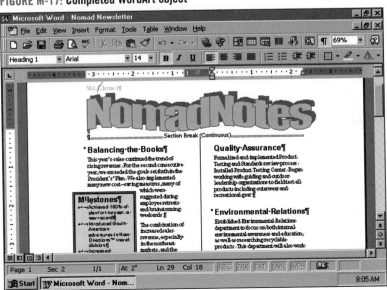

Modifying a WordArt Object

You can adjust the appearance of a WordArt object in a number of ways. For example, you can change the font style, format the text in bold, and change the font size. In addition, you can change the shape of the text, stretch or condense the text, change its line style, and even change the direction of the text. When you want to modify a WordArt object, you simply select the WordArt object by clicking over it. You can use the WordArt toolbar or WordArt on the Format menu to modify the object. ✐ Angela would like to experiment with other WordArt styles and other special effects for the masthead of the newsletter.

Steps 1234

1. **Select the WordArt object**
   The WordArt toolbar appears, as shown in Figure M-18. You can modify the style of the WordArt object using the various buttons on the toolbar.

2. **Click the WordArt Gallery button 🖼 on the WordArt toolbar**
   The WordArt Gallery dialog box appears, from which you can select a different style.

3. **Select the third option in the second row, then click OK**
   The WordArt object is displayed in the new style. Notice that you were not required to reenter the text. Not only can you modify the style, you can also modify the shape of your object. For example, you can choose from wavy, circular, vertical, or slanted shapes.

4. **Click the WordArt Shape button 🔤 on the WordArt toolbar, then select Double Wave 1 (seventh option in the third row)**
   The text appears in a wavy style. Even after you have modified the style and shape of your WordArt object, you can still modify the text.

5. **Click Edit Text on the WordArt toolbar**
   The Edit WordArt Text dialog box appears. You can adjust the text, font style, or font size.

6. **Delete the word Notes and retype it in capital letters, then click OK**
   The word "Notes" is formatted in all caps in the WordArt object. Using the WordArt toolbar, you can adjust the spacing between the letters in your object.

7. **Click the WordArt Character Spacing button 🔡 on the WordArt toolbar, then select Loose**
   The letters appear farther apart.

8. **Click anywhere outside the WordArt object**
   The WordArt toolbar is hidden. Compare your document to Figure M-19.

9. **Click the Save button 💾 on the Standard toolbar**

FIGURE M-18: WordArt toolbar

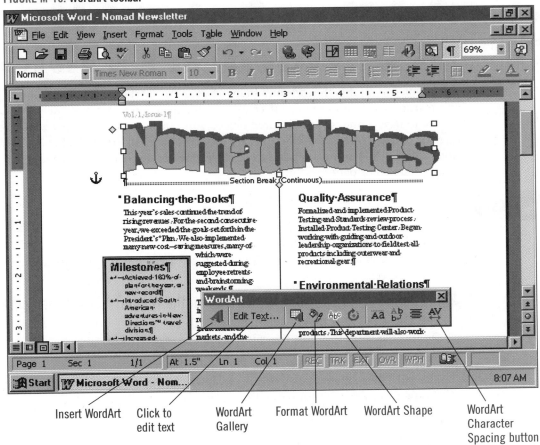

Insert WordArt   Click to   WordArt   Format WordArt   WordArt Shape   WordArt
                      edit text   Gallery   Character
                                                                       Spacing button

FIGURE M-19: Completed WordArt object

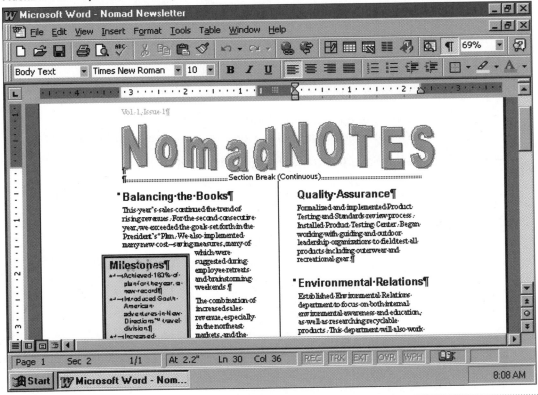

Adding Color Effects to a WordArt Object

Just as you can modify the style and shape of your WordArt object, you can also adjust the color and texture to add a dramatic effect. Word supplies various preset color patterns, or you can choose to have a one- or two-colored object. You can also choose from a wide selection of textures or patterns. All of these options are located in the Fill Effects dialog box. Angela would like to draw more attention to her title. She has decided to experiment with some of the Word preset color patterns.

Steps 1 2 3 4

1. **Select the WordArt object**
   The WordArt toolbar appears. With the object selected you can begin adding special effects to the object.

2. **Click the Format WordArt button** 🖌 **on the WordArt toolbar, then click the Colors and Lines tab if it is not already selected**
   On this tab you can adjust the color of the text in a WordArt object.

3. **Click the Color list arrow, then click Fill Effects**
   The Fill Effects dialog box appears, as shown in Figure M-20. In this dialog box you can choose from various textures and preset patterns.

4. **Click the Preset option button**
   With this option selected, you can choose from preset color patterns.

5. **Click the Preset colors list arrow, then select Desert**
   You can see a preview of the color pattern in the sample area.

6. **Click the Vertical option button, then in the Variants box click the option in the lower left corner**
   The sample area displays the pattern vertically.

7. **Click OK twice**
   The WordArt object is displayed with the new color pattern.

8. **Click anywhere outside the WordArt object**
   The WordArt toolbar is hidden. Compare your document to Figure M-21.

9. **Click the Save button** 💾 **on the Standard toolbar**

Time To
- Print
- Close

FIGURE M-20: Fill Effects dialog box

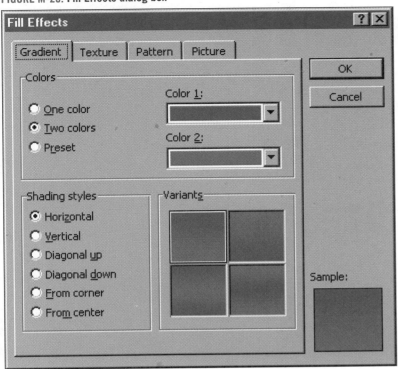

FIGURE M-21: Completed WordArt object

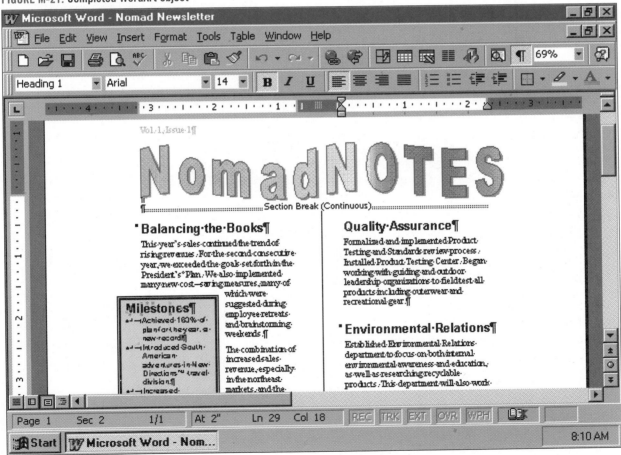

Word 97

Practice

▶ Concepts Review

Label each item of the newsletter shown in Figure M-22.

FIGURE M-22

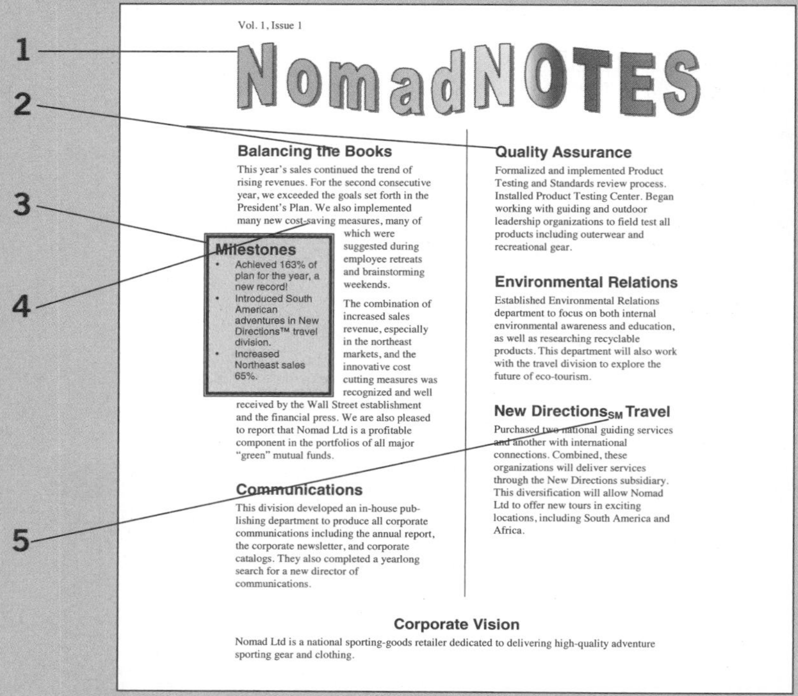

Vol. 1, Issue 1

NomadNOTES

Balancing the Books

This year's sales continued the trend of rising revenues. For the second consecutive year, we exceeded the goals set forth in the President's Plan. We also implemented many new cost-saving measures, many of which were suggested during employee retreats and brainstorming weekends.

The combination of increased sales revenue, especially in the northeast markets, and the innovative cost cutting measures was recognized and well received by the Wall Street establishment and the financial press. We are also pleased to report that Nomad Ltd is a profitable component in the portfolios of all major "green" mutual funds.

Milestones

- Achieved 163% of plan for the year, a new record!
- Introduced South American adventures in New Directions™ travel division.
- Increased Northeast sales 65%.

Communications

This division developed an in-house publishing department to produce all corporate communications including the annual report, the corporate newsletter, and corporate catalogs. They also completed a yearlong search for a new director of communications.

Quality Assurance

Formalized and implemented Product Testing and Standards review process. Installed Product Testing Center. Began working with guiding and outdoor leadership organizations to field test all products including outerwear and recreational gear.

Environmental Relations

Established Environmental Relations department to focus on both internal environmental awareness and education, as well as researching recyclable products. This department will also work with the travel division to explore the future of eco-tourism.

New Directions℠ Travel

Purchased two national guiding services and another with international connections. Combined, these organizations will deliver services through the New Directions subsidiary. This diversification will allow Nomad Ltd to offer new tours in exciting locations, including South America and Africa.

Corporate Vision

Nomad Ltd is a national sporting-goods retailer dedicated to delivering high-quality adventure sporting gear and clothing.

Match each of the following terms with the statement that best describes its function.

6. Text box	**a.** Allow you to size an object
7. Section	**b.** Formats text into columns using default settings
8. Sizing handles	**c.** Allows you to position text anywhere on the page
9. Column break	**d.** Allows you to format individual parts of a document with different settings
10. Columns button	**e.** Formats text in unique shapes, positions, and patterns
11. WordArt	**f.** Moves text from one column to the next

Select the best answer from the list of choices.

12. To view multiple columns in a document, you must

- **a.** Display the document in page layout view.
- **b.** Click Format on the menu bar, then click Columns and select the Show Formatting check box in the dialog box.
- **c.** Click the Columns button on the Standard toolbar and reapply the column formatting you want.
- **d.** Insert a column break somewhere in the column.

13. Which of the following is NOT an option in the Columns dialog box?

- **a.** Insert a vertical line between columns
- **b.** Display the document in normal view so you can see the columns
- **c.** Make columns of uneven widths
- **d.** Increase the space between columns

14. **The main benefit of inserting a section break in a document is**
   a. You can specify when you want text to start on a new page.
   b. You can redistribute the amount of text that appears in columns.
   c. You can create sections that contain identical page formatting.
   d. You can format different parts of the same document with different column and page setup settings.

15. **Which of the following is NOT true about text boxes?**
   a. You cannot position text boxes outside of the specified page margins.
   b. You can drag text boxes to different locations on the page.
   c. You can resize text boxes using the sizing handles.
   d. You can change the formatting of text boxes without affecting surrounding text outside of the frame.

16. **To insert a WordArt object**
   a. Click the Drawing toolbar and create text graphics using the Drawing program.
   b. Click Insert on the menu bar, click Picture, then click WordArt.
   c. Double-click any framed text to open the WordArt environment.
   d. Click Format on the menu bar, then click WordArt.

17. **Which of the following is NOT a way to modify a WordArt object?**
   a. Use the buttons on the WordArt toolbar
   b. Use the buttons on the Formatting toolbar
   c. Double-click the WordArt object
   d. Click Format, then click WordArt

18. **What is a nonbreaking space used for?**
   a. To format the document into columns
   b. To insert a continuous section break
   c. To prevent words in a phrase from separating at the end of a line
   d. To move text from one column to another

19. **What is NOT true of the Columns command?**
   a. You can modify column formatting for existing text.
   b. When you click the Columns button, the text is formatted into two columns by default.
   c. You can choose an uneven format for your columns.
   d. You can specify the amount of space between columns.

20. **An optional hyphen is used to**
   a. Create more even margins in a document.
   b. Prevent a hyphenated word from breaking at the end of the line.
   c. Increase the space between two columns.
   d. Break a word with a hyphen only if it doesn't fit on the line.

▶ Skills Review

1. **Arrange text in columns.**
   a. Start Word.
   b. Open the document named WD M-2 and save it as "Theater Art".
   c. Click the Columns button on the Standard toolbar, then drag to select three columns.
   d. Place the insertion point in front of the heading "Macbeth". Click Insert, then click Break.
   e. Click the Column break option button, then click OK.
   f. Place the insertion point in front of the heading "Hamlet", then press [F4] and save your work.

2. Create and format sections.

   a. Place the insertion point in front of the heading "Othello". Click Insert, then click Break.

   b. Click the Continuous option button, then click OK.

   c. Place the insertion point in section 1, click the Columns button on the Standard toolbar, then click one column.

   d. Place the insertion point before the paragraph mark above the heading "Still Can't Decide?" click Insert, then click Break.

   e. Click the Continuous option button, then click OK.

   f. Click the Columns button on the Standard toolbar, then click one column and save your work.

   g. Place the insertion point in section 2, click Format on the menu bar, then click Columns.

   h. In the Columns dialog box, click the Line between check box, then click OK.

   i. Save your changes.

3. Position text using text boxes.

   a. Select the entire paragraph near the beginning of the document in section 1, click Insert, then click Text Box.

   b. Drag the right center sizing handle to the left until the frame is about 1" wide. Drag the bottom center sizing handle until all the text can be seen.

   c. Position the pointer over a border of the frame until the pointer changes to the move pointer.

   d. Drag the framed text 1 ½ " to the left.

   e. Drag the framed text ½ " down. Continue positioning the framed text until it appears to the left of the main body of the document.

   f. Click the Center button on the Formatting toolbar.

   g. Click Format on the menu bar, then click Text Box.

   h. Click the Color list arrow in the Fill section, then select Sea Green. Click the color list arrow again, click Fill Effects, click from center on the Gradient tab, then click OK until you return to the document.

   i. Select the text in the text box, click the Font color list arrow on the Formatting toolbar, click White. Then click the Bold button on the Formatting toolbar. You might need to resize the text box.

   j. Save your work.

4. Create a WordArt object.

   a. Select the line with the text "Square Peg Theatre" and click the Cut button on the Standard toolbar.

   b. Click Insert, click Picture, then click WordArt.

   c. In the WordArt Gallery select the second option in the first row, then click OK.

   d. In the Edit WordArt Text box, press [Ctrl][V] to paste the text cut to the Clipboard, then click OK.

   e. Click the WordArt Shape button and click the Cascade Up shape (seventh option in the last row).

5. Modify the WordArt object.

   a. With the object still selected, click the Format WordArt button on the WordArt toolbar.

   b. On the Colors and Lines tab, in the Fill Color area, click the list arrow then click Sea Green. Click the Color list arrow again, click Fill Effects, click Horizontal on the Gradient tab, then click OK until you return to the document.

   c. Position the WordArt object at the top of the page above the three columns.

   d. Size the WordArt object as shown in Figure M-23.

   e. Click the WordArt Character Spacing button on the WordArt toolbar and select Very Tight.

   f. Click the WordArt Same Letter Heights button on the WordArt toolbar.

   g. Preview, save, and print the document.

   h. Close the file, then exit Word.

FIGURE M-23

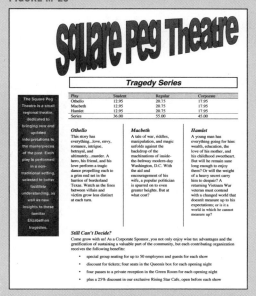

Independent Challenges

1. As committee co-chair, you need to draft a memo to the Middleburg Reunion Committee. After typing the text, you would like to add some interesting visual effects. Open a new document and save it as "Memo Art."

To complete this independent challenge:

1. Begin by typing the text of the memo, using Figure M-24 as your guide. Format the text in 14 pt type.
2. Insert a text box around the last paragraph.
3. Size and position the text box. Format the text box with a shaded background and double-lined border. Format the text in the text box as 24 pt, Arial, bold, italics, and center the text inside the text box.
4. Format the list in two columns. First insert a section break before the first item in the list and after the last item in the list.
5. Create a WordArt object using the third option in the last column of the WordArt Gallery. Size and position the WordArt object, as shown in Figure M-24.
6. Preview, save, and print the document, then close it.

FIGURE M-24

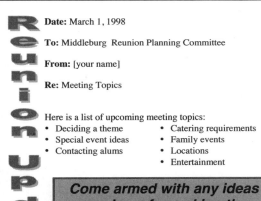

2. You would like to further enhance the appearance of the golf announcement for the Middleburg class reunion. To complete this independent challenge:

1. Create a new document using the text shown in Figure M-25 and save it as "Tournament Art".
2. To create the table, click the Insert Table button, then type the text shown in the figure. Use the Cell Height and Width command on the Table menu to center the entire table. Use the List1 preset option in the Table Autoformat dialog box to format the table.
3. Create a WordArt object using the first two lines in the title.
4. Select the third option in the first row of the WordArt Gallery.
5. Format the WordArt object with the preset rainbow color effects. Choose the Vertical style.
6. Drag the top sizing handle up to create a more dramatic arch.
7. Insert a text box object around the last five lines in the document.
8. Size the text box object and select a dashed line style.
9. Preview, save, and print the document, then close it.

FIGURE M-25

Dust off your clubs and sharpen your spikes for the

Middleburg Golf Classic! Compete for valuable prizes

and the admiration of your peers.

Where:	Middleburg Oaks Golf and Country Club
When:	Shot Gun Start at 7:30 a.m.
Who:	Mixed foursomes
HowMuch:	See below

Cost:	*Event:*
15.00	Single green fees
25.00	Couples green fees
5.00	Lunch
25.00	Dinner

Complete the attached order form (along with your check) to:

your name
Middleburg Reunion Co-chair
P.O. Box 2
Middleburg, MA 03411

3. As the marketing manager of a large computer company, you are responsible for producing an executive summary to the corporate report. Create a document that identifies the highlights of the past year. To save time, you start with a draft named WD M-3 and save it as "Corporate Art".

To complete this independent challenge:

1. Create a section break in the document (after the Financial Performance paragraph) and format the second section in two columns.
2. Insert a column break before the "Product Training" heading.
3. Insert a text box around the "Milestones" heading and bulleted items and format the text in Arial and bold. Add a teal green background to the text box. Size and position the text box to appear to the left of the Communications paragraph.
4. Create a WordArt object for the masthead, using the first style in the last row. Apply the Triangle Up shape to the WordArt object and apply very tight character spacing. Size the object to span the width at the top of the page.
5. Preview, save, and print the document, then close it. (*Hint*: When you print your document, you might see a message about the margins being outside the printable page. If this situation occurs, try to position the sidebar away from the left edge of the page.)

4. As an independent communications specialist, you have been asked to create an attractive newsletter for Celebrate Health, a nonprofit organization aimed at improving health awareness. Start by opening the draft document named WD M-4 and save it as "Health Art".

To complete this independent challenge:

1. Insert a section break after the heading "Current Topics".
2. Format section two in 2 uneven columns such that the left column is 2" wide and the right column is 2.75" wide.
3. Insert a text box around the heading "Whole Life Conference" and the following paragraph. Format the heading as 14 pt. Format the remaining text in the text box as 9 pt. Size and position the text box to appear at the bottom of the second column.
4. Create a WordArt object for the masthead, using the fourth option in the last column of the WordArt Gallery. Format the text for the object in Arial Black. Position and size the WordArt object so that it appears as a vertical sidebar that spans the length of the page.
5. Use your Web browser to locate sites related to any of the following topics: Organic farming, alternative medicine, or any other health and nutrition related issues or organizations. In your document, create a new heading called "Healthy Web Sites" and apply the Heading 1 style to it. In the following paragraph, provide a bulleted list of at least three different sites and corresponding descriptions. If you can't locate related sites, use your browser to go to http://www.course.com. From there, click Student Online Companions, then click the link for this textbook, then click the Word link for Unit M.
6. Create a text box for this topic and size and position it so it appears to the right of the text in the first section.
7. Preview, save, and print the document, then close it. (*Hint*: When you print your document, you might see a message about the margins being outside the printable page. If this situation occurs, try to position the object away from the left edge of the page.)

▶ Visual Workshop

As conference coordinator for Creative Consultants, Inc.'s creativity conference, you are responsible for developing an attractive document that describes the conference seminars to interested participants. Use the draft document WD M-5 to begin your program document. Figure M-26 serves as a guide for what your completed document should look like. Save the document with the name "Creative Art". Print the document before exiting Word.

FIGURE M-26

Creative Consultants, Inc.
Creativity Conference

Welcome to Creative Consultants, Inc Creativity Conference! This year's conference combines traditional creativity enhancing techniques with new methods tested in a variety of human endeavors. Learn how to become a more creative individual no matter what your field or interests. Today's sessions will help you:

❖Learn to use guided imagery to focus your creative energies.
❖Apply creativity enhancing techniques in everyday problem solving.
❖Learn how to find your creative "zone" and stay in the zone through to the completion of a project.
❖Discover how massage and relaxation techniques can enhance creativity.

Guided Imagination
Earth Room

Learn new techniques for finding the images that guide you towards your goals. Not all images work in every situation, so in this session you learn how to clarify your objectives to select the appropriate images. Structures for inter-weaving images are also identified for gaining heightened integration.

Creativity Every Day
Sky Room

Creativity is not just for the traditional "artists" or traditional "artistic" endeavors. Employing creative thinking and creative problem-solving can help us achieve success in everyday activities at work, at home, and even at play. In this session, learn how to think "outside of the lines" no matter what you do.

"Creative Consultants, Inc's creativity enhancing techniques have been used in every endeavor, including science, medicine, visual arts, music, and computer technology."
Beatrice Johnson
Massage World
June, 1998

The "Zone"
River Room

Sometimes our creativity comes unbidden, and if we are fortunate enough to take the time and energy to act on it, we are satisfied. But what to do when you "have" to be creative and your muse has abandoned you? In this session, we explore writer's block (and similar disabilities) in an effort to understand and triumph over them. Learn how to call up hidden stores of creativity, even when you feel dull and uninspired.

Enlightened Massage
Wind Room

View demonstrations of deep breathing, massage, and creative visualization exercises. Learn how various relaxation techniques can enhance your creative abilities. An informal dinner and discussion is scheduled after this final session.

Sign Me Up!
Please send me a conference registration packet. Enclosed is my check for $85.
Send self addressed envelope and check to:

Conference Coordinator
Creative Consultants, Inc
Pinewood Center
Pinewood, WI 54201

Creating
and Modifying Charts

- ▶ Understand charts and graphs
- ▶ Create a column chart from a table
- ▶ Change color and texture in a chart
- ▶ Create a pie chart
- ▶ Change orientation and proportions of a pie chart
- ▶ Create a pyramid chart
- ▶ Modify values in a chart
- ▶ Create a custom chart

A **chart** is a graphical representation of data often used to illustrate trends, relationships, or patterns. You can use a chart to accompany a table of numbers. Using the chart options in Word, you can specify the kind of chart you want to make, such as a line graph, a column chart, a pie chart, a three-dimensional chart, and so on. After you create your chart, you can modify it easily in the Graph window within Word. As part of Nomad Ltd's acquisition of Alpine Adventures, Angela will be giving a presentation to the board of directors. The presentation will include general tour and sales information. To better display this information, Angela would like to convert the tables of data into charts.

Understanding Charts and Graphs

Numbers might speak for themselves, but pictures speak a thousand words. When you present numbers in a table, your reader might not always spot their significance in the rows and columns of values. Charts and graphs help your reader analyze numbers and draw conclusions, because they help the reader visualize trends and make comparisons. Because the Microsoft graph feature provides many different kinds of charts and graphs from which to choose, it is useful to review the ones you are most likely to use and consider when you would use them. Figures N-1 and N-2 display some of the charts and graphs available in Word.

Details

 Line graphs are useful for illustrating trends. Each value is connected to the next value by a line.

 Area graphs are similar to line graphs, except that the area under the lines is filled with a color. Values for each item are represented in a unique color so you can distinguish different items from one another.

 XY (or scatter) charts are useful for identifying patterns or recognizing clusters of values, because each value is represented as a single dot. Values for each item are represented in a unique color so you can distinguish different items from one another.

 Column charts are useful when you want to compare values for different items side-by-side. Each value is represented as a vertical bar, and values for each item are represented in a unique color. Bar charts are similar to column charts, except that the values are displayed as horizontal (rather than vertical) bars. Pyramid charts are similar to bar and column charts except that data is displayed in pyramids rather than rectangles.

 Combination charts combine bar (or column) charts with line (or area) charts.

 Pie charts are useful for showing values in relation to other items and as part of a whole (as in a percentage). The values for each item are displayed in different colors to help you compare proportions. A doughnut chart is similar to a pie chart except that the center is not filled.

 For a more dramatic effect, you can also select a three-dimensional format for most of the charts.

 In addition, there are custom charts that combine elements of two or more of the standard charts, as shown in Figure N-2.

 You can also combine chart elements to create your own custom charts.

FIGURE N-1: Examples of types of charts and graphs available in Word

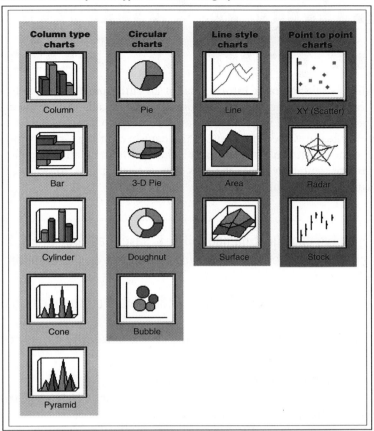

FIGURE N-2: Custom charts in Word

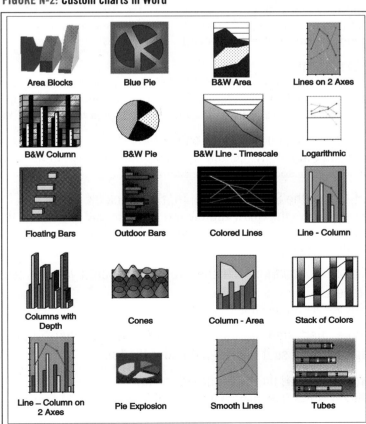

Creating a Column Chart from a Table

You can quickly display selected table information or an entire table as a chart by choosing the Chart command on the Insert menu. This command automatically inserts the default column chart based on the selected table information. You can then modify the chart type, color, text, placement, and other features. Because you use the datasheet in the Graph window to change values and labels in the chart, you can also insert a chart without creating a table first. The first table in the presentation shows the ages of tour participants. Angela will begin by displaying this information in a column chart.

1. Start Word, open the document named **WD N-1**, save it as **Tour Chart**, then, to show nonprinting characters, click the Show/Hide button ¶ on the Standard toolbar
   You first need to select the table.

2. Place the insertion point in the first table, click **Table** on the menu bar, then click **Select Table**
   This command selects the entire table. With the table selected, you are now ready to create a chart.

3. Click **Insert** on the menu bar, click **Picture**, then click **Chart**
   A column chart is inserted in the document, as shown in Figure N-3. The chart is shown in the Graph window. In this window, you have access to many chart buttons and options, which you can use to modify the chart. You can also modify the data in the datasheet, which is also shown in the Graph window. You cannot modify the text in your document when you are working in the Graph window. By double-clicking different parts of a chart you can change the color, position, and appearance of chart elements. You can also adjust the location of the legend (the key to the chart's data).

4. Double-click the **legend**
   The Format Legend dialog box opens. In this dialog box, you can modify the font, placement, and color of a legend. On the Placement tab you can adjust the location of the legend in relation to the chart. For example, you can move the legend to the top of the chart.

5. Click the **Placement tab**, click the **Top option button**
   On the Font tab you can modify the font style and size of the text in the legend, so that it matches the style of your document and is easier to read.

6. Click the **Font tab**, in the Size box select **10**, then click **OK**
   The legend appears above the chart, and the text in the legend appears in 10 pt and bold. Just as you can size pictures and graphics, you can also adjust the size of your graphs and charts to fit the document.

7. Drag the **right sizing handle** of the chart to the right until you can see all the bottom (x-axis) labels
   The x-axis labels appear on one line.

8. Click outside the chart area, position the pointer over the chart until it changes to ✛, and drag the **chart** so it is centered under the table

9. Click the **Save button** 🖫 on the Standard toolbar
   The Graph window closes. The chart is inserted in the document as shown in Figure N-4.

FIGURE N-3: Inserted chart in the Graph window

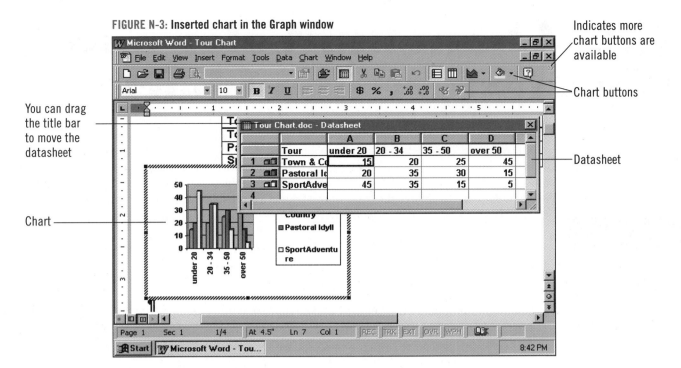

Indicates more chart buttons are available

Chart buttons

You can drag the title bar to move the datasheet

Datasheet

Chart

FIGURE N-4: Completed chart in document window

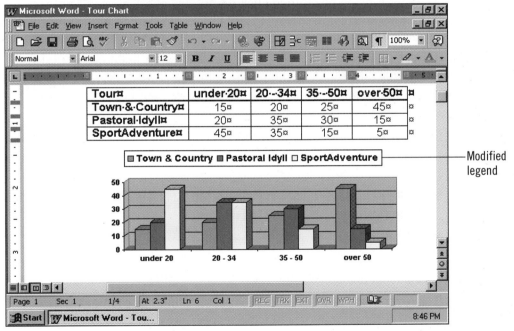

Tour¤	under·20¤	20·-·34¤	35·-·50¤	over·50¤	¤
Town·&·Country¤	15¤	20¤	25¤	45¤	¤
Pastoral·Idyll¤	20¤	35¤	30¤	15¤	¤
SportAdventure¤	45¤	35¤	15¤	5¤	¤

Modified legend

Viewing CourseHelp

The camera icon on the opposite page indicates there is a CourseHelp available for this lesson. CourseHelps are on-screen "movies" that bring difficult concepts to life, to help you understand the material in this book. Your instructor received a CourseHelp disk and should have installed it on the machine you are using.

Because CourseHelp runs in a separate window, you can start and view a movie even if you're in the middle of completing a lesson. Once the movie is finished, you can click the Word program button on the taskbar and continue with the lesson, right where you left off.

Changing Color and Texture in a Chart

Now that you have seen your chart in the document and your information appears as the kind of chart you want, you can improve the appearance of it. Unlike text in a document, a chart is a graphic object in Word, which is similar to a picture in a document. The chart itself is composed of several individual graphic objects, which you can modify. For example, you can change the color of all the columns related to a heading or change the color of just one column. ✐ Angela would like to change the color of the SportAdventure columns so they are easier to read. She has also decided to emphasize the largest values by changing the texture of these columns.

Steps

1. **Double-click the chart**
   The Graph window opens and the datasheet appears.

2. **Click once on one of the yellow SportAdventure columns, click the right mouse button, then click Format Data Series**
   The columns are selected when a small square appears in the center of each yellow column. The Format Data Series dialog box appears, as shown in Figure N-5.

3. **Select a green color, then click OK**
   Each yellow column changes to green. Notice the legend automatically changes to match the new color. You can also change the color of just one of the columns in a heading.

4. **Click on the green column above the under 20 heading, so that it is selected**
   Clicking once on a column selects the whole series. Clicking twice slowly selects just that data point, not the whole series. When a single column is selected, you can see its sizing handles (the small squares on the top, bottom, and sides).

5. **With the column selected, right click the column, then click Format Data Point**
   The Format Data Point dialog box opens. In this dialog box, you can modify the color and texture of a single column.

6. **Click Fill Effects, click the Pattern tab, select 75% dot pattern (fourth option in the second column), as shown in Figure N-6**

7. **Click OK twice**
   The column appears with the dot texture. Notice the legend and the other columns attached to the SportAdventure heading are not changed.

8. **Repeat steps 5 and 7 with the tallest column in each age category**
   Each of the columns you modified appears with the dot texture.

9. **Click outside the graph object area and save your changes to the chart**
   Compare your chart to Figure N-7.

Trouble?

If you double-click too quickly, the Format Data Series dialog box will open.

Trouble?

Where two tours have the same value, add a pattern to both columns.

FIGURE N-5: Format Data Series dialog box

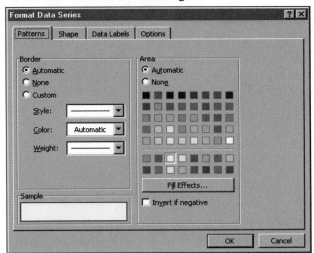

FIGURE N-6: Fill Effects dialog box

Select this pattern —

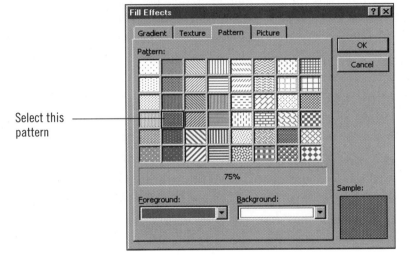

FIGURE N-7: Modified chart

Pattern —

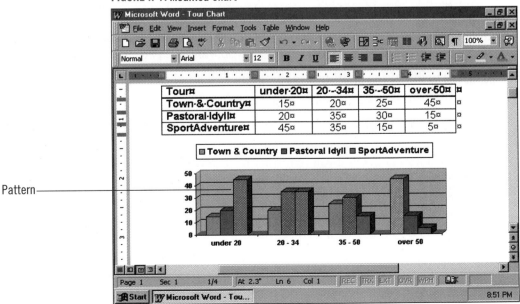

Word 97

Creating a Pie Chart

A pie chart is another kind of chart that is frequently used to compare values. It is different from a bar or column chart in that it represents values as part of a whole. Each value is represented as a wedge of the pie. All of the wedges add up to 100 percent, the entire pie reflecting a total of all the values. Because of its design, a pie chart displays values for only one row or column in a table. ▰ Angela would like to use a pie chart to illustrate the percent of travelers using Alpine Adventures in relation to other national travel services.

1. **Place the insertion point in the second table in the document, click Table, then click Select Table**
   With the data selected, you are ready to insert the graph in the document.

2. **Click Insert on the menu bar, click Picture, then click Chart**
   Because the column chart is the default graph, it appears in the document. Using the Chart Type button on the Graph toolbar, you can select the kind of chart you want to create.

QuickTip

To view the names of the charts, move the mouse over the icons.

3. **Click the Chart Type arrow, then select the 3-D Pie Chart**
   Notice the data in the chart is based on the first row of the datasheet as shown in Figure N-8. You can adjust the way a chart shows data by using the buttons on the Graph toolbar.

4. **Click the By Column button 🔲 on the Graph toolbar**
   The pie chart changes to show the data in the columns rather than the rows.

5. **Move the pointer over a wedge of the pie, right-click, then click Format Data Series**
   The Format Data Series dialog box appears. In this dialog box you can apply various options to your chart. For example, the numbers in the chart should be displayed as percentages.

6. **Click the Data Labels tab, click the Show percent option button, as shown in Figure N-9, then click OK**
   The percentages appear next to the related pie piece clarifying the data displayed in the chart.

7. **Move the pointer over the Alpine Adventures pie piece until you see the ScreenTips for each piece**
   Notice a message appears showing the name of the series, Number of Tour Participants, the name of the point, Alpine Adventures, the value, 305, and the percentage, 35%.

8. **Expand the width of the chart by dragging the size handles on either side of the outer object until the text in the legend appears on one line**

Time To

✔ Save

9. **Click outside the chart object, if necessary adjust the chart so that it matches Figure N-10, and save your changes to the chart**
   The Graph window closes and you return to the document window. Compare your graph to Figure N-10.

FIGURE N-8: **Pie chart based on data by rows**

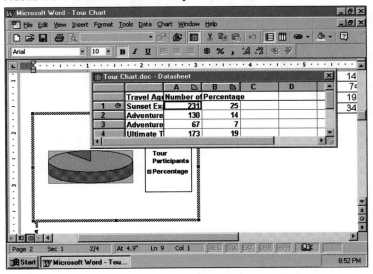

FIGURE N-9: **Format Data Series dialog box**

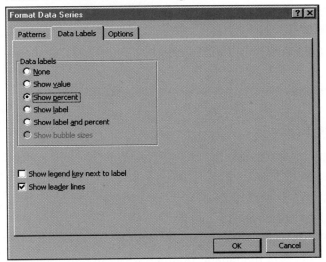

FIGURE N-10: **Completed pie chart**

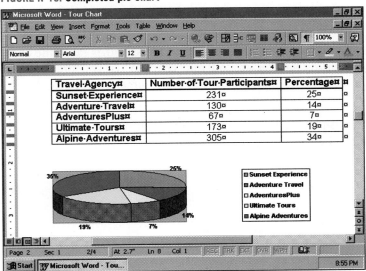

Changing Orientation and Proportions of a Pie Chart

Like the column chart you modified earlier, you can change the pie chart by adjusting the position of the legend title and other graph objects. You can adjust the orientation of a pie chart to better display a significant piece. You can modify the size of the chart and legend using the sizing handles of an individual selected object. ✐ Angela has decided her chart will have a better effect if the Alpine Adventures pie piece is placed toward the front. She will also size the chart so that it fills the width of the page.

Steps

1. **Double-click the pie chart to open the Graph window**
   The Graph window opens for you to modify the pie chart.

2. **Right-click on one of the pie pieces, then click Format Data Series**
   The Format Data Series dialog box opens. On the Options tab you can adjust the orientation of the chart by increasing or decreasing the angle.

3. **Click the Options tab, click the up arrow until the Degrees box reads 220, as shown in Figure N-11**
   You can see the change in orientation in the view area as you click the degree arrows.

4. **Click OK**
   The angle of the pie changes to 220 degrees.

5. **Click in the gray area called the plot area around the chart, then drag the right corner sizing handle until the chart is about 2" wide and 1" tall**
   Sizing the plot area affects only the chart and not the legend or white space around the chart.

6. **Drag the chart to the left so it does not cover the legend**
   You can also size the legend by selecting it and using the sizing handles.

7. **Click on the legend to select it, then size the legend to about 1" wide and 2" tall**
   Adjust the size of the legend until you can see all the text. Compare your chart to Figure N-12.

8. **Click in the white space around the chart, then drag the bottom center sizing handle down 1"**
   The white space around a chart and other text objects, such as the legend, is called the **chart area**. You now see two sets of sizing handles around your chart. When you size the chart area, you can change the size of both the chart and legend at the same time. Notice that the text in the legend is also sized proportionately.

9. **Click outside the chart area and save your changes to the chart**
   The Graph window is closed and you see the chart in the document window. Compare your chart to Figure N-13.

FIGURE N-11: **Options tab**

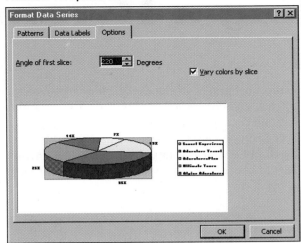

FIGURE N-12: **Selected chart area**

Chart area ─────

Data series ─────

Plot area ─────

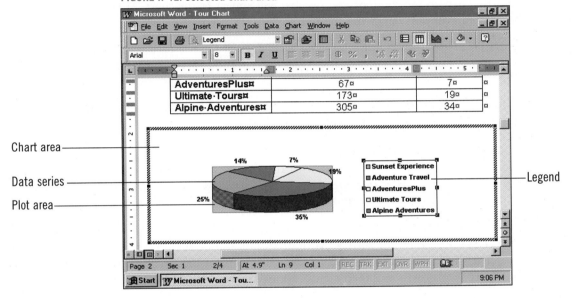

───── Legend

FIGURE N-13: **Modified pie chart**

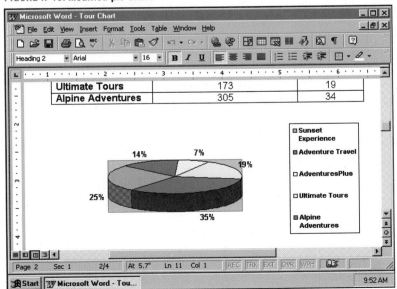

Creating a Pyramid Chart

A pyramid chart is similar to a column chart but the columns are shaped as pyramids. Pyramid charts come in various styles, such as stacked pyramids or 3-D pyramids. Like the pie chart, you can use a stacked pyramid chart to compare values. All the values related to a certain label are color coded and stacked in one pyramid. One of the Nomad Ltd market researchers has compiled a chart showing the 1998 tourism statistics sorted by continent visited and age of the tourist. ◢━━━ Angela would like to make these values easier to examine by inserting a stacked pyramid chart.

Steps

1. **In the third table in the document, select the first five columns (do not select the Total column)**
   Only the data in the columns you selected will appear in the chart. After the column chart is inserted, you can change the chart type.

2. **Click Insert on the menu bar, click Picture, then click Chart**
   Begin by sizing the chart area so it is easier to read, and to give yourself more space in which to work.

3. **Drag the bottom right corner sizing handle of the chart area down and to the right, so the chart area spans the width of the page**

4. **Click Chart on the menu bar, then click Chart Type**
   The Chart Type dialog box opens with the Standard Types tab displayed, as shown in Figure N-14. This tab offers a greater variety of standard chart types that are not available with the Chart Types button on the Graph toolbar.

5. **Scroll and select Pyramid in the Chart type box. In the Chart sub-type box, select 100% Stacked column with a pyramid shape, then click OK**
   The chart changes to show stacked columns. This type of chart is useful when showing total numbers of categories and their subcategories. You can also add titles to your chart or axes.

6. **Click Chart on the menu bar, click Chart Options, then click the Titles tab**
   The Chart Options dialog box contains various options related to titles, labels, axes, gridlines, tables, and legends.

7. **Type Tourism by Age in the Chart title box, then click OK**
   The new title appears at the top of the chart.

8. **Right-click on a pyramid in the chart, then click Format Data Series**
   The Format Data Series dialog box opens. Using the Options tab, you can adjust the gap width and gap depth of the columns or pyramids in your chart.

Time To

✔ Save

9. **Click the Options tab, in the Gap width box type 0, then click OK**
   The chart appears without gaps between the pyramids. Compare your chart to Figure N-15.

FIGURE N-14: Chart Type dialog box

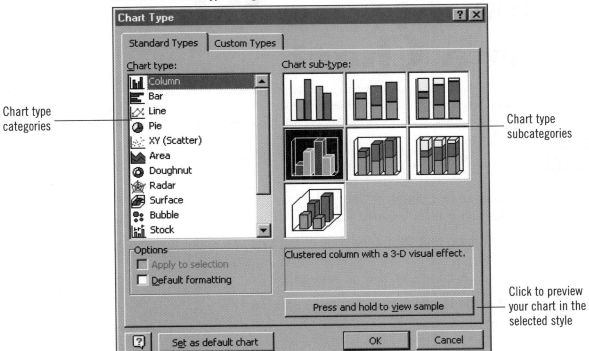

Chart type categories

Chart type subcategories

Click to preview your chart in the selected style

FIGURE N-15: Stacked pyramid chart

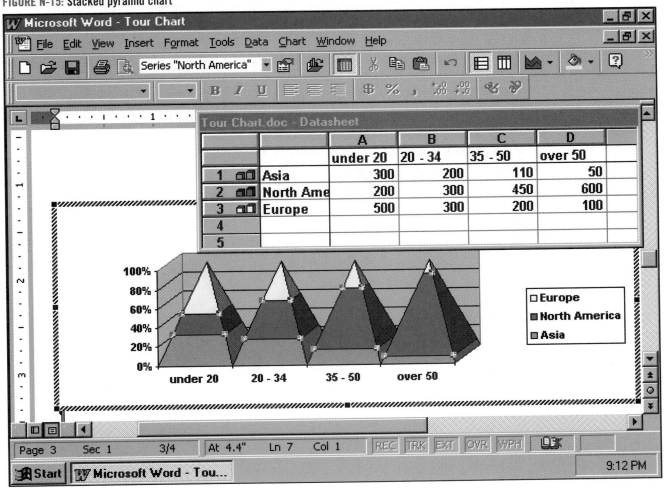

Modifying Values in a Chart

Using the datasheet, you can modify the values displayed in the chart. The chart is automatically updated when you enter new values in the datasheet. ✎ Angela's chart is based on rows and not columns, as it should be. Angela will modify some of the values, which are inaccurate.

Steps

1. Click the **By Column button** ⊞ on the Graph toolbar
   The chart changes to show data sorted by column. Now you can edit values in individual cells.

2. Click the cell at the intersection of the **Asia** and **Under 20** cells, type **100**, then click the **chart**
   The chart changes to show the new value.

3. Make the following changes in the datasheet:

Europe	Over 50	200
Europe	Under 20	700

4. Click the **chart**
   The new values are shown in the chart. When you have finished working in the datasheet, you can close or hide it to have a better view of your chart.

5. Click the **View Datasheet button** 🖽 on the Graph toolbar
   The datasheet is hidden. Clicking the View Datasheet button again will display the datasheet. Because the chart illustrates the information better than the table, you can remove this table from the document.

6. Click outside the chart area, select the entire table on this page, click **Table**, then click **Delete rows**
   The table no longer appears in the document. Compare your chart to Figure N-16.

7. Click the **Save button** 🖫 on the Standard toolbar

FIGURE N-16: Completed pyramid chart

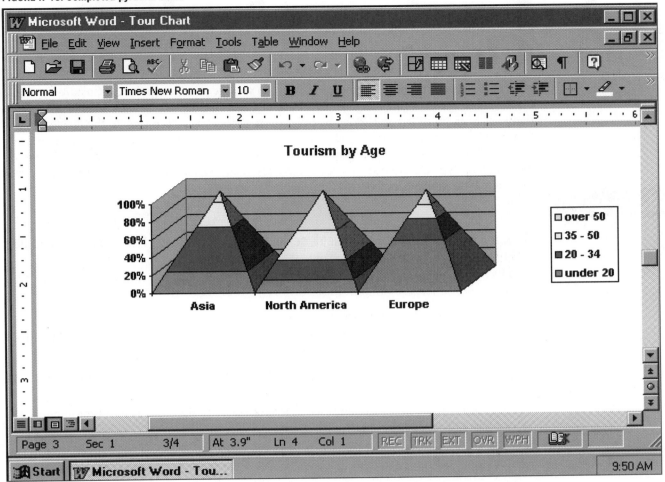

Editing values in the datasheet

The chart datasheet is designed to give you an easy way to edit values in a chart. The datasheet does NOT, however, update any calculations you might have used in the table. For example, if you change a value in a month column, you will need to enter a new value in the Total Year column. The datasheet will not recalculate your totals. In addition, the datasheet does not update the values in your table. If you change the values in the datasheet for a chart that is accompanied by a table, you need to enter new values in the table (and update any calculations in the table) to make the table match the values in the chart.

Creating a Custom Chart

You choose a chart type based on the kind of data you are presenting. On the Custom Types tab in the Chart Type dialog box, you can view and choose from built-in custom charts or charts that have been modified and added by other users. Adding a custom style to the dialog box can be very helpful after you have modified a chart and would like to use the same features again without repeating all the steps. ◀▬▬ Angela has viewed the chart types on the toolbar and on the Standard Type tab but does not see the chart type she wants. She will add a custom chart and make a few modifications.

Steps

1. **Scroll to the end of the document, select the last table, click Insert on the menu bar, click Picture, then click Chart**
   The default column chart appears in the Graph window. You can now apply the chart type you desire.

2. **Click Chart on the menu bar, then click Chart Type**
   The Chart Type dialog box appears. On the Custom Types tab, you can view and select from various custom charts.

3. **Click the Custom Types tab, scroll to and select the Columns with Depth custom chart as shown in Figure N-17, then click OK**
   The chart appears in the Columns with Depth style. With the correct chart type applied, you can size and modify the chart.

4. **Drag the lower right sizing handle of the outside chart object area down and to the right to span the width of the page**
   Use Figure N-18 as a guide for sizing the chart.

5. **Double-click on the legend, click the Placement tab, click the Top option button, then click OK**
   This text will appear across the top of the chart. You can also modify the labels on an axis.

6. **Double-click the text on the x-axis, in the Format Axis dialog box, click the Alignment tab, then click the Degrees up arrow until it shows 45**
   The category axis labels appear slanted at a 45-degree angle. You can add gridlines to make it easier to read the values in the chart. Next, decrease the font size of the text on the x-axis.

7. **Click the Font tab, in the Size box select 8, then click OK, then drag the bottom sizing handle until the label "Local Transportation" fits on one line**

QuickTip

You can also click the Value Axis Gridlines button 🗏 if you see it on the Graph toolbar.

8. **Click the y-axis on the chart, click Chart on the menu bar, click Chart options, then click the Gridlines tab, in the Value (Z) axis area, click the Major gridlines checkbox, then click OK**
   Gridlines appear in the chart for the Value axis. You can add gridlines for the category axis by clicking the Category Axis Gridlines on the Graph toolbar. To hide the gridlines, click the button again.

Time To

✔ Save
✔ Print
✔ Close
✔ Exit

9. **Click the cell in the upper left corner of the datasheet, click the Currency Style button 💲 on the Formatting toolbar, then click outside the chart**
   Clicking the left uppermost cell in a datasheet selects the entire datasheet. Both the datasheet and the chart appear with dollar signs. Compare your chart to Figure N-19.

FIGURE N-17: **Custom Types tab in Chart Type dialog box**

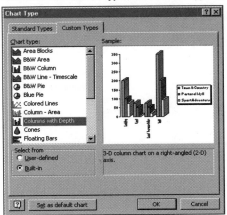

FIGURE N-18: **Columns with depth chart style**

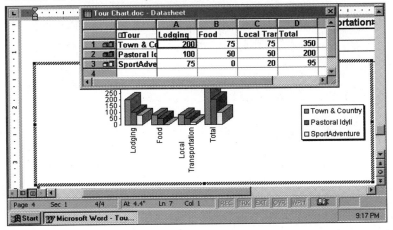

FIGURE N-19: **Completed chart**

Gridlines

Labels at
an angle

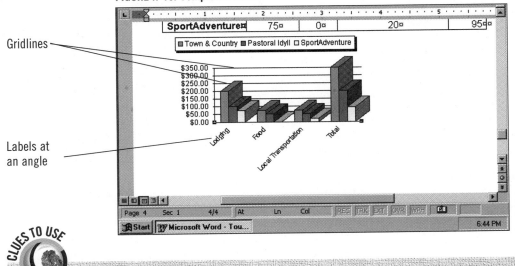

CLUES TO USE

Adding custom styles

You can add a style to the Custom Types tab in the
Chart Types dialog box, formatted the way you want.
With the selected chart, on the Custom Types tab,
click the User defined option button, then click Add.
You can enter the name and a description of the new

style and add the style. Also, located on the Custom
Chart tab is a button labeled Set as default chart. By
clicking this button, the selected chart style replaces
the column chart as the default style.

Word 97

Practice

► Concepts Review

Label each of the elements Figure N-20.

FIGURE N-20

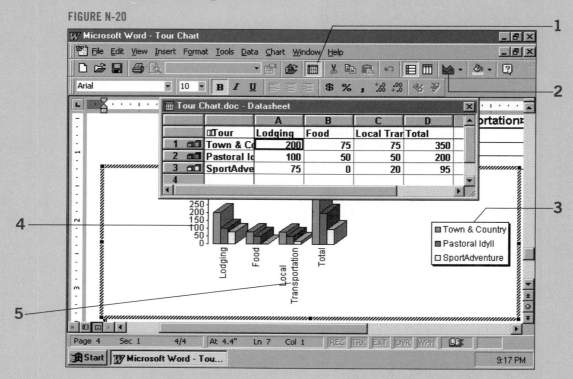

Match each of the following terms with the statement that best describes its function.

6. **Datasheet**
7. **Column chart**
8. **Legend**
9. **Chart Type button or command**
10. **Pie chart**

a. Used to compare values side-by-side
b. Displays the values a chart is based on
c. Offers various styles of charts that can be used
d. Displays values as parts of a whole
e. Serves as a visual key identifying how items are represented in a chart

Select the best answer from the list of choices.

11. **The Insert Chart command displays the**
    a. Chart dialog box.
    b. Chart Type dialog box.
    c. Chart in the default style.
    d. Chart Wizard.

12. **To modify a chart in Word, you**
    a. Click Insert on the menu bar, then click Object.
    b. Click the View Datasheet button on the Graph toolbar.
    c. Click Format on the menu bar, then click Chart.
    d. Double-click the chart to start the Graph program.

13. **Which of the following is NOT a way to modify the values displayed in a chart?**
    a. Click the View Datasheet button on the Graph toolbar.
    b. Double-click the chart object in the Graph program.
    c. Double-click a column in the datasheet to exclude values.
    d. Modify the values in the table in Word.

14. **Which of the following chart or graph types is most useful when you want to illustrate a trend?**
    a. Scatter chart
    b. Line graph
    c. Column chart
    d. Pie chart

► Skills Review

1. **Display data as a cylinder chart.**
   a. Start Word, then open the document named WD N-2 and save it as "Expense Chart".
   b. Select the table.
   c. Click Insert on the menu bar, click Picture, then click Chart.
   d. Click Chart on the menu bar, then click Chart Type.
   e. In the Chart Type column, scroll to and select Cylinder in the category box.
   f. Click the Press and hold to view sample button.
   g. Click OK.

2. **Modify text in a chart.**
   a. Select the Legend.
   b. Click Format on the menu bar, then click Selected Legend.
   c. Click the Placement tab.
   d. Click the Bottom option button, then click OK.
   e. Click Chart on the menu bar, then click Chart Options.
   f. Click the Titles tab, then type "Expense Report" in the Chart title box.
   g. Click OK.

3. **Modify color and size of a chart.**
   a. Drag the lower right sizing handle down and to the right so the chart is clearly visible.
   b. Click on the Taxis data series to select it.
   c. Click Format on the menu bar, then click Selected Data Series.
   d. Choose a bright green color, then click OK.
   e. Click outside the chart area.

4. **Create a pie chart.**
   a. Select the first two columns in the table.
   b. Click Insert on the menu bar, click Picture, then click Chart.
   c. Click the Chart Type arrow on the Graph toolbar, then click Pie Chart.
   d. Click outside the chart area.

5. **Modify values in a chart.**
   a. Double-click the pie chart to start the Graph program.
   b. Click the View Datasheet button on the Graph toolbar if the datasheet is not displayed already.
   c. Click the By Column button on the Graph toolbar.
   d. Click Chart on the menu bar, then click Chart Options.
   e. Click the Data Labels tab, click the Show percent option button, then click OK.

  f. Click outside the pie chart, then double-click the cylinder chart.

  g. Select the "January Airfare" cell, then type "457.56", then change Airfare Expense Total to 692.54.

  h. Select all the cells containing numeric values, then click the Currency Style button on the Formatting toolbar.

  i. Click Chart, click Chart Options, type "Revised January Airfare" in the chart title area, then click OK.

  j. Click outside the chart area.

  k. Select the table, click Table on the menu bar, then click Delete Rows.

6. Create a custom chart.

  a. Double-click the cylinder chart.

  b. Click Chart on the menu bar, then click Chart Type.

  c. Click the Custom Types tab, then review the different custom chart types.

  d. Click Smooth Lines.

  e. Click OK.

7. Change the axis labels.

  a. Double-click the Category axis labels.

  b. Click the Alignment tab and adjust the orientation to a 45° angle.

  c. Click the Font tab, change the font style to bold, then click OK.

  d. Double-click the Legend.

  e. Click the Font tab, change the font style to bold, then click OK.

  f. Click outside the chart area.

  g. Save and print the document, then exit Word.

▶ Independent Challenges

1. As the director of marketing for ReadersPlus publishing company, you are responsible for sales projections for the new beginners reading series called "Everyone Is a Reader." You have been asked to present these projections at the upcoming sales kickoff meeting. Begin by opening the draft document WD N-3 and saving it as "Readers Chart". Then create a chart based on the data presented in the table.

  To complete this independent challenge:

  1. Insert an (XY) Scatter Chart and display the data in rows, then exclude the Total column.
  2. Position the legend at the bottom of the chart.
  3. Adjust the chart width and height to fit the page.
  4. Select the y-axis and format the numbers as currency.
  5. Add a title "Regions" to the x-axis. Resize as necessary.
  6. Preview, save, print, then close the document.

2. As the conference coordinator for Educational Consultants, Inc, you are in charge of tracking the costs for an upcoming Creativity in Education Conference. You want to compare this year's conference costs with those of last year's conference. Open a new document and save it as "Education Chart". Using Figure N-21 as a guide for how the completed document should look, make the following changes.

To complete this independent challenge:

1. Insert a default column chart.
2. Use Figure N-21 as a guide to enter the text and values.
3. Adjust the font size of the legend to 9 pts and position it to the left of the chart.
4. Select the y-axis and format the numbers as currency.
5. Add a title called "Conference Costs" (Hint: Use the Chart Option command).
6. Size the chart and plot areas. Use the figure as a guide.
7. Adjust the Category Axis alignment to 45 degrees and change the font size to 9 pts.
8. Change the color of the Estimated data series to green.
9. Preview, save, print, then close the document.

FIGURE N-21

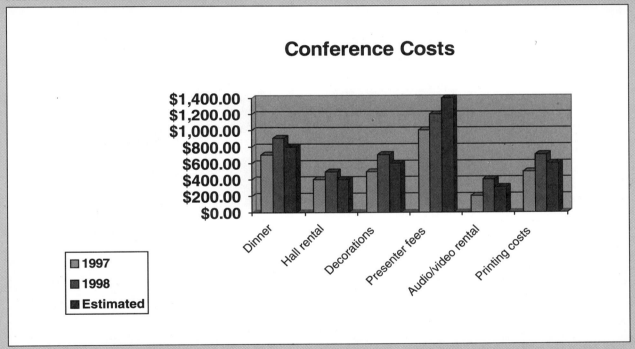

3. As a co-chairman of the entertainment committee for the Lake City class reunion, you are responsible for calculating attendance fees for the planned events. You want to create a visual graphic showing the distribution of attendees among all events. Another member of the committee has provided you with the number of classmates who have responded for specific events. Create a new document and save it as "Entertainment Chart".

To complete this independent challenge:

1. Create an exploded 3-D pie chart based on Figure N-22.
2. Display the data in columns.
3. Position the legend at the bottom of the chart.
4. Add the title "Entertainment Attendance".
5. Size the chart and plot areas.
6. Add data labels showing the value of each wedge.
7. Adjust the font size of the data labels to 9 pt. (*Hint*: Double-click on a data label to Format the Data Labels.)
8. Change the color of the Banquet wedge to bright red.
9. Preview, save, print, then close the document.

FIGURE N-22

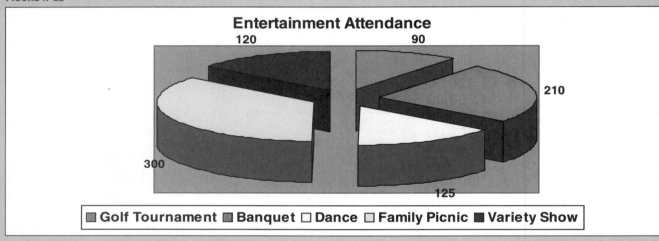

WEB WORK

4. As director of marketing for the Baroque Concert Series, you want to determine if the current number of registrations will cover the costs for upcoming events. Open the document named WD N-4 and save it as "Music Chart". To complete this independent challenge:

1. Create a chart similar to Figure N-23, based on the table provided.
2. Change the Series Attendance value to 101. Add the title and adjust the font size to 14 pt.
3. Display the data in columns, excluding the Cost and Total columns.
4. Add labels and percentages to the chart. Remove the legend.
5. Size the chart and plot areas. Use Figure N-23 as a guide.
6. Delete the table.
7. Use your Web browser to locate information concerning music that can be charted. For example, you could chart the Billboard rating of the top ten record albums and compare the current week to the previous week. On a new page in your document, create an appropriate new heading, for example, "Daily Ratings" followed by the date. Press [Enter] twice, then create a bar chart that displays the information. If you can't locate a related site, use your browser to go to http://www.course.com. From there, click Student Online Companions, click the link for this textbook, then click the Word link for Unit N. (*Hint*: It is sometimes easier to print a Web page and then copy the data into a Word table than to use the copy and paste function for a frame of data).
8. Preview, save, print, then close the document.

FIGURE N-23

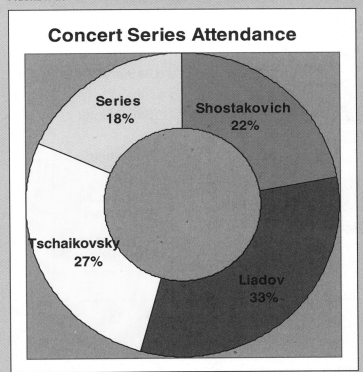

▶ Visual Workshop

As part of your responsibilities as the director of Valley SportsCenter health club, you have created a price list for club activities. Open the document named WD N-5 and save it as "Activity Chart". To help you recognize the percentage each activity contributes to the club's revenues, create a 3-D pie chart based on the data in the last column of the price list. Adjust the size and the color. Add a title. Compare your document to Figure N-24.

FIGURE N-24

Valley SportsCenter

Activity	Price	Sales	Total
Aerobic classes	$15.00	89	$1335.00
Basketball	$7.00	152	$1064.00
Racquetball	$10.00	123	$1230.00
Swimming	$10.00	236	$2360.00
Therapeutic massage	$30.00	56	$1680.00
DaySport Pass ("two-for-one")	$72.00	75	$5400.00
Total for First Quarter 1998		**731**	**$13069.00**

Activity Percentages

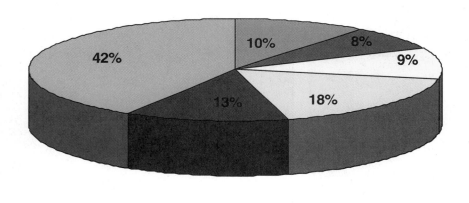

- ■ Aerobic classes
- ■ Basketball
- ☐ Racquetball
- ☐ Swimming
- ■ Therapeutic massage
- ■ DaySport Pass ("two-for-one")

Creating
and Using Forms

Objectives

- ► **Create a new template form**
- ► **Create text box form fields**
- ► **Specify calculations in form fields**
- ► **Create check box form fields**
- ► **Create drop-down form fields**
- ► **Add Help to form fields**
- ► **Prepare a form for a user**
- ► **Fill out a form as a user**

Forms in Word are similar to the familiar paper forms we use everyday. There are labeled blanks to be filled in and boxes to be checked, but Word forms have the added benefit of being able to be completed while you are in Word. By avoiding the use of paper forms, you not only save paper, but you also avoid having to decipher bad penmanship, and you can provide guidance for answering questions. In addition, you can create forms that provide a list of options from which a user can choose, and include help information for further instructions to the user when completing the form. Completing the weekly time sheet form is a dreaded task for employees at Nomad Ltd because its small blanks are difficult to complete. Repeated copying has caused much of the form to be illegible. The handwriting on the completed forms is also illegible, and inconsistent responses make it difficult to use the information the form is supposed to provide. Angela has decided to make this time-keeping activity simpler and more accurate by creating a form that everyone can use online.

Creating a New Template Form

When you create a form, you begin by creating a new template. A template is a special kind of document that contains standard text (also known as boilerplate text) and formatting that serves as a basis for new documents. By creating a form in a template, you allow users to complete the form without affecting the text, structure, or formatting of the form itself. Identifying the kind of information you want recorded on a form helps you determine which form fields you want to provide on the form. **Form fields** you can use are text boxes, check boxes and drop-down lists. The Forms toolbar makes it easy to create fields for your form. ✎ Using an existing time sheet (on paper), Angela is ready to start creating her form.

1. Start Word

2. Click File on the menu bar, then click New
   The New dialog box appears. Here you can indicate the type of document you want to create using existing templates or wizards. Because you want to create a form, indicate that you want to create a template first.

3. Click the Template option button in the lower right corner of the dialog box, then click OK
   A new document appears in the document window. The default name, Template1, appears in the title bar. To create a form, display the Forms toolbar so that you can use forms features.

4. Click View on the menu bar, click Toolbars, then click Forms
   The Forms toolbar appears in the document window. Because placing fields in a table makes it easy to align the fields, start your form by creating a table.

5. Press [Enter] to allow room for text at the top of the page, click the Insert Table button 🎛 on the Forms toolbar and click in the fourth square in the second row
   A table that is four columns wide by two rows appears in the document window.

6. Move the insertion point below the table, then press [Enter] to allow space before the next table, click the Insert Table button 🎛 on the Forms toolbar, then click in the fifth square in the third row
   Compare your document to Figure O-1. The first row in the second table will contain field names for the fields in the middle row of the form. After you create the fields in the middle row, you will copy the row to provide the seven rows the users will need to enter their hours worked each day.

7. Using Figure O-2 as a guide, type in the text for the form and field labels as indicated
   Remember to press [Tab] to move from cell to cell. Do not, however, press [Tab] in the last cell of the last row in a table. You will need to click in the first cell of the second table. The blank cells will contain the form fields you will enter later in the lesson.

8. Click the Save button 🖫 on the Standard toolbar, type Nomad Time Sheet in the File name box, then click Save
   Word saves your document as a template in the Templates folder in the Microsoft Office folder. If you choose to save your template to another location, you will not see it in the New dialog box.

FIGURE O-1: Blank cells in a table

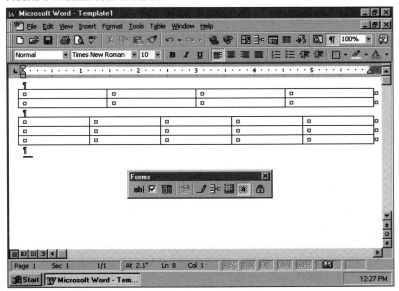

FIGURE O-2: Labeled cells in a table

Field labels—

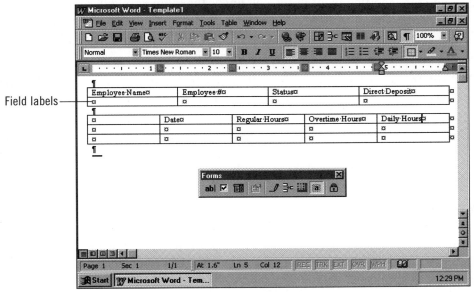

Designing effective forms

A major benefit of a form is that it provides ways to control and focus the user's attention on entering information (input), leaving the analysis and interpretation of the data (the output) to someone else. However, the form can also aid in the output part of the process. For example, in an order form, users can enter individual quantities of each product, and the form can include calculations that determine the total amount. When designing a form, take care to ensure that your questions (fields) allow the user to enter basic or raw information, so you can design the form to calculate data or allow analysts to interpret the input. Creating a new form in Word is a good opportunity to re-evaluate your information needs.

- Think about the information you want to gather in the form and who will use it.
- Determine how to make the form easy to complete, and reduce the chance for errors by selecting the form fields that are appropriate for the information being gathered.
- Determine what information needs to be grouped together and place those form fields next to each other.

Creating Text Box Form Fields

Text box form fields provide an area for users to enter text information in a field. By using a text box form field (rather than simply having a user enter text in a table cell) you can inform users of data entry errors they might have made. For example, you can restrict the user to a specific number of characters or specify that only numbers (rather than any character) or dates are valid entries. If the user enters an invalid response, the form will "beep" and display an error message, so that the user enters only correct responses. ✍ Angela would like each employee to enter his or her name, and employee ID number. For each day worked, employees should also enter the starting and ending time and hours. She will use text boxes to gather this information in the form.

Steps 123 4

1. With the insertion point in the cell under the label Employee Name in the first row, click the Text Form Field button abl on the Forms toolbar

   Five shaded dots appear in the cell that contained the insertion point, as shown in Figure O-3. Next, create another field for the employee number.

2. Place the insertion point in the cell under the label Employee # in the first row, click abl on the Forms toolbar

   You will enter fields for the other cells in this table later in this unit. For now, you can enter additional fields for entering time tracking information.

3. Place the insertion point in the cell under the heading Status, and click abl on the Forms toolbar, then repeat this step for the cells under the Date, Regular Hours, Overtime Hours, and Daily Hours columns

   The cell under the Date label will contain a date supplied by the user (the employee completing the form). You can format a text box form field to accept only dates and display all dates in the same format. You can specify such field options in the Form Field Options dialog box.

4. Select the cell under the heading Date, then click the Form Field Options button 🖻 on the Forms toolbar

   The Text Form Field Options dialog box appears. In this dialog box you can specify a number of options for the kind of information a user can enter in a field.

5. Click the Type list arrow, choose Date

   You can also indicate an acceptable format in which the date should be entered.

6. Click the Date format list arrow, choose the M/d/yy format from the list, as shown in Figure O-4, then click OK

   You will see no change in the form field, but the Date option you chose will ensure that the user enters the correct information using the correct format in this field. Similarly, you want to ensure that users enter the correct number of digits for their ID number in the Employee Number field.

7. Select the text field under the heading Employee # in the first row, then click the Form Field Options button 🖻 on the Forms toolbar

8. Click the Maximum Length up arrow until 5 appears in the box, then click OK

   You will see no change in the form field, but the Maximum Length option ensures that the user enters the correct number of characters. When you return to the document window, compare your form to Figure O-5.

9. Click the Save button 🖫 on the Standard toolbar

FIGURE O-3: **Text fields in a form**

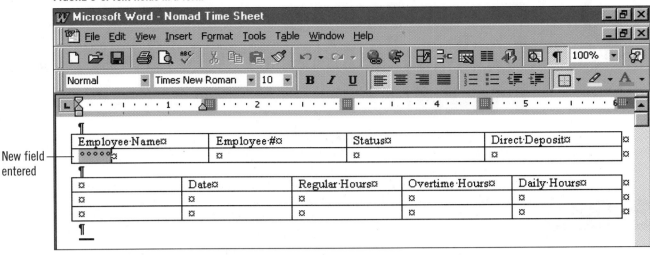

New field entered

FIGURE O-4: **Date options for a text form field**

Click to specify field option

Click to choose a date format

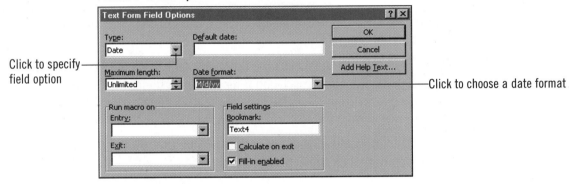

FIGURE O-5: **Text fields in a form**

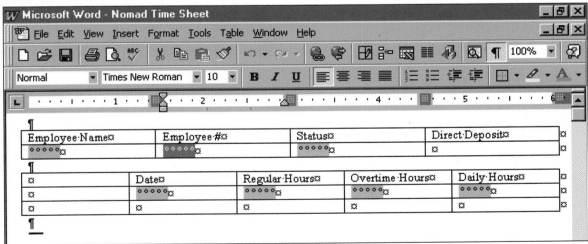

CLUES TO USE

Using date formatting in a text form field

The key to a successful form is consistency. Using the Date formatting feature in a text form field ensures that a date will be entered consistently, no matter who uses the form. Even if a user enters a date in another format, the form will re-format the entry automatically. For

example, if you have specified a 'm/d/yy' date format and the user enters June 1, 1998, the form will correct the entry to read 6/1/98. Also notice that additional date formatting options include the ability to accept hours and minutes in a date formatted text form field.

Specifying Calculations in Form Fields

In the same way that date formatting can ensure that dates are entered consistently and correctly, number formatting ensures that the user enters numbers in the correct format (for example, when entering dollar amounts). If you plan to use calculations in your form, you can use the **Calculate on Exit option** to update a calculation in another part of the form that uses the user's entry. Angela would like to calculate the total number of hours worked. The fields containing the user's entries for each day should be formatted to update any calculations.

Steps

1. **Select the field under the Regular Hours heading, then click the Form Field Options button on the Forms toolbar**
   The Text Form Field Options dialog box appears. Next, you will want the field that uses this value in a calculation to be updated (that is, recalculated) after the user makes an entry and exits this field.

2. **In the Field settings area, click the Calculate on exit check box, as shown in Figure O-6, then click OK. Repeat steps 1 and 2 for the fields under the Overtime Hours heading**
   With the two fields to be included in the total daily hours calculation properly formatted, you can now format the last field in the row to include the calculation itself.

3. **Select the last field in the row under the heading Daily Hours, then click on the Forms toolbar, click the Type list arrow, then click Calculation**
   With the calculation option set, you can enter the formula for the value you want to calculate. In this case, you want to add together the two values to the left of the current cell.

4. **In the Expression box, after the equal sign, type sum(left) as shown in Figure O-7, then click OK**
   Notice that "0" now appears in the field. Next display the Tables and Borders toolbar so that you have quick access to tables and border features.

5. **Click View on the menu bar, click Toolbars, click Tables and Borders**
   In the last row you will create the new fields that will contain the totals for the week. First, you will merge the first two cells in the last row, so that you can create a label for the total fields.

6. **Select the first two cells in the last row, click the Merge Cells button on the Tables and Borders toolbar, then type Total Hours**
   Now you can create the total field for the regular hours worked in the next column.

7. **Press [Tab], click the Text Form Field button on the Forms toolbar, then click on the Forms toolbar**

8. **In the Text Form Field Options dialog box, click the Type list arrow, then click Calculation**
   In the Expression box, you can enter an expression that refers to the range of cells that are above the current cell. When you refer to specific cells, enter the cell address, which is the column letter followed by the row number.

Time To

✔ Save

9. **Click in the Expression text box, type = sum(above), click OK, then repeat steps 6 through 8 in each of the next two cells**
   Compare your form to Figure O-8.

FIGURE O-6: Text form field number options

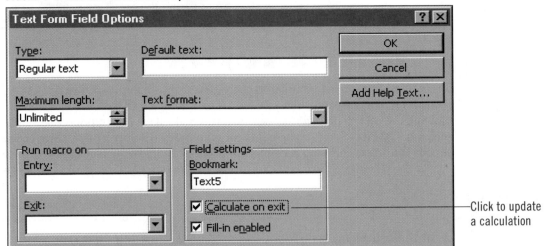

Click to update
a calculation

FIGURE O-7: Text form field calculation options

Current
option set

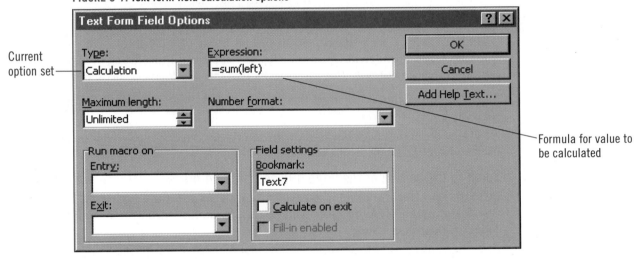

Formula for value to
be calculated

FIGURE O-8: Calculated field in a form

Total field

Merge Cells
button

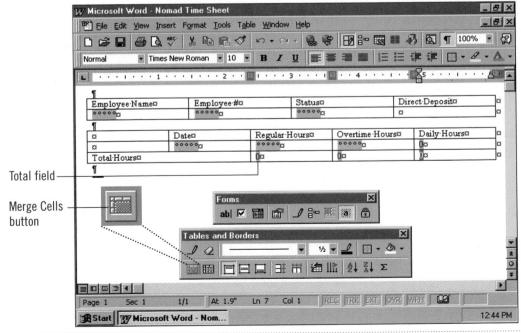

Creating Check Box Form Fields

Check boxes in a form are similar to check boxes you see in dialog boxes in a program like Word. You can use check boxes when you want a user to make selections from a set of options. Or by allowing the user to place an "x" in a box, you make it easy to respond to a single yes or no style question. ✏️ Because payments for employees who prefer that their checks be deposited directly into their checking accounts are processed differently from those who prefer to receive checks, the payroll department wants to be able to quickly identify direct deposit employees.

Steps 1 2 3 4

1. In the cell below the Direct Deposit label, click the Check Box Form Field button ☑ on the Forms toolbar
   A check box appears in the cell. If you anticipate that a check box is usually going to be checked by the user, you can specify that the check box is checked by default.

2. Click the Form Field Options button 📰 on the Forms toolbar
   The Check Box Form Field Options dialog box appears. In this dialog box, you can specify options for check boxes. In this case, specify that this check box is checked by default.

3. In the Default Value area, click the Checked option button, as shown in Figure O-9, then click OK
   A "x" appears in the check box in the form. Next, you can add more check boxes that will be used and completed by the payroll department.

4. Scroll to the bottom of the page if necessary and press [Enter] twice to create some extra space after the table, then type For Payroll Use Only and press [Enter]
   The fields you are about to create will be used by another department, which uses special codes for their internal use.

5. Click the Check Box Form Field button ☑ on the Forms toolbar, then press [Tab], type AB, and press [Enter]

6. Click ☑ on the Forms toolbar, then press [Tab], type CD, and press [Enter]

7. Click ☑ on the Forms toolbar, then press [Tab], type XW, and press [Enter]

Time To
✔ Save

8. Click ☑ on the Forms toolbar, then press [Tab], type YZ, and press [Enter]
   Compare your document to Figure O-10.

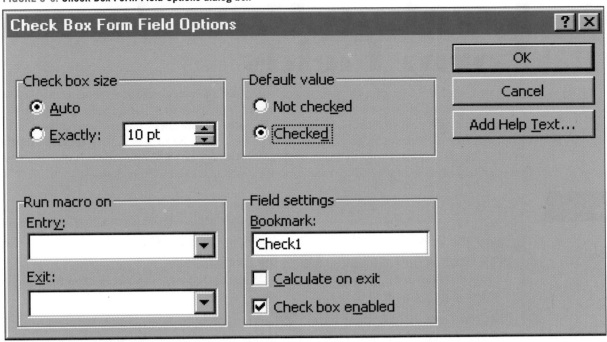

Check box
checked by default

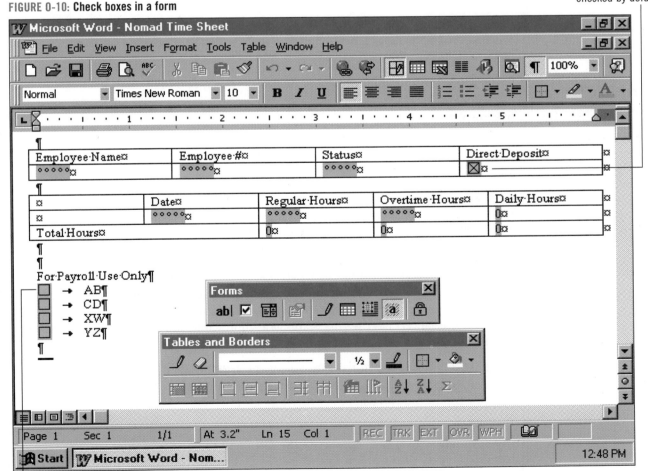

New check boxes

Creating Drop-down Form Fields

When you want the user of a form to select from a list of several options, using a drop-down field provides a list of options without requiring a lot of space in a form. In the actual form, a user sees an arrow next to a drop-down field. The user simply clicks the arrow to display a list of options from which to choose and then clicks the option he or she wants. Angela would like each employee to provide information about his or her employment status. Because there can be only one of several correct responses, Angela creates a drop-down field.

Steps

Trouble?

Take care to select the field, but not the entire cell and the end-of-cell marker.

1. **Select the field in the cell below the label Status (in the first table), then click the Drop-Down Form Field button 📇 on the Forms toolbar**
   A blank drop-down field appears in the form. With the field created, you can enter the options that you want to appear in the list.

2. **Click the Form Field Options button 📇 on the Forms toolbar**
   The Drop-Down Form Field Options dialog box appears. In this dialog box you can specify the options you want to appear in the list. In this case, the list will contain employment status options.

3. **In the Drop-down item box, type contractor, and then click Add**
   The first item in the list appears in the Items in drop-down list box. You can continue adding items to this drop-down list.

Trouble?

If you make a spelling mistake, you can remove an item by selecting it in the Items in drop-down list box and clicking Remove. Then re-enter the item.

4. **In the Drop-down item box, type the following items, and remember to click Add after each item:**
   temporary
   part-time
   full-time
   intern
   freelancer
   The first item that appears in the Items in drop-down list box is the default item that appears in this field when the user fills out the form. You can rearrange the items in the list so that the "full-time" option appears as the default item.

5. **In the Items in drop-down list box, select the full-time item, then click the Move up arrow until "full-time" appears at the top of the list, as shown in Figure O-11**
   You can also delete items from the list so that they do not appear in the drop-down field. Because a "freelancer" has the same status as a "contractor," you can remove the "freelancer" item from the list.

6. **In the Items in drop-down list box, select the freelancer item, then click Remove**
   The item no longer appears in the Items in drop-down list box. You have finished entering items for the drop-down list.

7. **Click OK**
   The drop-down form field appears in the form and the first item appears in the field by default. Compare your form to Figure O-12.

8. **Click the Save button 📇 on the Standard toolbar**

FIGURE O-11: **Drop-Down Form Field Options dialog box**

Type in items to be added to list

Click to add to list

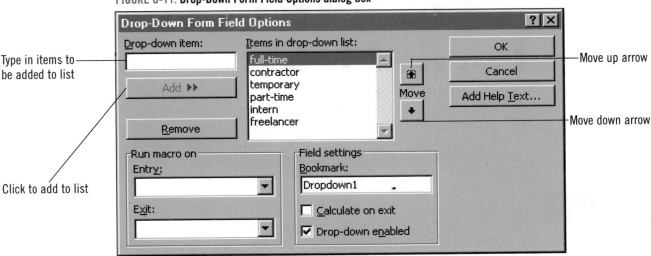

Move up arrow

Move down arrow

FIGURE O-12: **Drop-down field in a form**

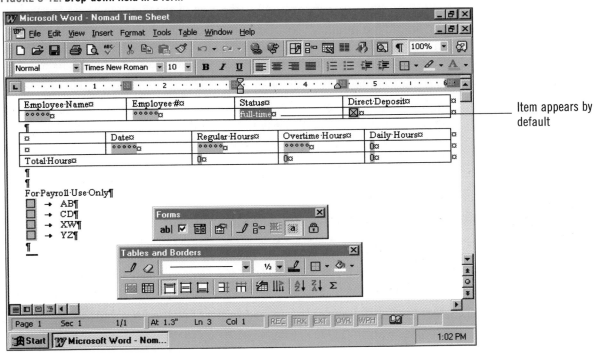

Item appears by default

Word 97

CLUES TO USE

Using other form fields

In addition to the form fields available on the Forms toolbar, you can add other kinds of form fields (called **controls**) to your forms. Some of these controls look very much like the controls you use in dialog boxes. For example, instead of typing in numbers in a text form field, you can use a spinner control which looks like this

, so that the user can click the arrows to specify a quantity in a field. These controls are available on the Control Toolbox toolbar, which you can display by clicking View from the menu bar, clicking Toolbars, and then clicking Control Toolbox.

Adding Help to Form Fields

Using form fields is one way to make a form easier to use. Another way to help a user understand how to complete a form is to provide help information and instructions. When a user selects a field for which help information is available, the user sees instructions or other information in the status bar. You also have the option to provide even more information, which appears when the user presses the [F1] function key. ▰▰▰▰ Angela wants to use the help feature to provide instructions for completing the form.

Steps

1. Select the text field for the **Employee Number**, then click the **Form Field Options button** 🖼 on the Forms toolbar

2. Click **Add Help Text** and click the **Status Bar tab** if necessary
   The Form Field Help Text dialog box appears. In this dialog box, you enter the text for two different kinds of help information. On the Status Bar tab, you enter the text the user will see when the user selects this field in the form.

3. Click the **Type your own option button** and in the Type your own text box, type **Enter your employee number.**, as shown in Figure O-13
   You can enter up to 130 characters. In the Help Key (F1) tab you can enter the information you want to appear when the user presses [F1] when completing this field.

4. Click the **Help Key (F1) tab**, then click the **Type your own option button** and in the Type your own text box, type **Your Employee Number is NOT the same as your Social Security number. In the Employee Number field, you must use the 6-digit number that appears in the Comments field on your pay stub.**
   Because you can enter up to 255 characters, use (F1) help when you wish to provide more than a single line of information. The text you enter on this tab appears when the user presses [F1] while the field is selected.

5. Click **OK** to return to the Text Form Field Options dialog box, then click **OK** to return to the form
   You do not see any change in the form, but the help information you entered has been applied to the field. With the fields in the form complete, you can now create additional rows of fields in the form so that the user can enter hours worked for up to seven days.

6. Select the second row of the second table, click the **Copy button** 🖼 on the Standard toolbar

7. Deselect the row and with the insertion point in the cell above **Total Hours**, click the **Paste button** 🖼 on the Standard toolbar six times

8. In the first column for each new row, enter abbreviations for each day of the week, starting with **Mon.** for Monday
   Compare your form to Figure O-14. Now you can save your changes.

9. Click the **Save button** 🖼 on the Standard toolbar

FIGURE O-13: **Status Bar help text**

Use to provide larger amounts of text (up to 255 characters)

You can enter up to 130 characters

FIGURE O-14: **Additional rows in the form**

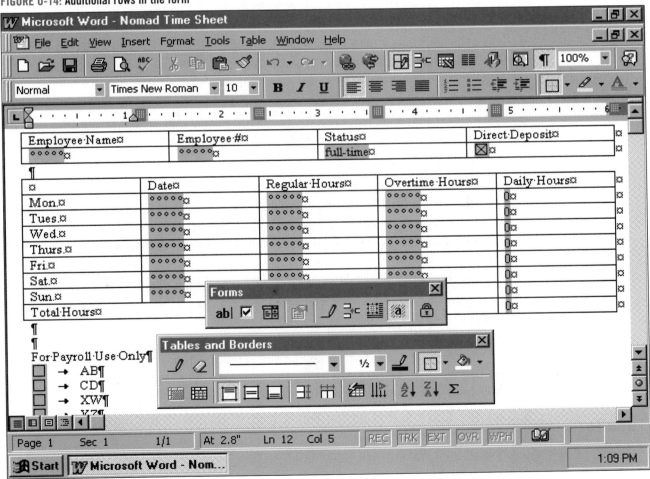

Preparing a Form for a User

With the fields entered in the form, you use a variety of screen and table features to improve the appearance of the form. For example, so that the user sees all of the form when he or she first opens the document, you can save the form with a specific magnification setting. You can hide the shaded fields in the form and use a preset format with the Table AutoFormat command. Most importantly, you can protect the form, so that the user does not change it (other than filling in the fields) as he or she fills it in. Angela wants to prepare the form for use by an employee. First she will hide the shading in the form fields.

Steps

1. With the insertion point in the second table, click the Form Field Shading button on the Forms toolbar

The fields are no longer shaded. Next, you can add lines and shading to the form.

2. Click Table AutoFormat on the Tables and Borders toolbar

In the Table AutoFormat dialog box, select the preset formatting you want to apply to the table.

3. Click List 4, then click OK

The table is formatted with lines and shading, as shown in Figure O-15. To make the form look more interesting, rotate the days of the week in the first column.

4. Select the cells containing the days of the week, right-click anywhere in the selected area, then click Text Direction, click the left box, then click OK

In the Text Direction dialog box you can specify the orientation of text in a cell. With the text oriented vertically, you can specify how it should be aligned in each cell.

5. With the text still selected, click the Align Top button on the Formatting toolbar, click the Font Size list arrow, click 14, then click the Bold button **B** on the Formatting toolbar

6. Select all the cells that will contain hours, click the Font Size list arrow, click 16, click **B**, then adjust the width of each of the columns by dragging the boundaries between columns, as shown in Figure O-16

So that the user sees the entire form when he or she opens the form, display the form in the page width magnification.

7. Click the Zoom list arrow on the Standard toolbar, then click Page Width

This information is saved when you save the form. So that the user does not make any changes to the form, you need to protect it. In addition, your form must be protected before any help information is displayed.

8. Click the Protect Form button on the Forms toolbar

Now that you have finished developing the form, you can hide the Forms toolbar and the Tables and Borders toolbar. Then save your changes and close the document.

Time To

☞ Save
☞ Close

9. Click the Close button on the Forms toolbar, then click the Close button on the Tables and Borders toolbar

Compare your document to Figure O-17.

FIGURE O-15: Formatted form

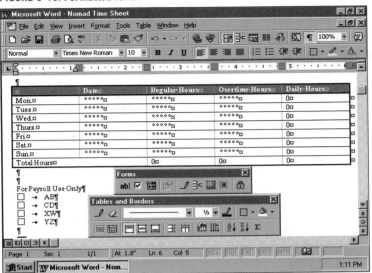

FIGURE O-16: Adjusted column widths

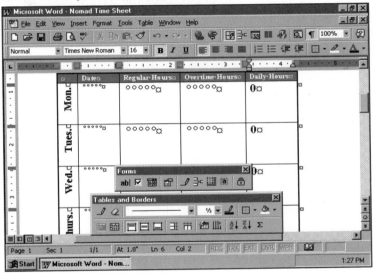

FIGURE O-17: Completed form

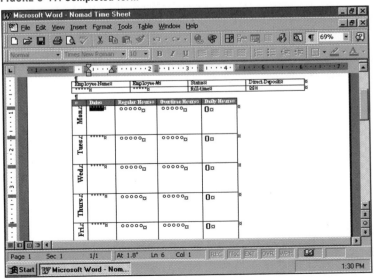

Filling Out a Form as a User

After you have completed entering and formatting fields in the form, you can test your form by attempting to use it as a user would. To begin using a form, you create a new document based on the form template you created. Angela is ready to test the form before she shares it with her employees.

Steps

1. **Click File on the menu bar, then click New**
   The New dialog box appears. You want to create a new document using the form template you created in this lesson. Save the new document before you complete the form.

2. **Double-click Nomad Time Sheet, click the Save button** 💾 **on the Standard toolbar; then in the File name box, type My Time Sheet**
   The form document appears in the document window. You can complete the form as a user would by using the fields displayed.

3. **In the Employee Name field, enter your name**
   Your name appears in the form. Now you can move to the next field.

4. **Press [Tab] to move to the next field, Employee #, then type 12343**
   The insertion point moves to the next field in which you can enter information. Because the form is protected you cannot select any of the text in it. Notice the text that appears in the status bar. Next, display the [F1] help information.

5. **Press [F1]**
   The help information appears in a help window, as shown in Figure O-18.

6. **Click OK to close the help window, then press [Tab] to move to the next field**
   Next use the drop-down field to specify your employment status.

7. **Click the Status list arrow, as shown in Figure O-19, and choose intern**

8. **Complete the remaining fields in the form as indicated in Figure O-20**

Time To
- ✔ Save
- ✔ Print
- ✔ Close the document
- ✔ Exit Word

FIGURE O-18: Help information in a form

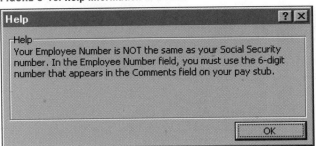

—— Press F1 to get Help window

Help

Help
Your Employee Number is NOT the same as your Social Security number. In the Employee Number field, you must use the 6-digit number that appears in the Comments field on your pay stub.

OK

FIGURE O-19: Drop-down field

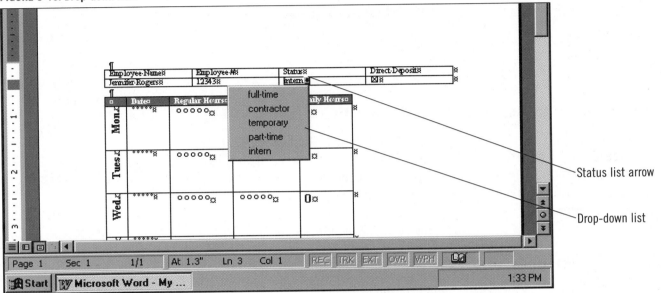

—— Status list arrow

—— Drop-down list

FIGURE O-20: Completed time sheet

Employee Name	Employee #	Status	Direct Deposit
Jennifer Rogers	12343	intern	☒

	Date	Regular Hours	Overtime Hours	Daily Hours
Mon.	6/1/98	8	2	10
Tues.	6/2/98	6	0	6
Wed.	6/3/98	8	2	10
Thurs.	6/4/98	6	0	6
Fri.	6/5/98	8	1	9
Sat.	6/6/98	0	0	0
Sun.	6/7/98	0	0	0
Total Hours		36	5	41

For Payroll Use Only
☐ AB
☐ CD
☐ XW
☐ YZ

Practice

▶ Concepts Review

Label and describe each of the parts of the toolbar shown in Figure O-21.

FIGURE O-21

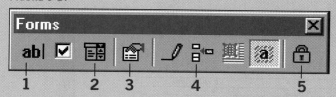

Match each of the following descriptions with the term that it describes best.

6. Template
7. Drop-down form field
8. Table AutoFormat
9. Text box form fields
10. Protect Form

a. An area to enter text information in a field
b. Preset formatting that can be applied to a table
c. A type of document that contains standard text and formatting that is a basis for new documents
d. A feature that protects a form from changes
e. Provides a list of options in a form

Select the best answer from the list of choices.

11. Which of the following is true about drop-down form fields?
    a. Until the user makes a selection in a drop-down form field, the field appears blank.
    b. Items in the drop-down list cannot be removed after you've entered them.
    c. The order in which items appear in the list cannot be changed.
    d. A drop-down field provides a list of options in a form.

12. To create a template:
    a. Click File on the menu bar, then click Template.
    b. Click File on the menu bar, click New, then click the template option button.
    c. Click the New button on Standard toolbar.
    d. You must have a form created first.

13. Which statement best describes the Protect Form function?
    a. The information cannot be changed after it has been protected.
    b. The form must not be protected before any help information is displayed.
    c. You can use the Protect Form button instead of the Save button.
    d. Once the form is protected, you must enter a password to unprotect it.

14. In the Forms toolbar you can:
    a. Merge cells.
    b. Save your changes.
    c. Add checkboxes.
    d. Change text direction.

► Skills Review

1. Create a form.

a. Start Word. Click File on the menu bar, then click New.

b. Click the Template option button in the lower right corner of the dialog box, then click OK.

c. Click View on the menu bar, click Toolbars, then click Forms.

d. With the insertion point at the top of the page, type "Office Automation" and press [Enter], then type "Needs Assessment Form", then press [Enter] twice.

e. Select the 2 lines of text, click the Outside Borders button, then click the Center button.

f. Below the title, press [Enter] twice, then click the Insert Table button and create a table that is two columns wide and three rows high. Enter the following items in the cells in the first column: "Employee Name:", "Department Number:", "Category:".

g. Click below the table, press [Enter] to allow space before the next table, click the Insert Table button and create a table that is four columns wide and 11 rows high. Select the first two cells in the first row, click Table on the menu bar, then click Merge Cells. Beginning with the second row, decrease the cell width of the first column to about 1 inch.

h. Enter text in the cells according to the table below:

I create or edit the following document types:	how often each week?	hours to create or edit:
Interoffice memos		
Letters to a single client		
Letters to multiple clients		
Internal reports		
Financial summaries		
Charts and graphs		
Desktop publishing or creative documents		
Overheads/transparencies		
Other:		
	Total Hours:	

i. Drag the column boundaries to size the columns so that all the text appears on one line.

j. Click the Save button and save the form with the name Office Survey, then click Save.

2. Create text box form fields.

a. Place the insertion point in the cell next to the label "Employee Name" in the first row, then click the Text Form Field button on the Forms toolbar.

b. Repeat step 2a for the cell next to the Department Number field. In the second table, insert text form fields in each cell in the last column and next to the label "Other" near the end of the table.

c. Select the cell next to the "Department Number" label, then click the Form Field Options button.

d. Click the Maximum Length up arrow until 2 appears in the box, then click OK.

e. Click the Save button on the Standard toolbar.

3. Specify calculations in form fields.

a. Select the first field under the "Hours to create or edit" heading, then click the Form Field Options button on the Forms toolbar.

b. Click the Type list arrow, click Number, then in the Default Number box, type 0.

c. In the Field settings area, click the Calculate on exit check box, then click OK.

d. Repeat steps 3a through 3c for all (except the last) cells in the column.

e. Select the last field in the column, then click the Form Field Options button.

f. Click the Type arrow, click Calculation, then in the Expression box, type = sum(above), then click OK.

4. Create check box form fields.

   a. In the first cell of the second row in the second table, click the Check Box Form Field button on the Forms toolbar.

   b. Repeat step 4a for each cell in this column of the table, excluding the last row.

5. Create drop-down form fields.

   a. Place the insertion point in the cell next to the label "Category" (in the first table), then click the Drop-Down Form Field button on the Forms toolbar, then click the Form Field Options button.

   b. In the Drop-Down item box, type "supervisor," and then click Add. Type the following items. Remember to click Add after each item: "secretary"; "paralegal"; "attorney"; "analyst".

   c. Click OK to close the dialog box.

   d. In the cell under the "How often each week" heading (in the second table), click the Drop-Down Form Field button on the Forms toolbar, then click the Form Field Options button on the Forms toolbar.

   e. In the Drop-Down item box, type "twice/week", and then click Add. Type the following items. Remember to click Add after each item: "three/week", "once/week", "daily", "once/month", "none", "once/quarter", "once/year".

   f. In the Items in Drop-Down List box, select the "daily" item, then click the Move up arrow until it appears at the top of the list. Move the "once/week" item to above the "twice/week" item.

   g. In the Items in Drop-Down List box, select the "none" item, click Remove, then Click OK.

   h. Select and copy this field to the remaining cells in this column, excluding the cell next to the "other" label.

   i. Click the Save button on the Standard toolbar.

6. Add Help to form fields.

   a. Select the first check box in the first column of the second table, then click the Form Field Options button.

   b. Click Add Help Text and click the Status bar tab if necessary.

   c. In the Type your own text box, type "Click the check box for each type of document you create."

   d. Click the Help key (F1) tab, and in the Type your own text box, type "You can check as many document types as you wish. If a document type you use is not included on this form, click the Other check box, then in the Other field enter the name and description of the document."

   e. Click OK to return to the Form Field Options dialog box, then click OK to return to the form.

   f. Save your changes to the form.

7. Prepare a form for a user.

   a. With the insertion point in the second table, click the Form Field Shading button on the Forms toolbar.

   b. Click Table on the menu bar, then click Table AutoFormat.

   c. Click Grid 8, then click OK.

   d. In the first table, adjust the column width of the second column so the table is as wide as the second table.

   e. Click the Zoom list arrow on the Standard toolbar, then click Page Width.

   f. Click the Protect Form button on the Forms toolbar.

   g. Click the Save button on the Standard toolbar, then close the template.

8. Fill out a form as a user.

   a. Click File on the menu bar, click New, then double-click Office Survey.

   b. Save the form as Analyst Survey, then in the Employee Name field, enter your name.

   c. Press [Tab], in the Department Number field, type "33", then press [Tab], click the Category arrow, then click paralegal.

   d. Click the first check box and notice the text that appears in the status bar, then press [F1] and read the message.

   e. Click OK to close the help window, press [Tab] to move to the next field, then click the arrow in the next column, click once/week, then press [Tab] and enter 4 in the last column.

   f. Complete the form by checking the check boxes for different kinds of documents, specifying the frequency of the document and the hours spent creating or editing this document. (There are no right or wrong responses in these fields).

   g. Save your document and print it, then exit Word.

▶ Independent Challenges

1. You've been asked to coordinate and plan this summer's company picnic. Because you can't stage the entire event yourself, you've decided to recruit volunteers to help you. These volunteers will form a committee for the picnic. Create an online form that your co-workers can complete at their desks. Use Figure O-22 as a guide.

To complete this independent challenge:

1. Create a new template document and save it as Committee Sign Up Form.
2. Give your form the title Company Picnic Committee Sign Up Form. Center the title and format the text in Times New Roman, 18 pts, bold, and italic.
3. Create a table that is three rows by four columns.
4. Type in the field labels shown in the figure. Note that "Food" is not a label. Format the text in Arial Black, 14 pts. Apply double-spaced paragraph formatting, align the text, and adjust the column width as shown in Figure O-22.
5. In the last row of the second column, insert a drop-down form field. Supply the following items to the field: Clean-up, Entertainment, Prizes, Announcements, and Food. Arrange the items so that "Food" is the default entry.
6. In the remaining cells in the second and fourth columns, insert text form fields.
7. Add a check box several lines below the table. Add the following help text to the check box that appears in the status bar: "Attend this meeting and receive a customized baseball cap and T-shirt!"
8. After the check box, press [Tab], then add the following text: "I want to help, but I am not able to attend the organizational meeting on October 3rd."
9. Protect, save, and close the form.
10. Complete the form as you wish, then preview, save, and print the document, then close it.

FIGURE O-22

Company Picnic Committee Sign Up Form			
Name:		Extension:	
Department:		Home Phone:	
Committee:	Food	E-mail address:	

☐ I want to help, but I am not able to attend the organizational meeting on October 3rd.

2. Your company, CompuTech Trainers, provides computer training to corporate customers. To gather information from students about the effectiveness and quality of the training, you've decided to create a form that the students can complete at their computers after finishing a class. You will create a form based on a paper form already in use.

To complete this independent challenge:

1. Open the student file WD O-1 and save the document as CompuTech Trainers. Be sure to specify the Document template file type in the Save as type box in the Save as dialog box.
2. Insert text form fields in all the blank cells except the cell next to the Course label.

3. In the cell next to the Course label, insert a drop-down form field and enter the following items in the list: Computer Basics, Application Basics, Beyond the Basics, and Tips and Tricks.

4. In the Date field, specify a date field type and the MMMM d, yyyy format.

5. In the Rating column, apply the Calculate on exit option to each of the fields except the Evaluation Score field. Specify that the default value should be one (1) for each of these fields. (*Tip*: Specify the options for one field, then copy it to the remaining cells.)

6. In the Evaluation Score field, specify a Calculation field type and the sum(above) formula to provide a total.

7. Protect, save, and close the form.

8. Complete the form as you wish, then preview, and save the completed form with the name Basic Evaluation. Print the document, then close it.

3. High-Tech Towers is a hotel that delivers high-quality, personalized customer service by taking advantage of the latest technologies. As the customer service manager, you want to ensure that the mini-fridge in each guest's room is stocked with the items each guest prefers. To accomplish this goal, you decide to convert a paper form to an online form that the guests can complete on the computer in their room.

To complete this independent challenge:

1. Open the student file WD O-2 and save the document as a template with the name High-Tech Towers.

2. In the cell next to the Credit Card label, insert a drop-down form field and enter the following items in the list: Universal, CardAmerica, and MasterExpress.

3. Insert a check box in the cells in front of each item in the Item column. Each cell should be checked.

4. In the Option column insert a drop-down form field in each cell.

5. For each drop-down list, supply a list of options for each item. For example, in the mineral water column type at least three different flavors of the beverage. Arrange the options in alphabetical order.

6. Insert text form fields in the remaining blank fields. Specify that the Room# field should be limited to 3 characters. Specify that the Acct # should be a number field type.

7. Protect, save, and close the form.

8. Complete the form as you wish, then preview, and save the completed form with the name My Hotel Preferences. Print the document, then close it.

4. Personal Surfers is an Internet-based news service that sends news information to its clients. As the subscription manager, you must keep track of the items requested by subscribers. An online form that subscribers complete will make your job much easier.

To complete this independent challenge:

1. Create a new template document and save it as MyWeb News.

2. Give your form the title text shown in Figure O-23. Format the text in Times New Roman, 14 pt, bold, and italic.

3. Create two tables as shown in Figure O-23.

4. Type in the field labels and align them as shown in the figure for both tables. Format the text in Times New Roman, 12 pts, bold. Select each table, then apply double-spaced paragraph formatting to each table.

5. In the first column of the second table, insert a check box for each item in the Item column.

6. In the second column, insert a text form field in each cell. Specify a number field type, a default number of "0" and click the Calculate on exit check box.

7. In the cell to the left of the Total Charge column, specify a calculation field type. Include a calculation that is a total of the column multiplied by .99 (the cost for each retrieval). The formula is =sum(above)*.99.
8. In the Option column insert a drop-down form field in each cell.
9. For each drop-down list, supply a list of at least three options, arranged in alphabetical order.
10. For the check box next to the Favorites item, add help information that instructs the user to provide up to three internet addresses in the last three fields in the Option column.
11. In each of the last three cells in the Option column, insert a text form field for Web addresses.
12. Protect, save, and close the form.
13. Log on to the Internet and use your browser to locate three of your favorite news source Web sites. If you can't locate a site on your own, use your browser to go to http://www.course.com. From there, click Student Online Companions, then click the link for this textbook, then click the Word link for Unit O. Then view the three news sources. (Tip: you can select the URL and copy it to the clipboard.)
14. Complete the form as you wish, but be sure to include the web addresses of your favorite news sources.
15. Preview and save the completed form with the name Web Preferences. Print the document, then close it.

FIGURE O-23

Personal Surfers Web Service
News and Information Preferences

Name:	Amelia Masters	E-mail Address:	amaster@mynet.com
Credit Card	CardAmerica	Acct #	1234-435-322-332
Exp. Date	Sep-99		

Click the check box for each item you want sent to you.
Then make a selection from the Options list.

	Retrieval Limits	Item	Options
☒	1	Sports	all
☒	1	International news	conflict
☒	2	National news	society
☒	1	Entertainment	movies
☒	3	Favorites	http://www.cnn.com/WORLD/index.html http://www.jpost.com/News/Article-0.html http://www.jpl.nasa.gov/galileo/
	$5.94	**Total Charge**	

▶ Visual Workshop

As the compensation administrator in a company that provides financial and accounting consultants, you want to make it easy for the consultants to complete their travel expense form so that they can get reimbursed promptly. By providing the consultants with a form they can complete online, you give the consultants the ability to complete the form while they are out of the office. They can then e-mail you their completed forms. Create an online form that looks like the form shown in Figure O-24. Save the form with the name CPA Group. Complete the form as a user and save the completed form with the name CPA Form.

FIGURE O-24

The CPA Group
Weekly Expense Report Form

| Name: | | Social Security#: | |
| ABA #: | | AutoSavings Plan? | ☒ |

Parking		Meals		Transportation		Lodging	
Date	**Amount**	**Date**	**Amount**	**Date**	**Amount**	**Date**	**Amount**
	$0.00		$0.00		$0.00		$0.00
	$0.00		$0.00		$0.00		$0.00
	$0.00		$0.00		$0.00		$0.00
	$0.00		$0.00		$0.00		$0.00
	$0.00		$0.00		$0.00		$0.00
	$0.00		$0.00		$0.00		$0.00
	$0.00		$0.00		$0.00		$0.00
	$0.00		$0.00		$0.00		$0.00
Subtotals	$0.00		$0.00		$0.00		$0.00
Total Expenses	$0.00						

Customizing
Word with AutoText and Macros

- ► **Create and insert AutoText entries**
- ► **Create AutoCorrect exceptions**
- ► **Record a macro**
- ► **Run a macro**
- ► **Modify a macro**
- ► **Add Visual Basic commands to a macro**
- ► **Create a custom toolbar**
- ► **Use a custom toolbar**
- ► **Manage custom features**

Word offers many features that allow you to customize commands to better meet your needs. For example, you can use AutoText to quickly insert frequently used words and phrases by typing only a few characters. Or, you can create macros to automate Word procedures that you perform frequently and that require a series of steps (such as menu and dialog box selections). A **macro** is a set of instructions that performs a series of tasks in the order you specify. For example, if you often need to save a document and print only the current page, you can record your mouse movements and selections and save them as a macro. By default, your macros are available to all documents, but you can also store macros within a specific document. In addition, you can assign a button to a macro and add the button to a custom toolbar. ✎ Angela customizes Word to her needs by creating AutoText entries, AutoCorrect exceptions, and macros, which she adds to a custom toolbar.

Creating and Inserting AutoText Entries

Using AutoText you can store entries for text you use frequently in documents. A standard closing to a letter, a request for information, or a company name are examples of text for which you might create an AutoText entry. With the AutoText command, you can assign a short name to selected words, sentences, paragraphs, or entire pages of text you use frequently. Then you can insert an AutoText entry by typing the short name and pressing [F3]. You can also add an AutoText entry to the AutoText menu on the Insert menu. ✐ Angela creates and inserts AutoText entries for "NomadNotes" and the company name.

Steps

1. Start Word, open the document named WD P-1, then save it as NomadNotes Practice

2. Select the text NomadNotes in the first paragraph
   With the text selected, you are ready to create an AutoText entry.

3. Click Insert on the menu bar, click AutoText, then click New
   The Create AutoText dialog box opens, as shown in Figure P-1. When the selected text is rather long, Word provides a suggested short name. In this case, however, the newsletter name is only one word, so the suggested short name is the same as the AutoText entry itself. You can always replace the suggested name with one of your own.

4. With the text NomadNotes selected, type nn, then click OK
   Your typing replaces the existing short name suggested in the name box. The dialog box closes and the AutoText entry is stored in the default template and will be available in any document you create.

5. Press [Ctrl][End] to place the insertion point at the end of the document, press [Spacebar], type To learn about the details of each tour day, see next month's issue of, then press [Spacebar]
   AutoText entries you create are available from the AutoText menu.

6. Click Insert on the menu bar, click AutoText, then click nn
   The text "NomadNotes" appears in the document. Another way to insert an AutoText entry is to use the short name.

7. Type a period(.), press [Spacebar], type nn, then press [F3]
   After typing an AutoText short name, pressing [F3] inserts the text associated with the short name.

Time To
✔ Save

8. Press [Spacebar], then continue typing will lead you through the steps of planning the perfect vacation.
   Compare your document to Figure P-2.

FIGURE P-1: Create AutoText dialog box

FIGURE P-2: Inserted AutoText entries

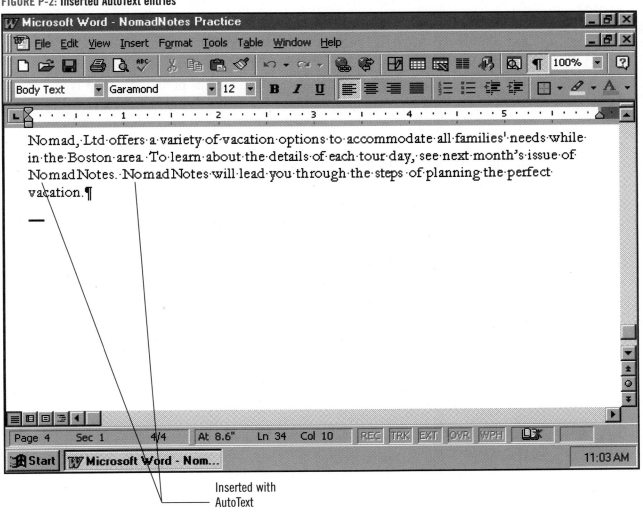

Inserted with
AutoText

Creating AutoCorrect Exceptions

When you type a period after a word, in most cases the AutoCorrect feature automatically capitalizes the next word you type, because a period usually identifies the end of a sentence, and the next word should be capitalized. Abbreviations are exceptions to this convention. For example, when a company name ends in "Inc." the first word after the name should not always be capitalized. As a result, Word includes hundreds of AutoCorrect exceptions to handle these situations. To handle exceptions not provided in Word, you can customize the AutoCorrect feature by creating your own AutoCorrect exceptions. In an article about sight-seeing in Boston, Angela wants to use "Mass." as an abbreviation for Massachusetts. She creates an AutoCorrect exception so that the next word is not automatically capitalized.

1. **Click Tools on the menu bar, then click AutoCorrect**
   The AutoCorrect dialog box appears, as shown in Figure P-3. In this dialog box you can create and delete AutoCorrect entries. You also have the option to create AutoCorrect exceptions.

2. **Click Exceptions, click the First Letter tab (if it is not already selected)**
   The AutoCorrect Exceptions dialog box appears, as shown in Figure P-4.

3. **In the Don't capitalize after: box, type Mass., then click Add**
   This new AutoCorrect exception has been added.

Trouble?

If you see a message asking if you want to replace an existing AutoCorrect exception, click Yes.

4. **Click OK, then click OK to return to the document**
   Now you can test your new AutoCorrect exception.

5. **Place the insertion point at the start of the current paragraph, then type Boston, Mass. isn't a city as much as it is an experience. Press [Spacebar]**
   Notice that the "i" in "isn't" is not capitalized, as shown in Figure P-5. If you share your computer with others, you need to delete this AutoCorrect exception.

6. **Click Tools on the menu bar, click AutoCorrect, then click Exceptions**
   You can delete AutoCorrect exceptions in this dialog box.

7. **Type Mass., click Delete, then click OK twice to return to the document**
   You have removed the AutoCorrect entry. Now you can verify that you have removed the AutoCorrect entry.

8. **Press [Spacebar] then type Mass. isn't**
   Notice that the "i" is capitalized. Now delete the text.

9. **Select the text you just typed and press [Delete]**

Time To

☑ Save

FIGURE P-3: AutoCorrect dialog box

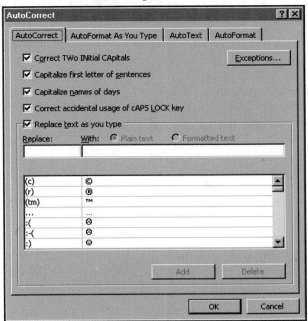

FIGURE P-4: AutoCorrect Exceptions dialog box

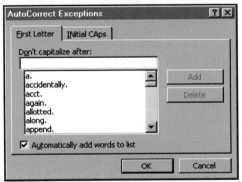

FIGURE P-5: AutoCorrect exception

AutoCorrect exception

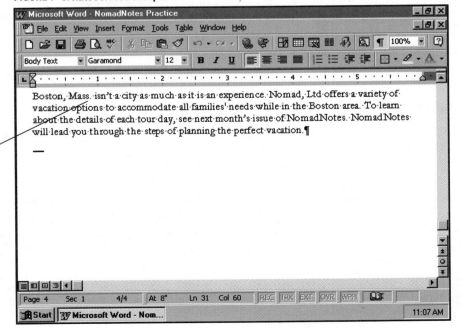

Word 97

Recording a Macro

When you discover you are using a series of commands on a regular basis, you have a good reason to create a macro. By recording these steps in a macro, you can run the macro whenever you need to perform the operation. Because Word can perform the operation faster than you can move the mouse, macros save you time. Also, Word will never make an error when you run the macro, provided that you record the steps accurately. With the Macro command, you provide a name for the macro you are about to record. You specify how you will run the macro, and then you begin recording your mouse actions. If you need to stop recording while you explore a new option or prepare for the next step, you can click the Pause button to temporarily stop recording your actions. When you are ready to continue, click the Pause button to resume. After recording your macro, you click the Stop button. ◢ When Angela is working on draft versions of her documents, she often needs to print only the current page. Because she frequently forgets to save her document before printing it, Angela would like her macro to save the document as well.

QuickTip

A fast way to start recording a macro is to double-click "REC" in the status bar.

1. Click Tools on the menu bar, click Macro, then click Record New Macro

The Record Macro dialog box opens, as shown in Figure P-6. In this dialog box, you give the new macro a name and description.

2. In the Macro name box, type PrintThisPage, then in the Description box, type This macro saves the document and prints the current page, then click OK

Macro names can be up to 25 characters long, and must not include spaces. After you close the dialog box you return to the document. Notice the macro toolbar appears in the document window as shown in Figure P-7, along with the new pointer.

3. Click the Save button 🖫 on the Standard toolbar

Word records the Save command in the macro.

4. Click File on the menu bar, then click Print

The Print dialog box opens. You specify the options you want your macro to use while printing.

5. In the Page range area click the Current page option button and click OK

The current page of the document prints on your printer. After the last step, you must stop the macro recorder.

6. Click the Stop button ■ on the Macro Record toolbar

The pointer returns to the default pointer shape and the Macro toolbar closes.

CLUES TO USE

Planning a macro

Because you cannot use the mouse to record selecting text in your macro, you need to plan a macro carefully before you record it. Here are some general guidelines for recording a macro:

• Give the macro a descriptive name and write a brief description of what it should do.
• Determine whether you want to use a menu or the keyboard to run the macro.
• Practice the steps you want to record in your macro and write them down. Your notes, such as those shown in Figure P-8, will guide you as you record the steps in the macro. Notice these notes

include general steps, and then the more specific commands required to carry them out.

• Determine if this macro should be available to all documents, only documents created with a specific template, or only the current document.
• It is a good idea to work in practice documents (not an important document that you need for your everyday work). Using a practice document allows you to experiment freely with your macro without being concerned about making changes you might not be able to reverse later.

FIGURE P-6: Record Macro dialog box

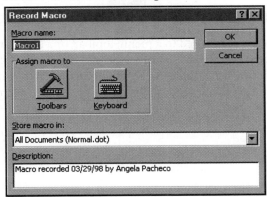

FIGURE P-7: Macro buttons

Macro toolbar —

Stop button —

Pause button —

Status bar
indicates you
are recording
a macro

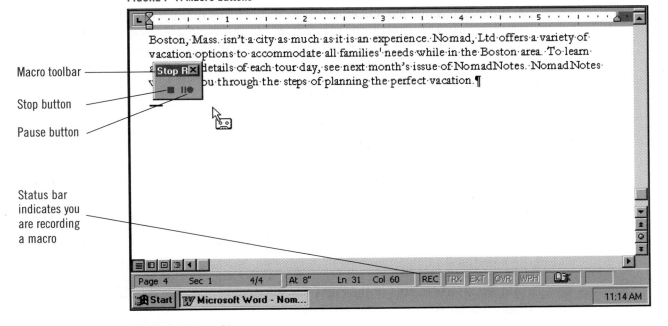

Boston, Mass. isn't a city as much as it is an experience. Nomad, Ltd offers a variety of vacation options to accommodate all families' needs while in the Boston area. To learn [a]bout details of each tour day, see next month's issue of NomadNotes. NomadNotes [takes y]ou through the steps of planning the perfect vacation.¶

Page 4   Sec 1   4/4   At 8"   Ln 31   Col 60   REC TRK EXT OVR WPH

Start   Microsoft Word - Nom...   11:14 AM

FIGURE P-8: Macro Plan

Macro Plan

Name:	PrintThisPage
Description:	This macro saves the document and prints the current page.
GENERAL STEPS:	SPECIFIC COMMANDS
1. Save the document	Click Save button
2. Print the current page	File, Print
	Click Current page
	Close dialog box
How to run it:	Keyboard shortcut and toolbar button

Running a Macro

If the macro you want to run is not assigned to a menu, toolbar, or a keyboard shortcut, you can run the macro from the Macros dialog box. Simply select the macro from the Macro Name list and click the Run button. You can also double-click a macro in the list to run it. ✐ Angela would like to test her macro using two methods. First she will test the macro from the menu.

Steps

1. **Click Tools, click Macro, then click Macros**
   The Macros dialog box opens, as shown in Figure P-9.

2. **In the Macro Name list, click the PrintThisPage macro, then click Run**
   The macro you recorded runs. It saves the document and prints only the current page. Instead of running the macro from a menu, you can assign a keyboard shortcut to your macro.

3. **Click Tools, click Customize, then click Keyboard**
   The Customize Keyboard dialog box opens. In this dialog box, you can assign a key combination to commands and macros.

4. **In the Categories list, scroll to and click Macros**
   A list of macros appears in the Macros box. Depending on the macros already created on your computer, your list might look different. You will save your keyboard shortcut in the current document.

5. **Click the Save changes in list arrow, then click NomadNotes Practice**
   Now you can assign a key combination to a selected macro.

6. **Be sure the PrintThisPage macro is selected, as shown in Figure P-10**

7. **With the insertion point in the Press new shortcut key box, press [Alt][P], click Assign, then click Close**
   The dialog box closes. Now you can close the Customize dialog box.

8. **Click Close to return to the document**

9. **Press [Ctrl] [Home] to move the insertion point to the first page in the document, then press [Alt][P]**
   The macro you recorded runs again, saving the document and printing only the current page. Compare your document to Figure P-11.

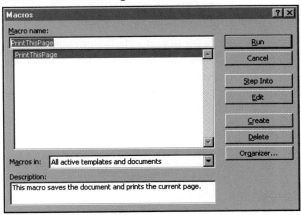

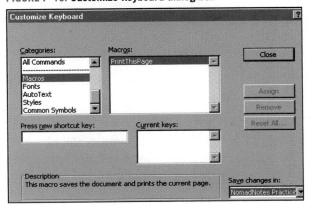

FIGURE P-11: **First page prints**

INSIDE THE BOSTONIAN WORLD

It's a cliché to say a city defies definition. But in this case, the cliché is simply truth. History. Culture. Sports capital. Business center. Haute couture and counterculture. Which Boston will you visit? Nomad, Ltd offers vacation planning to meet everyone's needs. See details in the monthly newsletter NomadNotes.

HISTORY

There's the historical Boston—the Boston you can't miss, and wouldn't want to. The city of Paul Revere, Benjamin Franklin, the Boston Tea Party, the Freedom trail, Copp's Hill and the King's Chapel Burying Grounds, and the USS Constitution. Visit the Old South Meeting House, dine at the Union Oyster House or Warren Tavern (which George Washington frequented), and stop at the restored Faneuil Hall or Quincy Marketplaces.

NIGHT LIFE

Boston's night scene features every kind of music from rock to blues to baroque to irish lballads. Or simply stroll the cobblestone streets listening to Boston's street musicians and performance artists. And one thing is for sure—there's a Boston that's perfect for you!

CLASS

Then there's the stately, though slightly snobby, Boston of Beacon Hill brown-stones where it is said the Lowells spoke only to the Cabots, and the Cabots only spoke to God. This is the Boston of the symphony, the ballet, and the Head of Charles sailing regatta; the Boston whose library in Copley Square deserves to be toured with an art curator. The Boston whose Back Bay mansions now house cultural institutions such as the French Library and the Goethe Institute. Don't miss:

- **Mapparium** (inside-out glass globe of the world) at the Christian Science Center
- **Glass flower** exhibit at Harvard

CULTURE

Thinking more along the lines of the trendy, cultural, artsy Boston? Then head for the Museum of Fine Arts or the Isabella Stewart Gardener Museum. As you walk Tremont Street in the Theater District take your pick of Broadway hits at the Wang Center for the Performing Arts, the Charles Playhouse, and other theaters big and small. Just a short subway ride away is Harvard Square in Cambridge—the land of hecutting-edge, the tbastion of counterculture that skirts the ivy-covered halls of Harvard Yard. Don't miss:

- **The Boston Pops**, especially the July 4₄concert at the Hatch Shell
- **Open rehearsal** , of the Boston Symphony Orchestra on Wednesday evening or Thrusday morning

Modifying a Macro

After you have recorded a macro, you might discover you wish to make changes to some part of it. You can modify a macro in the Microsoft Visual Basic window. In this window, you see the Visual Basic equivalent of your actions and selections when you recorded the macro. You can easily change the options you selected or add text to your macro. ✎ Angela would like to make a few adjustments to her macro, so she edits the macro.

Steps

Trouble?
If you do not see the New Macros (Code) window, click View on the menu bar, then click Code.

1. **Click Tools on the menu bar, click Macro, then click Macros**
   The Macros dialog box opens. The PrintThisPage macro appears in the dialog box. Begin by selecting the macro so you can edit it.

2. **In the Macro name list, select PrintThisPage, then click Edit**
   The macro appears in the Microsoft Visual Basic window, as shown in Figure P-12. In this window, you can modify the macro.

3. **Click the Close button of the Project window (on the left), then click the Maximize button of the New Macros (Code) window (on the right)**
   You can now see more of the macro code.

4. **In the New Macros (Code) window, select the 1 after the Copies option, then type 2**
   The number after the equal sign of the Copies option in the Application PrintOut command specifies how many copies to print. This value is now set to "2," as shown in Figure P-13. Before running the macro, save your work and return to your Word document.

5. **Click the Save button 💾 on the Standard toolbar**
   After you have finished modifying the macro, you can return to the Word document without closing the Microsoft Visual Basic window.

6. **Click the View Microsoft Word button on the Standard toolbar**
   The macro window is minimized, and you return to the NomadNotes Practice document.

7. **Press [Ctrl][End] to move the insertion point to the last page, then press [Alt][P]**
   Word prints two copies of the current page.

FIGURE P-12: **Macro in Microsoft Visual Basic window**

Project window
displays file
location of macro

Code window
displays Visual
Basic code for
the macro

Properties window
displays list of
macros you can edit

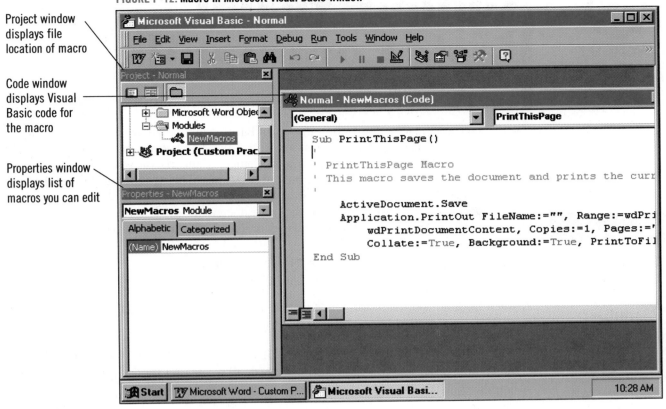

FIGURE P-13: **Edited macro**

View Microsoft
Word button

Code to save
the document

Code to print
the document

Revised number of
copies to print

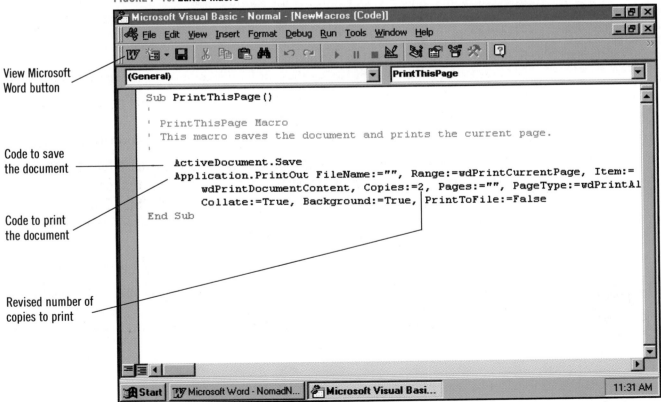

Adding Visual Basic Commands to a Macro

When you record a macro, Word stores the Visual Basic code for each operation. Visual Basic is a programming language with which you can control Word operations in a macro. You do not need to know much about Visual Basic to make changes to the macros you record. In fact, the built-in Help system for Visual Basic not only provides instructions about using specific commands, but it also includes examples of Visual Basic code that you can copy and paste into your macros.  Angela wants to preview the entire document as part of her macro. She will use the Help system to learn about the Visual Basic commands she needs to insert in her macro.

1. **Click the Microsoft Visual Basic button on the taskbar**
   The macro appears in the Microsoft Visual Basic window.

2. **Click Help on the menu bar, click Contents and Index, on the Contents tab double-click Microsoft Word Visual Basic Reference**

3. **Double-click Shortcut to Microsoft Word Visual Basic Reference, double-click Microsoft Word Visual Basic Reference, double-click Methods, then scroll to and double-click P**
   The features for which you can view Visual Basic help information are organized by general category, and then alphabetically within each category.

4. **Scroll to and double-click PrintPreview Method**
   The help window for the Print Preview topic appears, as shown in Figure P-14. Here you can read about using this command.

5. **Read the description of the command, then click Example**
   In the Example window, you can see the code for this command and copy it to your macro.

6. **In the PrintPreview Method Example window, select the text that begins If... through the last line End If, then press [Ctrl][C] to copy the text.**
   With the code copied to the clipboard, you can close the help windows and return to your macro.

7. **Click the Close button in each of the help windows until you return to the Visual Basic window, place the insertion point at the end of the line that contains the Save command, press [Enter], then click the Paste button on the Standard toolbar**
   Each command must appear on a line by itself. Compare your macro to Figure P-15.

8. **Click the Save button 🔲 on the Standard toolbar**
   After you have finished modifying the macro, close the Microsoft Visual Basic window.

9. **Click File on the menu bar, click Close and Return to Microsoft Word, then press [Alt][P] to run your macro**
   This command displays the current page in the Print Preview window while the macro continues.

Trouble?

If you see an error message that Word cannot locate the help file, it means that Visual Basic Help information was not installed on your computer. You need to run the Word setup program and add Visual Basic Help Reference to the installed features on your computer. If you cannot install Visual Basic Help Reference, continue by placing the insertion point at the end of the line that contains the "Save" command, press [Enter], then type the text shown in Figure P-15.

Time To

✔ Close the Preview window
✔ Save

FIGURE P-14: **Print Preview Method Help topic**

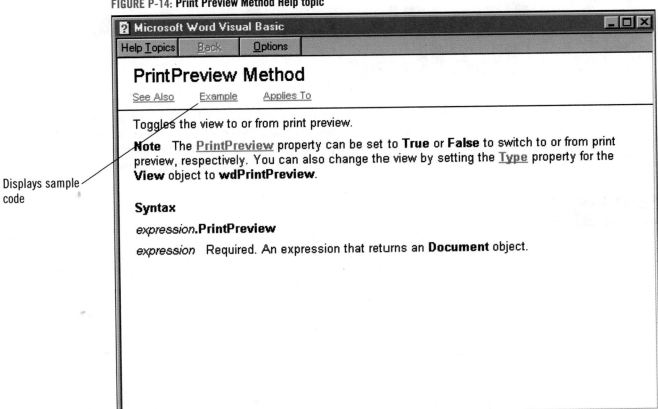

Displays sample code

FIGURE P-15: **Preview code in macro**

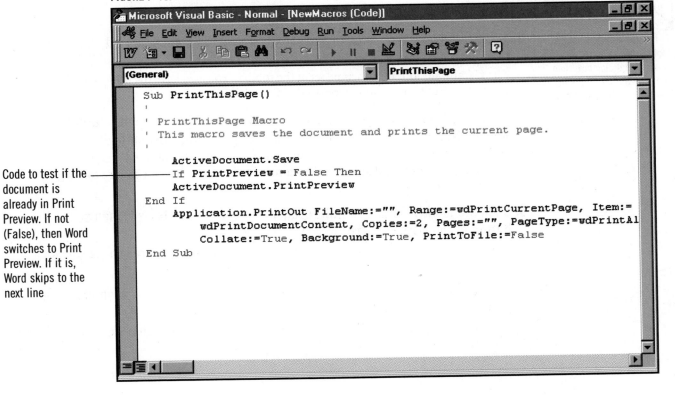

Code to test if the document is already in Print Preview. If not (False), then Word switches to Print Preview. If it is, Word skips to the next line

Creating a Custom Toolbar

You are probably already familiar with the Standard and Formatting toolbars in Word. In addition, there are other toolbars you can display and use. In Word, you can modify all the toolbars by adding and deleting buttons on them. You can also create your own custom toolbars that contain buttons for your favorite features, including your own macros. Angela would like to create her own toolbar that contains useful editing and printing features.

1. Click View on the menu bar, click Toolbars, then click Customize

The Customize dialog box opens. In this dialog box you can select toolbars you wish to view or choose to create a new toolbar.

2. Click New

The New Toolbar dialog box appears. In this dialog box, you name your new toolbar.

3. In the Toolbar name box, type Nomad Toolbar, then click OK

The new toolbar appears without any buttons, as shown in Figure P-16. Using the Customize dialog box you can select the buttons and commands you want on your custom toolbar. You can drag the dialog box to the side if it obscures your view of the toolbar window.

4. Click the Commands tab, then in the Categories list, click Edit

A group of buttons that represent editing commands appears on the tab.

5. Click the Repeat button ↻ and drag it to the Nomad Toolbar

6. In the Categories list, scroll to and click Fonts, in the Commands list, click Garamond, then drag it to the Nomad Toolbar

The Garamond font button appears in the toolbar. You also have the option of placing a button to represent a custom macro on the new toolbar.

7. In the Categories list, scroll to and click the Macros category, select Normal.NewMacros.PrintThisPage, then drag it to the custom toolbar

Macros you can place on the toolbar appear in the right side of the dialog box. The toolbar now contains a button displaying the name of the macro. You can choose to assign a different button design to the macro.

8. Click the Modify Selection button, click Change Button Image, then select the first button in the sixth row ▥

When you have finished adding buttons to your new toolbar, you can change the toolbar so that the macro name does not appear next to the button.

9. Click the Modify Selection button, click Text Only (in Menus), then click the Close button

Compare your toolbar to Figure P-17. Now you can edit your document and work with the new toolbar.

QuickTip

To remove a button from a toolbar, you must display the Customize dialog box, then drag the button off the toolbar back to the dialog box.

Time To

✔ Save

FIGURE P-16: Creating a custom toolbar using the Customize dialog box

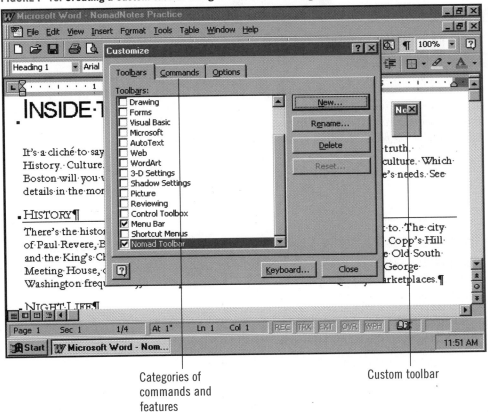

Categories of
commands and
features

Custom toolbar

FIGURE P-17: Completed custom toolbar

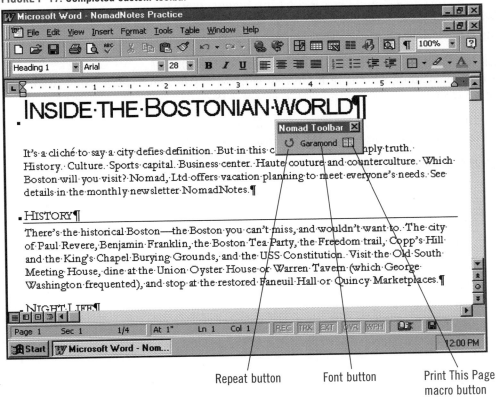

Repeat button

Font button

Print This Page
macro button

Using a Custom Toolbar

You can use a custom toolbar in the same way you use other toolbars in Word, by simply clicking the button you want. You can also position your custom toolbar anywhere in the document window. For example, you can "dock" it in place at the top of the document window, below the other Word toolbars. ▰▰▰ Angela is ready to use her new toolbar.

Steps 1234

Trouble?

If the toolbar disappears, you have dragged the toolbar too far. Look to the right edge of the Standard toolbar and drag the double bars down slightly.

1. Drag the Nomad Toolbar to the top of the document window (just above the ruler) and release the mouse

When you release the mouse, the toolbar is docked below the Formatting toolbar, as shown in Figure P-18. You can experiment with placing the toolbar.

2. Select the title of the document, then click the Garamond font button

The font is changed to the Garamond style.

3. Select the text the in the title of the document, then press [Delete]

You can use the buttons on the Nomad Toolbar to continue editing text.

4. Select the text ian at the end of the word "Bostonian," then click the Repeat button ⟳ on the Nomad Toolbar

Clicking this button repeats the last command.

5. Select the text World and click ⟳ on the Nomad Toolbar

The title now reads "Inside Boston." Next, you can print only this page of the document using the macro button.

6. Click the Print This Page button ▦ on the Nomad Toolbar

The document appears in the Print Preview window as Word saves, then prints, two copies of this page. Compare your document to Figure P-19.

7. Click the Close button on the Preview toolbar

After completing the edits to the document, save your work.

8. Click the Save button 🖫 on the Standard toolbar

▶ WD P-16   **CUSTOMIZING WORD WITH AUTOTEXT AND MACROS**

FIGURE P-18: Docked toolbar

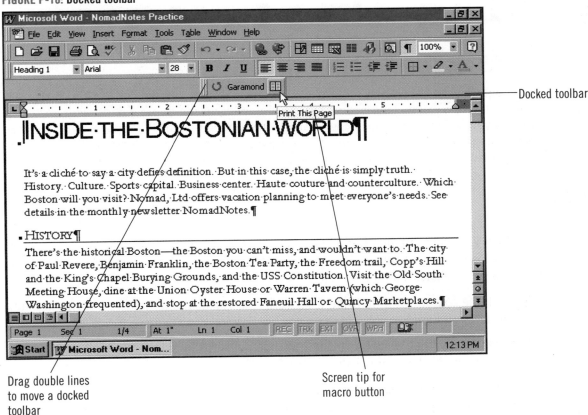

Docked toolbar

Drag double lines to move a docked toolbar

Screen tip for macro button

FIGURE P-19: Completed document

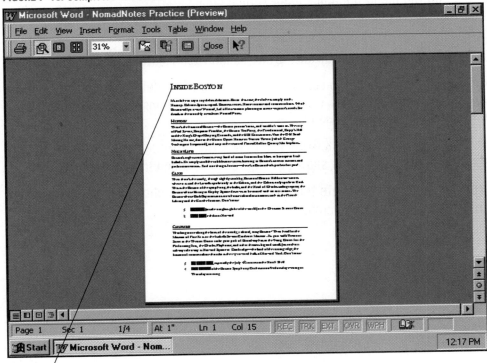

Text edited with custom toolbar

Managing Custom Features

Although you can always hide toolbars you no longer want to display, you can also completely remove toolbars you no longer need. You can also move macros to other documents and delete macros you no longer require. Angela has learned that the PC Support staff at Nomad is planning to customize every employee's Word toolbar to provide the same features that are on her Nomad Toolbar. As a result, Angela no longer needs her custom toolbar and macro.

Steps 1234

1. **Click View on the menu bar, click Toolbars, then click Customize**
   The Customize dialog box opens. In this dialog box, you can choose to hide or delete customized toolbars. You cannot, however, delete toolbars provided by Word.

2. **Click the Toolbars tab to bring it forward, then clear the Nomad Toolbar check box**
   The Delete button is enabled in the dialog box, as shown in Figure P-20.

3. **Click Delete, then click OK to confirm that you want to delete this toolbar**
   Clicking this button removes the toolbar from Word.

4. **Click Close in the Toolbars dialog box**
   Even though the toolbar containing the macro has been deleted, the macro itself is still available in the template.

5. **Click Tools on the menu bar, click Macro, then click Macros**
   The Macro dialog box opens. Begin by selecting the macro you would like to delete.

6. **Select the PrintThisPage macro**
   The Delete button is enabled in the dialog box, as shown in Figure P-21.

7. **Click Delete, then click Yes to confirm that you want to delete this macro**
   The custom toolbar and macro have been deleted and are no longer available in any document. You can also delete AutoText entries.

8. **In the Macros dialog box, click Organizer, click the AutoText tab, in the In Normal box scroll to and select nn, as shown in Figure P-22, then click Delete**

9. **Confirm that you want to delete this AutoText entry, then click Close in each dialog box until you return to your document**

Time To

✔ Save
✔ Close
✔ Exit

FIGURE P-20: Deleting custom toolbars

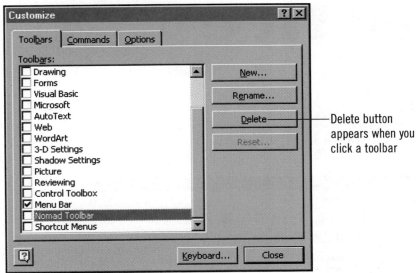

Delete button appears when you click a toolbar

FIGURE P-21: Deleting macros

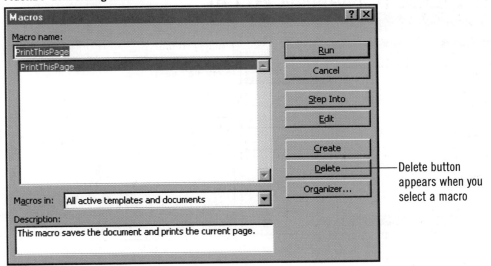

Delete button appears when you select a macro

FIGURE P-22: Organizer dialog box

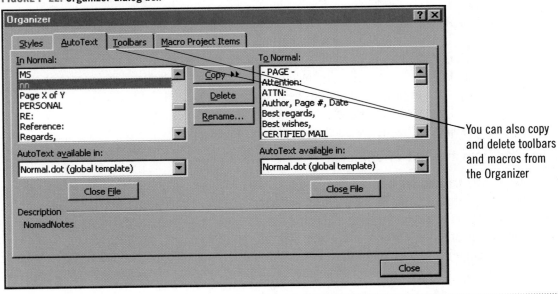

You can also copy and delete toolbars and macros from the Organizer

Practice

▶ Concepts Review

Label each of the elements of the screen shown in Figure P-23.

FIGURE P-23

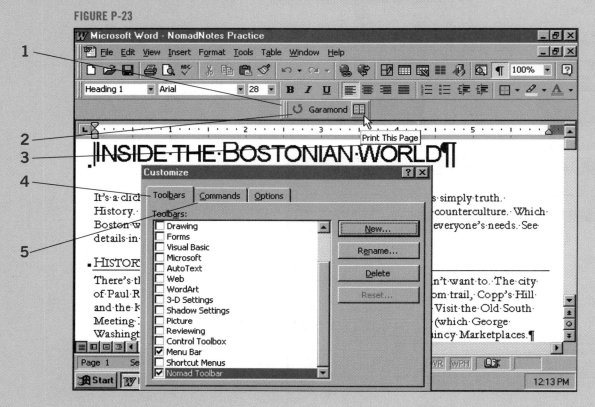

Match each of the following terms with the statement that best describes its function.

6. **Docked toolbar**
7. **Microsoft Visual Basic window**
8. **Macro**
9. **Pause button**
10. **Macro toolbar**
11. **AutoText**

a. Appears when you are recording a macro
b. Toolbar displayed below Formatting toolbar at the top of the document window
c. Collection of Word commands performed in a sequence to automate tasks
d. Used to temporarily stop recording keystrokes or selections in a macro so that you can prepare or set up the next macro command
e. Displays Visual Basic commands to be edited in a macro
f. Inserts frequently used text when you press [F3]

Select the best answer from the list of choices.

12. Which of the following is NOT true about AutoText entries?
a. You do not need to create AutoText entries for the preset entries available on the AutoText menu.
b. You can store AutoText entries to be used only in a specific document or in all documents.
c. You should use long names and real words to name your AutoText entry for easier identification.
d. The AutoText command can either insert an AutoText entry, or if text is selected, create a new entry.

13. If you do not want Word to automatically capitalize the first word after period, you can

   a. Record a macro.

   b. Create an AutoText entry.

   c. Create an AutoText exception.

   d. Create an AutoCorrect exception.

14. Which of the following is NOT a way to create a new macro?

   a. Click Tools on the menu bar, click Macro, then click Record New Macro.

   b. Click the Record button on the Macro toolbar.

   c. Click Tools on the menu bar, then click Record Macro.

   d. Double-click "REC" in the status bar.

▶ Skills Review

1. Create and insert an AutoText entry.

   a. Open the document WD P-2, then save the document with the name "Orientation Macro" (this document will serve as both your macro plan and a practice test document).

   b. In the Name box, type "SwitchToLandscape". Select the text "SwitchToLandscape".

   c. Click Insert on the menu bar, click AutoText, then click New. Type "stl", then click Add.

   d. In the Description box, type "The stl" then press [F3].

   e. Finish typing the sentence "macro changes the orientation to landscape and adjusts the margins."

2. Finish the plan for a macro to change the orientation from portrait to landscape and adjust the margins.

   a. Next to step 1 in the General Steps column, type "Change orientation" .

   b. Press [Tab] to move to the Specific Commands column and type "Click File, Page Setup, Paper Size, Landscape" .

   c. Press [Tab] to move to the General Steps column, and after the "2" type "Change margins".

   d. Press [Tab] to move to the Specific Commands column and type "Click Margins, Top 1, Bottom 1, Left .5, Right .5".

   e. Save your document.

3. Record and test a macro.

   a. Click Tools on the menu bar, click Macro, then click Record New Macro.

   b. In the Record Macro Name box, type "SwitchToLandscape", then in the Description box, type a description.

   c. Click the Keyboard button. Press [Alt][L], click Assign, then click Close.

   d. Click File on the menu bar, click Page Setup, then click Paper Size. Click the Landscape option button.

   e. Click the Margins tab, and in the Top margin box enter "1", in the Bottom margin box enter "1", in the Left margin box enter ".5", in the Right margin box enter ".5", then click OK. (If you receive a message stating that the margins are outside the printable area, click Ignore.)

   f. Click the Stop button on the Macro Record toolbar.

   g. Click the Print Preview button on the Standard toolbar to verify that the document now appears in the landscape orientation. Click the Close button to return to the document window.

   h. Click the Undo button and select the Page Setup command to verify the results of the macro were reversed.

4. Edit a macro.

   a. Click Tools on the menu bar, click Macro, then click Macros.

   b. Select SwitchToLandscape and click the Edit button.

   c. In the second line, place the insertion point after the "1" after the TopMargin=InchestoPoints, and type ".5".

   d. Place the insertion point after End With and press [Enter], then type the following, making sure you press [Enter] where indicated. Do not type the word itself.

      If PrintPreview = False Then [Enter]

      ActiveDocument.PrintPreview [Enter]

      End If [Enter]

   e. Click the Save button on the Standard toolbar. If you are asked to replace the existing Normal template, click Yes.

   f. Click File on the menu bar, then click Close and Return to Microsoft Word.

   g. Press [Alt][L], then click the Close button on the Preview toolbar.

FIGURE P-24

5. Customize a toolbar.
   a. Click View on the menu bar, click Toolbars, then click Customize. Click the New button.
   b. In the Toolbar Name box, type "Utilities" and click OK.
   c. On the Commands tab, in the Categories list, be sure File is selected and drag the Close button to the new toolbar.
   d. In the Categories list, select View. Click the Show All button and drag it to the custom toolbar.
   e. In the Categories list, scroll to and select the Macros category.
   f. Select Normal.NewMacros.SwitchToLandscape macro and drag it to the Utilities toolbar.
   g. Click Modify Selection, Change Button Image, then select the second button in the fifth row.
   h. Click Modify Selection, then click Text Only (in Menus).
   i. Click Close and compare your toolbar to Figure P-24.

6. Use a new toolbar.
   a. Open the document named WD P-3 and save it as "Overhead Macro". Verify that the Show/Hide button is off.
   b. Drag the Utilities toolbar to the top of the document window (just above the ruler) and release the mouse.
   c. Click the Show All button on the Utilities toolbar, then click the Switch to Landscape button on the Utilities toolbar.
   d. Click the Close button on the Preview toolbar. Reposition the callouts as required.
   e. Optional: Adjust the right-aligned tab in the footer so the text is aligned with the right margin of the document.
   f. Click the Close button that you placed on the Utilities toolbar, then click Yes to save your changes.

7. Delete a toolbar and a macro.
   a. Click View on the menu bar, click Toolbars, then Customize.
   b. On the toolbar tab, click the Utilities check box, then click the Delete button.
   c. Click OK, then click Close in the Toolbars dialog box.
   d. Click Tools on the menu bar, click Macro, then Macros.
   e. Select the SwitchToLandscape macro, click Delete, then click Yes to confirm that you want to delete this macro.
   f. Click Close in the Macro dialog box, click File on the menu bar, then click Exit.
   g. Click Yes if you are asked to save your changes.

► Independent Challenges

1. As communications coordinator for Mountain Top Tours, you find yourself repeatedly typing the company name and inserting a header with the company name. You decide to create an AutoText entry for the company name and a macro to insert the header. To begin this independent challenge, open a new document and save it as "Header Macro".

To complete this independent challenge:

1. Type the company name "Mountain Top Tours" and select this text (do not select the paragraph mark).
2. Create an AutoText entry for the company name. Type "mtt" for the entry name.
3. In the Record Macro dialog box, type the name "CompanyHeader" and a brief description.
4. Record the macro: Click View, click Header and Footer. Type "mtt", then press [F3]. Press [Tab] twice, then click Insert AutoText on the Header and Footer toolbar, then click Page. Click close on the Header and Footer toolbar, then click the Stop button on the Record Macro toolbar.
5. Assign the macro to a toolbar.
6. Open one of the documents you created at any time in this course and test the macro.
7. Review the macro in the Microsoft Visual Basic window, then print it.
8. Delete the new macro.
9. Use the Organizer feature to copy the AutoText entry created in this Independent Challenge from the global template (NORMAL) to the Header Macro document, then delete the AutoText entry from the global template.
10. Save and close all open documents.

2. You are the academic dean at a small liberal arts college. Together with the president, you have drafted a memo to all students outlining registration policy. You decide to create a more interesting document by reformatting the memo with bullets and new indents. Because this is one of many memos you write, you decide to create a macro. Open the document WD P-4 and save it as "Bullets Macro".

To complete this independent challenge:

1. Plan a reformatting macro that selects a paragraph, then format it with bullets and a left indent of 0.5 inches.
2. Move the cursor to the paragraph numbered 1 under "Financial Obligations Include" and record the reformatting macro you planned. (*Hint:* As the first step of the macro, press the [Home] key to move to the beginning of the sentence.)
3. Name the macro "Bullets", enter a description of the macro, then assign a keyboard shortcut, [Alt][B].
4. Test your macro on the other numbered paragraphs.
5. Review the macro in the Visual Basic Editor window, then print it. Do not save the macro, but save the Bullets Macro document before closing it.

3. As an intern for a newsletter editor, your job is to collect and organize a clip art library. The clip art library requires each graphic to have a colorful box border, as well as to fit on one page. You have just received a document with useful seasonal clip art in which the graphics need to be scaled down to fit on one page. Since this is one of many clip art documents with which you will be working, you decide to create a macro.

To complete this independent challenge:

1. Open the document WD P-5 and save it as "Graphics Macro".
2. Select the first graphic and record a macro named "ScalePicture".
3. Click Format, then click Picture, and on the Size tab type "71" then click OK.
4. Click Format, Borders and Shading, click the Box preset border, click the color arrow and choose Red, click the width arrow and choose 45, then click OK.
5. Customize the Formatting toolbar by placing the macro on this toolbar, and assign the macro to a new button.
6. Edit the macro by typing "50" after "Width" and after "Height" in the Microsoft Visual Basic window.
7. Test your macro on the other graphics in the document, using your macro button.
8. Review the macro in the Macro Editor, print it, then remove the button from the toolbar and delete the macro.

WEB WORK

4. As a communications coordinator, you find yourself frequently hiding the ruler, the Standard toolbar, and the Formatting toolbar to see as many lines of your document as possible. You then have to redisplay the ruler and toolbars to actually edit the document. To help speed up the process, you decide to create two macros. The first macro, called "TurnOff", turns off the ruler, the Standard toolbar, and the Formatting toolbar. The second macro, called "TurnBackOn", redisplays these features.

To complete this independent challenge:

1. You want to investigate using the web for marketing for your company. Use your Web browser to locate a site related to web marketing. Copy text from a web page, paste it into a new document, and save it as "Web Marketing Practice". If you can't locate a related site use your browser to go to http://www.course.com. From there, click Student Online Companions, click the link for this textbook, then click the Word link for this unit.
2. Record a macro named "TurnOff", by clicking View on the menu bar, clicking Toolbars, then clicking the toolbars you want to hide. Hide the ruler by clicking the Ruler command on the View menu.
3. Assign the macro to a new toolbar called "Proofing". Choose the Down Arrow button in the Customize dialog box on the Proofing toolbar.
4. Record a macro named "TurnBackOn" by reversing the steps you performed in step 2.
5. Assign this macro to the new toolbar. Choose the Up Arrow for the macro button.
6. Test TurnOff macro; then press [Alt][Print Scrn] to copy the image of the screen to the Clipboard. Insert a page break, then paste the image into the document.
7. Test TurnBackOn macro; then press [Alt][Print Scrn] to copy an image of the screen to the Clipboard. Insert a page break, then paste the image into the document. Then print the document.
8. Review the macros in the Microsoft Visual Basic window.
9. Delete the tool bar and macros, save, close, and print the document.

▶ Visual Workshop

As a member of the marketing team, you often route draft documents to other team members for review. When you print the draft document, it must include your name and the title of the document in the header. The footer contains the date and the page number. When you print the final copy, you delete all text from the header, and the date from the footer, leaving only the page number. You decide to create a macro called "Draft Macro" that inserts draft information, prints the draft document, then deletes the draft information. (*Hint:* As you record the macro, remember to use keyboard shortcuts to select words and whole sentences for deletion. You may also want to insert AutoText (using the Header and Footer toolbar) for the document name, date, and page number.) You also decide to create and customize a Drafting toolbar. The Drafting toolbar will contain the new macro button of your choice, as well as two very useful editing buttons, Repeat Last Command and the Find command. Review the macro in the Microsoft Visual Basic window and then print it. Compare your macro and toolbar to Figures P-25 and P-26. Delete the macro and the Drafting toolbar before exiting Word.

FIGURE P-25

FIGURE P-26

```
Sub DraftMacro()
'
' DraftMacro Macro
' Macro recorded 03/24/98 by Jennifer Swanson
'
    If ActiveWindow.View.SplitSpecial <> wdPaneNone Then
        ActiveWindow.Panes(2).Close
    End If
    If ActiveWindow.ActivePane.View.Type = wdNormalView Or ActiveWindow. _
        ActivePane.View.Type = wdOutlineView Or ActiveWindow.ActivePane.View.Type _
        = wdMasterView Then
        ActiveWindow.ActivePane.View.Type = wdPageView
    End If
    ActiveWindow.ActivePane.View.SeekView = wdSeekCurrentPageHeader
    NormalTemplate.AutoTextEntries("Created by").Insert Where:=Selection.Range
    Selection.TypeText Text:=vbTab & vbTab
    NormalTemplate.AutoTextEntries("Filename").Insert Where:=Selection.Range
    If Selection.HeaderFooter.IsHeader = True Then
        ActiveWindow.ActivePane.View.SeekView = wdSeekCurrentPageFooter
    Else
        ActiveWindow.ActivePane.View.SeekView = wdSeekCurrentPageHeader
    End If
    Selection.Fields.Add Range:=Selection.Range, Type:=wdFieldDate
    Selection.TypeText Text:=vbTab & vbTab
    Selection.Fields.Add Range:=Selection.Range, Type:=wdFieldPage
    ActiveWindow.ActivePane.View.SeekView = wdSeekMainDocument
    Application.PrintOut FileName:="", Range:=wdPrintAllDocument, Item:= _
        wdPrintDocumentContent, Copies:=1, Pages:="", PageType:=wdPrintAllPages, _
        Collate:=True, Background:=True, PrintToFile:=False
    If ActiveWindow.View.SplitSpecial <> wdPaneNone Then
        ActiveWindow.Panes(2).Close
    End If
    If ActiveWindow.ActivePane.View.Type = wdNormalView Or ActiveWindow. _
        ActivePane.View.Type = wdOutlineView Or ActiveWindow.ActivePane.View.Type _
        = wdMasterView Then
        ActiveWindow.ActivePane.View.Type = wdPageView
    End If
    ActiveWindow.ActivePane.View.SeekView = wdSeekCurrentPageHeader
    Selection.EndKey Unit:=wdLine, Extend:=wdExtend
    Selection.Delete Unit:=wdCharacter, Count:=1
    If Selection.HeaderFooter.IsHeader = True Then
        ActiveWindow.ActivePane.View.SeekView = wdSeekCurrentPageFooter
    Else
        ActiveWindow.ActivePane.View.SeekView = wdSeekCurrentPageHeader
    End If
    Selection.MoveRight Unit:=wdWord, Count:=1, Extend:=wdExtend
    Selection.Delete Unit:=wdCharacter, Count:=1
    ActiveWindow.ActivePane.View.SeekView = wdSeekMainDocument
End Sub
```

Accessories Built-in programs that come with Windows 95 that you can use for day-to-day tasks.

Active program The program that is running (that is, open).

Active window A window that you are currently using. If a window is active, its title bar changes color to differentiate it from other windows and its program button in the taskbar is highlighted.

Check box Clicking this square box in a dialog box turns an option off or on.

Click To press and release the left mouse button once quickly.

Clipboard Temporary storage space that contains information that has been cut or copied.

Close Use to quit a program or remove a window from the desktop. The Close button usually appears in the upper-right corner of a window.

Command Directive that provides access to a program's features.

Command button In a dialog box, a button that carries out an action. A command button usually has a label that describes its action, such as Cancel or Help. If the label is followed by an ellipses, clicking the button displays another dialog box.

Context-sensitive help Information related to your current task. An example of context-sensitive help in Windows is the What's This? feature.

Control Panel A Windows utility for changing computer settings, such as desktop colors or mouse settings.

Copy To copy information in a file and place it on the Clipboard to be pasted in another location.

Cursor The blinking vertical line in a document window such as WordPad, which indicates where text will appear when you type. Also known as the insertion point.

Cut To remove information from a file and place it on the Clipboard.

Cut and paste To move information from one place to another using the Clipboard as the temporary storage area.

Desktop An on-screen version of a desk that provides workspace for different computing tasks.

Dialog box A window that opens in which you enter information needed to carry out a command. Many commands display dialog boxes in which you must select options before Windows can carry out the command.

Disk label Name that you assign to a disk using the Properties dialog box.

Document window Displays the current document.

Double-click To press and release the left mouse button twice quickly.

Drag To point at an item, press and hold the left mouse button, move the mouse to a new location, then release the mouse button.

Drive Device which reads and saves files on a disk. Floppy drives read and save files on floppy disks. Hard drives read and save files on your built-in hard disk.

Edit To change the contents of a file without having to recreate it.

File A collection of information that has a unique name, distinguishing it from other files.

File hierarchy A logical order for folders and files that mimics how you would organize files and folders in a filing cabinet.

File management A skill to organize and keep track of files and folders.

Folder A collection of files and other folders that helps you organize your disks.

Font The design of a set of characters (i.e., Times New Roman).

Format Change the appearance of information but not the actual content.

Graphical user interface (GUI) An environment made up of meaningful symbols, words, and windows in which you can control the basic operation of a computer and the programs that run on it.

Help button A button in a Help window that when clicked jumps to a dialog box or opens a program to answer your question.

Highlight When an icon is shaded differently indicating it is selected. See also Select.

Horizontal scroll bar Moves your view from side to side in a window.

Icon Graphical representation of files and other screen elements.

Insertion point The blinking vertical line in a document window such as WordPad, which indicates where text will appear when you type. Also known as the cursor.

Keyboard shortcut A keyboard alternative for executing a menu command (i.e., [Ctrl][X] for Cut).

List box A box in a dialog box containing a list of items. To choose an item, click the list arrow, then click the desired item.

Maximize To enlarge a window so it takes up the entire screen. There is usually a Maximize button in the upper-right corner of a window.

Menu A list of available commands in a program.

Menu bar Provides access to most of a program's features through commands.

Minimize To reduce the size of a window. There is usually a Minimize button in the upper-right corner of a window. Clicking the Minimize button shrinks the window to an icon.

Mouse A hand-held input device that you roll on your desk to position the mouse pointer on the Windows desktop. See also Mouse pointer.

Mouse buttons The two buttons on the mouse (right and left) that you use to make selections and issue commands.

Mouse pointer The arrow-shaped cursor on the screen that follows the movement of the mouse as you roll the mouse on your desk. You use the mouse pointer to select items, choose commands, start programs, and edit text in applications. The shape of the mouse pointer changes depending on the program and the task being executed.

My Computer Use to view the files that are available on your computer and how they are arranged. The icon appears on the desktop.

Object An item (such as a file or folder) in a window. In task-oriented programs, objects are also graphics or text from another program.

Open Action which describes starting a program or displaying a window that was previously closed. Also used to describe a program that is currently running, but not necessarily displayed in an active window.

Operating system Controls the basic operation of your computer and the programs you run on it.

Option button (also called radio button) A small circle in a dialog box that you click to select an option.

Pattern A design that will display as your desktop background.

Point To move the mouse pointer to position it over an item on the desktop. Also a unit of measurement used to specify the size of text.

Pop-up menu The menu that appears when you right-click an item on the desktop. Also known as a shortcut menu.

Program Task-oriented software that you use for a particular kind of work, such as word processing or database management. Microsoft Access, Microsoft Excel, and Microsoft Word are all programs.

Program button The button that appears on the taskbar, representing a minimized (but still running) program.

Properties The characteristics of a specific element (such as the mouse, keyboard, or desktop display) that you can customize.

Radio button (also called option button) A small circle in a dialog box that you click to select an option.

RAM (random access memory) The memory that programs use to perform necessary tasks while the computer is on. When you turn the computer off, all information in RAM is lost.

Recycle Bin An icon that appears on the desktop that represents a temporary storage area for deleted files. Files will remain in the Recycle Bin until you empty it.

Restore To reduce the window to its previous size before it was maximized. There is usually a Restore button in the upper-right corner of a window.

Right-click To press and release the right mouse button once quickly.

Run To operate a program.

Screen saver A moving pattern that fills your screen after your computer has not been used for a specified amount of time.

Scroll bar A bar that appears at the bottom and/or right edge of a window whose contents are not entirely visible. Each scroll bar contains a scroll box and two scroll arrows. You click the arrows or drag the box in the direction you want the window to move.

Scroll box Located in the vertical and horizontal scroll bars and indicates your relative position in a window. See also Horizontal scroll bar and Vertical scroll bar.

Select When you click and highlight an item in order to perform some action on it. See also Highlight.

Shortcut A link that you can place in any location that gives you instant access to a particular file, folder, or program on your hard disk or on a network.

Shortcut menu The menu that appears when you right-click an item on the desktop. Also known as a pop-up menu.

Shut down The action you perform when you have finished your Windows work session. After you perform this action it is safe to turn off your computer.

Start button A button on the taskbar that you use to start programs, find files, access Windows Help and more.

Taskbar A bar at the bottom of the screen that contains the Start button and shows which programs are running

Text box A box in a dialog box in which you type text.

Title bar The area along the top of the window that contains the filename and program used to create it.

Toolbar Contains buttons that allow you to activate a command quickly.

ToolTip A description of a toolbar button that appears on your screen.

Triple-click To press and release the left mouse button three times quickly. In some programs, this action causes an entire line to be selected.

Vertical scroll bar Moves your view up and down through a window.

Wallpaper An image that is in the same format as Windows 95 Paint files that will display as your desktop background.

Window A rectangular frame on a screen that might contain icons, the contents of a file, or other usable data.

Windows Explorer Use to manage files, folders, and shortcuts; more powerful than My Computer and allows you to work with more than one computer, folder, or file at once.

Alignment   The horizontal position of text within the width of a line or between tab stops. There are four kinds of alignment in Word: left aligned (the default), centered, right-aligned, and justified.

Application   See *program*.

Automatic Save   A feature that automatically saves document changes in a temporary file at specified intervals. If power to the computer is interrupted, the changes in effect from the last save are retained. Enabled by default, you can turn off this feature by clicking Tools then Options.

AutoCorrect   A feature that automatically corrects a misspelled word. Word provides several entries for commonly misspelled words, but you can add your own.

AutoFormat   A feature that improves the appearance of a document by applying consistent formatting and styles based on a default document template or a document template you specify. The AutoFormat feature also adds bullets to lists and symbols for trademarks and copyrights where necessary.

AutoShape   A shape (circle, rectangle, triangle, callout, among others) that you can create by clicking the AutoShape button on the Drawing toolbar and dragging the pointer.

AutoText entry   A stored text or graphic you want to use again.

Bookmark   A named location in a document. Bookmarks allow you to jump to specific locations, create hyperlinks, and include ranges of pages in an index.

Border   A straight vertical or horizontal line between columns in a section, next to or around paragraphs and graphics, or in a table. You can assign a variety of widths to a border.

Bullet   A small graphic, usually a round or square dot, often used to identify items in a list.

Callout   A graphic element used to label or point to an item in a document. It consists of text and a line pointing to the item.

Cell   The basic unit of a table, separated by gridlines. In a table, the intersection of a row and a column forms one cell.

Cell reference   Identifies a cell's position in a table. Each cell reference contains a letter (A, B, C and so on) to identify its column and a number (1, 2, 3 and so on) to identify its row.

Character style   A stored set of font format settings.

Chart   Visual or graphical representation of numerical data.

Click   To press and release a mouse button in one motion.

Clipboard   A temporary storage area for cut or copied text or graphics. You can paste the contents of the Clipboard into any Word document or into a file of another Microsoft Windows application, such as Microsoft Excel. The Clipboard holds the information until you cut or copy another piece of text or a graphic.

Comment   Text that appears in a pop-up window when you position the pointer near a comment identifier. Double-clicking the comment identifier allows you to edit the comment text. In earlier versions of Word this feature was called "annotations".

Crop   To cut away the parts of a graphic you don't want to appear.

Cut   To remove selected text or a graphic from a document so you can paste it to another place in the document or to another document. The cut information is placed in a temporary storage area called the Clipboard. The Clipboard holds the information until you cut or copy another piece of text or a graphic.

Data source   the document containing the variable information to be used with the mail merge feature.

Dialog box   A box that displays the available command options for you to review or change.

Document window   A rectangular portion of the screen in which you view and edit a document. When you enlarge a document window to maximum size, it shares its borders and title bar with the Word program window.

Drag   To hold down the mouse button while moving the mouse.

Drive   The mechanism in a computer that read a disk to retrieve and store information. Personal computers often have one hard disk drive labeled C and two drives labeled A and B that read removable floppy disks.

Edit To add, delete, or change text and graphics.

Extend selection To lengthen a selection. When you extend a selection, it grows progressively larger each time you press [F8]. To shrink the selection, press [Shift] + [F8]. When you extend a selection, you can also use the arrow keys, or any of the other keys that move the insertion point within text, to enlarge or shrink the selection.

Field Variable information in a document that is supplied by a file or by Word. In a mail merge operation individual items (such as a name or state) are stored in fields in the data source. A merge field inserted in the main document (such as a form letter) instructs Word to provide that field's contents from the data source. A Word field is variable information provided by Word. For example, if you insert the Filename field in a footer, the document's file name appears in the footer.

File A document that has been created, then saved, under a unique file name. In Word, all documents and pictures are stored as files.

Folders Subdivisions of a disk that work like a filing system to help you organize files.

Font A name given to a collection of characters (letters, numerals, symbols, and punctuation marks) with a specific design. Arial and Times New Roman are examples of font names.

Font effects Refers to enhanced formatting you can apply to text, such as small caps, all caps, hidden text, strikethrough, subscripted, or superscripted, shadow, and engraved, among others.

Font size Refers to the physical size of text, measured in points (pts). The bigger the number of points, the larger the font size.

Font style Refers to whether text appears as bold, italicized, or underlined, or any combination of these formats.

Footer The text that appears at the bottom of every page.

Form A special document in which you can create blanks and controls so that a user can complete a form online.

Format The way text appears on a page. In Word, a format comes from direct formatting and the application of styles. The four types of formats are character, paragraph, section, and document.

Formatting toolbar A bar that contains buttons and options for the most frequently used formatting commands.

Global template In Word, a template with the file name NORMAL.DOT that contains default menus, AutoCorrect entries, styles and page setup settings. Documents use the global template unless you specify a custom template. See also *template*.

Graphics A picture, chart, or drawing in a document.

Graphic object An element in a document that can be moved, sized, and modified without leaving Word.

Gridlines The dotted lines that separate cells in a table. Gridlines do not print. You can alternately hide and display gridlines with the Gridlines command on the Table menu.

Hanging indent A paragraph format in which the first line of a paragraph starts farther left than the subsequent lines.

Header and footer A header is text or graphics that appear at the top of every page in a section. A footer appears at the bottom of every page. Headers and footers often contain page numbers, chapter titles, dates, and author names. Headers and footers appear in the header or footer pane for editing.

Hidden text A character format that allows you to show or hide designated text. Word indicates hidden text by underlining it with a dotted line. You can select or clear the Hidden Text option with the Options command on the Tools menu. You can omit hidden text during printing.

Horizontal ruler A graphical bar displayed across the top of the document window in all views. You can use the ruler to indent paragraphs, set tab stops, adjust left and right paragraph margins, and change column widths in a table. You can hide this ruler by clicking View then Ruler.

HTML Hypertext Mark Up Language. Language that formats a document so that it can be viewed on the Internet.

Hyperlink Specially formatted text that allows you to jump to another location in a document or open another document by simply clicking the hyperlink.

Indent The distance between text boundaries and page margins. Positive indents make the text area narrower than the space between margins. Negative indents allow text to extend into the margins. A paragraph can have left, right, and first-line indents.

Word 97

Insertion point Vertical blinking line on the Word screen that shows your current location and where text and graphics are inserted. The insertion point also determines where Word will begin an action.

Landscape A term used to refer to horizontal page orientation; opposite of "portrait," or vertical, orientation.

Legend A key to the symbol or colors used to represent data in a chart or graph.

Line break Mark inserted where you want to end one line and start another without starting a new paragraph.

Line spacing The height of a line of text, including extra spacing. Line spacing is often measured in lines or points.

Macro A collection of commands and keystrokes performed in a sequence that you record and store to perform repetitive tasks.

Mail merge The ability to create personalized form letters or labels by combining boilerplate text with variable information.

Main document In the mail merge process the main document is the document containing the boilerplate text, the text that is the same in each version of the merged document.

Margin The distance between the edge of the text in the document and the top, bottom, or side edges of the page.

Menu bar Lists the names of the menus that contain Word commands. Click a menu name on the menu bar to display a list of commands.

Non-printing characters Marks displayed on the screen to indicate characters that do not print, such as tab characters or paragraph marks. You can control the display of special characters with the Options command on the Tools menu, and the Show/Hide ¶ button on the Standard toolbar.

Normal view The view you see when you start Word. Normal view is used for most editing and formatting tasks.

Object A table, chart, graphic, equation, or other form of information you create and edit with an application other than Word, but whose data you insert and store in a Word document.

Options The choices available in a dialog box.

Overtype An option for replacing existing characters one by one as you type. You can select overtype by pressing the [Insert] key or by selecting the Overtype option with the Options command on the Tools menu. When you select the Overtype option, the letters "OVR" appear in the status bar at the bottom of the Word window.

Page break The point at which one page ends and another begins. A break you insert (created by pressing [Ctrl] + [Enter]) is called a hard break; a break determined by the page layout is called a soft break. A hard break appears as a dotted line and is labeled Page Break. A soft break appears as a dotted line without a label.

Page layout view A view of a document as it will appear when you print it. Items such as headers, footnotes, and framed objects appear in their actual positions, and you can drag them to new positions. You can edit and format text in page layout view.

Paragraph style A stored set of paragraph format settings.

Paste To insert cut or copied text into a document from the temporary storage area called the Clipboard.

Path Drive, folder, and file name. For example, the complete path for Microsoft Word might be C:\WINWORD\WINWORD.EXE.

Point size A measurement used for the size of text characters. There are 72 points per inch.

Portrait A term used to refer to vertical page orientation; opposite of "landscape," or horizontal, orientation.

Program A software application that performs specific tasks, such as Microsoft Word or Microsoft Excel.

Program window A window that contains the running application. The window displays the menus and provides the workspace for any document used within the application. The application window shares its borders and title bar with document windows that are fully enlarged.

Record The entire collection of fields related to an item or individual, contained in the data source.

Redo The ability to repeat reversed actions or changes, usually editing or formatting actions. Only reversed changes can be repeated with the redo feature.

Repetitive text   Text that you use often in documents.

Resize   the ability to change the size of an object (such as framed text or a graphic) by dragging sizing handles located on the sides and corner of the selected object.

Resolution   Refers to size of your monitor's screen display. Resolution is measured in pixels, such as a typical resolution is 640 × 480. The illustrations in this book were taken on a computer with this resolution. Because a higher resolution results in more space visible on the screen and smaller text, your screen might not exactly match the illustrations in this book if you are using a higher resolution. You can change the resolution of the monitor using the Control Panel on the Start menu.

Sans serif font   A font whose characters do not include serifs; the small strokes at the ends of the characters. Arial is a sans serif font.

ScreenTip   When you move the pointer over a button, the name of the button is displayed and a brief description of its function appears in the status bar. In earlier versions of Word, this feature was called "ToolTips".

Scroll bar   A graphical device for moving vertically and horizontally through a document with a mouse. Scroll bars are located at the right and bottom edges of the document window. You can display or hide scroll bars with the Horizontal scroll bar and Vertical scroll bar check boxes, on the View tab of the Options dialog box (Tools menu).

Section   A part of a document separated from the rest of the document with a section break. By separating a document into sections, you can use different page and column formatting in different parts of the same document.

Selection bar   An unmarked column at the left edge of a document window used to select text with the mouse. In a table, each cell has its own selection bar at the left edge of the cell.

Serif font   A font that has small strokes at the ends of the characters. Times New Roman and Palatino are serif fonts.

Shading   The background color or pattern behind text or graphics.

Soft return   A line break created by pressing [Shift] + [Enter]. This creates a new line without creating a new paragraph.

Spreadsheet program   A software program used for calculations and financial analysis.

Standard toolbar   The topmost row of buttons that perform some of the most frequently used commands.

Status bar   Located at the bottom of the Word window, it displays the current page number and section number, the total number of pages in the document, and the vertical position (in inches) of the insertion point. You also see the status of commands in effect. The status bar also displays descriptions of commands and buttons as you move around the window.

Style   A group of formatting instructions that you name and store, and are able to modify. When you apply a style to selected characters and paragraphs, all the formatting instructions of that style are applied at once.

Style area   An area to the left of the selection in which the names of applied styles are displayed. You can display the style area using the Options command for View options on the Tools menu.

Style Gallery   A feature that allows you to examine the overall formatting and styles used in a document template. With the Style Gallery you can also preview your document formatted in the styles from a selected template.

Table   One or more rows of cells commonly used to display numbers and other items for quick reference and analysis. Items in a table are organized into rows and columns. You can convert text into a table with the Insert Table command on the Table menu.

Tab stop   A measured position for placing and aligning text at a specific place on a line. Word has four kinds of tab stops, left-aligned (the default), centered, right-aligned, and decimal.

Template   A special kind of document that provides basic tools and text for creating a document. Templates can contain the following elements: styles, AutoText items, macros, customized menu and key assignments, and text or graphics that are the same in different types of document.

Text box   A box you add to mark an area of text or graphic in a document so that you can easily position it on a page. Once you insert an object into a frame, you can drag it to the position you want in page layout view.

Text flow   Refers to paragraph formatting which controls the flow of text across page breaks. Controling text flow prevents awkward breaks within paragraph or ensure that related paragraph appear together on the same page.

Title bar   The horizontal bar at the top of a window that displays the name of the document or application that appears in that window. Until you save the document and give it a name, the temporary name for the document is DOCUMENT1.

Toolbar A graphical bar with buttons that perform some of the most common commands in Word, such as opening, copying, and printing files.

Undo The ability to reverse previous actions or changes, usually editing or formatting actions. Actions from the File menu cannot be reversed. You can undo up to 100 previous actions from the time you opened the document.

Version The saved changes stored with a document. By saving versions of a document you can revert a document to an earlier stage of editing.

Vertical alignment The placement of text on a page in relation to the top, bottom, or center of the page.

Vertical ruler A graphical bar displayed at the left edge of the document window in the page layout and print preview views. You can use this ruler to adjust the top and bottom page margins, and change row height in a table.

View A display that shows certain aspects of the document. Word has several views: normal, outline, online, page layout, full screen, and print preview.

View buttons Appear in the horizontal scroll bar. These buttons allow you to display the document in one of four views: normal, page layout, online and outline.

Web page A document stored in HTML format that you can view on the Internet.

Web site A collection of Web pages you can view on the Internet.

Window A rectangular area on the screen in which you view and work on documents.

Wizard An on-line coach you use to create documents. When you use a wizard to create a document, you are asked questions about document preferences, and the wizard creates the document according to your specifications.

WordArt The ability to format text into interesting and creating shapes, orientations and patterns.

Word processing program A software program used for creating documents efficiently. Usually includes features beyond simple editing, such as formatting and arranging text and graphics to create attractive documents, as well as the ability to merge documents for form letters and envelopes.

Word-wrap Automatic placement of a word on the next line. When you type text and reach the right margin or indent, Word checks to see if the entire word you type fits on the current line. If not, Word automatically places the entire word on the next line.

Index

Index

defined, WD H-1
inserting, WD H-2-3
modifying, WD H-4-5
Clipboard
copying objects to, W B-8-9
for copying text, WD B-6
defined, W B-8
for moving text, WD B-8
Clip Gallery dialog box, WD H-2-3
Close All command, WD G-16
Close button, W A-18, W A-19
exiting Word with, WD A-16
collaboration, WD L-1-17
accepting and rejecting changes, WD L-10-11
bookmarks, WD L-14-15
comparing documents, WD L-8-9
defined, WD L-1
hyperlinks, WD L-16-17
inserting comments, WD L-2-3
saving versions of documents, WD L-4-5
tracking, WD L-6-7, WD L-12-13
collapsing, heading levels, WD K-6, WD K-7
color
background in text boxes, WD M-10, WD M-11
in charts, WD N-6-7
effects, in WordArt objects, WD M-16-17
of scrolling text background, WD J-12
of shapes, WD H-8-9
Color list arrow, for formatting text, WD C-4
color palette, in Paint, W B-4
Colors and Lines tab, WD H-4
column breaks, WD M-5
column charts, WD N-2
creating from tables, WD N-4-5
custom, WD N-16-17
legends for, WD N-4
columns, WD M-1, WD M-2-7
arranging text in, WD M-1, WD M-2-3
customizing with Draw Table button, WD D-14-15
distributing evenly, WD D-16
editing text in, WD M-4-5
formatting, WD M-2-3, WD M-6-7
inserting and deleting, in tables, WD D-6-7
line between, WD M-6, WD M-7
moving text in, WD M-4-5
sorting by, WD D-10-11
sorting by more than one, WD D-11
space between, WD M-6, WD M-7
width of, WD M-6-7
Columns command, WD M-6-7
Columns with Depth custom chart, WD N-16-17
Columns dialog box, WD M-6-7
column width, forms, WD O-14
combination charts, WD N-2
command buttons, in dialog boxes, W A-13
comment markers, WD L-2
Comment pane, WD L-2-3
comments, WD L-2-3
deleting, WD L-2
displaying, WD L-2, WD L-3
identifiers, WD L-2
inserting in documents, WD L-2-3
numbers, WD L-2
Common Tasks toolbar, WD I-8

Compare Documents dialog box, WD L-8
Compare Documents and Track Changes, WD L-1
comparing documents, WD L-4, WD L-5, WD L-8-9
continuous breaks, WD M-2, WD M-5
Control Panel, W A-10-11
controls, WD O-11
Control Toolbox toolbar, WD O-11
Copy button, on Standard toolbar, WD B-6
copying
files, W B-14-15
formatting, with Format Painter, WD C-2
text, WD A-2, WD B-6-7
copy and paste, WD I-2
CourseHelp, WD B-9
viewing, WD G-3, WD N-4, WD N-5
cover pages, fax, WD I-16-17
Create AutoText dialog box, WD P-2-3
Create Data Source dialog box, WD G-4-5
Create from File tab, WD H-14, WD H-15
Create Labels dialog box, WD G-12-13, WD I-4, WD I-5
criteria
multiple selection, WD G-14-15
for selecting records to merge, WD I-6
cropping, graphics, WD H-5
Currency Style, WD I-14
in charts, WD N-16
custom charts, WD N-2, WD N-3
creating, WD N-16-17
custom graphics, *See also* graphics
creating, WD H-6-7
modifying, WD H-8-9
Customize dialog box, WD P-14-15, WD P-18
Customize Keyboard dialog box, WD P-8-9
custom toolbars
creating, WD P-14-15
deleting, WD P-18-19
removing buttons from, WD P-14
using, WD P-16-17
Cut command, W B-15, WD B-8, WD E-6
cutting
files, W B-14, W B-15
text, WD M-4

▶ D

database files, as data source for mailing
labels, WD I-4-5
data fields, *See also* fields
defined, WD G-2
Data Form dialog box, WD G-6, WD G-7
datasheets
editing values in, WD N-15
hiding/viewing, WD N-14
data source
creating, WD G-4-5
defined, WD G-2, WD G-4
editing, WD G-7
entering records in, WD G-5-7
data sources, attaching Access database as, WD I-4-5
date
formatting, in text form fields, WD O-4-5

inserting in footers, WD E-8-9
Date and Time dialog box, WD A-10, WD G-2
deleting
comments, WD L-2
custom toolbars, WD P-18-19
files, W B-10, W B-18-19
macros, WD P-18-19
shortcuts, W B-20
text, WD A-10-11, WD M-4
demoting, headings, WD K-8-9
descending sorts, of tables, WD D-10, WD D-11
Desert fill effect, WD H-10
desktop
defined, W A-2
elements of, W A-3
managing files on, W B-20-21
Details button, on My Computer toolbar, W B-12,
W B-13
Details command, on Control Panel View menu,
W A-10, W B-12
dialog boxes, W A-12-13
defined, W A-12
typical items in, W A-13
Different first page check box, WD E-16
Different odd and even check box, WD E-16
dimmed commands, on menus, W A-11
Display as icon option, WD I-13
Distribute Columns Evenly button, WD D-16
Document Map, WD A-3, WD F-12-13, WD K-7
documents
aligning text with tabs, WD C-6-7
arranging text in, WD M-1-17
AutoText in, WD P-1-5
borders, WD C-16-17
bulleted lists, WD C-14-15
charts in, WD N-1-17
closing, WD A-16
collaborating with, WD L-1-17
deleting text in, WD A-10-11
entering text in, WD A-8-9
formatting, WD C-1-17
forms in, WD O-1-17
inserting text in, WD A-10-11
large, *See* large documents
macros in, WD P-6-15
numbered lists, WD C-14-15
opening, WD B-4-5
paragraph alignment, WD C-8-9
paragraph indention, WD C-10-11
paragraph spacing, WD C-12-13
planning, WD B-2-3
printing, WD A-16
Print Preview, WD A-16-17
replacing text in, WD A-12-13
saving, WD A-8-9
saving with new name, WD B-4-5
shading, WD C-16-17
sharing information among, WD I-1-17
tone of, WD B-2
document window, WD A-6-7
double-clicking, with mouse, W A-4, W A-5
double line borders, around graphics, WD H-4
double-underlining, WD L-6, WD L-7
doughnut charts, WD N-2

Index

drop-down, WD O-10-11
text box, WD O-4-5
Form Field Shading option, WD O-14
forms, WD O-1-17
  appearance of, WD O-14-15
  calculated form fields, WD O-6-7
  check box form fields, WD O-8-9
  column width, WD O-14
  controls, WD O-11
  date options, WD O-4-5
  defined, WD O-1
  drop-down form fields., WD O-10-11
  effective, planning, WD O-3
  field labels, WD O-2
  filling out, WD O-16-17
  form fields, WD O-2
  instructions in form fields, WD O-12-13
  preparing for users, WD O-14-15
  protecting, WD O-14
  templates for, WD O-2-3
  text box form fields, WD O-4-5
  time sheet, WD O-2-3
Forms toolbar, WD O-2
Formula command, WD D-8-9
Formula dialog box, WD D-8, WD D-9
formulas, built-in, for table calculations, WD D-8-9
form Web pages, creating, WD J-6-7
fractions, AutoFormat, WD F-16-17
Free Rotate button, WD H-10

►G

Gradient tab, WD H-10
grammar correction, WD A-9, WD B-10-11
graphical user interface (GUI), W A-1
graphics, WD H-1-17, *See also* clip art; custom
graphics; shapes
  AutoShapes, WD H-12-13
  borders around, WD H-4
  callouts, WD H-16-17
  clip art, WD H-2-5
  creating hyperlinks on, WD J-14
  cropping, WD H-5
  custom, WD H-6-9
  fill effects, WD H-10-11
  inserting from other programs, WD H-14-15
  positioning, WD H-12-13
  sizing, WD H-2, WD H-3
  special effects, WD H-10-11
  text wrapping around, WD H-4, WD H-12-13
graphs, *See also* charts
  area, WD N-2
  line, WD N-2
  types of, WD N-2-3
Graph window, WD N-4-5
Grayscale, for graphics, WD H-4
green wavy lines
  hiding, WD C-2
  potential grammatical errors identified by, WD C-9
gridlines, for charts, WD N-16-17
grouping, shapes, WD H-8-9

►H

handouts, WD I-10
Hanging Indent Marker, WD C-10
hanging indents, WD C-11
hard disks, W B-2
hard page breaks, WD E-2
Header and Footer toolbar, WD E-6, WD E-8-9, WD K-12
  buttons, WD E-9
  formatting in multiple sections, WD E-14-15
header row, WD D-10, WD G-2, WD G-5
headers
  changing formatting in, WD E-14-15
  creating for specific pages, WD E-16-17
  defined, WD E-6
  formatting, WD E-6-7
  formatting for specific pages, WD E-16-17
  inserting, WD E-6-7
heading levels
  collapsing, WD K-6, WD K-7
  expanding, WD K-6, WD K-7
  showing and hiding, WD K-4, WD K-6, WD K-7
  styles, WD K-2, WD K-3
headings
  demoting, WD K-8-9
  moving, WD K-6, WD K-7
  promoting, WD K-8-9
  styles, WD K-2, WD K-3
  in Web pages, WD J-8
heading styles
  applying, WD F-6
  AutoFormat, WD F-16-17
  checking, WD F-4
  moving to headings with, WD F-12-13
  replacing, WD F-14-15
  spacing before headings, WD F-6
Help, W A-16-17
  adding to form fields, WD O-12-13
  menu commands, WD A-15
  Office Assistant, WD A-14-15
  Visual Basic Help Reference, WD P-12
  What's This pointer, WD A-15
Help button (?), W A-17
Help Key (F1), WD O-12
Help Topics dialog box, W A-17
hiding, *See also* showing; viewing
  heading levels, WD K-4, WD K-6, WD K-7
Highlight Changes dialog box, WD L-6, WD L-7
home pages, WD J-2
horizontal lines, in Web pages, WD J-10
horizontal ruler, WD A-6-7
horizontal scroll bar, WD A-6-7, W A-14-15
HTML
  saving documents as, WD J-10
  viewing code, WD J-16, WD J-17
hyperlinks, *See also* linking
  bookmarks for, WD L-14, WD L-16
  creating, WD I-2, WD L-16-17
  on graphics, WD J-14
  in Web pages, WD J-2, WD J-14-15
hyphens
  nonbreaking, WD M-6
  optional, WD M-6

►I

icons
  defined, W A-1, W A-2
  displaying objects as, WD I-13
  selecting with mouse, W A-4
Image Control button, WD H-4
Increase Indent button, WD C-10, WD C-14
indenting paragraphs, WD C-10-11, WD F-14-15
indexes
  bookmarks in, WD K-15
  creating, WD K-14-15
  formatting, WD K-14-15
Index and Tables dialog box, WD K-10-11
Insert Hyperlink button, WD L-16
Insert Hyperlink dialog box, WD J-14
inserting text, WD A-10-11
insertion point, WD A-4
Insert Merge Field dialog box, WD G-8
Insert Subdocument dialog box, WD K-16
Insert Table command, WD O-2
  on Standard toolbar, WD D-2, WD D-4-5
  on Table menu, WD D-2
Internet, WD J-1, *See also* Web pages; Web sites
Isosceles Triangle, WD H-6-7
Italic button, WD C-2

►J

justification, WD C-8-9

►K

keyboard shortcuts, W A-11
  assigning styles to, WD F-9

►L

Label Options dialog box, WD G-12, WD I-4
labels
  creating for main documents, WD G-12-13
  data source for, WD I-4-5
  field, for forms, WD O-2
  formatting, WD G-16-17
  merged to new document, WD G-14-15
  Print Preview, WD G-16
landscape orientation, WD E-12-13
large documents, WD K-1-17
  creating in outline view, WD K-2-3
  defined, WD K-1
  editing in outline view, WD K-4-5
  indexes, WD K-14-15
  master documents, WD K-16-17
  numbering pages in multiple sections, WD K-12-13
  organizing in outline view, WD K-6-7
  promoting and demoting headings in, WD K-8-9
  tables of contents, WD K-10-11
Large Icons, My Computer toolbar, W B-12

Index

objects
  copying onto Clipboard, W B-8-9
  defined, WD I-2
  displaying as icons, WD I-13
  Excel
    inserting into documents, WD I-12-13
    modifying, WD I-14-15
  PowerPoint, inserting in documents, WD I-10-11
  WordArt
    adding color effects to, WD M-16-17
    arranging text in, WD M-1, WD M-12-17
    creating, WD M-12-13
    fonts, WD M-14-15
    modifying, WD M-14-15
odd page breaks, WD M-5
Odd Page Header box, WD E-16
Office Assistant, WD A-10, WD A-14-15
  in Spelling and Grammar dialog box, WD B-10
OLE, *See* Object Linking and Embedding (OLE)
One Page button, on Print Preview toolbar, WD B-14
online Help, *See* Help
Open Data Source dialog box, WD G-12
Open dialog box, WD B-4, WD B-5
opening documents, WD B-4-5
  multiple, WD B-6, WD B-7
operating systems, W A-3
optional hyphens, WD M-6
Organizer dialog box, WD P-18, WD P-19
orientation, *See also* page orientation
  of pie charts, WD N-10-11
  of text in cells, WD O-14
orphans, controlling, WD E-3
outlines
  creating presentations from, WD I-8-9
  formatting, WD C-4
outline view
  creating documents in, WD K-2-3
  editing documents in, WD K-4-5
  master documents, WD K-16
  organizing documents in, WD K-6-7
  Outlining toolbar, WD K-4, WD K-6
  options, WD K-6, WD K-7, WD K-8
ovals, drawing, WD H-6-7
OVR indicator, WD A-10

▶P

page breaks, WD M-5
  controlling, WD E-2-3
  hard, WD E-2
  inserting, WD E-2, WD K-14
page formatting, WD E-1-17, *See also* formatting;
  formatting documents
  defined, WD E-1
  document margins, WD E-4-5
  footers, WD E-8-9, WD E-10-11, WD E-14-15
  headers, WD E-6-7, WD E-14-15
  headers for specific pages, WD E-16-17
  in multiple sections, WD E-14-15
  page orientation, WD E-12-13
  text flow between pages, WD E-2-3
Page Layout View, WD A-6, WD E-8, WD K-12

viewing master documents and subdocuments in,
  WD K-16
Page Number Format dialog box, WD K-13
page numbering
  alignment, WD K-12
  in footers, WD E-8-9
  format of, WD K-12-13
  in multiple sections, WD K-12-13
Page Numbers dialog box, WD K-12
page orientation
  changing, WD E-12-13
  landscape, WD E-12-13
  portrait, WD E-12-13
pages
  controlling text flow between, WD E-2-3
  previewing, WD E-4-5
Page Setup dialog box, WD E-4, WD E-12, WD E-16
Paint
  creating files, W B-4-5
  inserting graphics from, WD H-14-15
  modifying objects, WD H-14
  saving files, W B-6-7
  toolbox tools, W B-5
  working with WordPad and, W B-8-9
Paper Size options, WD E-12-13
Paragraph dialog box, WD C-9, WD C-10
paragraphs
  alignment, changing, WD C-8-9
  formatting, defined, WD C-1
  indenting, WD C-10-11
  preventing page breaks between, WD E-3
  preventing page breaks within, WD E-3
  spacing, WD C-12-13
Paragraphs command, line and page breaks, WD E-2-3
paragraph styles
  applying, WD F-4, WD F-8-9
  creating, WD F-8
  defined, WD F-4
  displaying names of, WD F-10-11
password dialog box, W A-2
paste, WD I-2, WD M-4, *See also* copy and paste
Paste button, WD B-6, WD B-8, WD E-6
Paste Link command, WD I-2, WD I-10
Pause button, macros, WD P-6, WD P-7
pictures. *See* clip art; graphics
Picture toolbar, WD H-2, WD H-4-5
pie charts, WD N-2
  creating, WD N-8-9
  defined, WD N-8
  modifying, WD N-10-11
  orientation of, WD N-10-11
  proportions of, WD N-10-11
  3-D, WD N-8-9
planning
  documents, WD B-2-3
  macros, WD P-6, WD P-7
  Web sites, WD J-2-3
pointer trail, mouse, W A-12
pointing, W A-4, W A-5
pop-up menus, displaying, W A-4, W A-5
portrait orientation, WD E-12-13
positioning, graphics, WD H-12-13
PowerPoint, WD I-8-11
  creating presentations from outlines, WD I-8-9

objects, inserting in documents, WD I-10-11
presentations
  creating from outlines, WD I-8-9
  file size, WD I-10
  inserting into documents, WD I-10-11
Preset colors, WD H-10
previewing, *See also* Print Preview
  documents, WD B-14-15, WD A-16-17
  files, W B-10, W B-17
  pages, WD E-4-5
  Web pages, WD J-16-17
Print command, WD B-16
Print dialog box, WD F-11, WD B-16, WD B-17
printers, merging to, WD G-10
printing
  documents, WD A-16-17, WD B-16-17
  options, WD B-16
  styles, WD F-11
Print Preview, WD B-14-15, *See also* previewing
  keyboard shortcut, WD B-14
  labels, WD G-16
  merged documents, WD G-10
Professional Memo template, WD F-4, WD F-5
programs
  closing, W A-18-19
  defined, W A-2
  starting in Microsoft Windows 95, W A-6-7
Programs menu, launching Word with, WD A-4
promoting, headings, WD K-8-9
proofreading, documents, WD A-2, WD B-10-11
Properties dialog box, W B-16, WD E-11
proportions, of pie charts, WD N-10-11
Protect Form option, WD O-14
protection, forms, WD O-14
pyramid charts, WD N-2, WD N-12-13
  stacked column, WD N-12-13

▶Q

Query Options, mail merge, WD G-14-15, WD I-6-7
Quick View command, W B-17

▶R

radio buttons, in dialog boxes, W A-13
random access memory (RAM), W B-6
recording macros, WD P-6-7
Record Macro dialog box, WD P-6, WD P-7
records, mail merge
  defined, WD G-2, WD G-4, WD G-6
  entering in data source, WD G-5-7
  merging selected, WD G-14-15
  selecting for merging, WD I-6-7
Recycle Bin, W B-18
  icon, W A-2
  size of, resetting, W B-18
Redo Typing feature, WD A-12
red wavy lines
  hiding, WD C-2
  potential spelling errors identified by, WD C-9

Reject Change option, WD L-10-11
Replace dialog box, WD B-12
replacing, *See also* finding and replacing
options for, WD B-13
styles, WD F-14-15
text, WD A-12-13, WD B-12-13
restoring files, W B-18-19
reviewing documents, WD B-14-15
multiple reviewers, WD L-11
Reviewing toolbar, WD L-10-11
right-aligned tab marker, WD C-6, WD C-7
right alignment, WD C-8
right-clicking, W A-4, W A-5
Right-handed radio button, W A-12
Right Indent Marker, WD C-10
Roman numerals, in numbered lists, WD C-14
rotate handles, WD H-10
rows
calculating totals for, WD I-14
creating, WD D-2
customizing with Draw Table button, WD D-14-15
height of, WD D-5
inserting and deleting, WD D-6-7, WD D-14-15, WD I-14
ruler, adjusting margins with, WD E-5

▶ S

Same as Previous button, WD E-14-15
sans serif fonts, WD C-3
Save As dialog box, WD A-8, WD A-9, WD B-4, WD G-4
Save as HTML command, WD J-10
Save In list arrow, W B-6
Save as type list arrow, W B-6
Save Version dialog box, WD L-4, WD L-5, WD L-8
saving
documents, WD A-8, WD A-9
documents with new name, WD B-4-5
files with presentations, WD I-10
files with spreadsheets, WD I-12, WD I-14
Paint files, W B-6-7
versions of documents, WD L-4-5, WD L-9
scatter (XY) charts, WD N-2
ScreenTips, WD A-6-7
customizing, WD A-7
scroll bars, WD A-6-7, W A-14-15
scroll boxes, W A-14-15
scrolling text
background color, WD J-12
borders, WD J-12
speed of, WD J-12, WD J-13
in Web pages, WD J-12-13
Scrolling Text dialog box, WD J-12-13
section breaks, WD M-2, WD M-3, WD M-5
defined, WD E-12
page orientation and, WD E-12-13
sections, multiple, changing formatting in, WD E-14-15
Select Browse Object button, WD F-12
selecting
files and folders, W B-15
text, WD A-12-13
selection bar, in tables, WD D-7

selection criteria, multiple, WD G-14-15
Send command, inserting presentations in documents with, WD I-10
serif fonts, WD C-3
shading, WD C-16-17
defined, WD C-16
in documents, WD C-17
Shading Color list arrow, WD C-16
shadows, WD F-6
shapes, *See also* clip art; custom graphics; graphics
adding color to, WD H-8-9
aligning, WD H-9
drawing, WD H-6-7
grouping, WD H-8-9
sizing, WD H-9
sharing information among programs, WD I-1-17
faxes, WD I-16-17
linking and embedding, WD I-2-3
Mail Merge, WD I-4-7
presentations, WD I-8-11
spreadsheets, WD I-12-15
shortcuts
adding to Start menu, W B-21
creating, W B-20-21
creating folders for, W B-20
creating for Word, WD A-4
defined, WD A-4, W B-20
deleting, W B-20
double-clicking, WD A-4
Show All Headings option, WD K-4, WD K-6
Show First Line Only option, WD K-4
Show Formatting button, WD K-4
Show Heading options, WD K-4
showing, *See also* viewing
heading levels, WD K-4, WD K-6, WD K-7
nonprinting characters, WD A-12
Shrink to Fit button, on Print Preview toolbar, WD B-14
sidebars
creating, WD M-8-9
defined, WD M-8
sizing
callouts, WD H-16
charts, WD N-4, WD N-8, WD N-10
graphics, WD H-2, WD H-3
shapes, WD H-9
text boxes, WD M-8, WD M-9
windows, W A-8-9
WordArt objects, WD M-12, WD M-13
Slide Layout dialog box, WD I-8
Slide Sorter view, WD I-8, WD I-9
small caps, WD F-6
Small Icons
Control Panel View menu, W A-10
My Computer toolbar, W B-12
Snap to Grid, WD H-9
Sort dialog box, WD D-11
sorting
by more than one column, WD D-11
information in tables, WD D-10-12
order of, WD D-10, WD D-11
spacing
adjusting, WD F-4
between lines, WD C-12-13
between paragraphs, WD C-12-13
special effects, applying to graphics, WD H-10-11

spelling correction, WD A-2, WD A-9, WD B-10-11
Spelling and Grammar dialog box, WD B-10-11
spinner controls, WD O-11
Split Cells dialog box, WD D-16-17
spreadsheets
calculations, WD I-14
inserting in documents, WD I-12-13
linking to documents, WD I-12-13, WD I-14
modifying, WD I-14-15
square text wrapping, around graphics, WD H-4
stacked column charts, pyramid, WD N-12-13
standard text, WD O-2
Standard toolbar, WD A-6-7
Start button, W A-2
launching Word with, WD A-4
Start menu, W A-6-7
adding shortcuts to, W B-21
categories, W A-6
status bar, WD A-6-7
Stop button, macros, WD P-6, WD P-7
strikethrough formatting, WD L-6-7
Style area, displaying style names in, WD F-10-11
Style dialog box, WD F-2, WD F-8, WD F-9, WD F-10
Style Gallery, WD F-2, WD F-4
style list, WD F-2, WD F-4
styles, *See also* formatting; formatting documents; heading styles; page formatting
assigning keyboard shortcuts to, WD F-9
character styles, WD F-2-3
checking, WD F-4
custom, for charts, WD N-16-17
defined, WD F-1
displaying names of, WD F-10-11
headings, WD K-2
modifying, WD F-6-7, WD F-10
moving around with, WD F-12-13
paragraph styles, WD F-4, WD F-8-9, WD F-10-11
printing, WD F-11
replacing, WD F-14-15
tables of contents, WD K-10
subdocuments, WD K-16-17
defined, WD K-16
working with, WD K-17
subscripts, in text boxes, WD M-10
superscripts
AutoFormat, WD F-16-17
in text boxes, WD M-10, WD M-11
Switch Between Headers and Footers button, WD E-14
symbols
replacing, WD F-4
in text boxes, WD M-10

▶ T

tab leaders, tables of contents, WD K-10, WD K-11
Table AutoFormat, WD D-12-13, WD D-16, WD O-14
tables, WD A-2, WD D-1-17
calculating data in, WD D-8-9
converting text to, WD D-4-5
creating, WD D-2-3
creating column charts from, WD N-4-5
customizing with Draw Table button, WD D-14-15
defined, WD D-1

Index